ベルセルク

BERSERK 17

BY
KENTARO MIURA

三浦建太郎

TRANSLATION
DUANE JOHNSON

LETTERING AND RETOUCH
REPLIBOOKS

DARK HORSE MANGA

DMP
Digital Manga Publishing

PUBLISHERS
MIKE RICHARDSON, DARK HORSE MANGA
HIKARU SASAHARA, DIGITAL MANGA PUBLISHING

EDITORS
CHRIS WARNER, DARK HORSE MANGA
FRED LUI, DIGITAL MANGA PUBLISHING

COLLECTION DESIGNERS
DAVID NESTELLE
KRYSTAL HENNES

ART DIRECTOR
LIA RIBACCHI

English-language version produced by
DARK HORSE MANGA and DIGITAL MANGA PUBLISHING.

BERSERK vol. 17 by KENTARO MIURA

Dark Horse Manga
A division of Dark Horse Comics, Inc.
10956 SE Main Street
Milwaukie OR 97222

darkhorse.com

Digital Manga Publishing
1487 West 178th Street, Suite 300
Gardena CA 90248

dmpbooks.com

To find a comics shop in your area, call the Comic
Shop Locator Service toll-free at 1-888-266-4226

First edition: May 2007

ISBN-10: 1-59307-742-4
ISBN-13: 978-1-59307-742-6

10 9 8 7 6 5 4 3 2 1
Printed in Canada

BERSERK

ベルセルク⑰

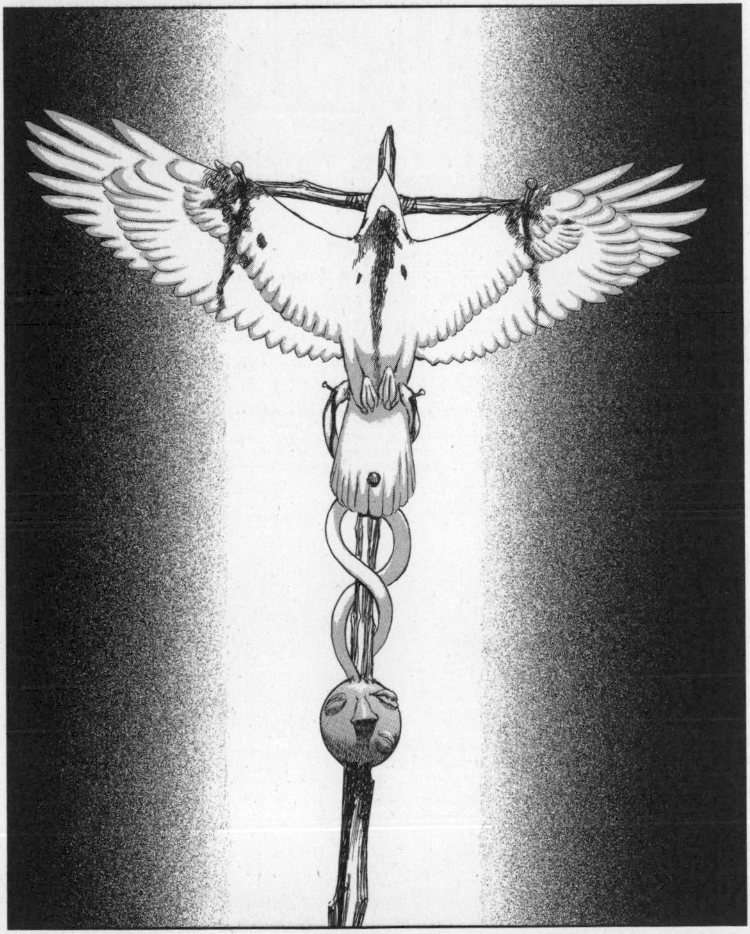

三浦建太郎

ベルセルク 17

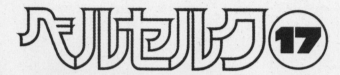

CONTENTS

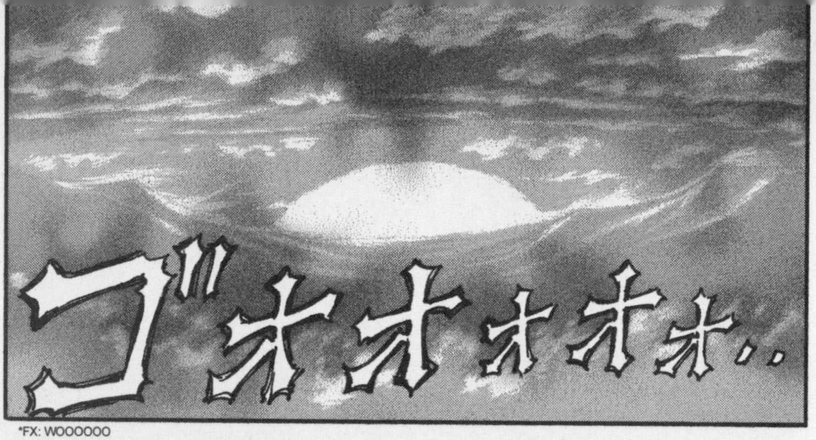
ゴオオォオオォ‥
*FX: WOOOOOO

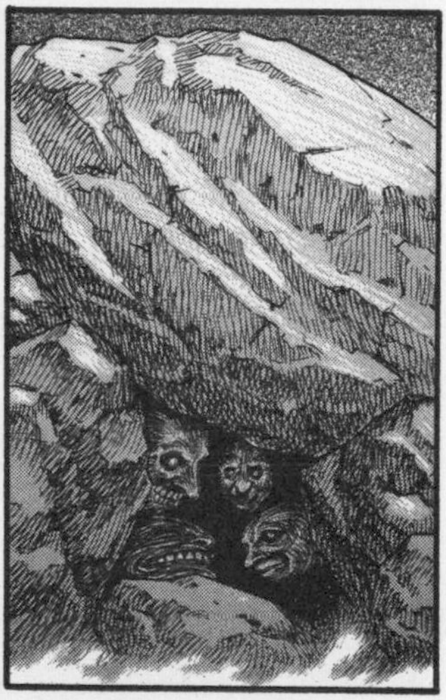

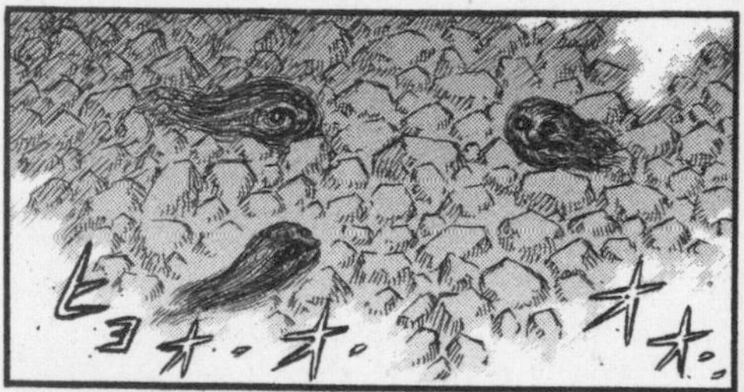
*FX: HYOOOOOOO

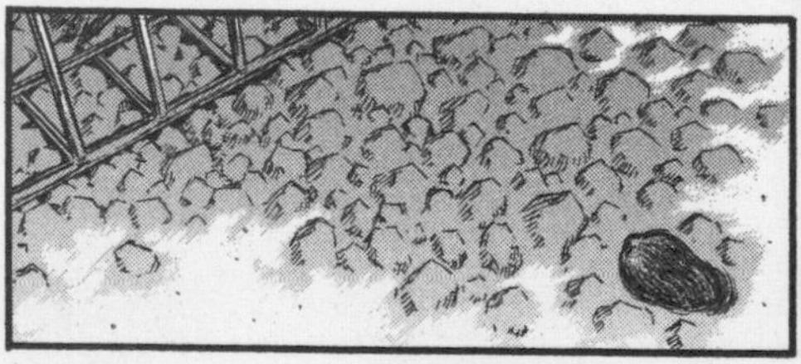

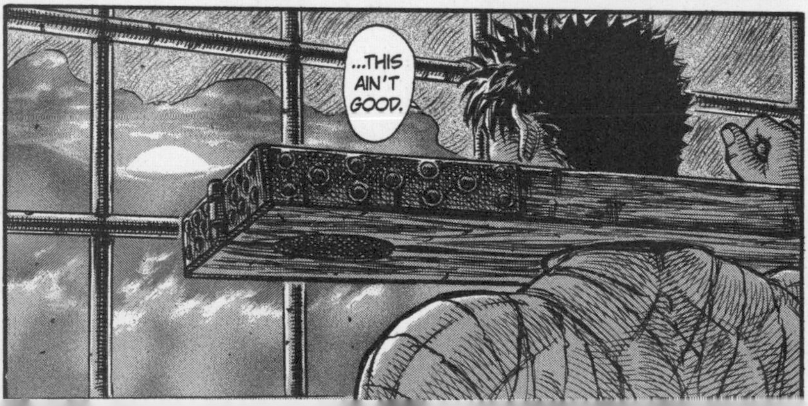
...THIS AIN'T GOOD.

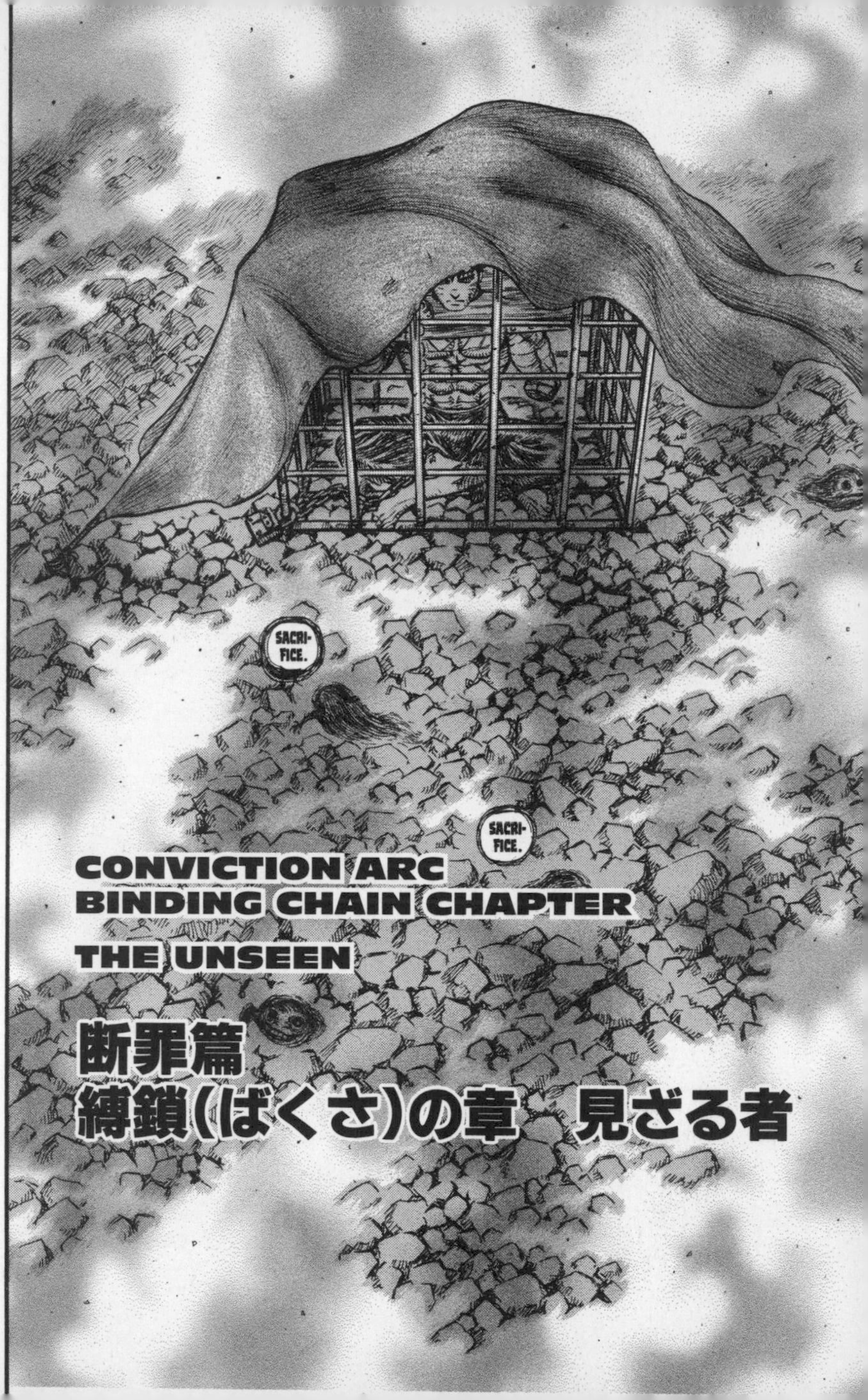
SACRI-
FICE.
SACRI-
FICE.

CONVICTION ARC
BINDING CHAIN CHAPTER
THE UNSEEN

断罪篇
縛鎖(ばくさ)の章　見ざる者

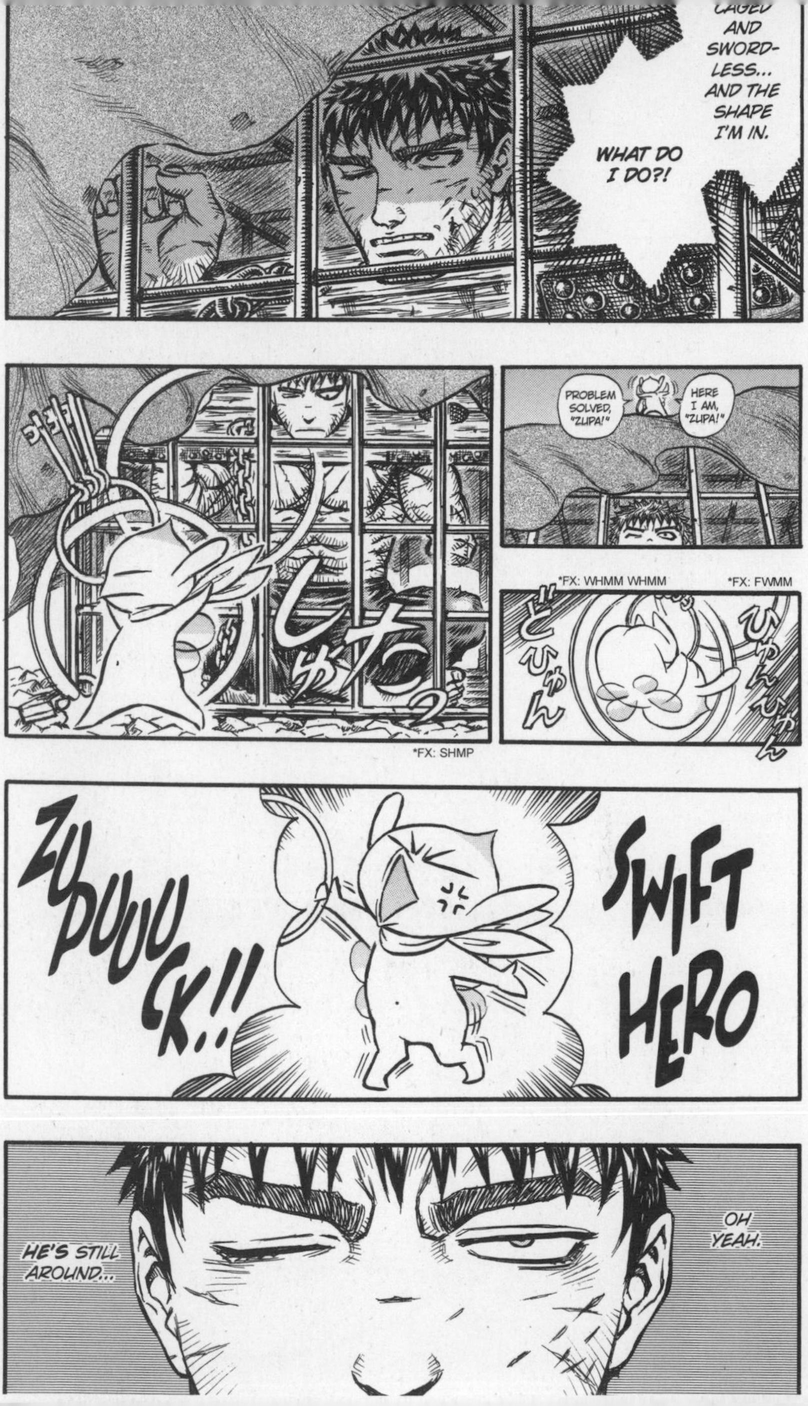
CAGED AND SWORDLESS... AND THE SHAPE I'M IN.
WHAT DO I DO?!
HERE I AM, "ZUPA!"
PROBLEM SOLVED, "ZUPA!"
ひゅんひゅん
*FX: FWMM
どひゅん
*FX: WHMM WHMM
しゅたっ
*FX: SHMP
SWIFT HERO
ZUPUUUCK!!
OH YEAH.
HE'S STILL AROUND...

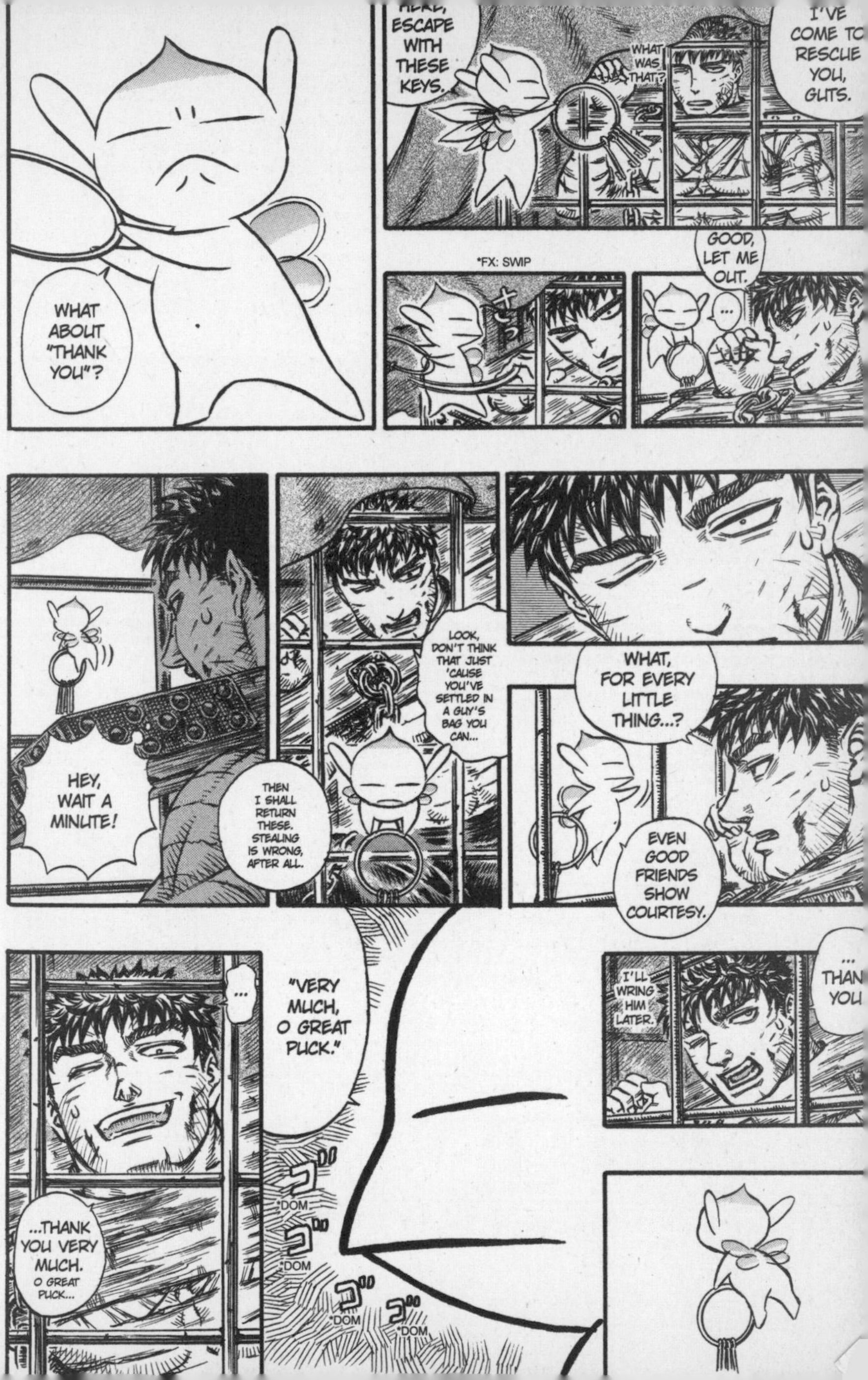
I'VE COME TO RESCUE YOU, GUTS.
ESCAPE WITH THESE KEYS.
WHAT WAS THAT?
GOOD, LET ME OUT.
...
*FX: SWIP
WHAT ABOUT "THANK YOU"?
WHAT, FOR EVERY LITTLE THING...?
EVEN GOOD FRIENDS SHOW COURTESY.
LOOK, DON'T THINK THAT JUST 'CAUSE YOU'VE SETTLED IN A GUY'S BAG YOU CAN...
THEN I SHALL RETURN THESE. STEALING IS WRONG, AFTER ALL.
HEY, WAIT A MINUTE!
... THAN YOU
I'LL WRING HIM LATER.
"VERY MUCH, O GREAT PUCK."
*DOM
*DOM
*DOM
*DOM
...
...THANK YOU VERY MUCH. O GREAT PUCK...

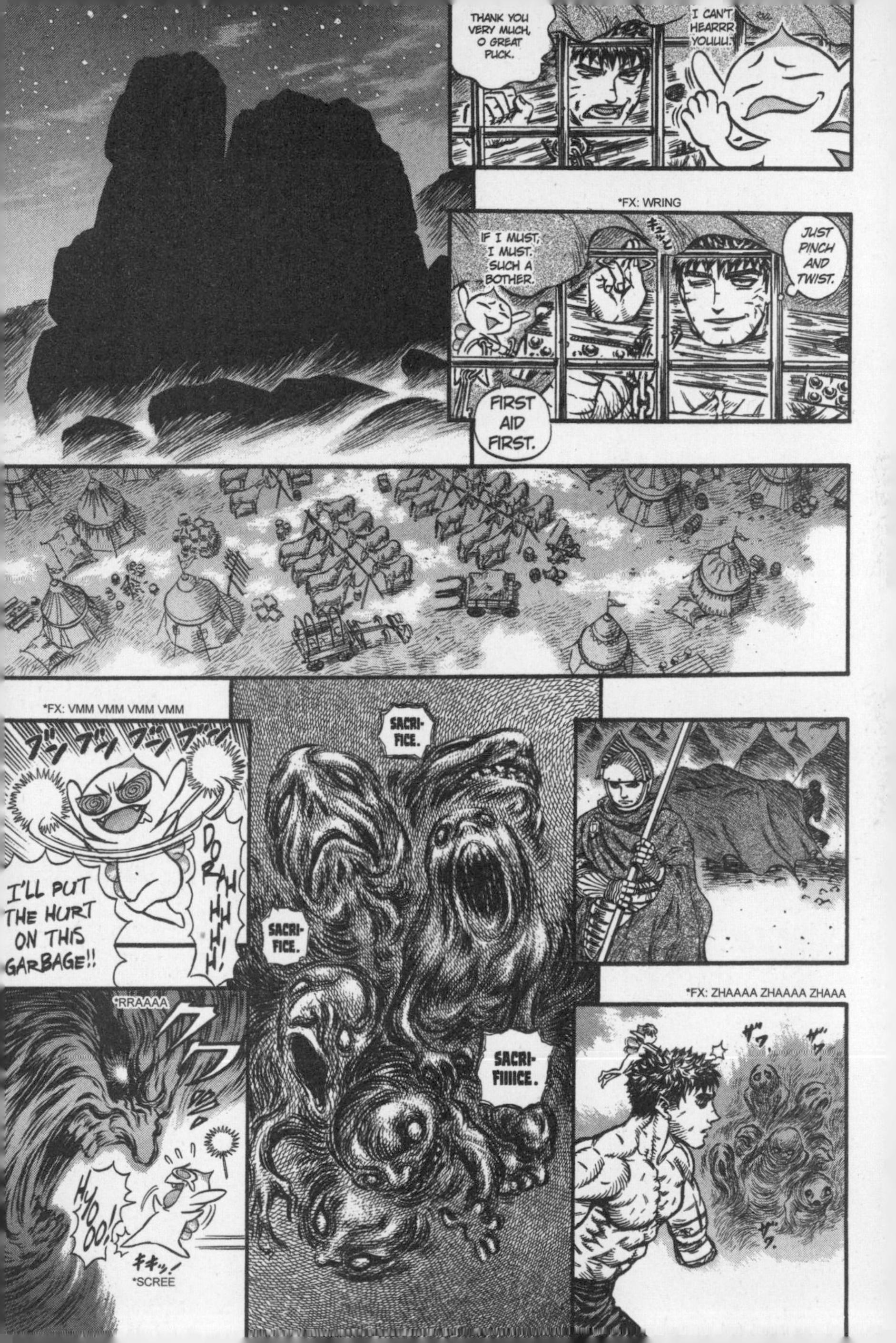
I CAN'T HEARRR YOUUU.
THANK YOU VERY MUCH, O GREAT PUCK.
*FX: WRING
JUST PINCH AND TWIST.
IF I MUST, I MUST. SUCH A BOTHER.
FIRST AID FIRST.
*FX: ZHAAAA ZHAAAA ZHAAA
SACRI-FICE.
SACRI-FICE.
SACRI-FIIIICE.
*FX: VMM VMM VMM VMM
DORAHHHHH!
I'LL PUT THE HURT ON THIS GARBAGE!!
*RRAAAA
HYOOO!
*SCREE

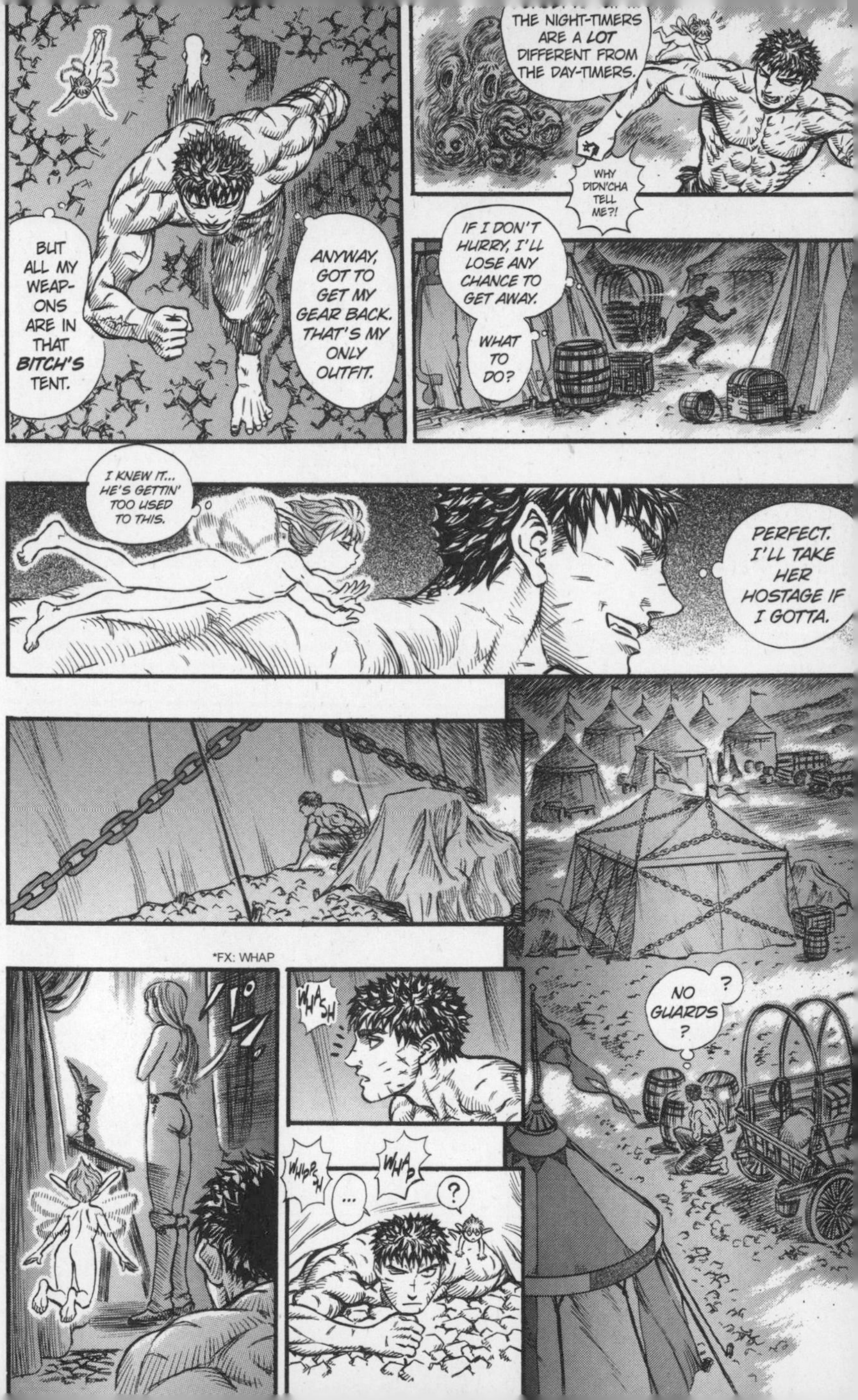
THE NIGHT-TIMERS ARE A LOT DIFFERENT FROM THE DAY-TIMERS.
WHY DIDN'CHA TELL ME?!
IF I DON'T HURRY, I'LL LOSE ANY CHANCE TO GET AWAY.
WHAT TO DO?
ANYWAY, GOT TO GET MY GEAR BACK. THAT'S MY ONLY OUTFIT.
BUT ALL MY WEAP-ONS ARE IN THAT BITCH'S TENT.
PERFECT. I'LL TAKE HER HOSTAGE IF I GOTTA.
I KNEW IT... HE'S GETTIN' TOO USED TO THIS.
NO GUARDS ? ?
*FX: WHAP
WHASH
WHAP
...
?

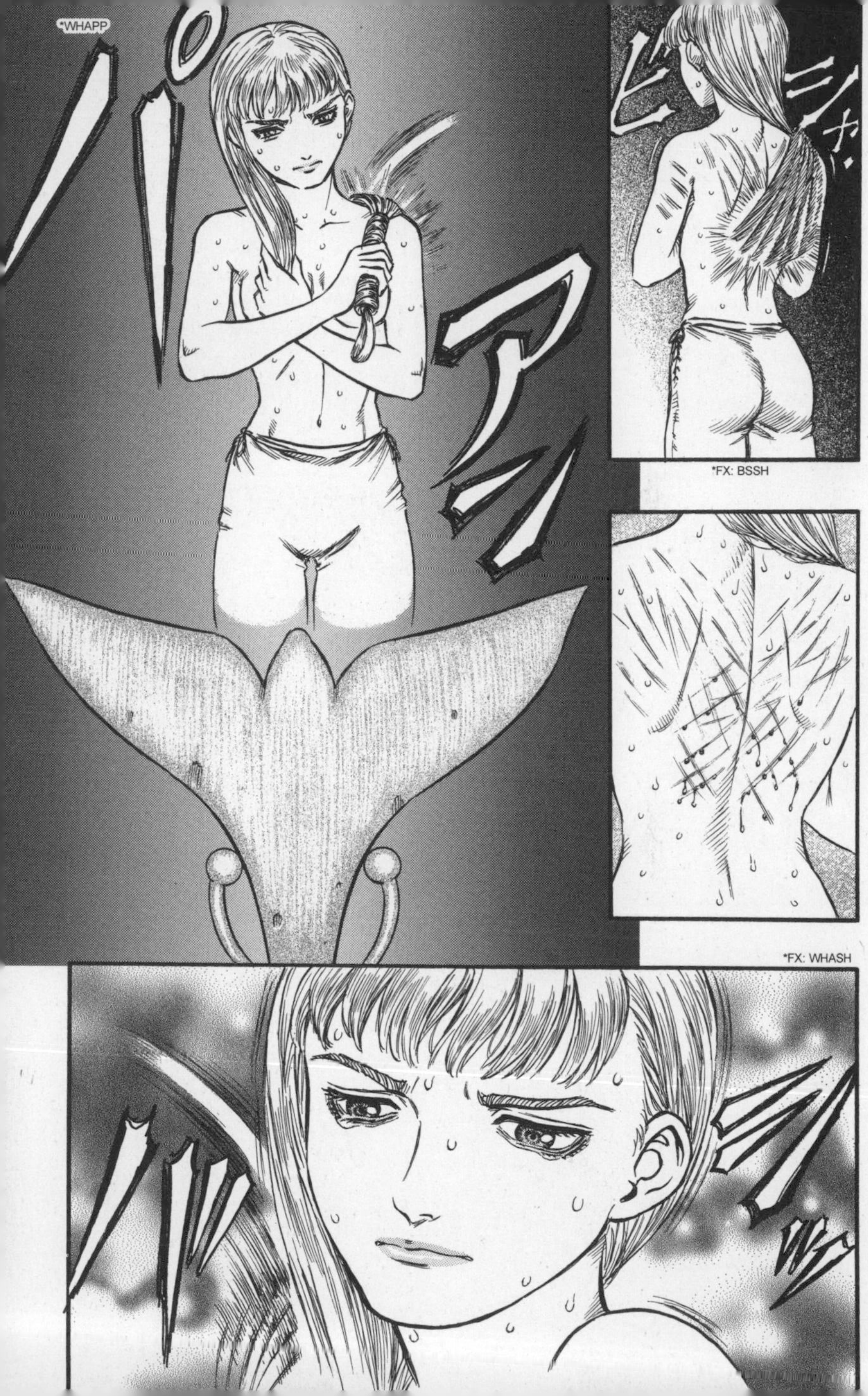
*FX: BSSH
*FX: WHASH
*WHAPP
パァン

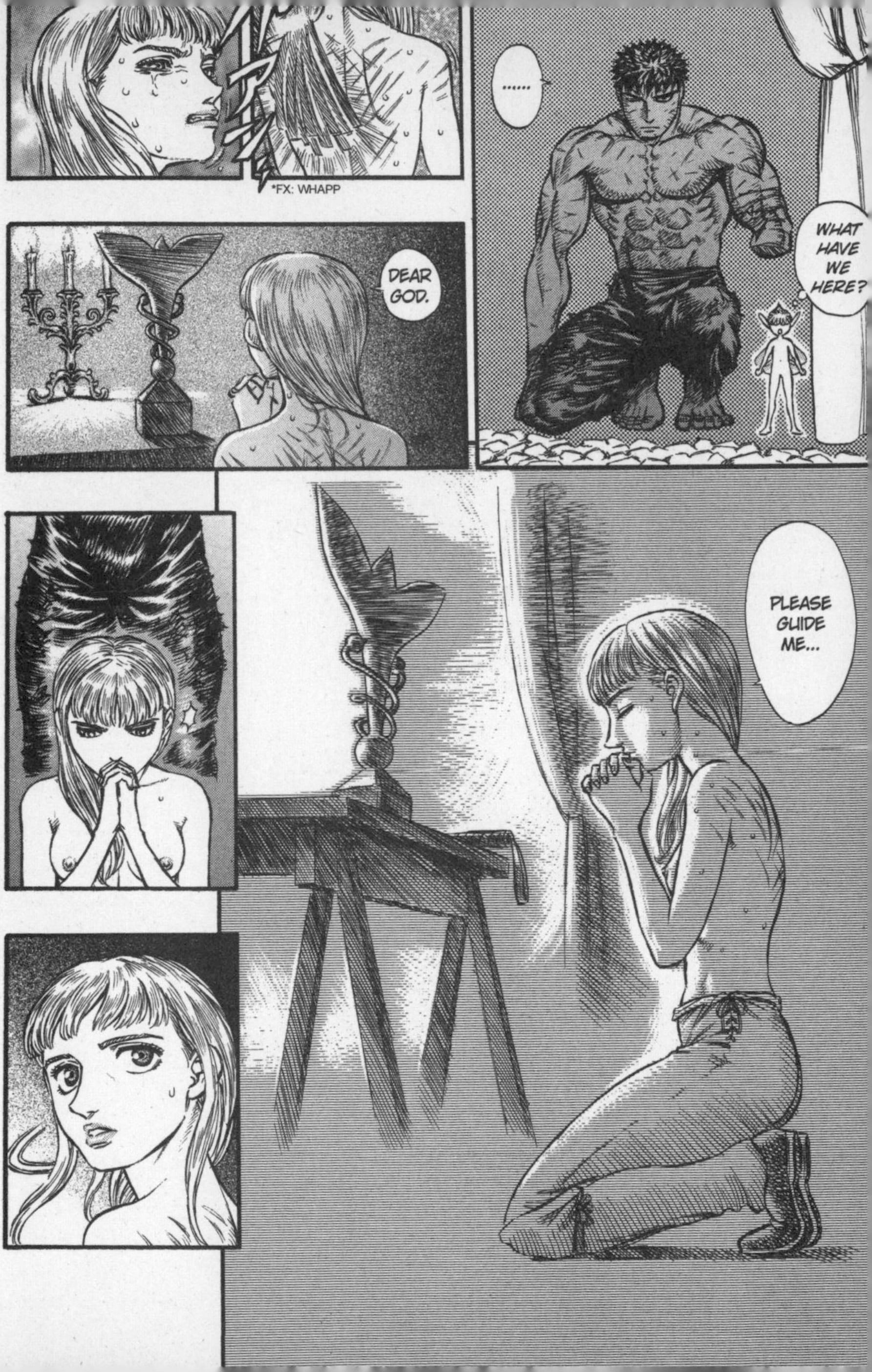
......
WHAT HAVE WE HERE?
*FX: WHAPP
DEAR GOD.
PLEASE GUIDE ME...

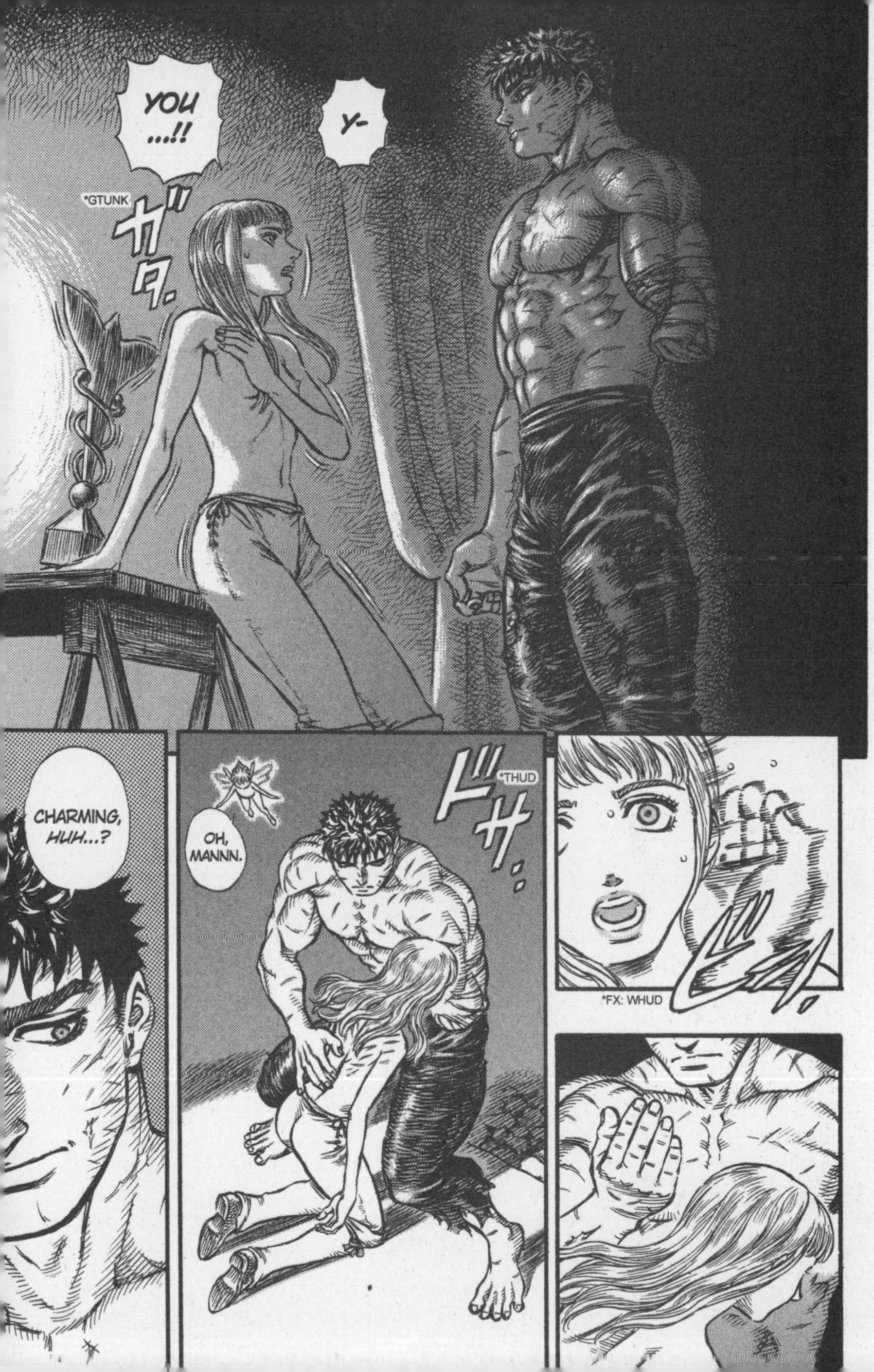
Y-
YOU ...!!
ガタ
*GTUNK
*FX: WHUD
ドサ
*THUD
OH, MANNN.
CHARMING, HUH...?

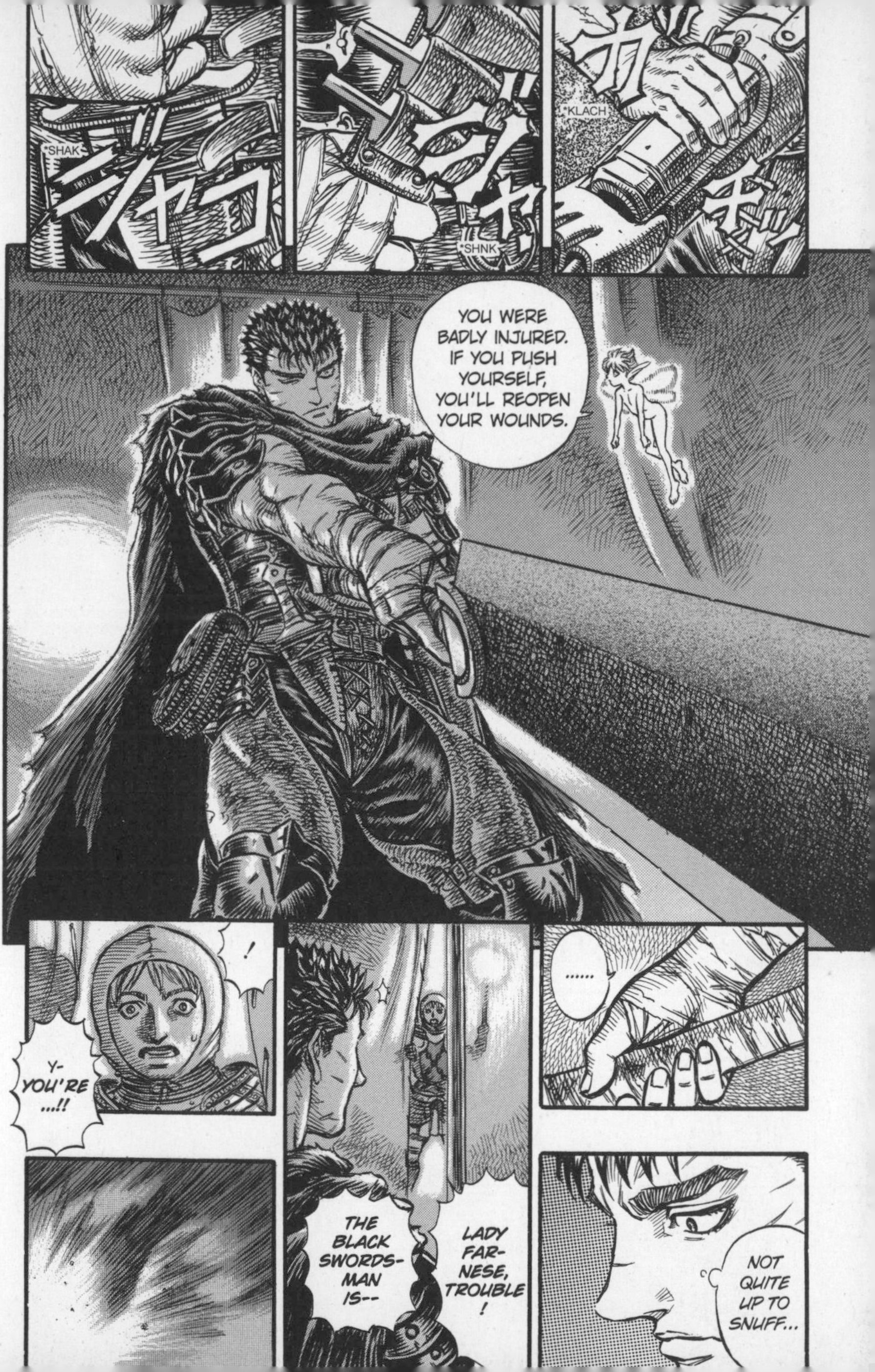
*KLACH
*SHNK
*SHAK
YOU WERE BADLY INJURED. IF YOU PUSH YOURSELF, YOU'LL REOPEN YOUR WOUNDS.
......
NOT QUITE UP TO SNUFF...
LADY FARNESE, TROUBLE!
THE BLACK SWORDSMAN IS--
!
Y- YOU'RE ...!!

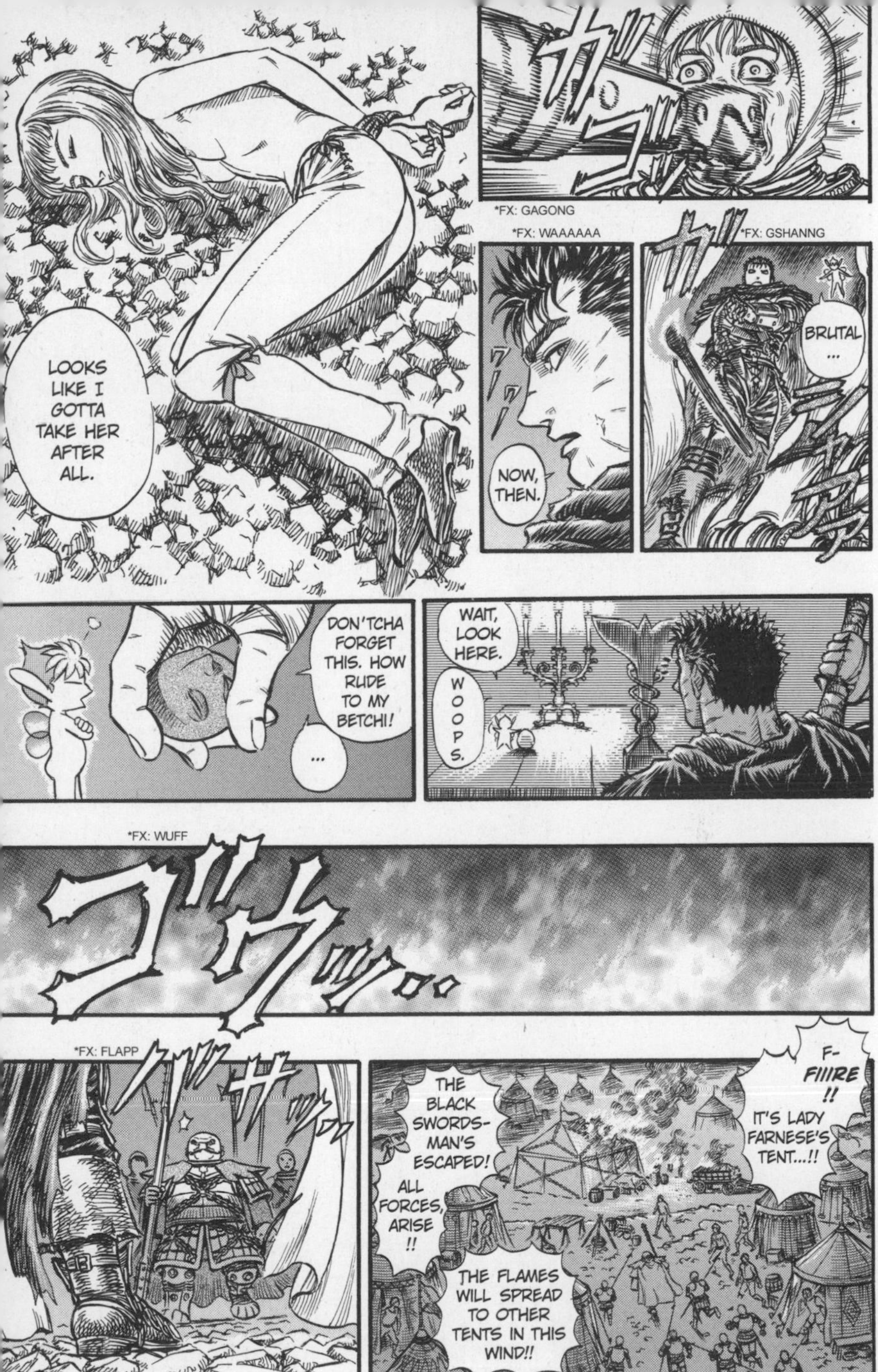
*FX: GAGONG
*FX: GSHANNG
BRUTAL ...
*FX: WAAAAAA
NOW, THEN.
LOOKS LIKE I GOTTA TAKE HER AFTER ALL.
WAIT, LOOK HERE.
WOOPS.
DON'TCHA FORGET THIS. HOW RUDE TO MY BETCHI!
...
*FX: WUFF
F- FIIIRE !!
IT'S LADY FARNESE'S TENT...!!
THE BLACK SWORDS-MAN'S ESCAPED!
ALL FORCES, ARISE !!
THE FLAMES WILL SPREAD TO OTHER TENTS IN THIS WIND!!
*FX: FLAPP

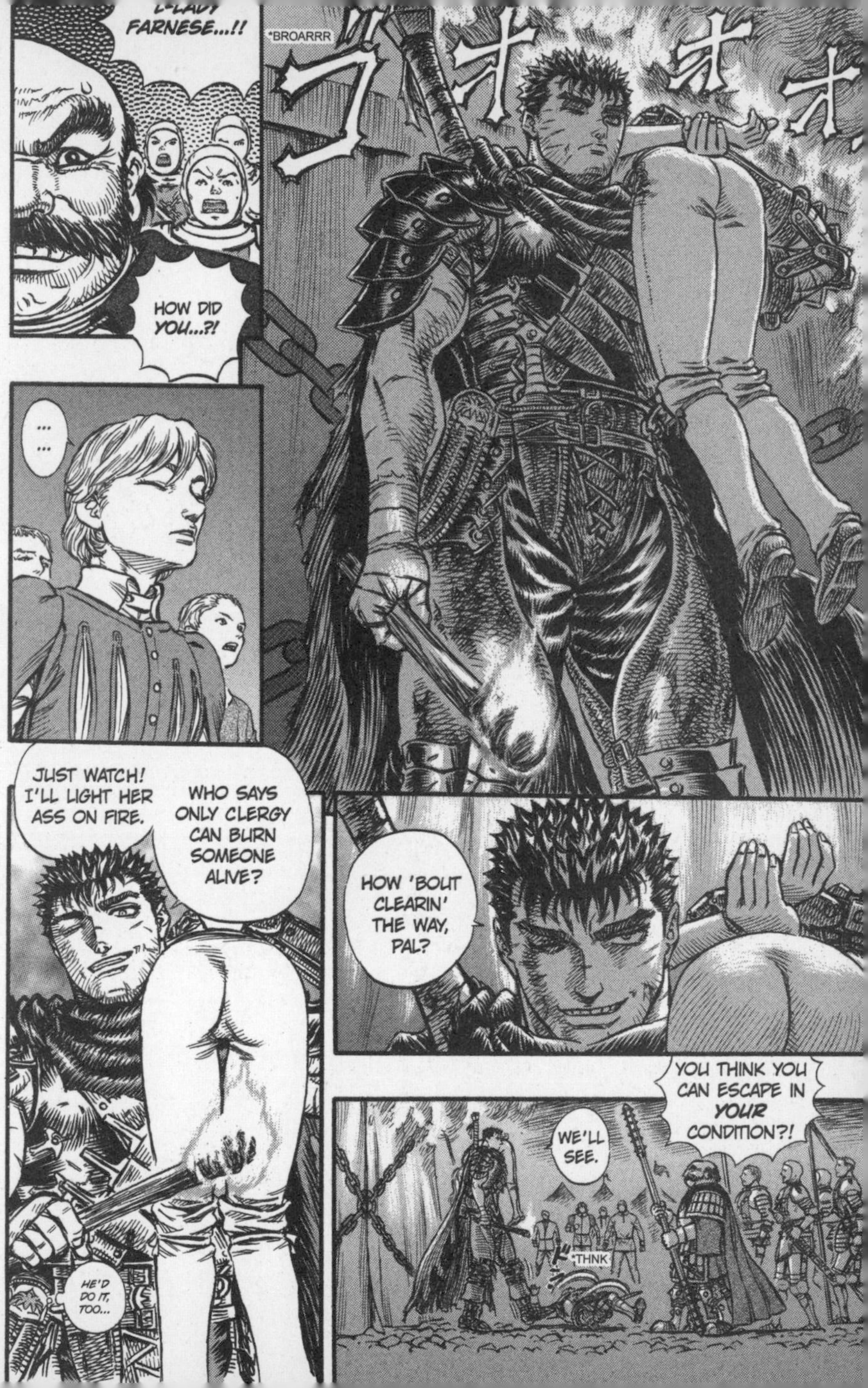
*BROARRR
L-LADY FARNESE...!!
HOW DID YOU...?!
... ...
HOW 'BOUT CLEARIN' THE WAY, PAL?
YOU THINK YOU CAN ESCAPE IN YOUR CONDITION?!
WE'LL SEE.
*THNK
WHO SAYS ONLY CLERGY CAN BURN SOMEONE ALIVE?
JUST WATCH! I'LL LIGHT HER ASS ON FIRE.
HE'D DO IT, TOO...

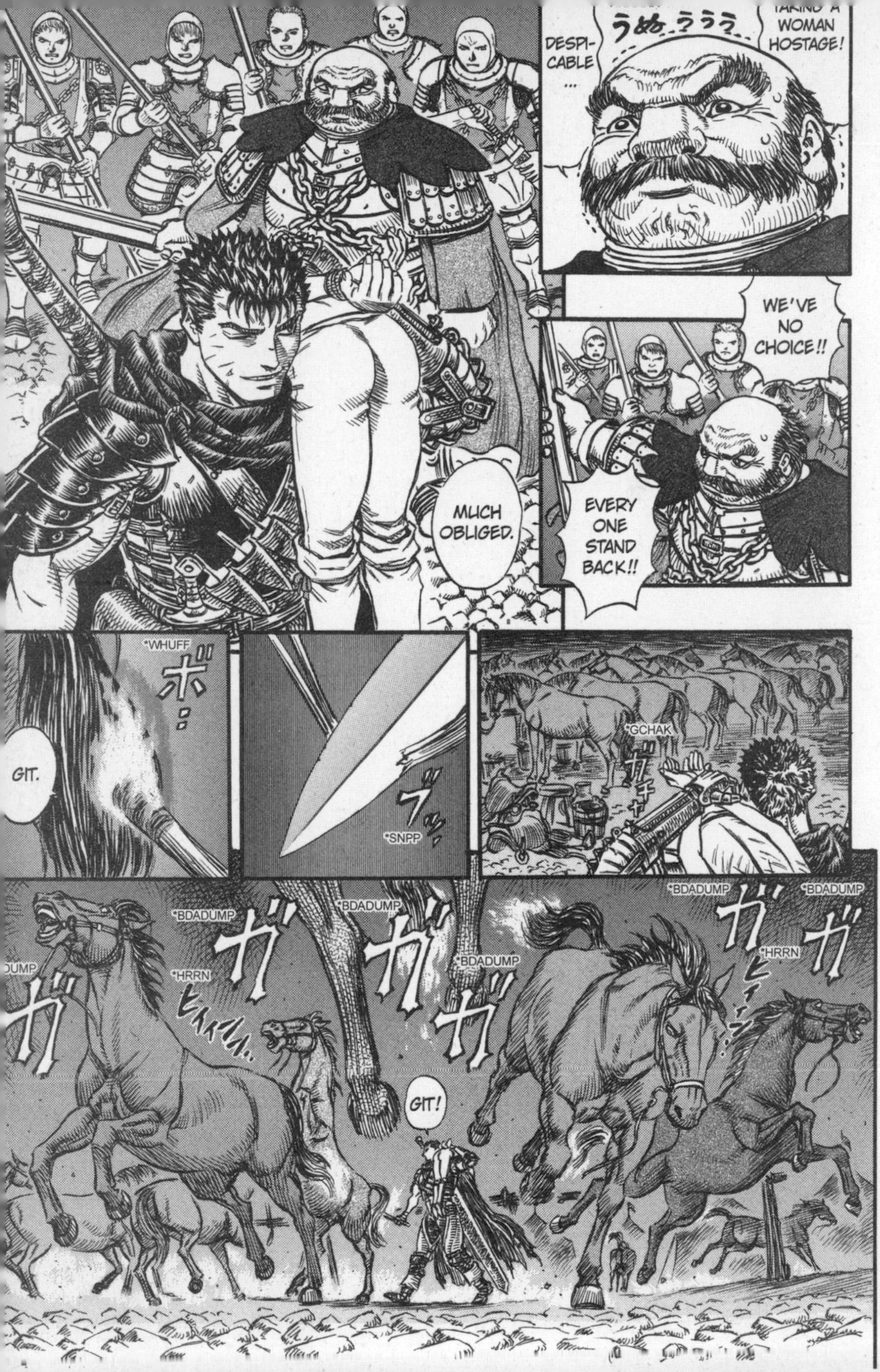

TAKING A WOMAN HOSTAGE!
うぬ…ううう…
DESPI-CABLE …
WE'VE NO CHOICE!!
EVERY ONE STAND BACK!!
MUCH OBLIGED.
*GCHAK
*SNPP
*WHUFF
GIT.
*BDADUMP
*BDADUMP
*HRRN
*BDADUMP
GIT!
*BDADUMP
*HRRN
*BDADUMP
DUMP

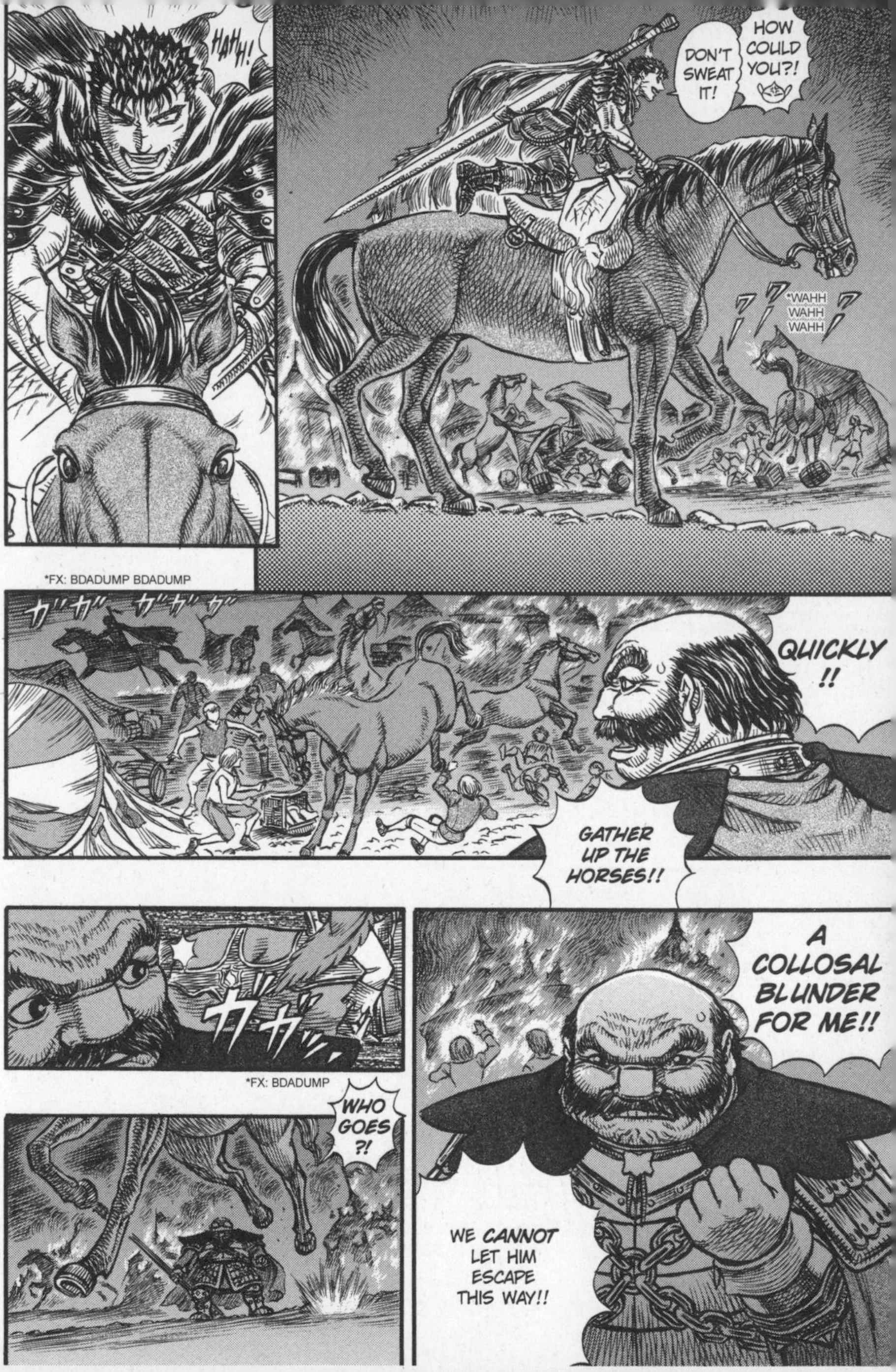
HOW COULD YOU?!
DON'T SWEAT IT!
*WAHH WAHH WAHH
HAHH!
*FX: BDADUMP BDADUMP
QUICKLY!!
GATHER UP THE HORSES!!
A COLLOSAL BLUNDER FOR ME!!
WE CANNOT LET HIM ESCAPE THIS WAY!!
*FX: BDADUMP
WHO GOES?!

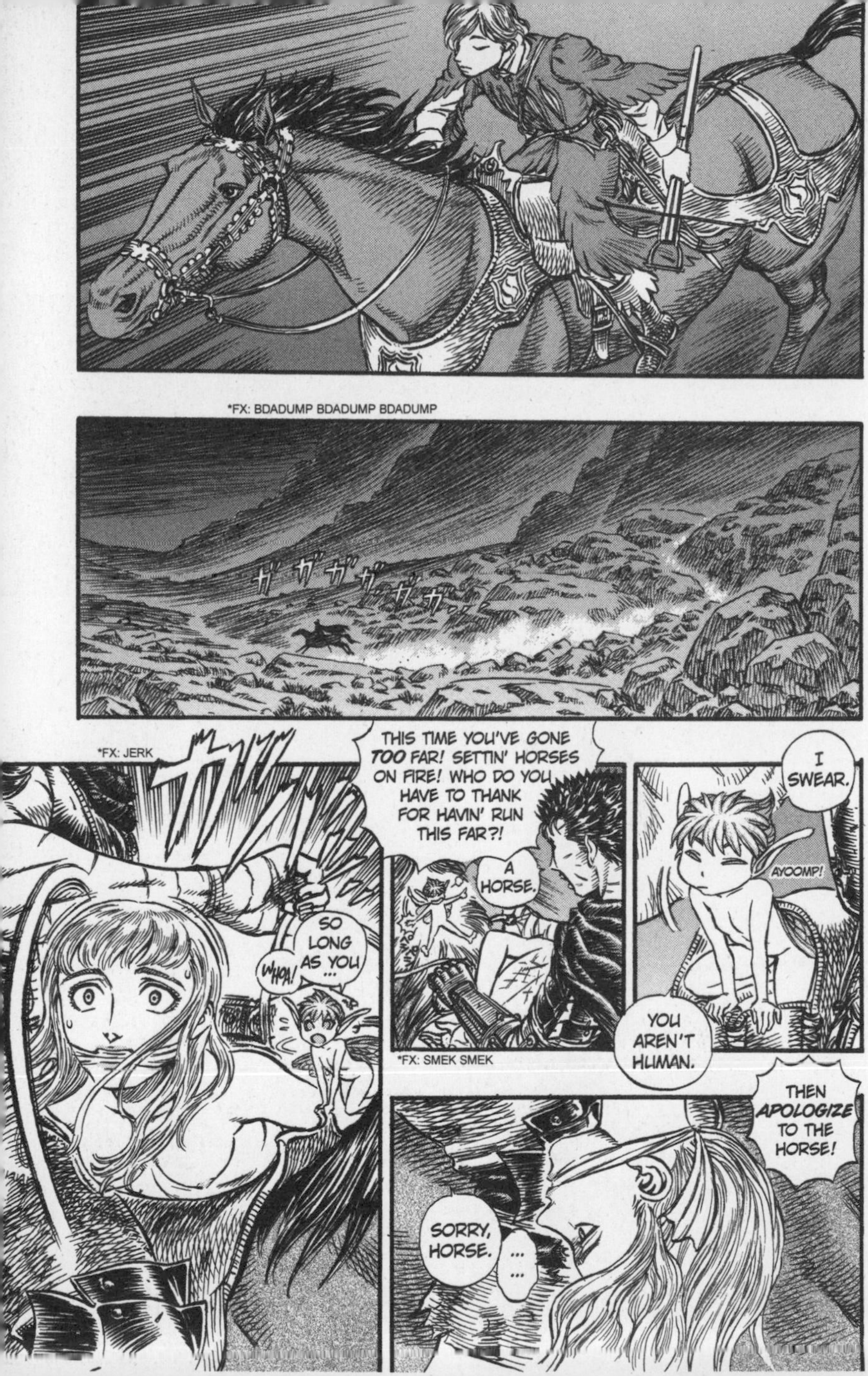
*FX: BDADUMP BDADUMP BDADUMP
ガガガガガガ
I SWEAR.
AYOOMP!
YOU AREN'T HUMAN.
THIS TIME YOU'VE GONE *TOO* FAR! SETTIN' HORSES ON FIRE! WHO DO YOU HAVE TO THANK FOR HAVIN' RUN THIS FAR?!
A HORSE.
*FX: SMEK SMEK
THEN *APOLOGIZE* TO THE HORSE!
SORRY, HORSE.
... ...
*FX: JERK
WHOA!
SO LONG AS YOU ...

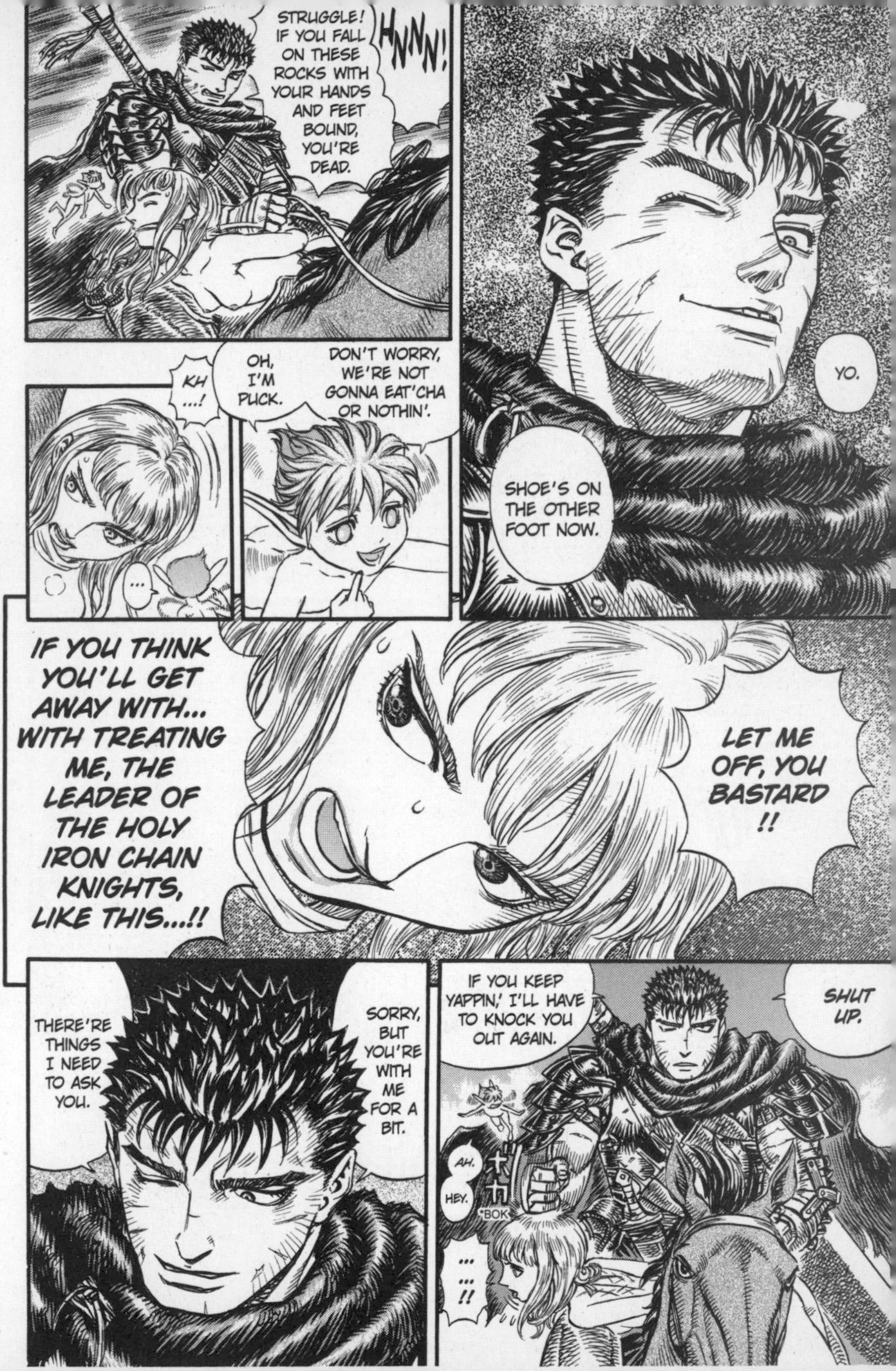
YO.
SHOE'S ON THE OTHER FOOT NOW.
HNNN!
STRUGGLE! IF YOU FALL ON THESE ROCKS WITH YOUR HANDS AND FEET BOUND, YOU'RE DEAD.
DON'T WORRY, WE'RE NOT GONNA EAT'CHA OR NOTHIN'.
OH, I'M PUCK.
KH ...!
...
LET ME OFF, YOU BASTARD !!
IF YOU THINK YOU'LL GET AWAY WITH... WITH TREATING ME, THE LEADER OF THE HOLY IRON CHAIN KNIGHTS, LIKE THIS...!!
SHUT UP.
IF YOU KEEP YAPPIN,' I'LL HAVE TO KNOCK YOU OUT AGAIN.
AH.
HEY.
*BOK
... ... !!
SORRY, BUT YOU'RE WITH ME FOR A BIT.
THERE'RE THINGS I NEED TO ASK YOU.

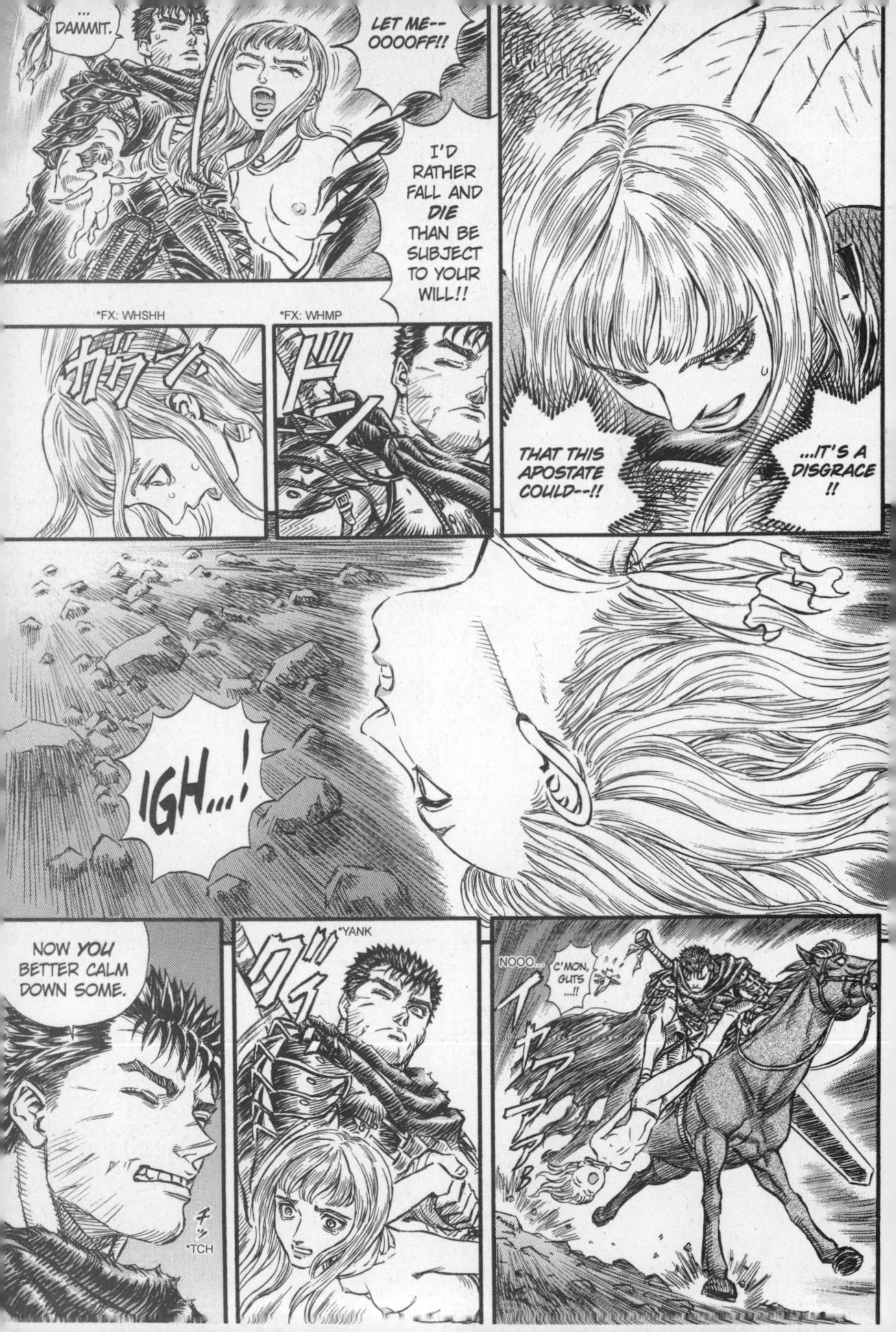
...IT'S A DISGRACE !!
THAT THIS APOSTATE COULD--!!
LET ME-- OOOOFF!!
I'D RATHER FALL AND DIE THAN BE SUBJECT TO YOUR WILL!!
... DAMMIT.
*FX: WHMP
*FX: WHSHH
IGH...!
C'MON, GUTS ...!!
NOOO...
*YANK
NOW YOU BETTER CALM DOWN SOME.
*TCH

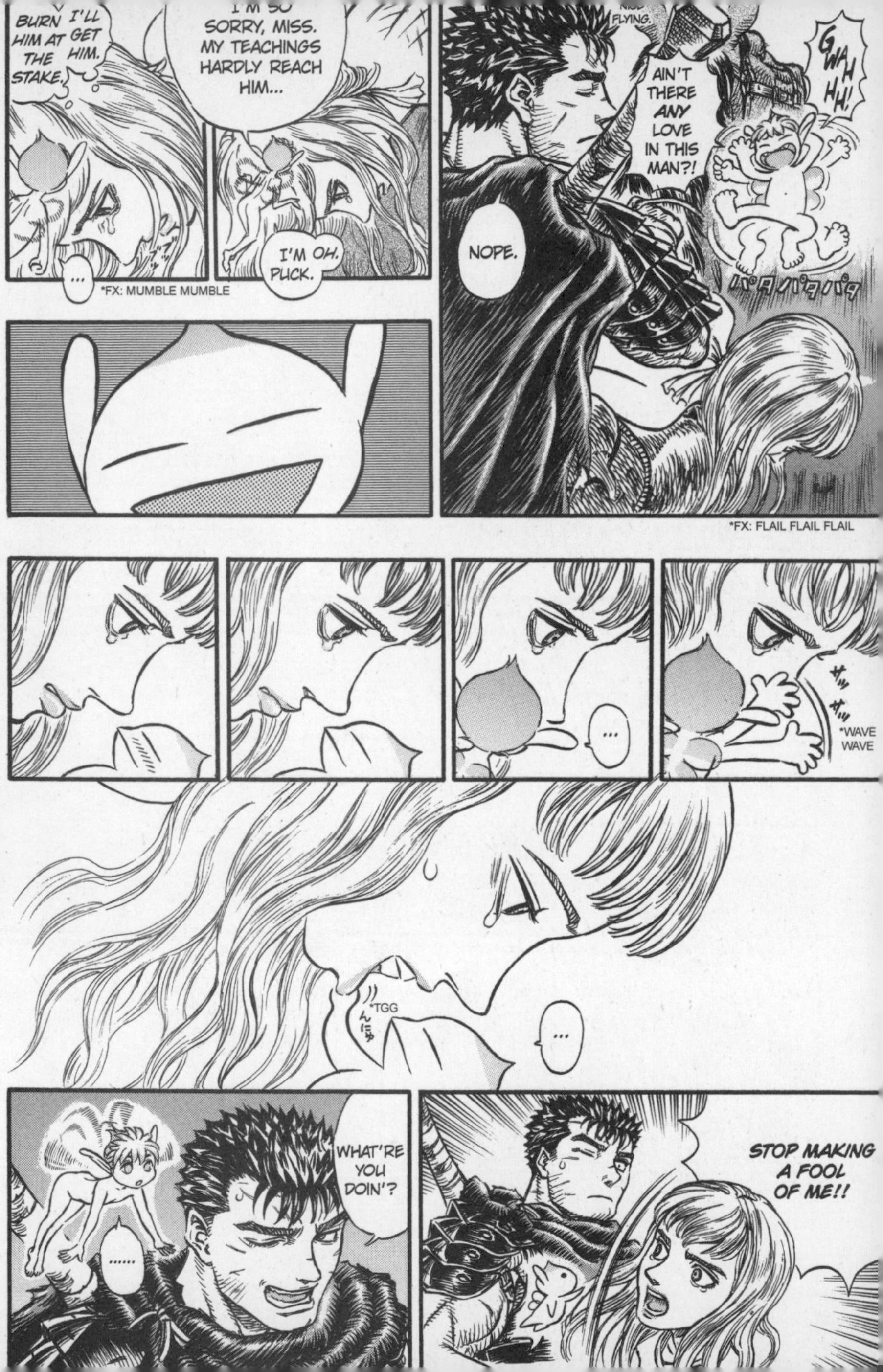
FLYING.
GWAHHH!
AIN'T THERE ANY LOVE IN THIS MAN?!
NOPE.
パタパタパタ
*FX: FLAIL FLAIL FLAIL
I'M SO SORRY, MISS. MY TEACHINGS HARDLY REACH HIM...
I'M PUCK.
OH.
I'LL GET HIM.
BURN HIM AT THE STAKE.
...
*FX: MUMBLE MUMBLE
*WAVE WAVE
...
*TGG
...
STOP MAKING A FOOL OF ME!!
WHAT'RE YOU DOIN'?
......

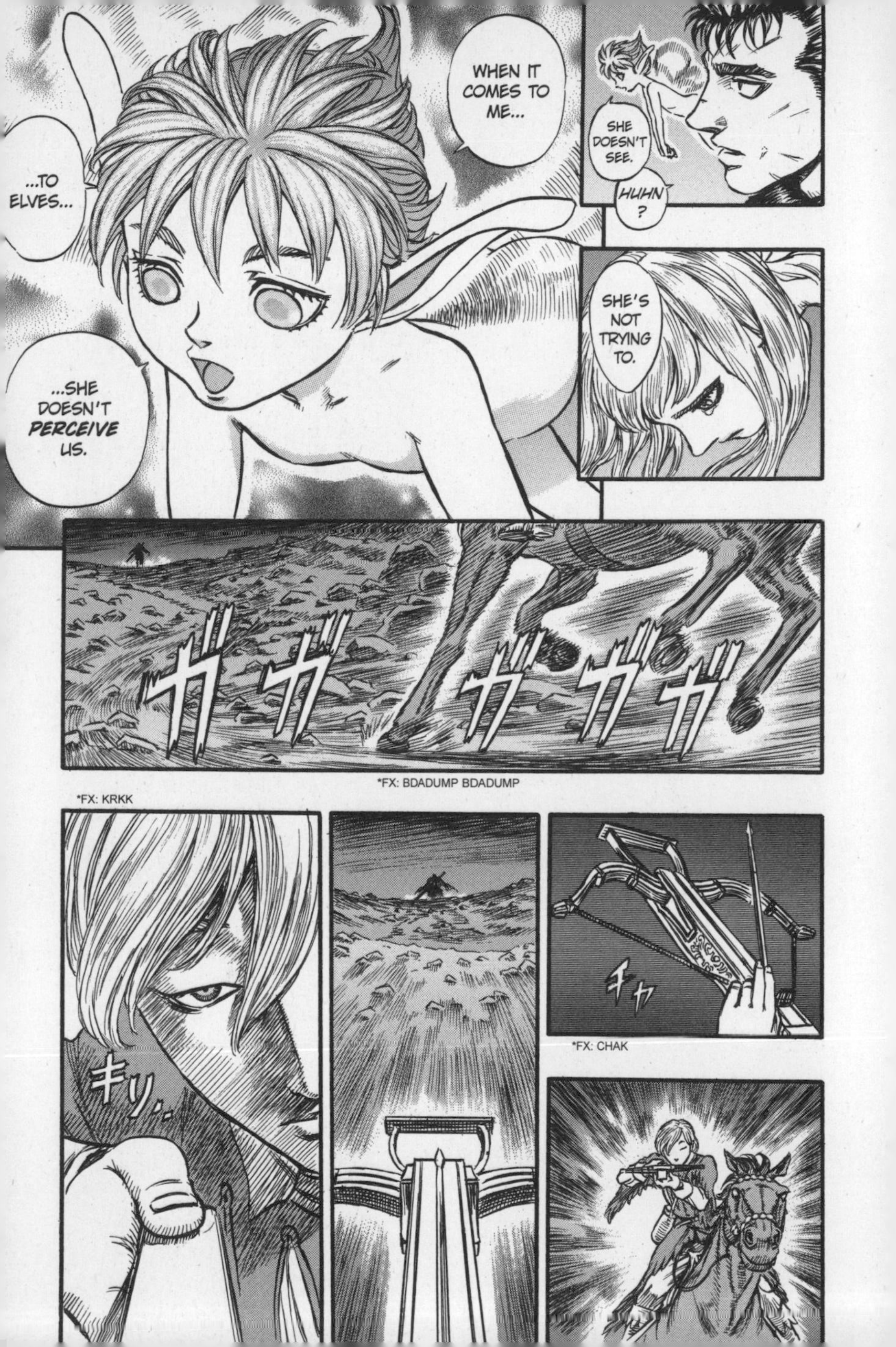
SHE DOESN'T SEE.
HUHN?
SHE'S NOT TRYING TO.
WHEN IT COMES TO ME...
...TO ELVES...
...SHE DOESN'T PERCEIVE US.
*FX: BDADUMP BDADUMP
*FX: CHAK
*FX: KRKK

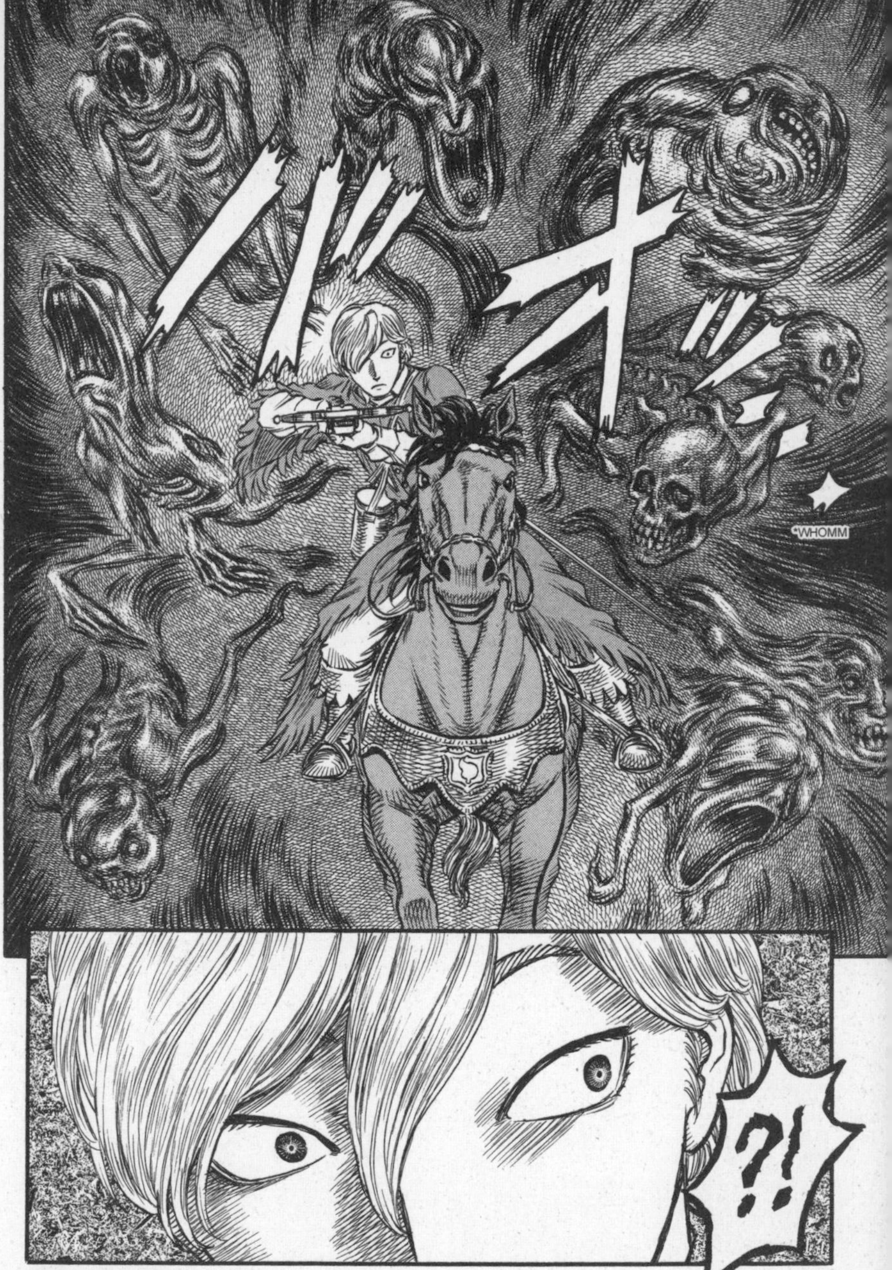
*WHOMM
?!

CONVICTION ARC
BINDING CHAIN CHAPTER
THE UNSEEN: END

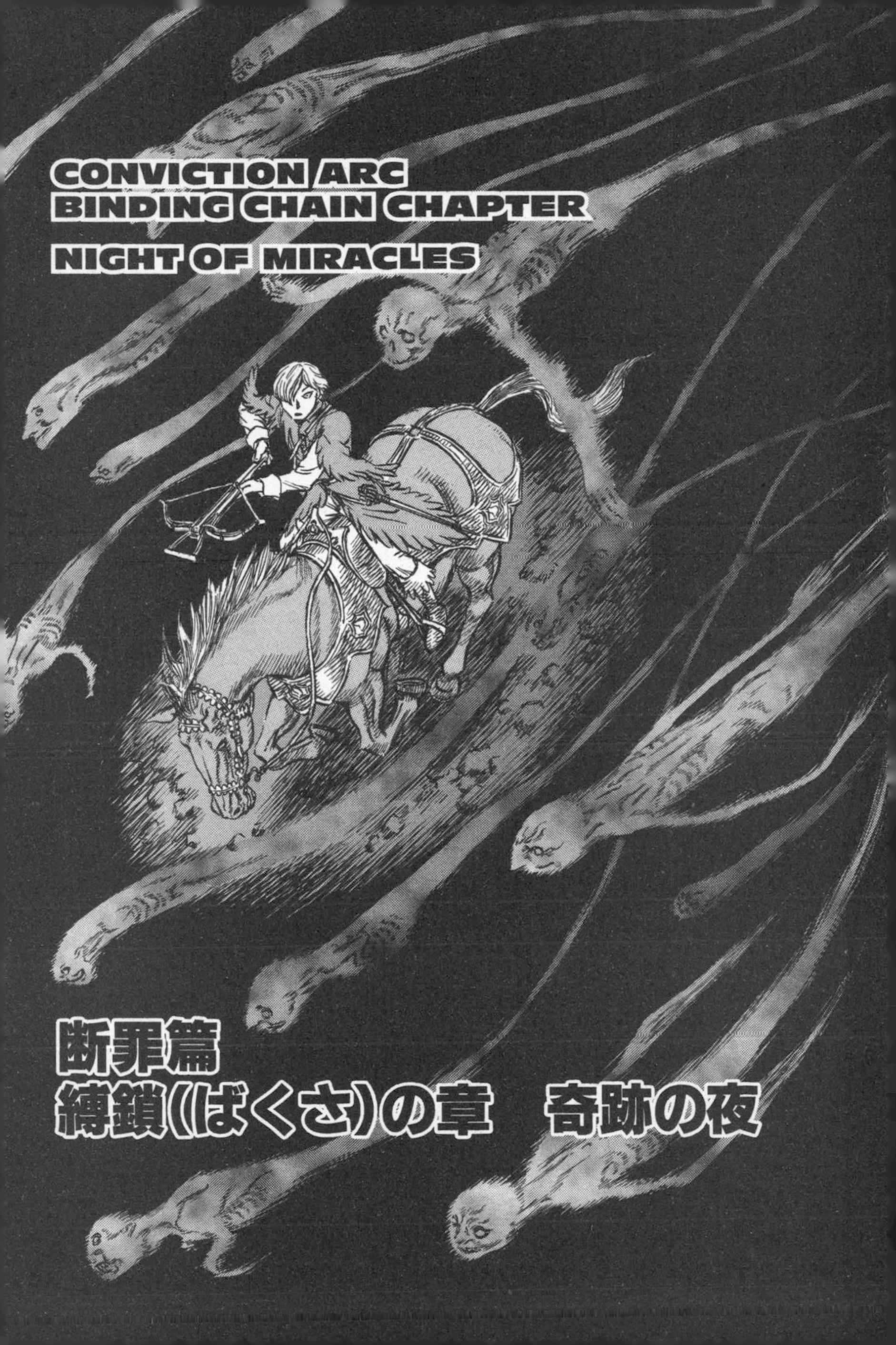
CONVICTION ARC
BINDING CHAIN CHAPTER
NIGHT OF MIRACLES
断罪篇
縛鎖(ばくさ)の章　奇跡の夜

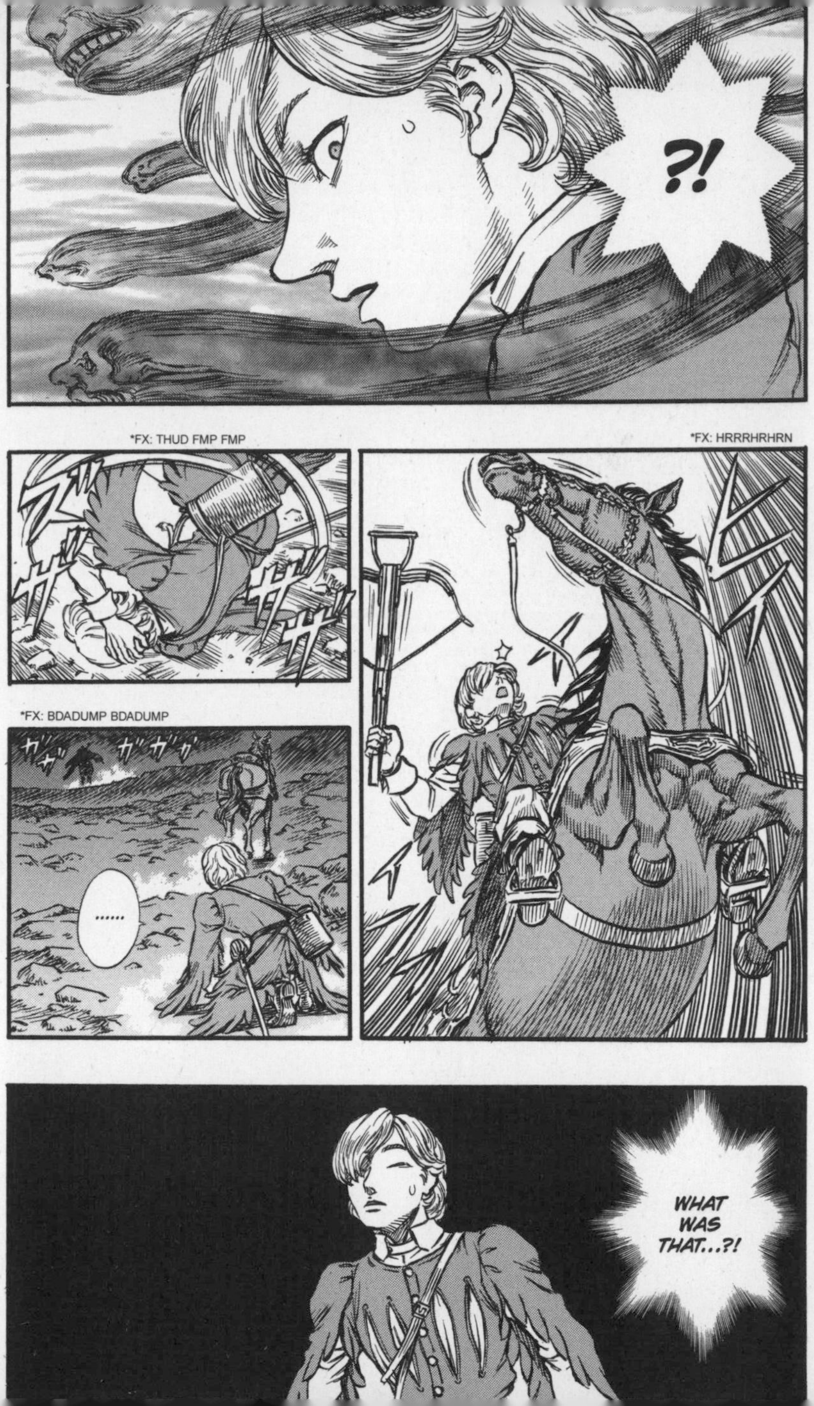
?!
*FX: HRRRHRHRN
*FX: THUD FMP FMP
*FX: BDADUMP BDADUMP
......
WHAT WAS THAT...?!

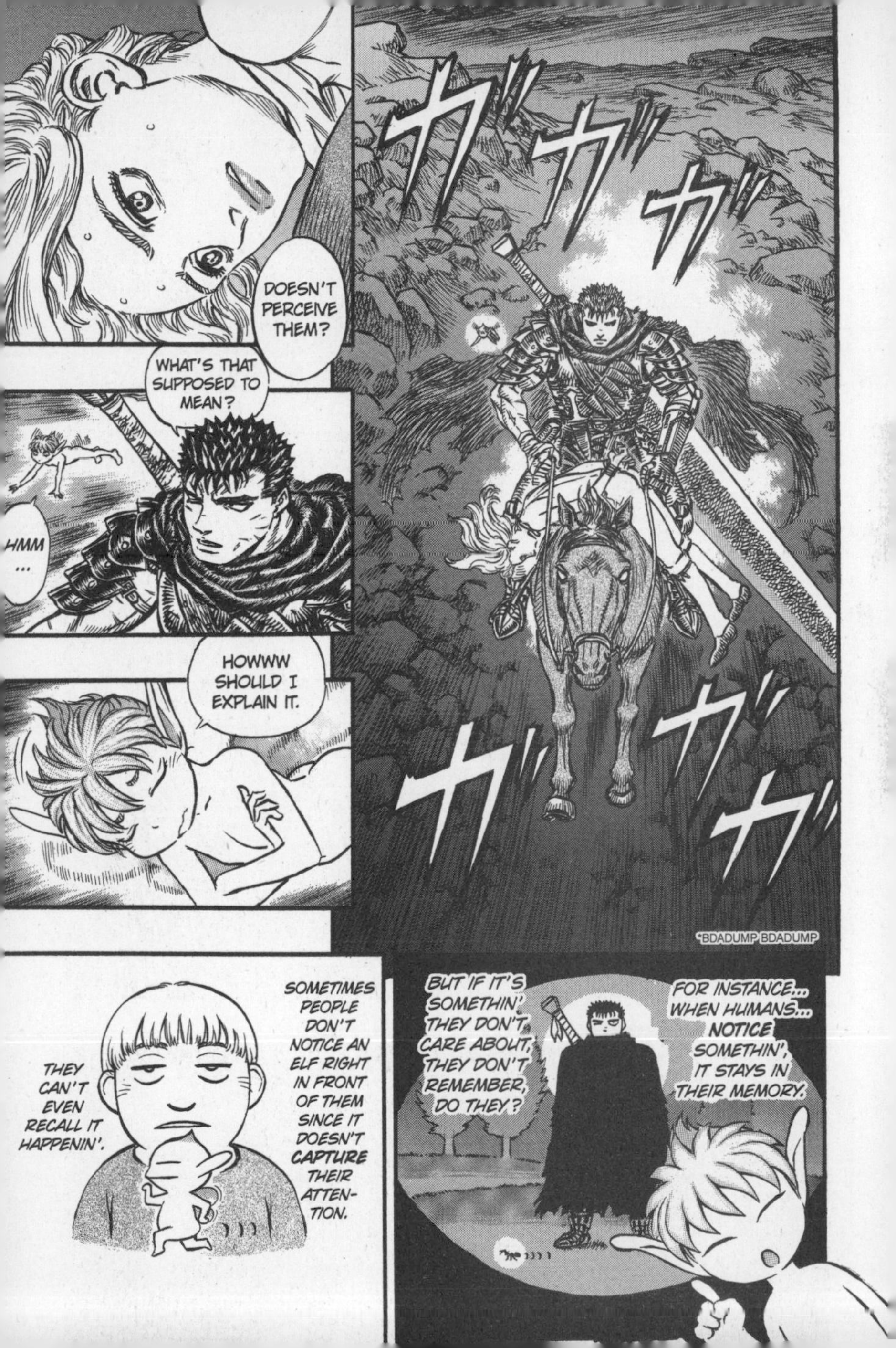
*BDADUMP BDADUMP
DOESN'T PERCEIVE THEM?
WHAT'S THAT SUPPOSED TO MEAN?
HMM ...
HOWWW SHOULD I EXPLAIN IT.
FOR INSTANCE... WHEN HUMANS... NOTICE SOMETHIN', IT STAYS IN THEIR MEMORY.
BUT IF IT'S SOMETHIN' THEY DON'T CARE ABOUT, THEY DON'T REMEMBER, DO THEY?
SOMETIMES PEOPLE DON'T NOTICE AN ELF RIGHT IN FRONT OF THEM SINCE IT DOESN'T CAPTURE THEIR ATTEN-TION.
THEY CAN'T EVEN RECALL IT HAPPENIN'.

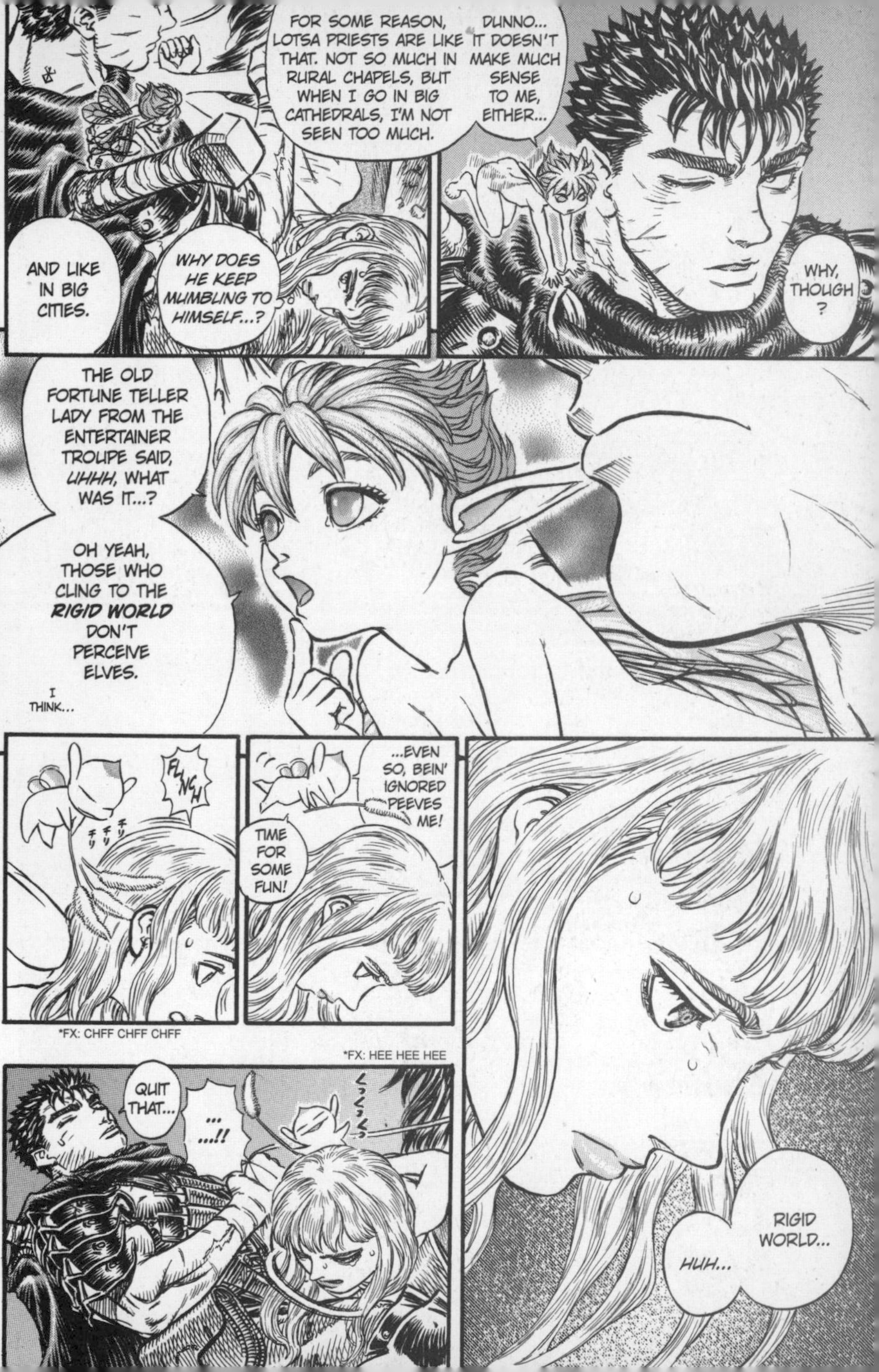
WHY, THOUGH?
DUNNO... IT DOESN'T MAKE MUCH SENSE TO ME, EITHER...
FOR SOME REASON, LOTSA PRIESTS ARE LIKE THAT. NOT SO MUCH IN RURAL CHAPELS, BUT WHEN I GO IN BIG CATHEDRALS, I'M NOT SEEN TOO MUCH.
AND LIKE IN BIG CITIES.
WHY DOES HE KEEP MUMBLING TO HIMSELF...?
THE OLD FORTUNE TELLER LADY FROM THE ENTERTAINER TROUPE SAID, UHHH, WHAT WAS IT...?
OH YEAH, THOSE WHO CLING TO THE RIGID WORLD DON'T PERCEIVE ELVES.
I THINK...
RIGID WORLD...
HUH...
...EVEN SO, BEIN' IGNORED PEEVES ME!
TIME FOR SOME FUN!
*FX: HEE HEE HEE
FLINCH
チリチリ
*FX: CHFF CHFF CHFF
QUIT THAT...
...
...!!
くっくっ

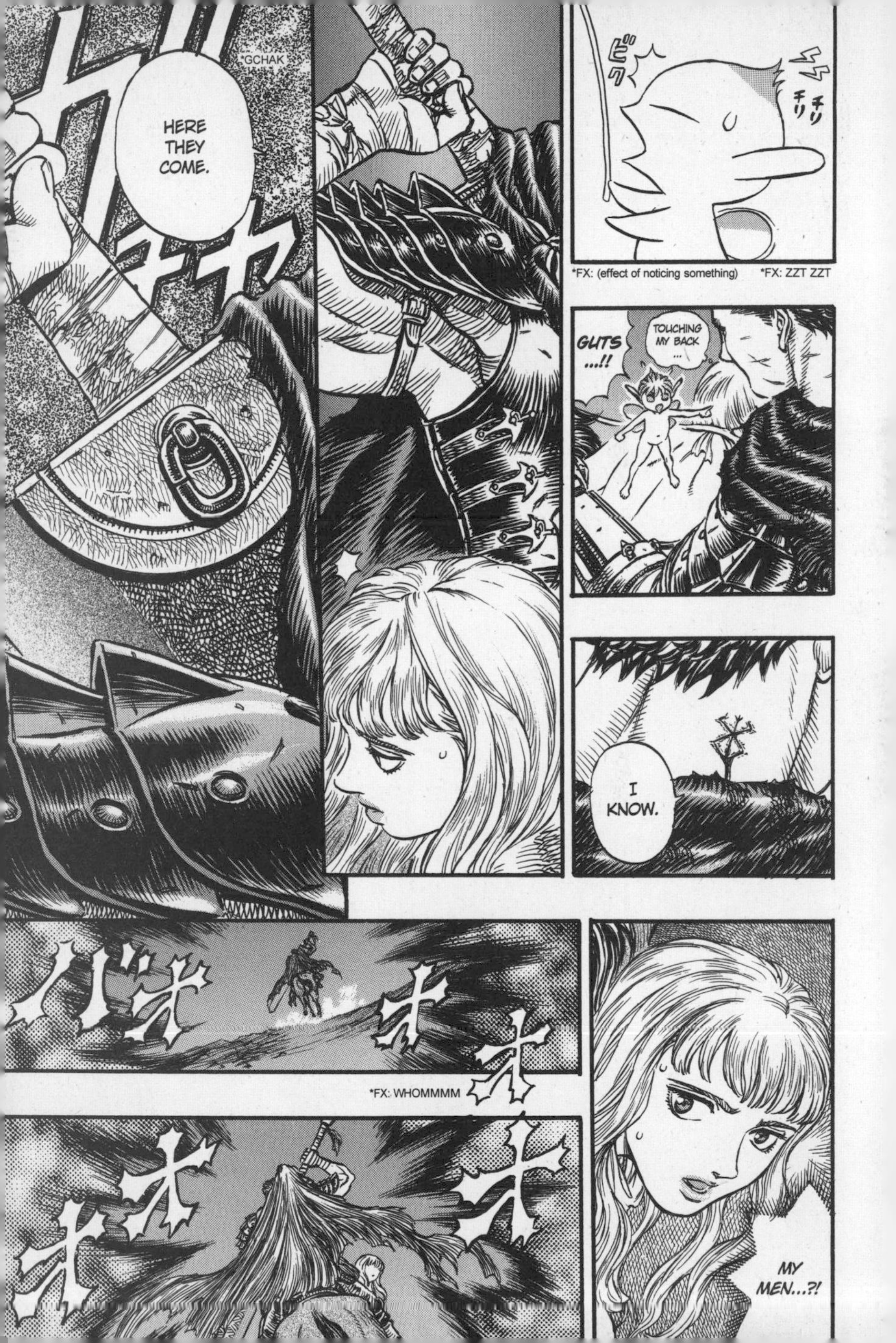
*FX: (effect of noticing something)
*FX: ZZT ZZT
GUTS ...!!
TOUCHING MY BACK ...
I KNOW.
*GCHAK
HERE THEY COME.
MY MEN...?!
*FX: WHOMMMM

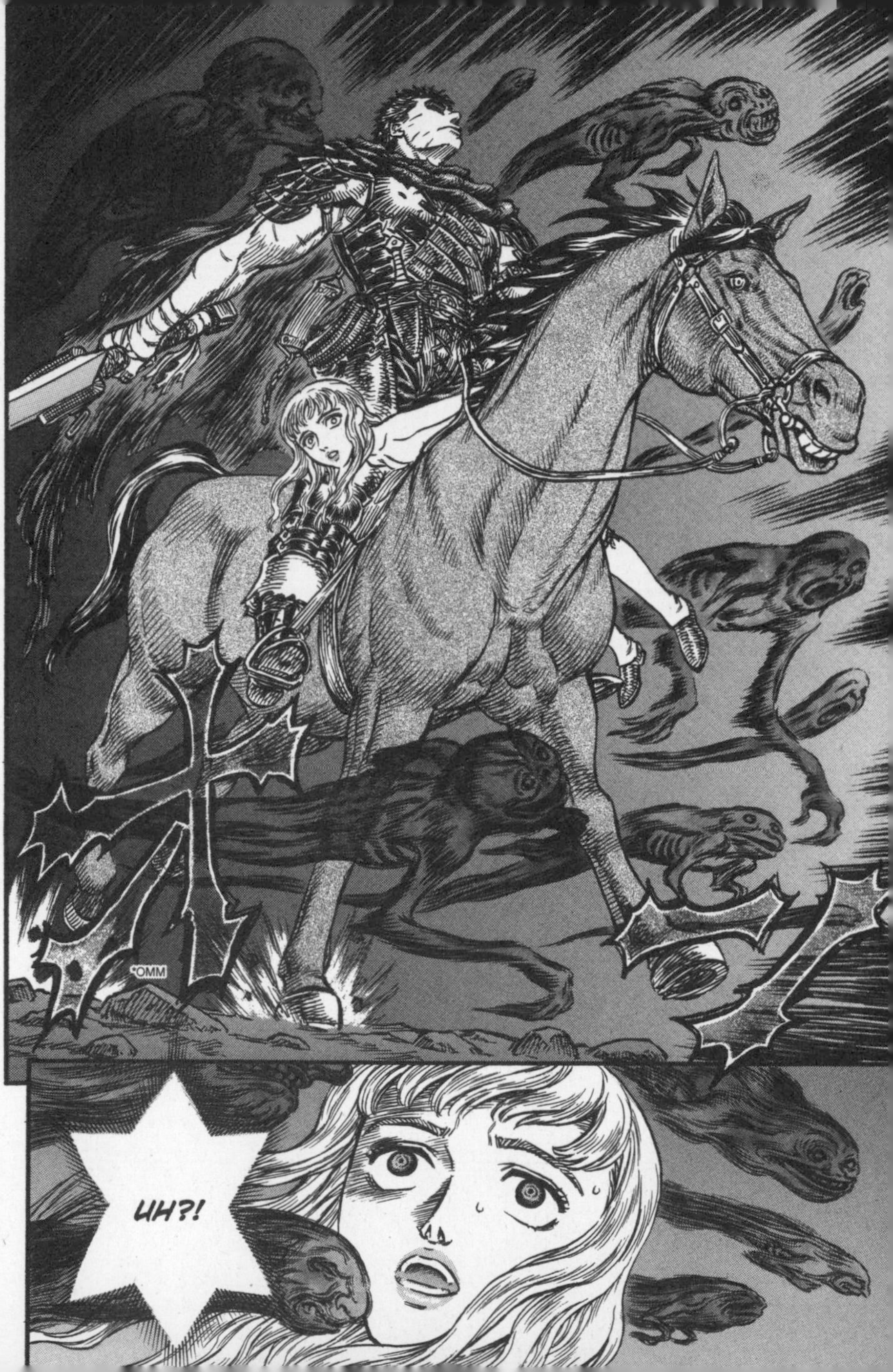
*OMM
UH?!

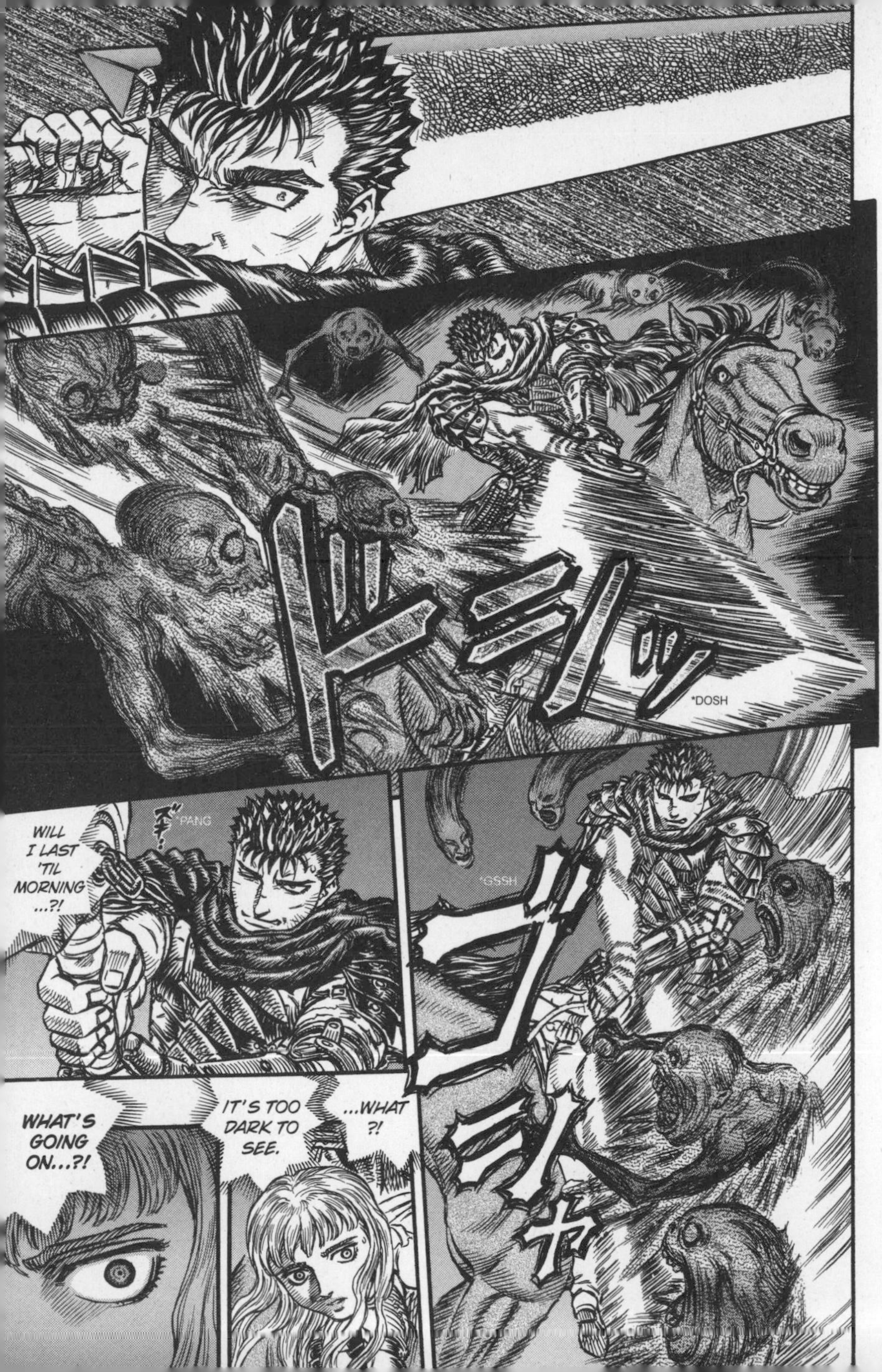
*DOSH
*GSSH
PANG
WILL I LAST 'TIL MORNING ...?!
...WHAT ?!
IT'S TOO DARK TO SEE.
WHAT'S GOING ON...?!

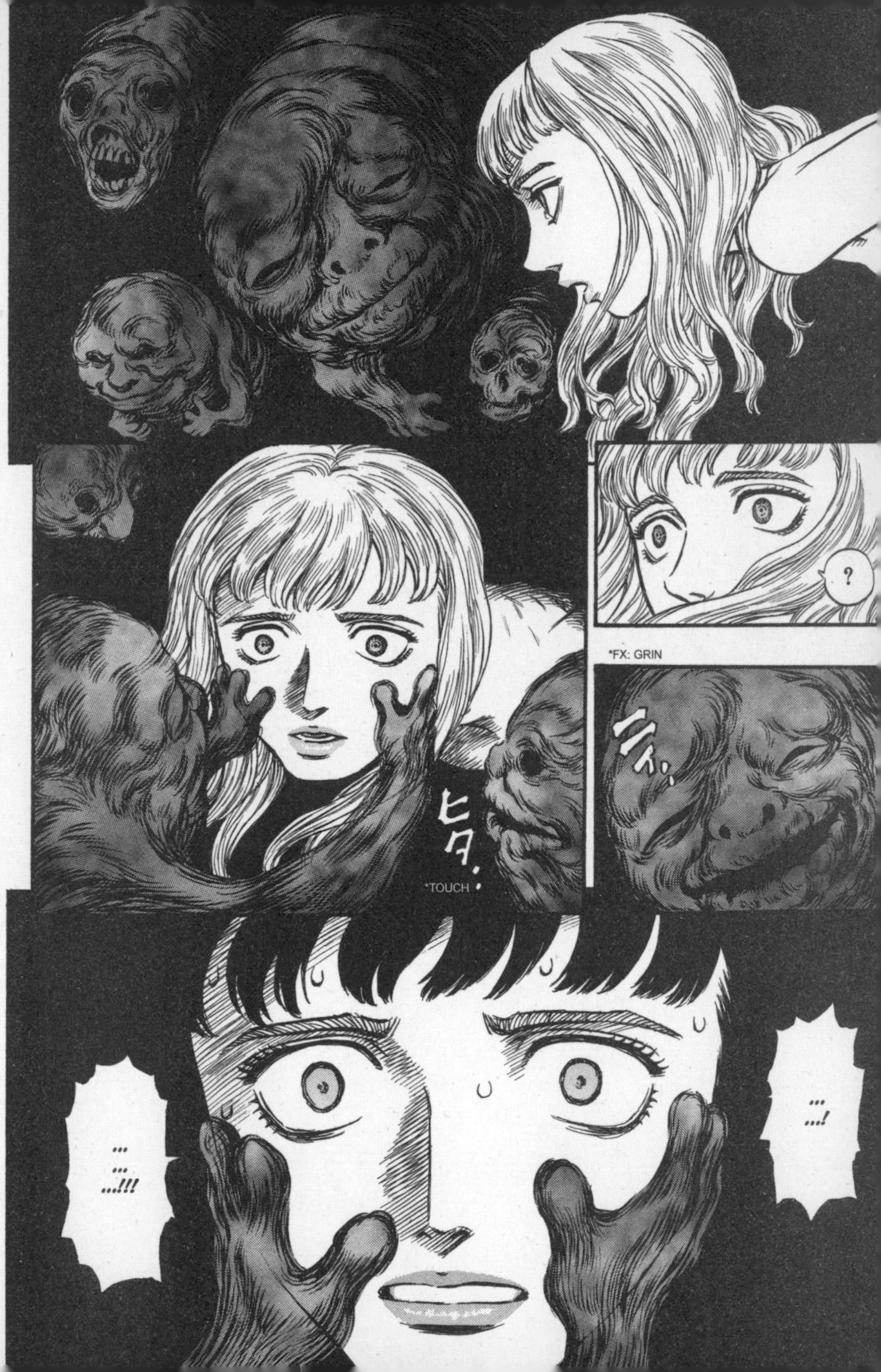
?
*FX: GRIN
ニィ
ヒタ
*TOUCH
...
...!
...
...
...!!!

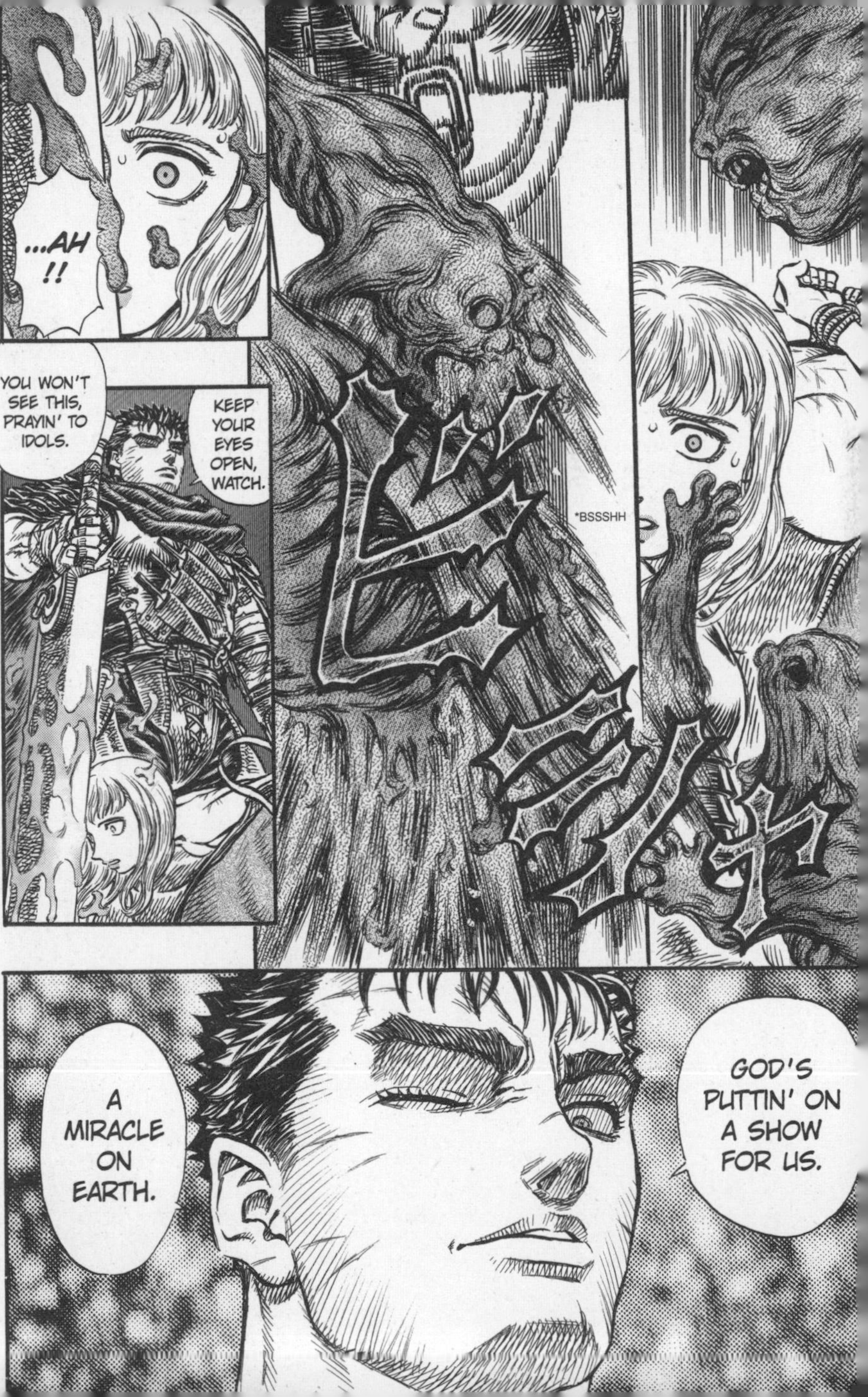
*BSSSHH
...AH !!
KEEP YOUR EYES OPEN, WATCH.
YOU WON'T SEE THIS, PRAYIN' TO IDOLS.
GOD'S PUTTIN' ON A SHOW FOR US.
A MIRACLE ON EARTH.

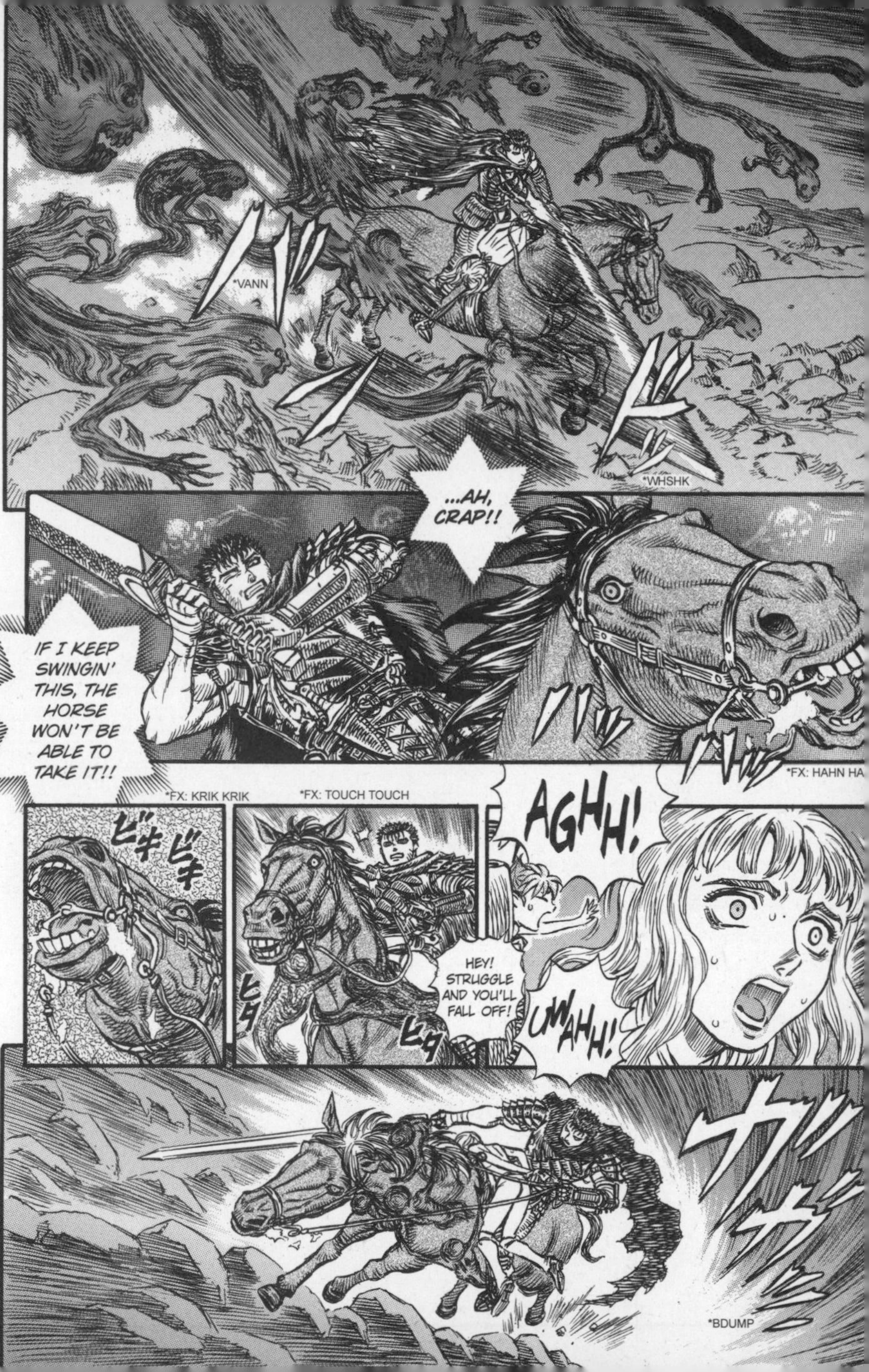
*VANN
*WHSHK
...AH, CRAP!!
IF I KEEP SWINGIN' THIS, THE HORSE WON'T BE ABLE TO TAKE IT!!
*FX: HAHN HA
AGHH!
HEY! STRUGGLE AND YOU'LL FALL OFF!
UWAHH!
ヒタ
ヒタ
*FX: TOUCH TOUCH
ビキ
ビキ
*FX: KRIK KRIK
*BDUMP

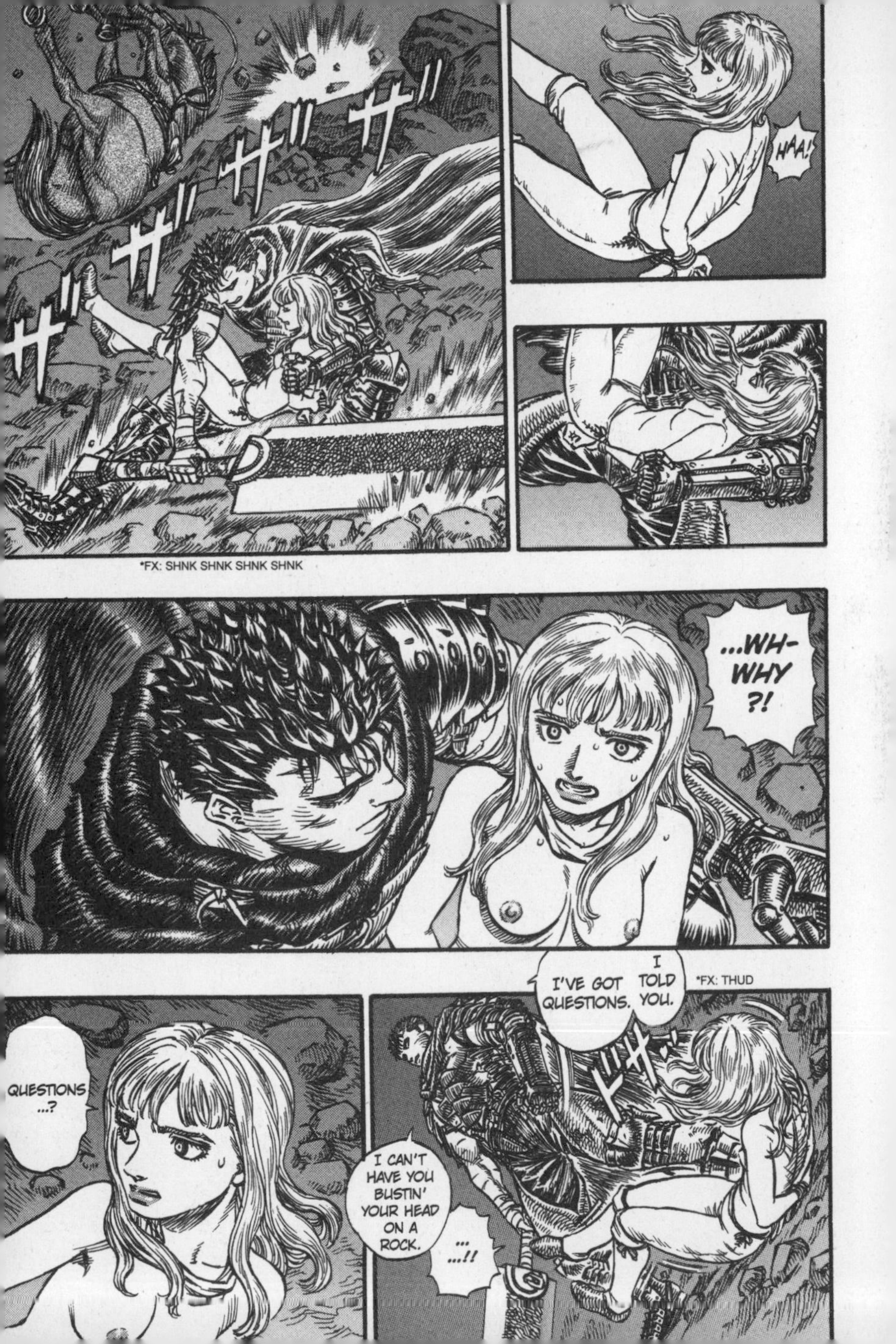
HAA!
*FX: SHNK SHNK SHNK SHNK
...WH- WHY ?!
I TOLD YOU.
I'VE GOT QUESTIONS.
*FX: THUD
I CAN'T HAVE YOU BUSTIN' YOUR HEAD ON A ROCK.
... ...!!
QUESTIONS ...?

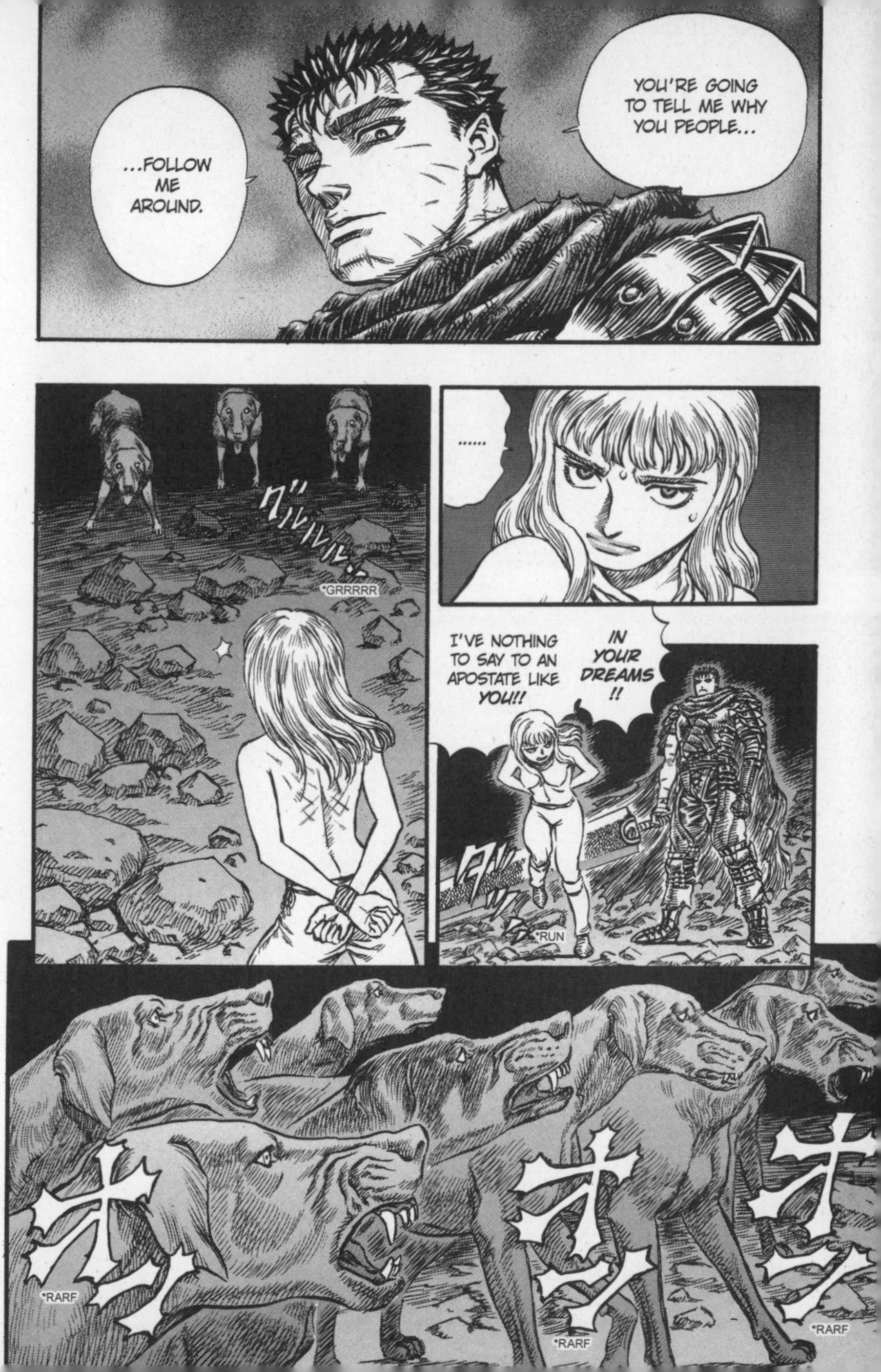
YOU'RE GOING TO TELL ME WHY YOU PEOPLE...
...FOLLOW ME AROUND.
......
IN YOUR DREAMS!!
I'VE NOTHING TO SAY TO AN APOSTATE LIKE YOU!!
*RUN
*GRRRRR
*RARF
*RARF
*RARF

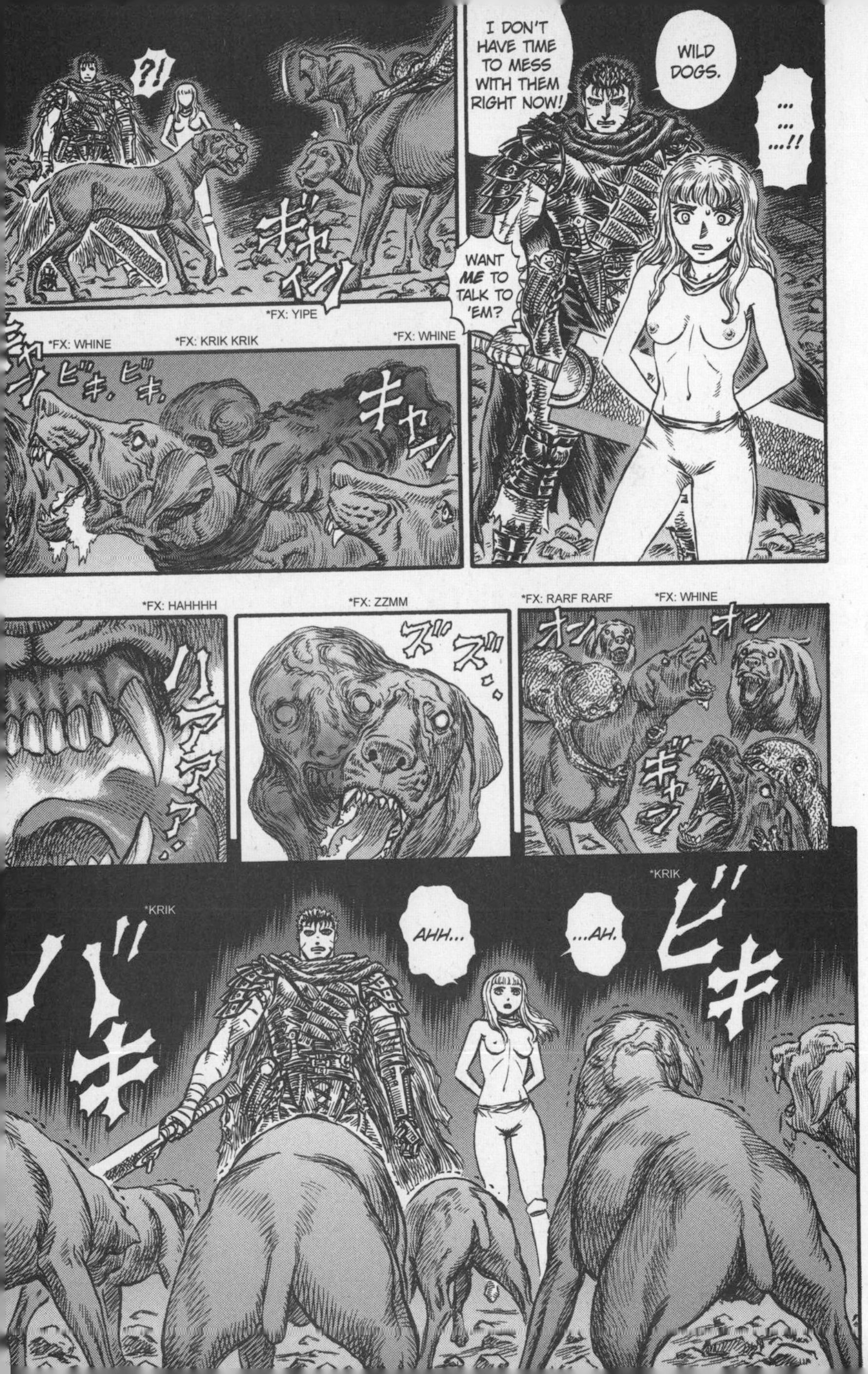
WILD DOGS.
... ...!!
I DON'T HAVE TIME TO MESS WITH THEM RIGHT NOW!
WANT *ME* TO TALK TO 'EM?
?!
*FX: YIPE
*FX: WHINE
*FX: KRIK KRIK
*FX: WHINE
*FX: WHINE
*FX: RARF RARF
*FX: ZZMM
*FX: HAHHHH
*KRIK
...AH.
AHH...
*KRIK

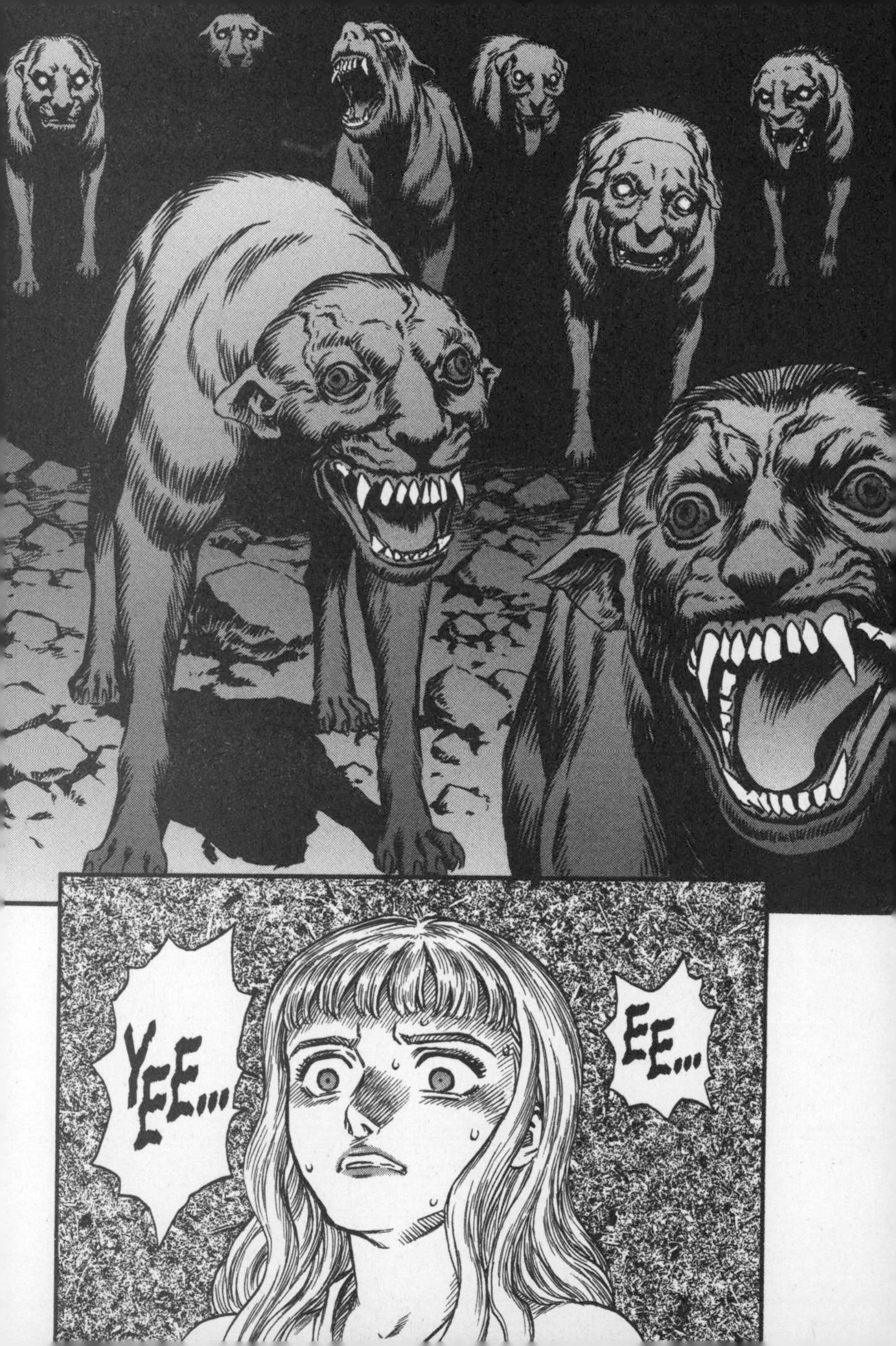
YEE...
EE...

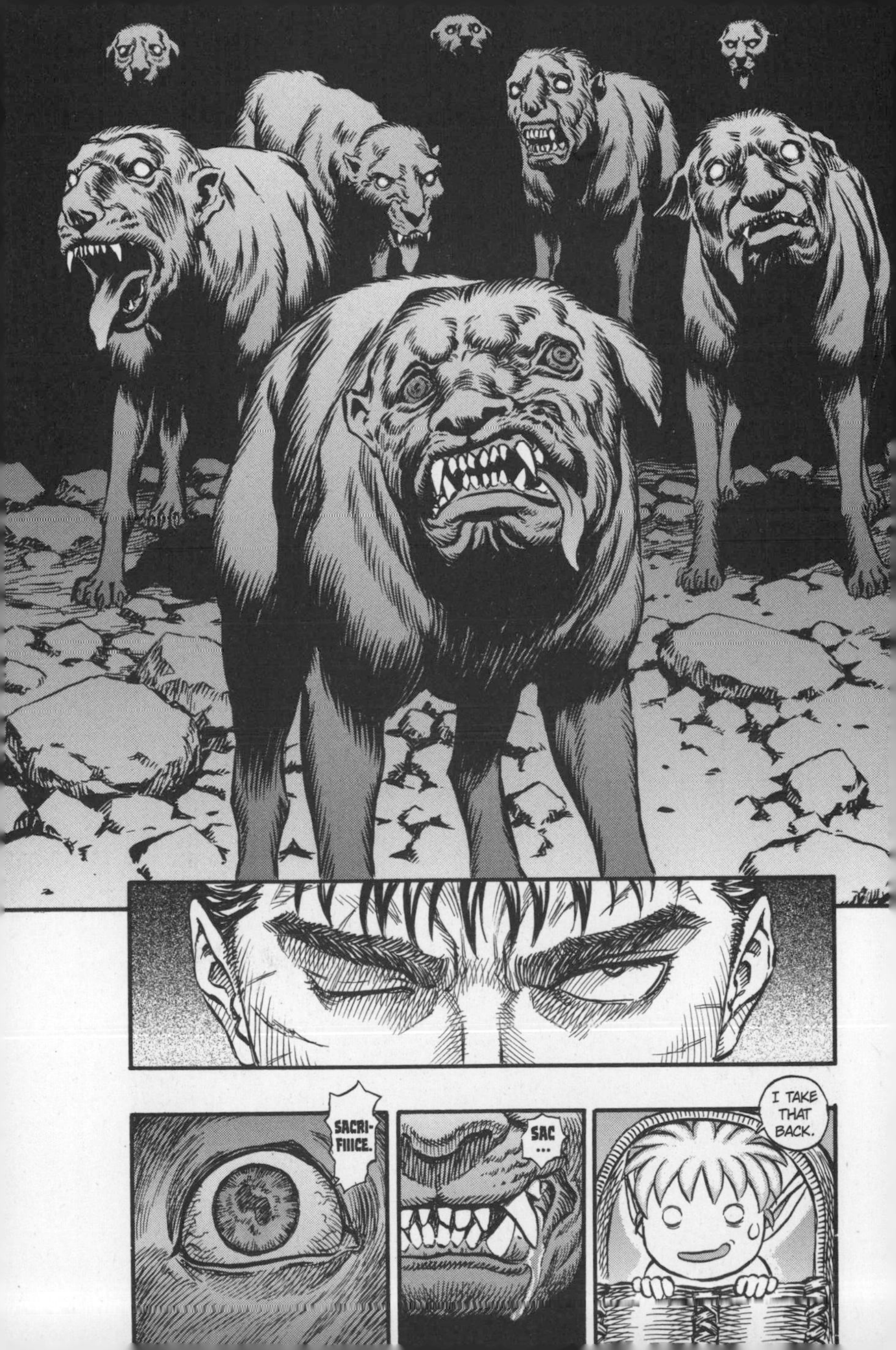
I TAKE THAT BACK.
SAC ...
SACRI-FIIICE.

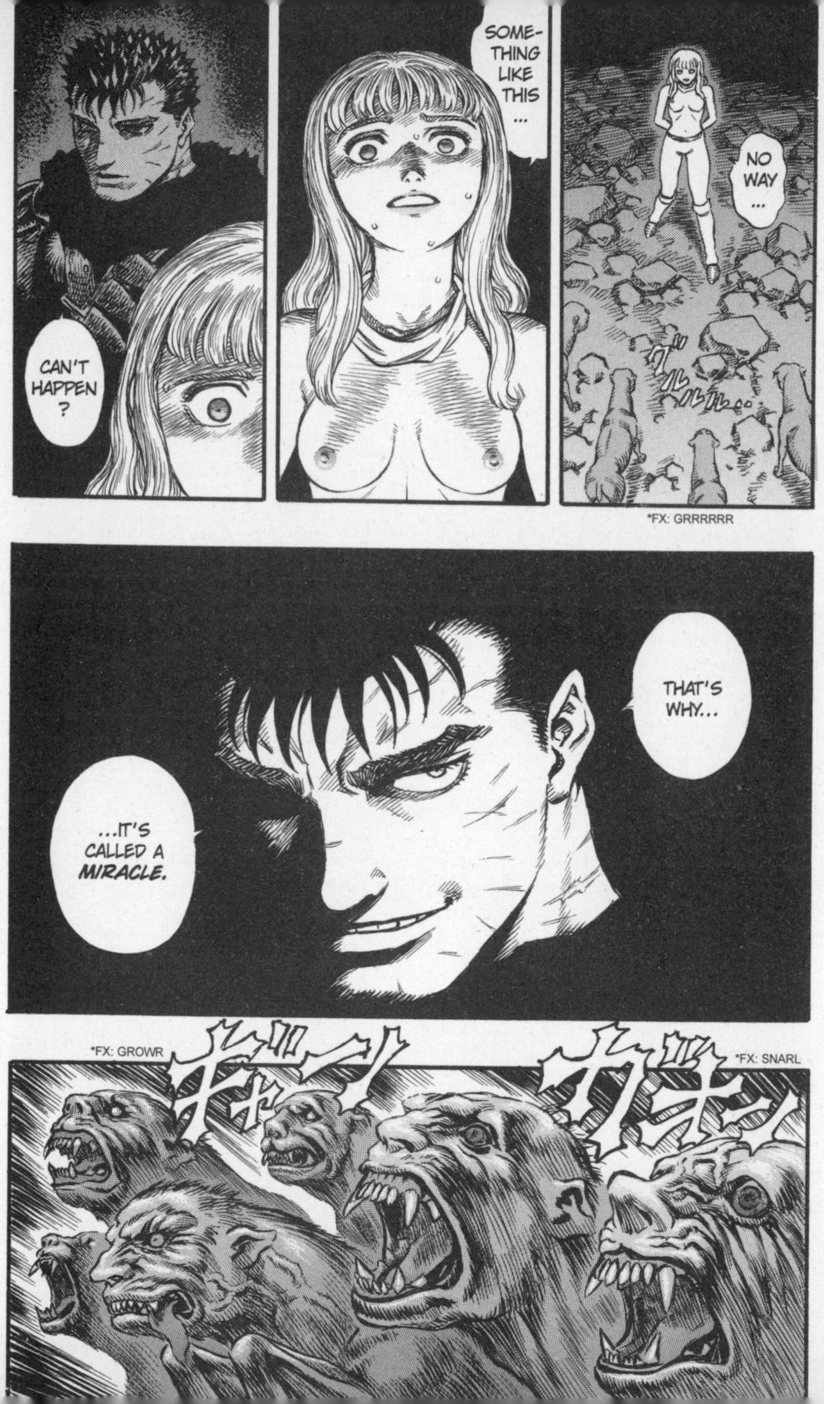
NO WAY ...
*FX: GRRRRRR
SOMETHING LIKE THIS ...
CAN'T HAPPEN ?
THAT'S WHY...
...IT'S CALLED A MIRACLE.
*FX: SNARL
*FX: GROWR

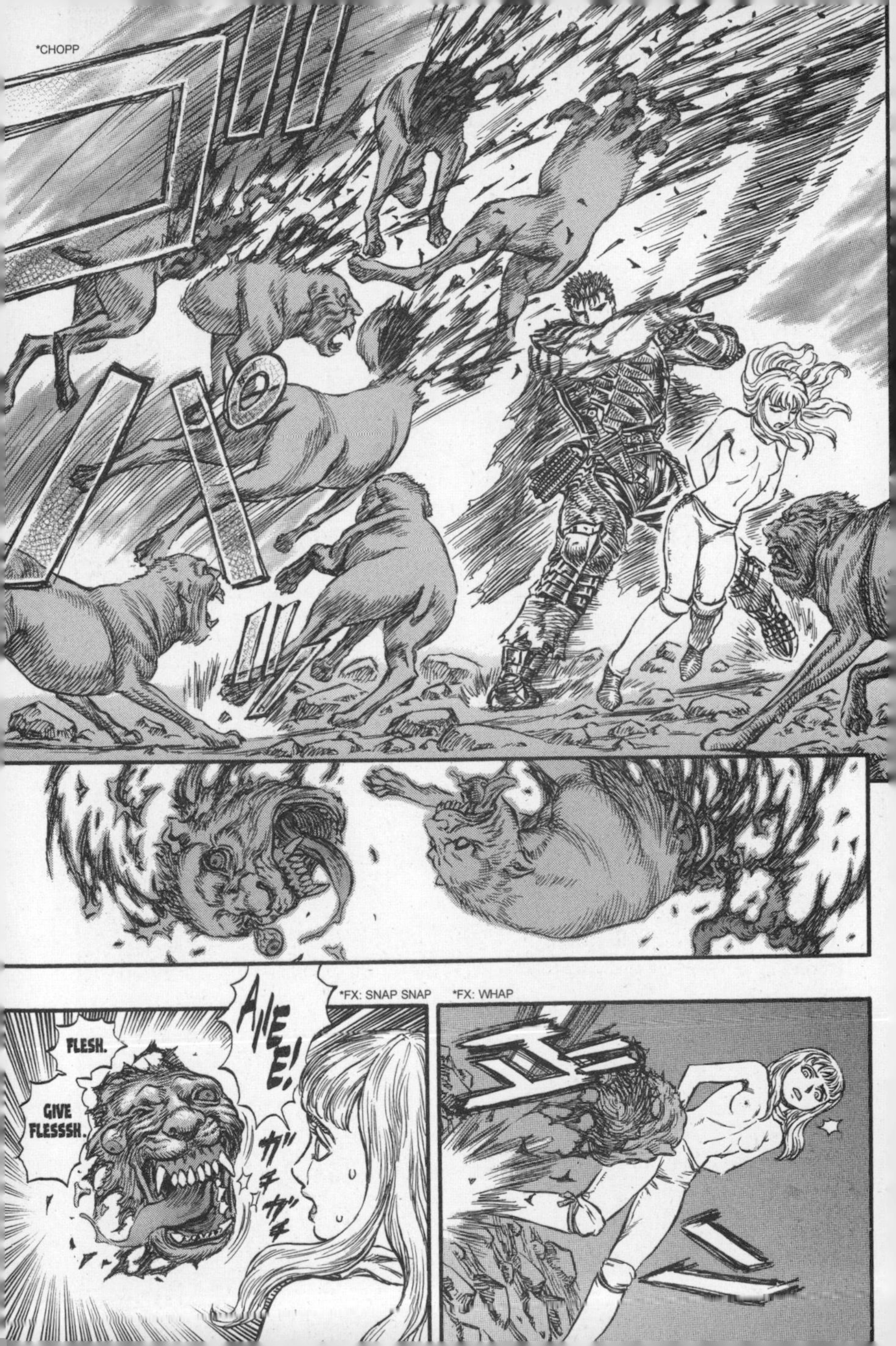
*CHOPP
*FX: WHAP
*FX: SNAP SNAP
AIEEE!
FLESH.
GIVE FLESSSH.

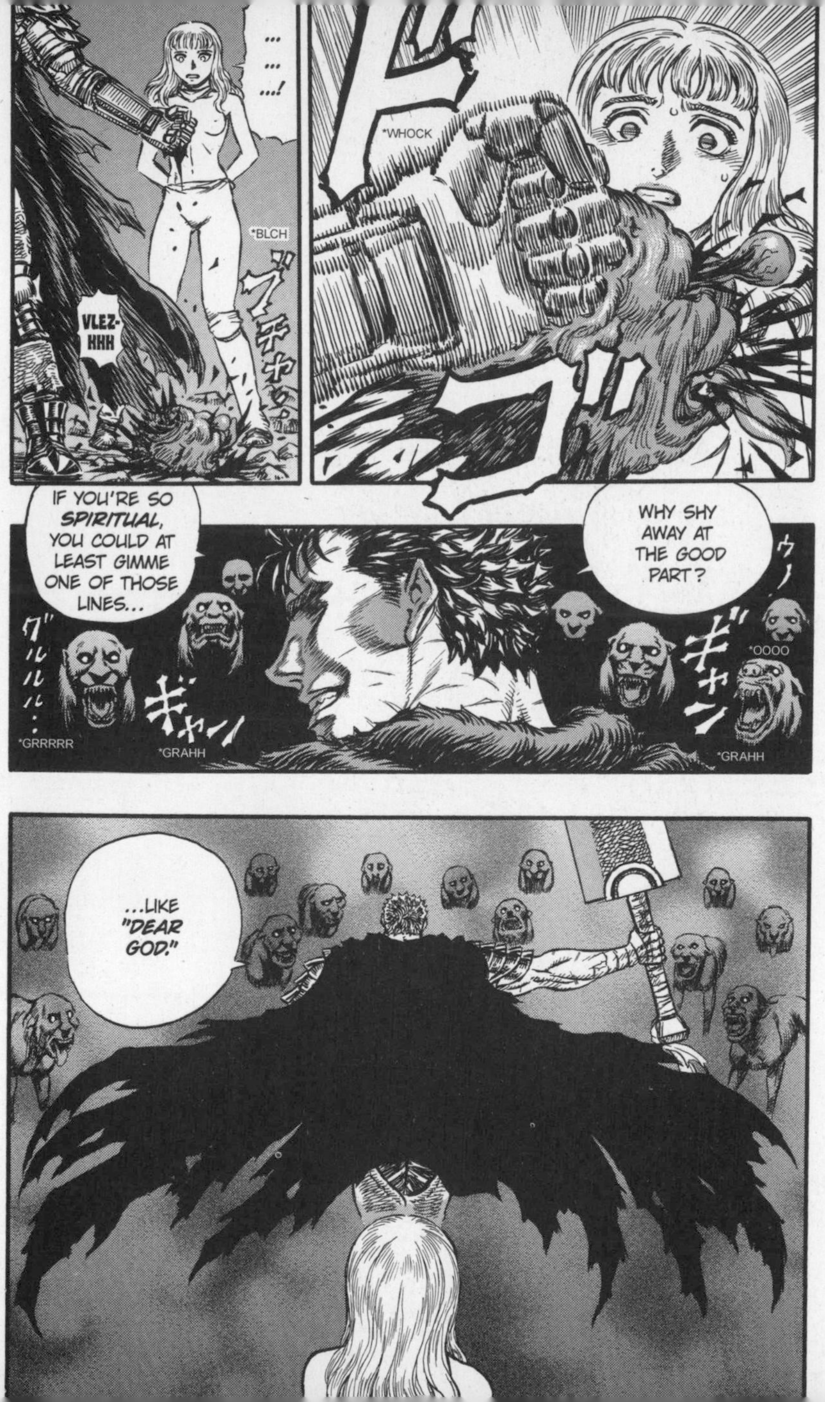

*WHOCK
...
...
...!
*BLCH
VLEZ-HHH
WHY SHY AWAY AT THE GOOD PART?
*OOOO
*GRAHH
IF YOU'RE SO ***SPIRITUAL***, YOU COULD AT LEAST GIMME ONE OF THOSE LINES...
*GRAHH
*GRRRRR
...LIKE ***"DEAR GOD."***

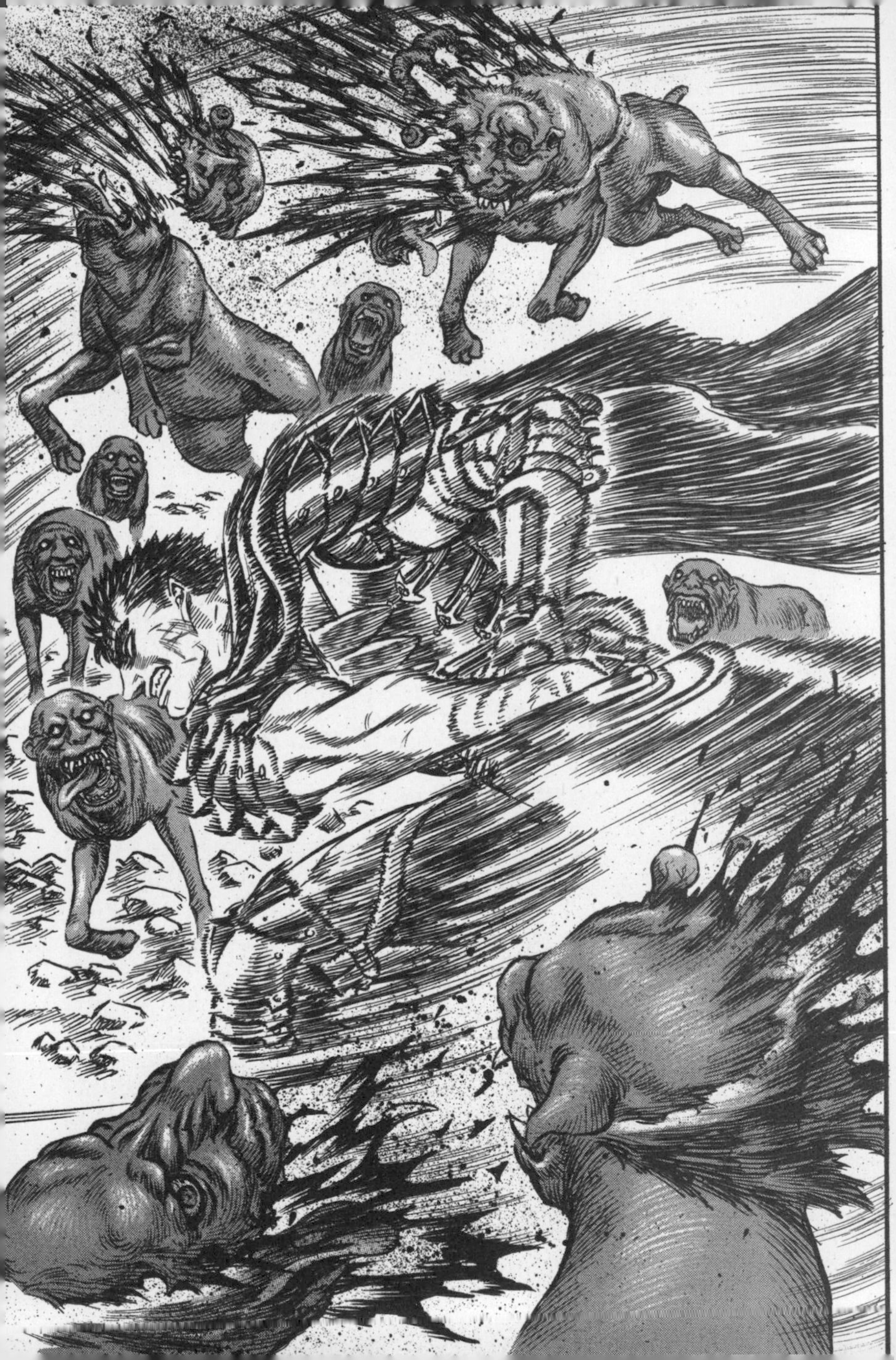

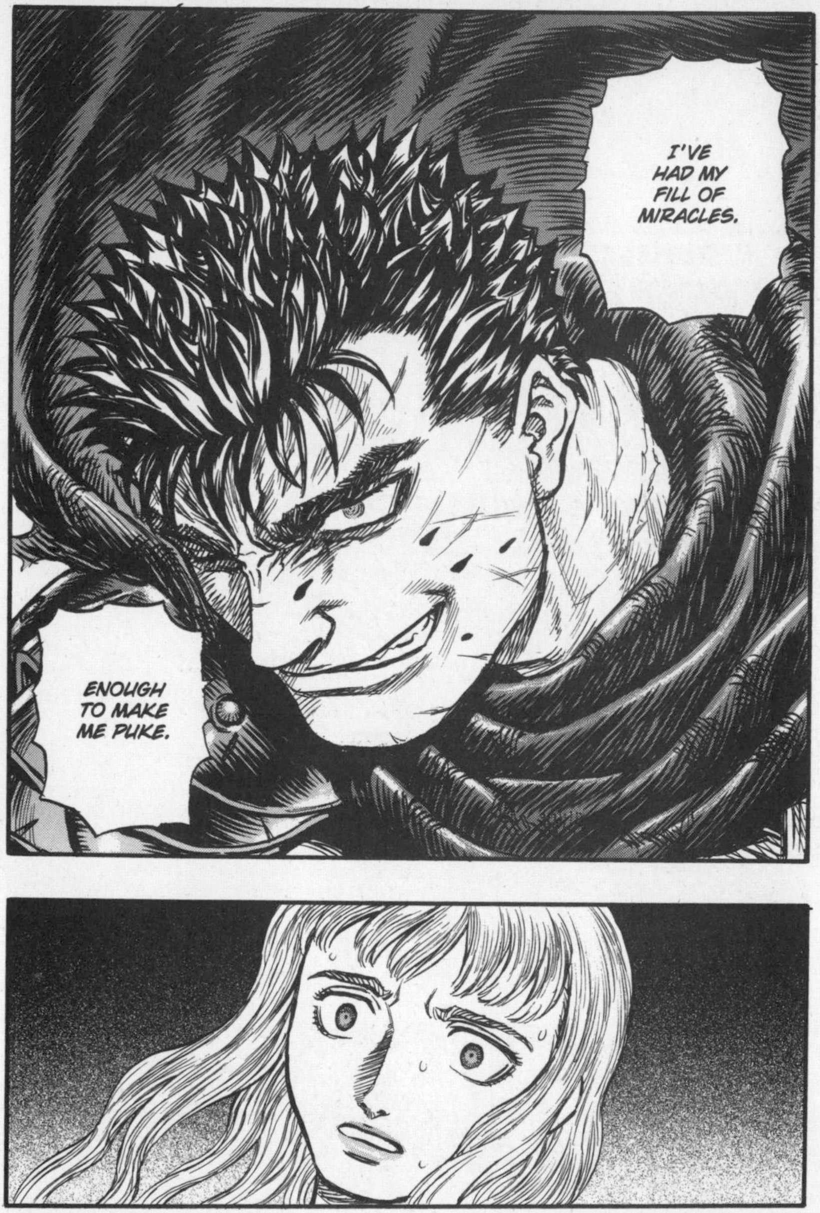
I'VE HAD MY FILL OF MIRACLES.
ENOUGH TO MAKE ME PUKE.

CONVICTION ARC
BINDING CHAIN CHAPTER

NIGHT OF MIRACLES: END

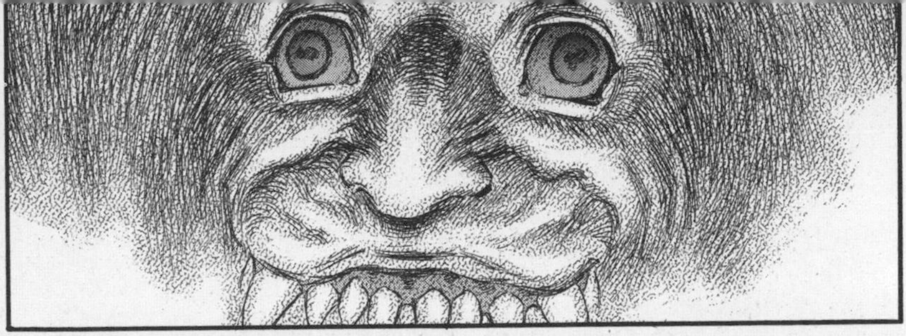

CONVICTION ARC

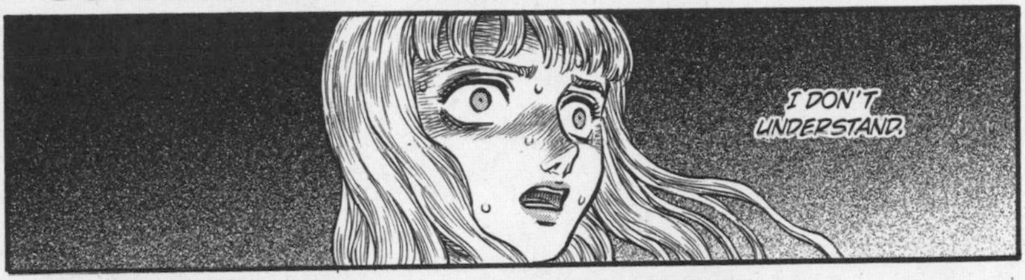
I DON'T UNDERSTAND.

BINDING CHAIN CHAPTER

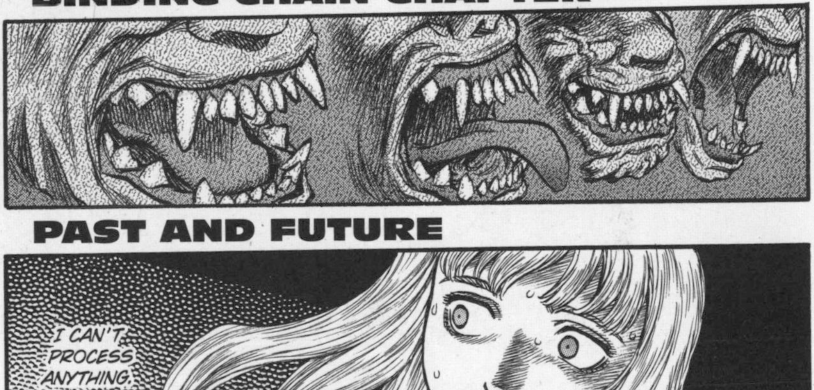

PAST AND FUTURE

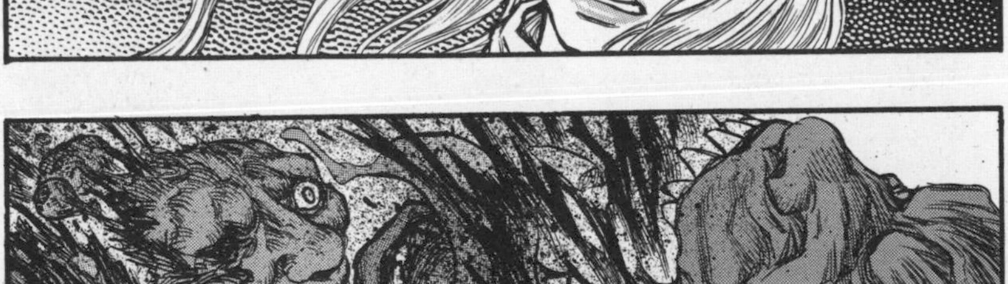
I CAN'T PROCESS ANYTHING.

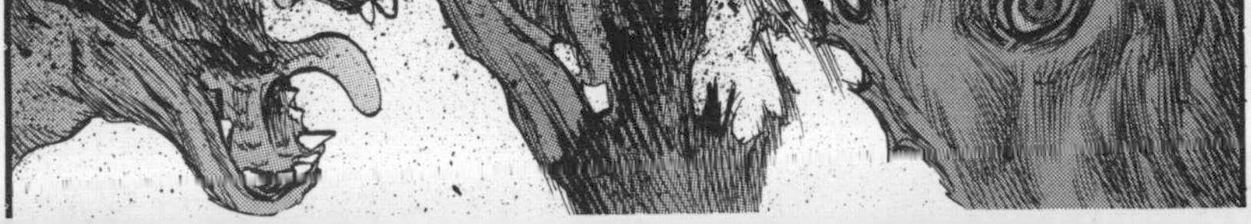

断罪篇 縛鎖(ばくさ)の章 去来

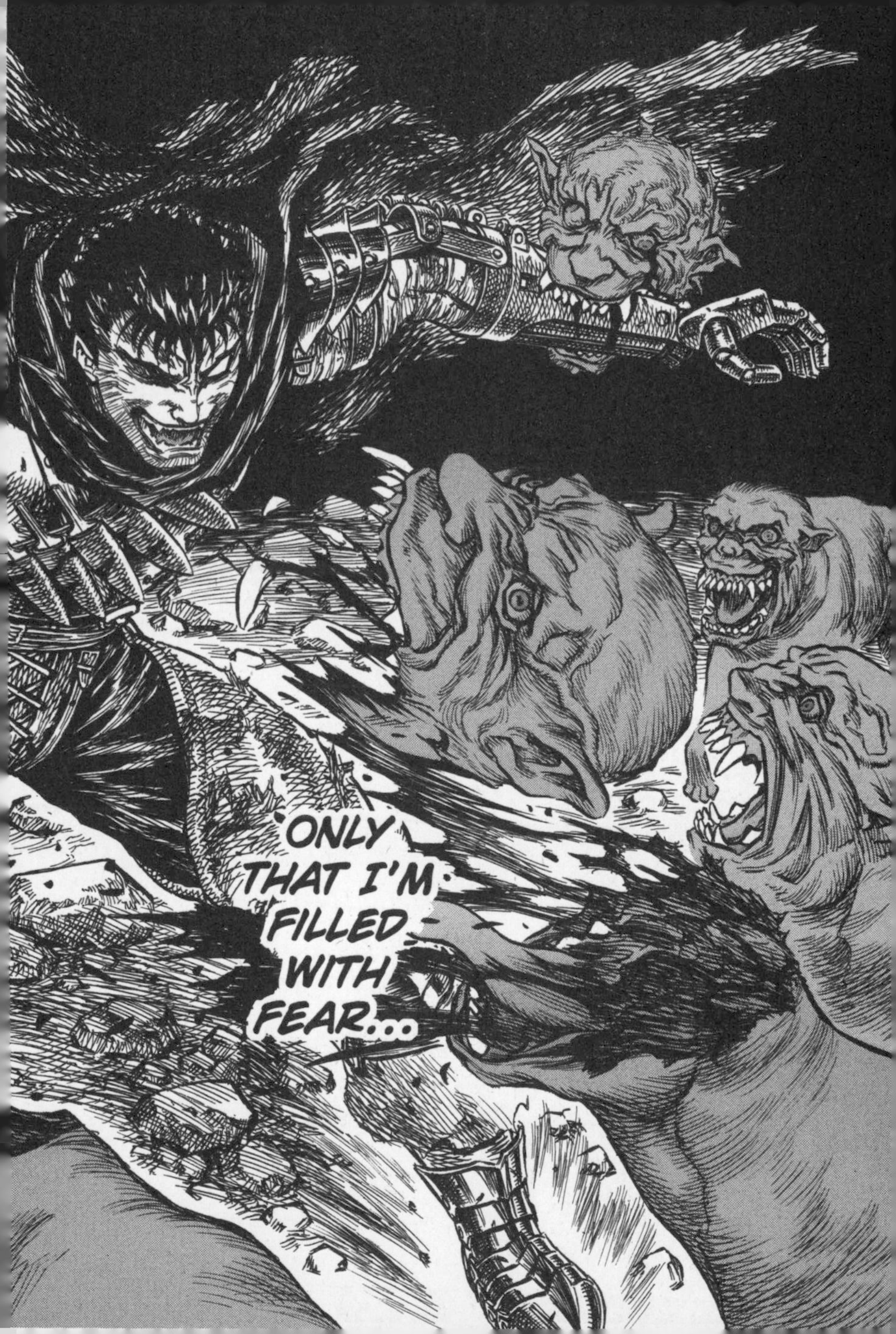
ONLY THAT I'M FILLED WITH FEAR...

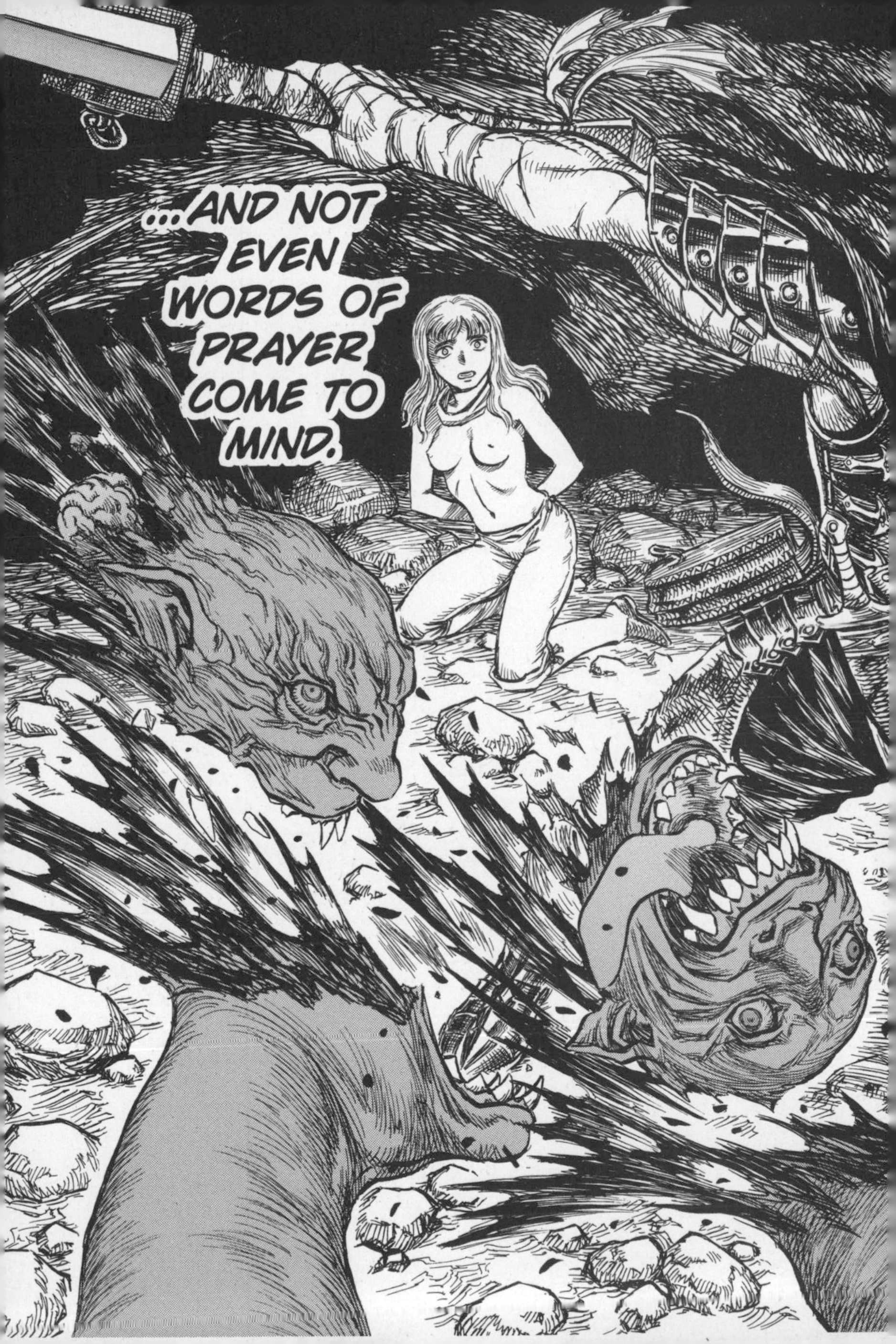
...AND NOT EVEN WORDS OF PRAYER COME TO MIND.

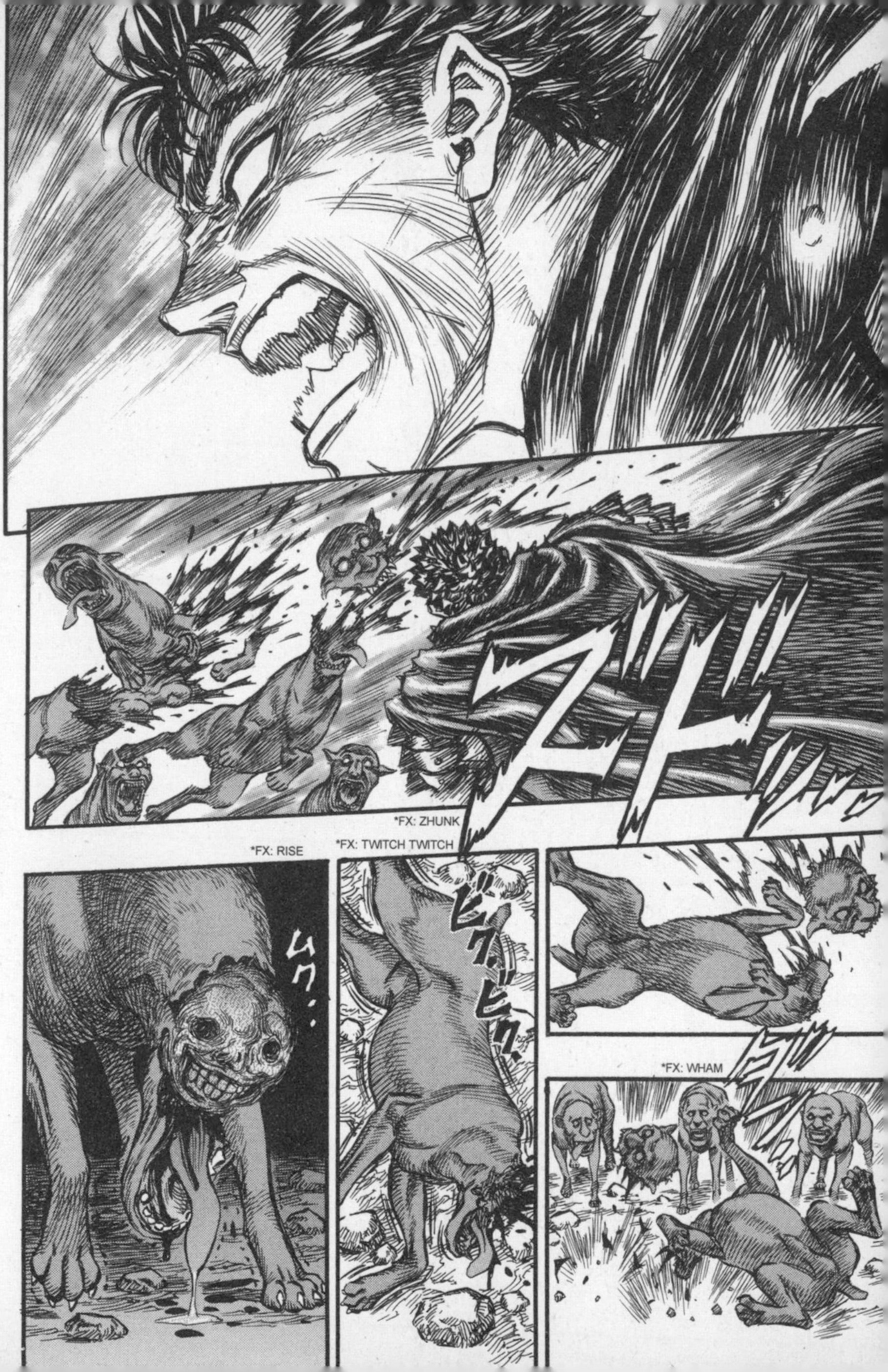
*FX: ZHUNK
*FX: WHAM
*FX: TWITCH TWITCH
*FX: RISE

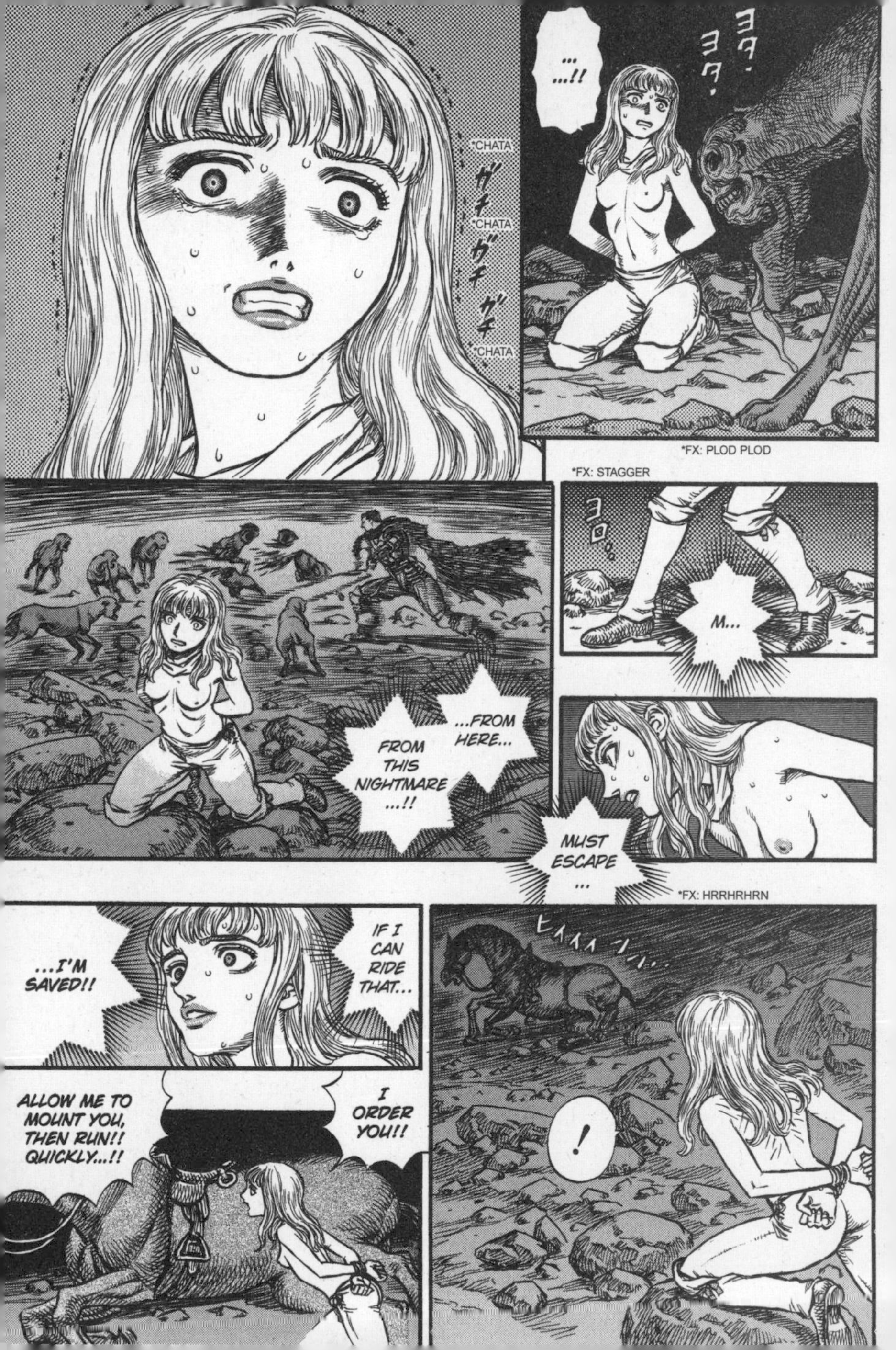
…
…!!
ヨタ ヨタ
*FX: PLOD PLOD
ガチ ガチ ガチ
*CHATA
*CHATA
*CHATA
*FX: STAGGER
M…
MUST ESCAPE …
…FROM HERE…
FROM THIS NIGHTMARE …!!
*FX: HRRHRHRN
!
IF I CAN RIDE THAT…
…I'M SAVED!!
I ORDER YOU!!
ALLOW ME TO MOUNT YOU, THEN RUN!! QUICKLY…!!

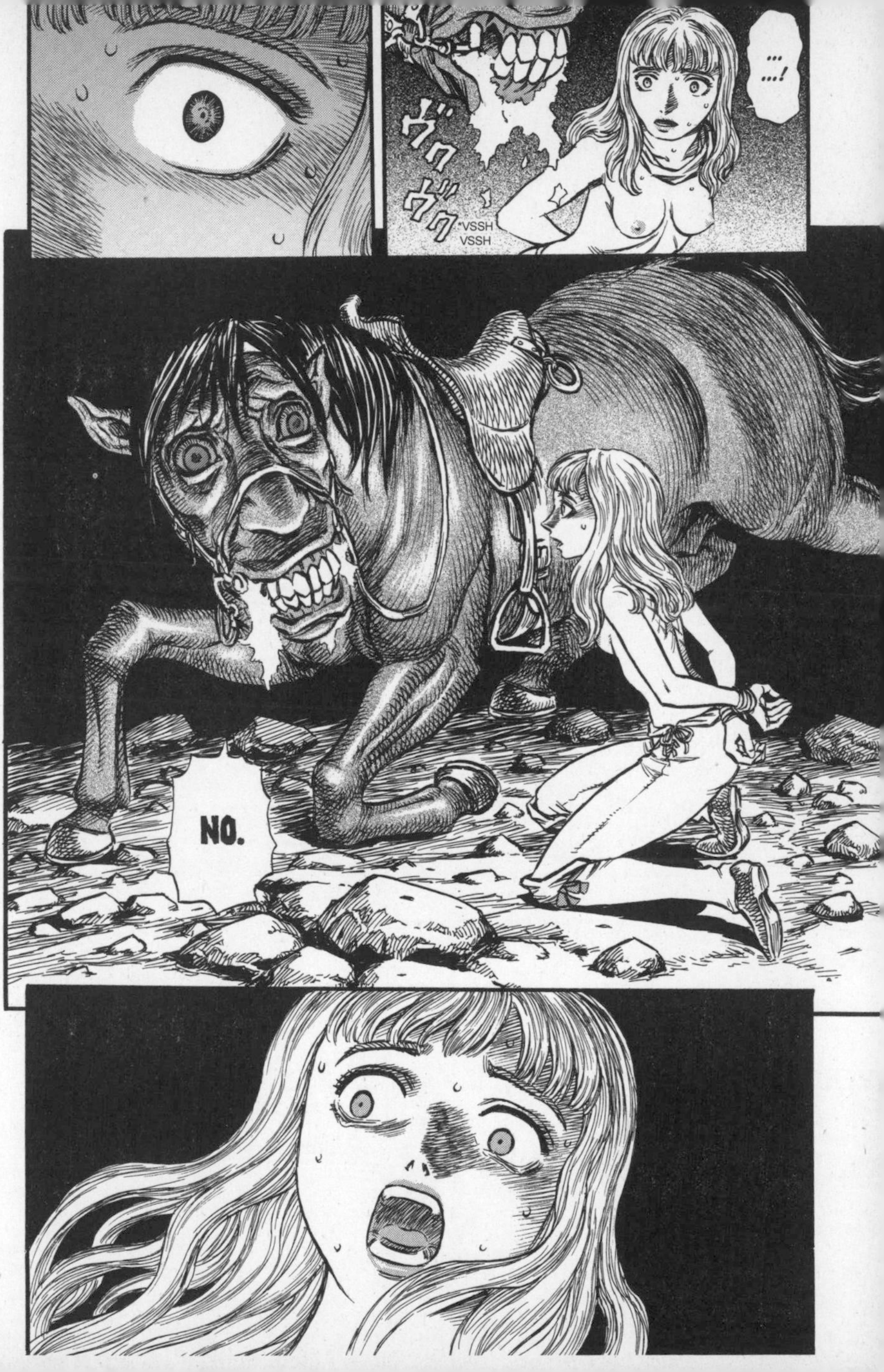
... ...!
ヴクヴク
*VSSH VSSH
NO.

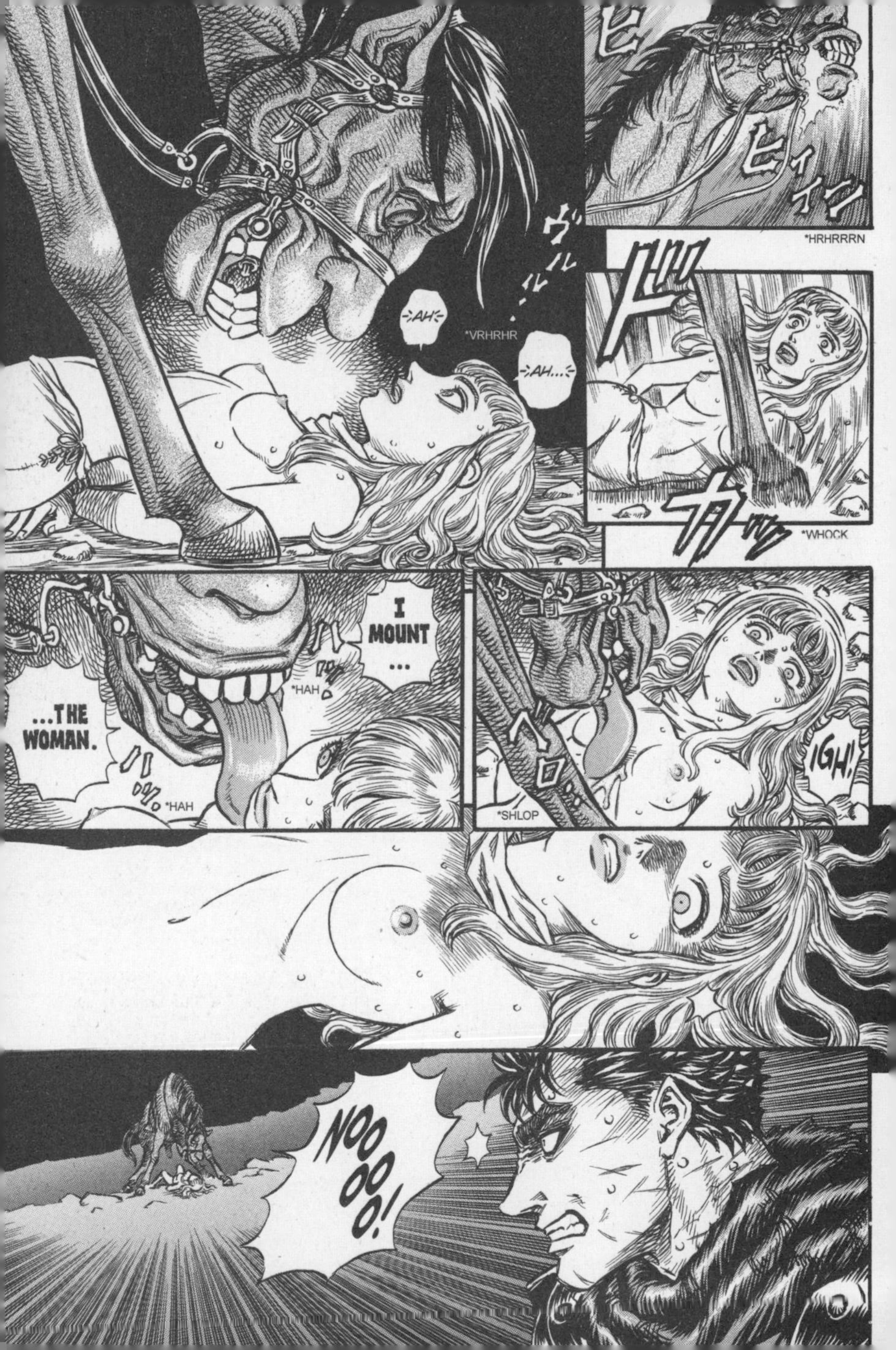
ヒ
ヒィイイ
*HRHRRRN
ドッ
ガッ
*WHOCK
ヴルル!
*VRHRHR
AH
AH...
*SHLOP
IGH!
I MOUNT ...
*HAH
...THE WOMAN.
*HAH
NOOOOO!

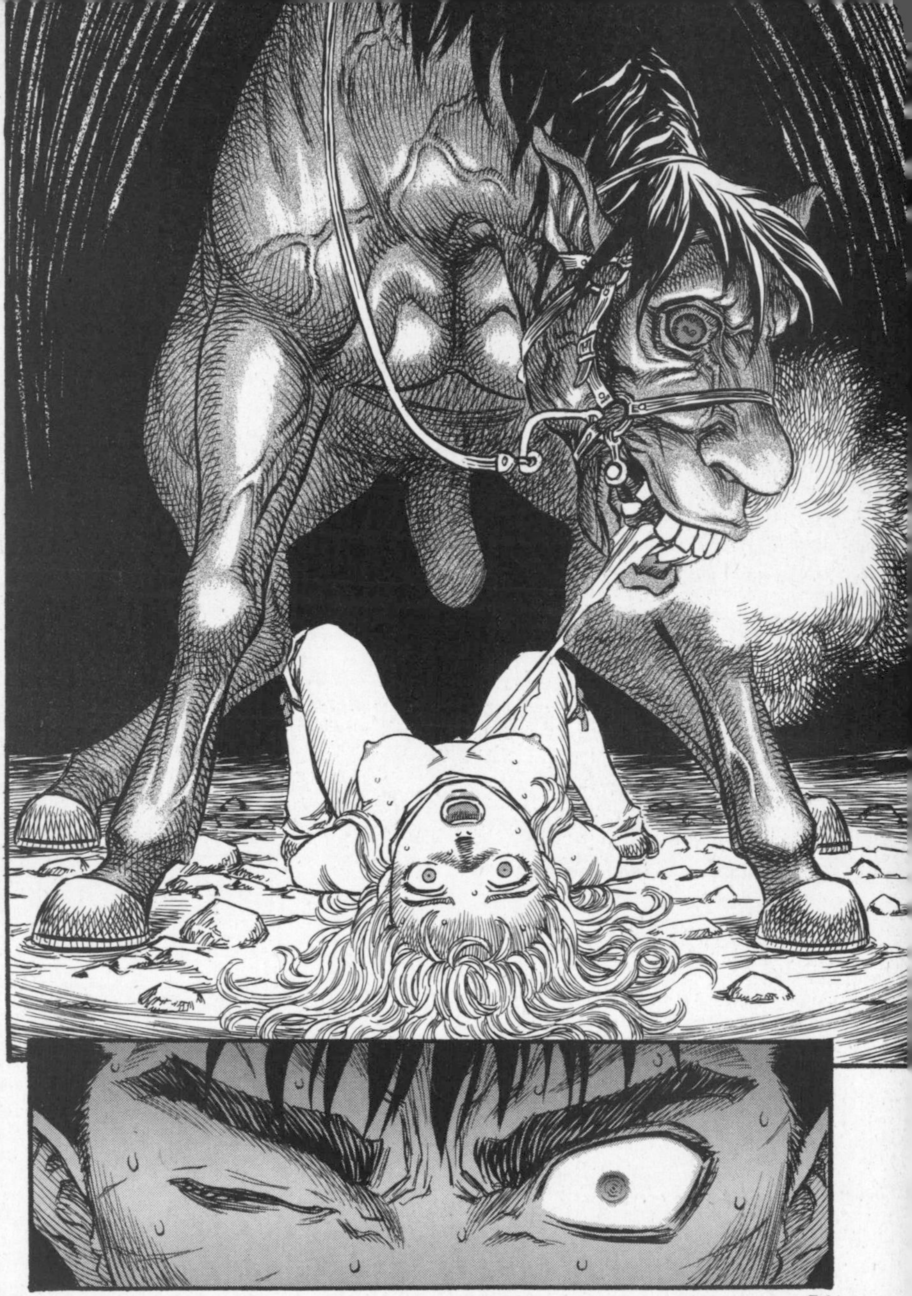

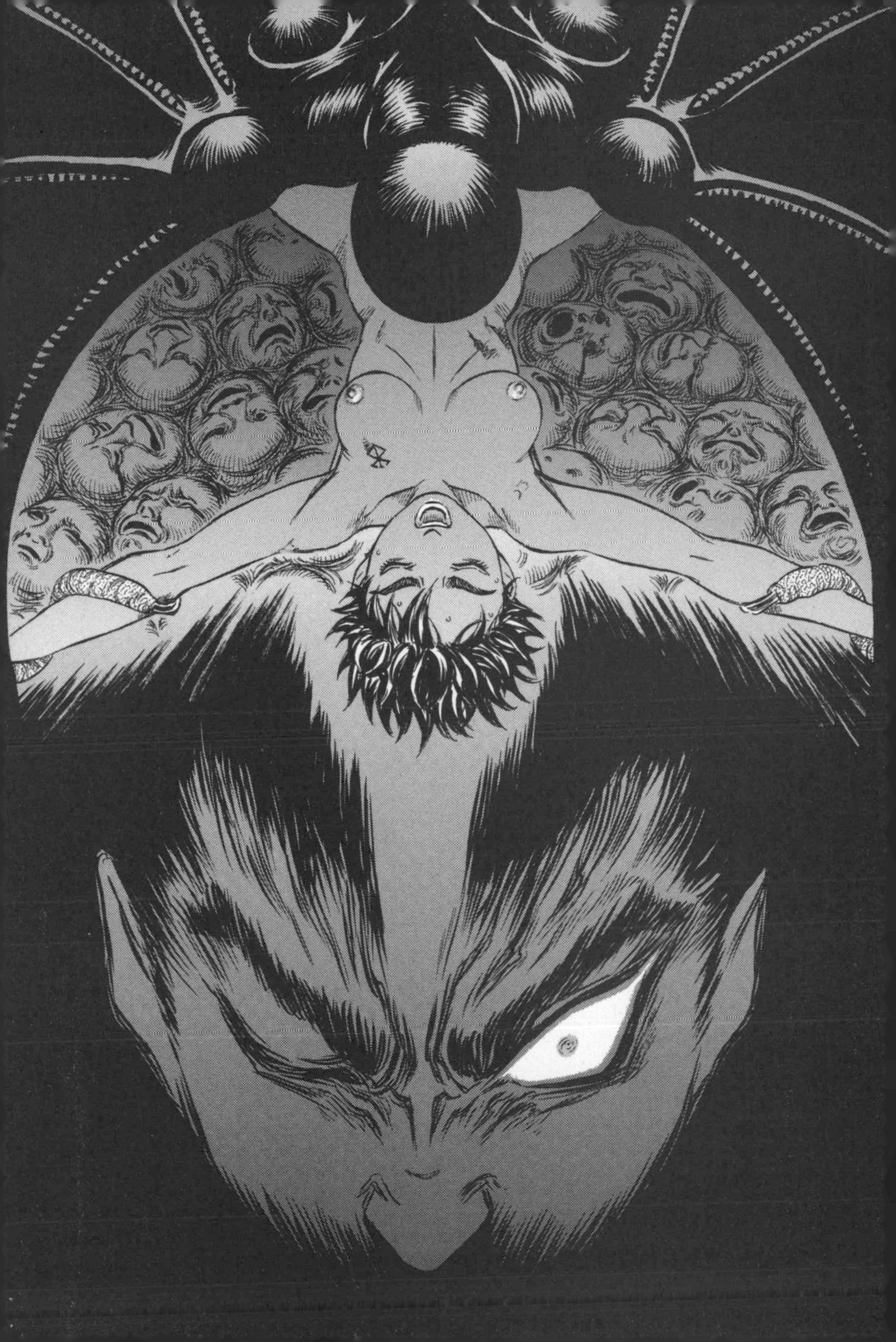

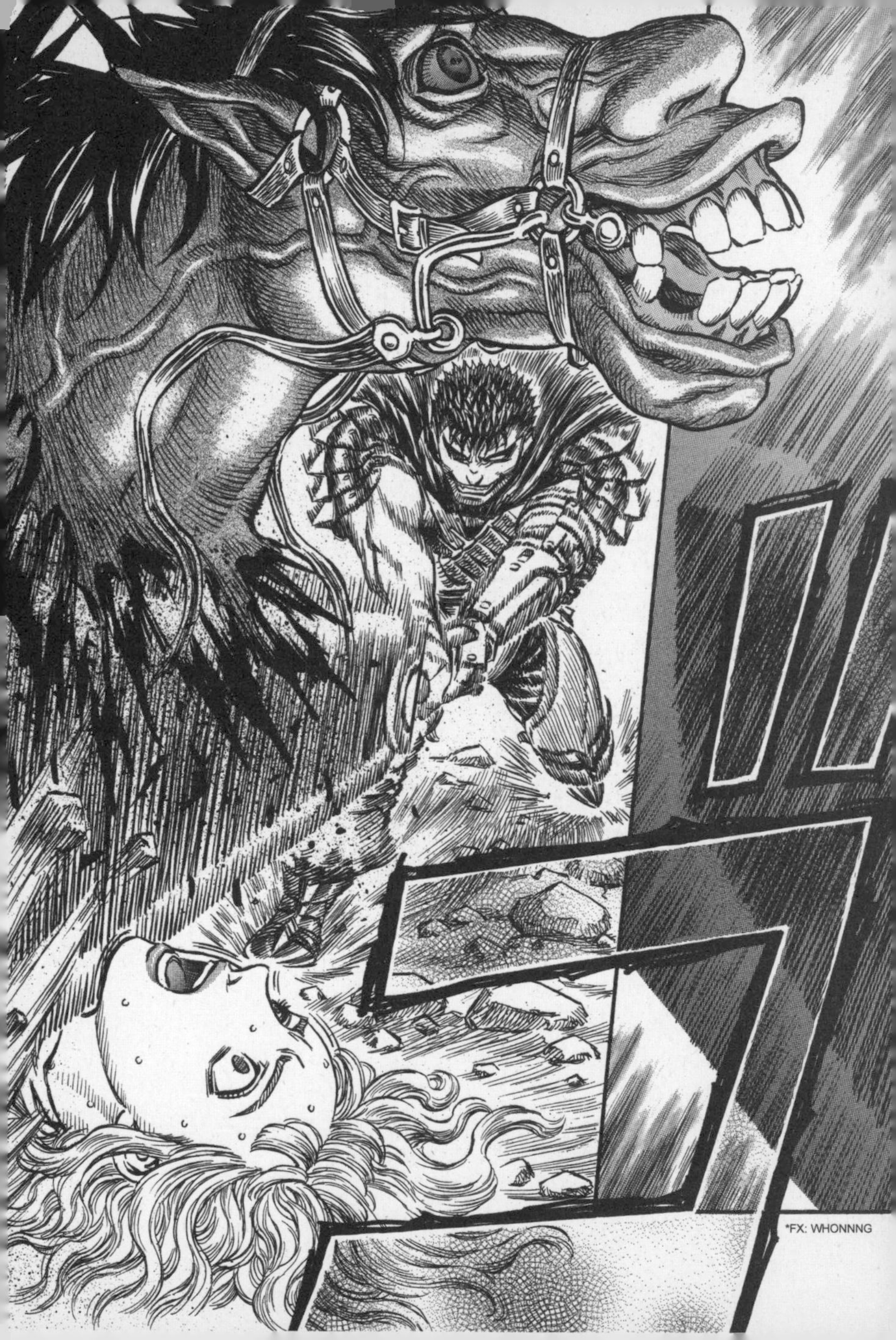
*FX: WHONNNG

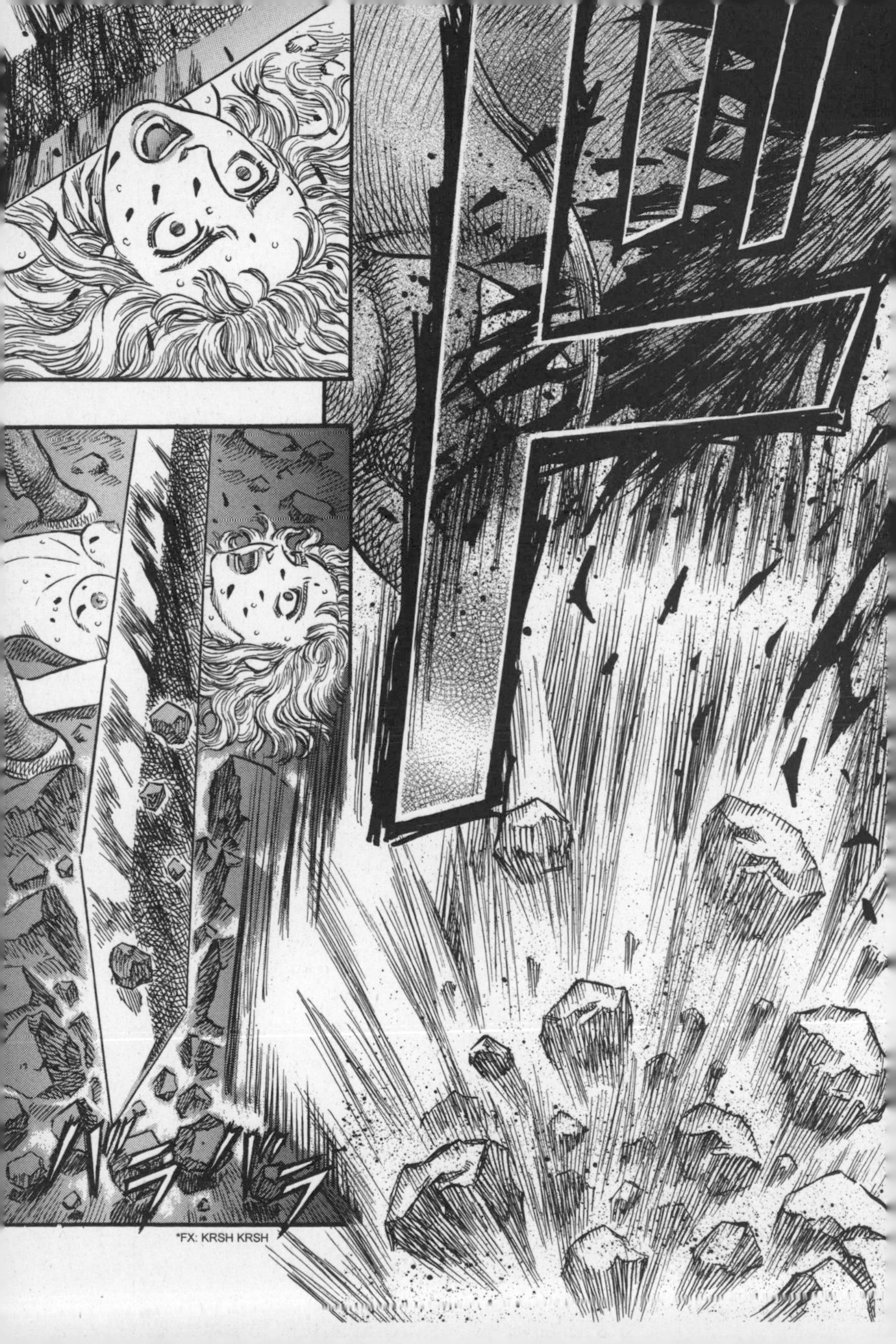
*FX: KRSH KRSH

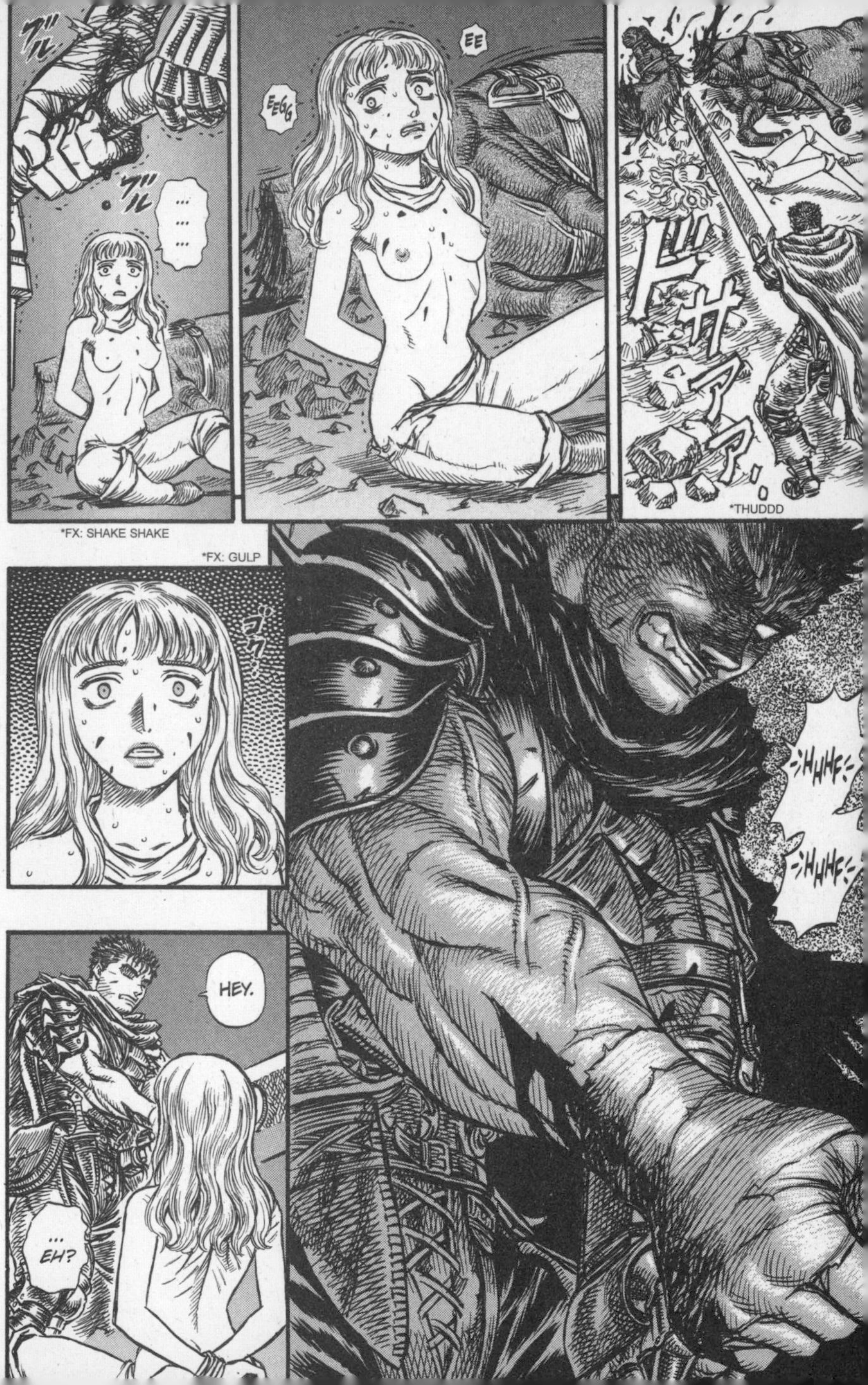
*THUDDD
EE
EEGG
...
...
...
*FX: SHAKE SHAKE
HHHF
HHHF
*FX: GULP
HEY.
...
EH?

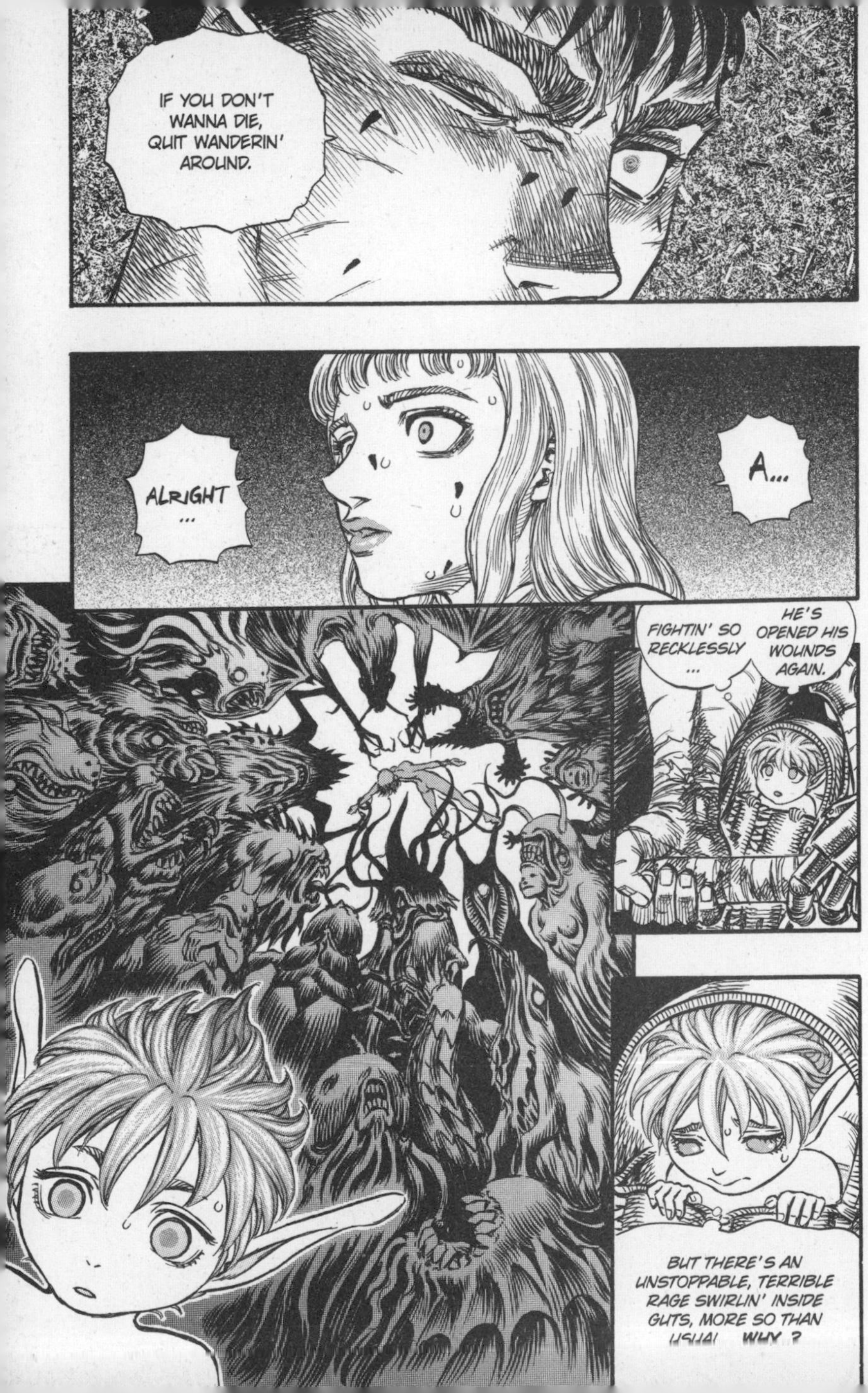
IF YOU DON'T WANNA DIE, QUIT WANDERIN' AROUND.
A...
ALRIGHT ...
HE'S OPENED HIS WOUNDS AGAIN.
FIGHTIN' SO RECKLESSLY ...
BUT THERE'S AN UNSTOPPABLE, TERRIBLE RAGE SWIRLIN' INSIDE GUTS, MORE SO THAN USUAL WHY ?

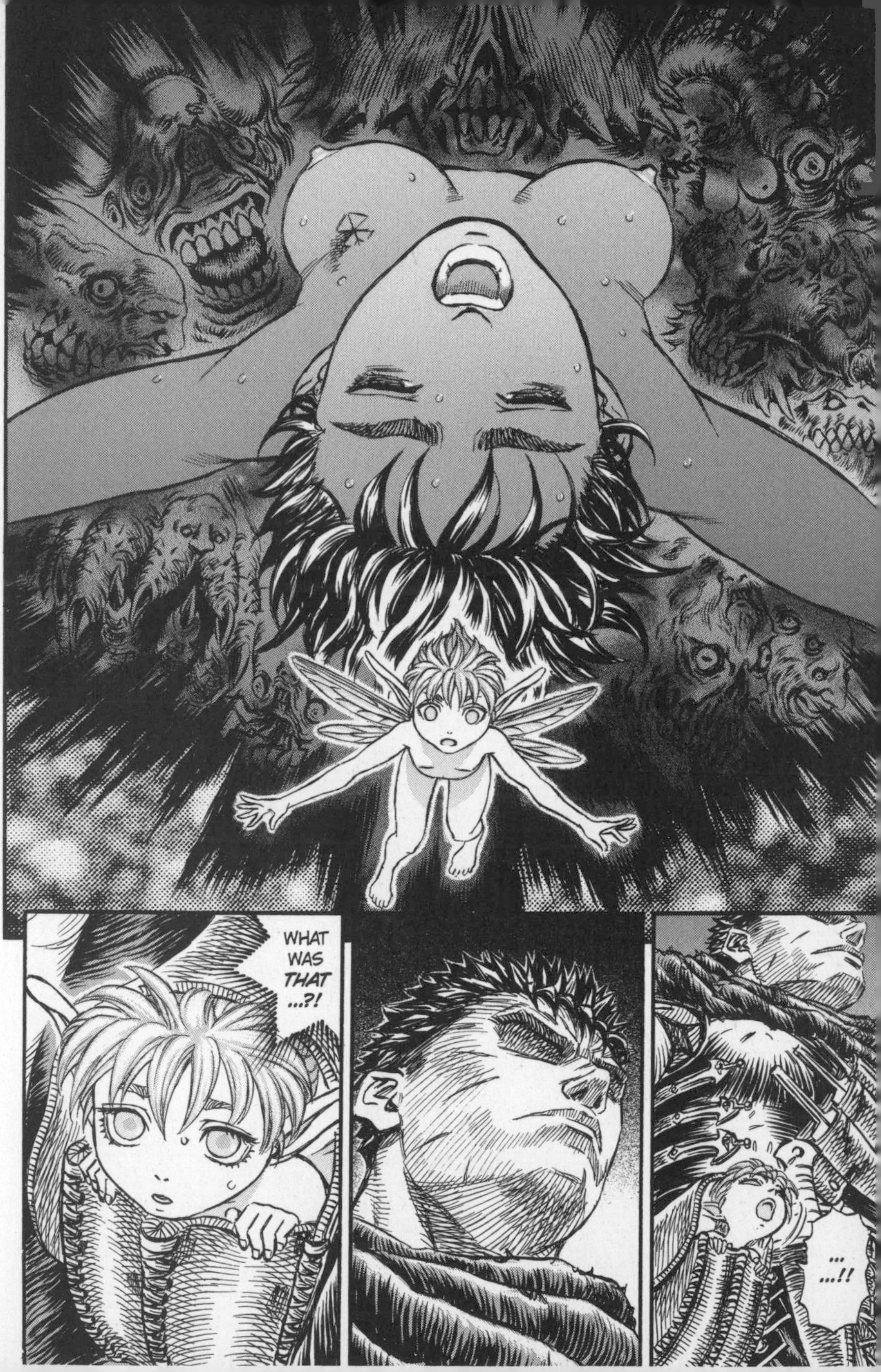
...
...!!
WHAT WAS *THAT* ...?!

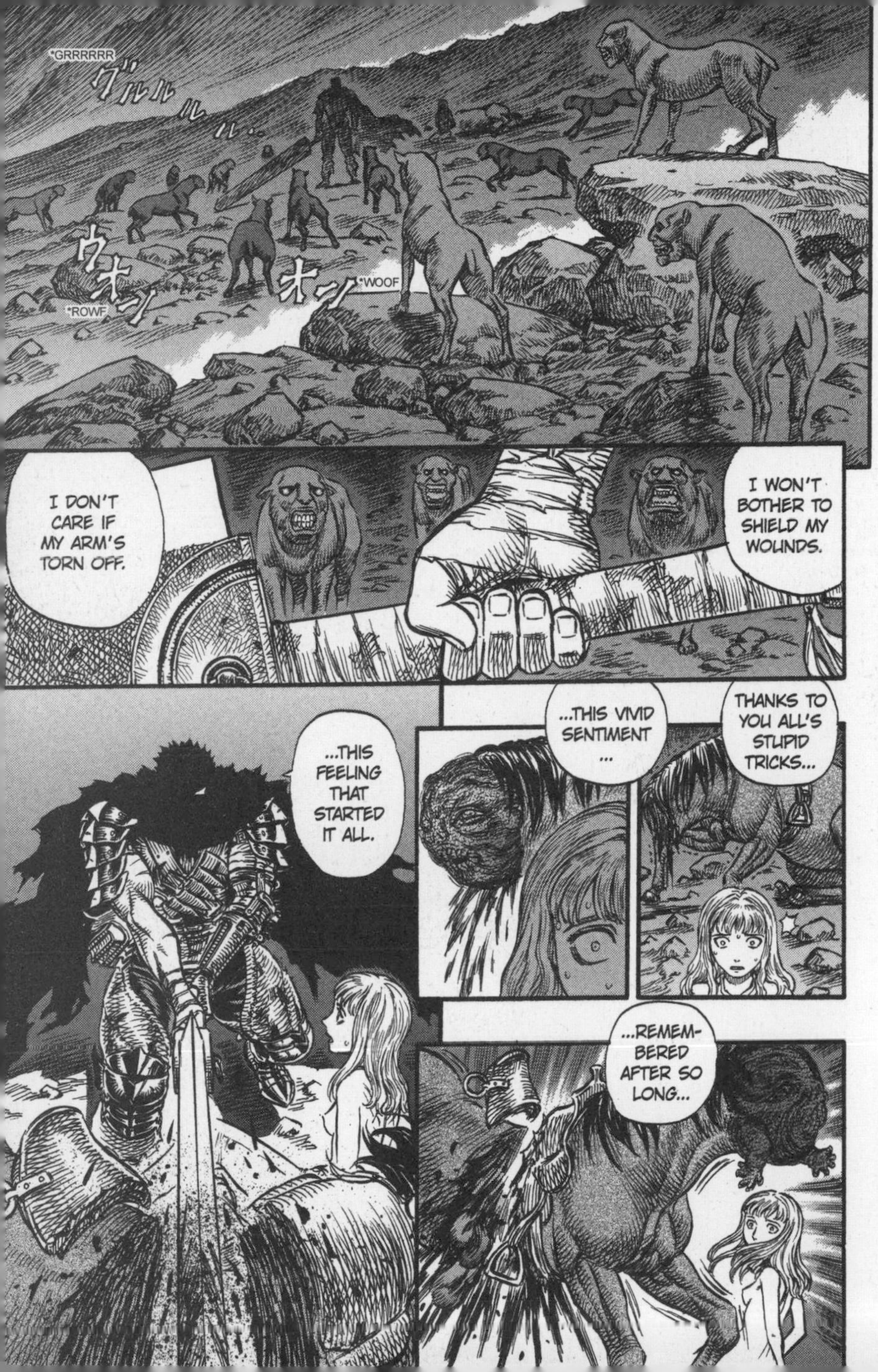
*GRRRRRR
*WOOF
*ROWF
I WON'T BOTHER TO SHIELD MY WOUNDS.
I DON'T CARE IF MY ARM'S TORN OFF.
THANKS TO YOU ALL'S STUPID TRICKS...
...THIS VIVID SENTIMENT ...
...REMEMBERED AFTER SO LONG...
...THIS FEELING THAT STARTED IT ALL.

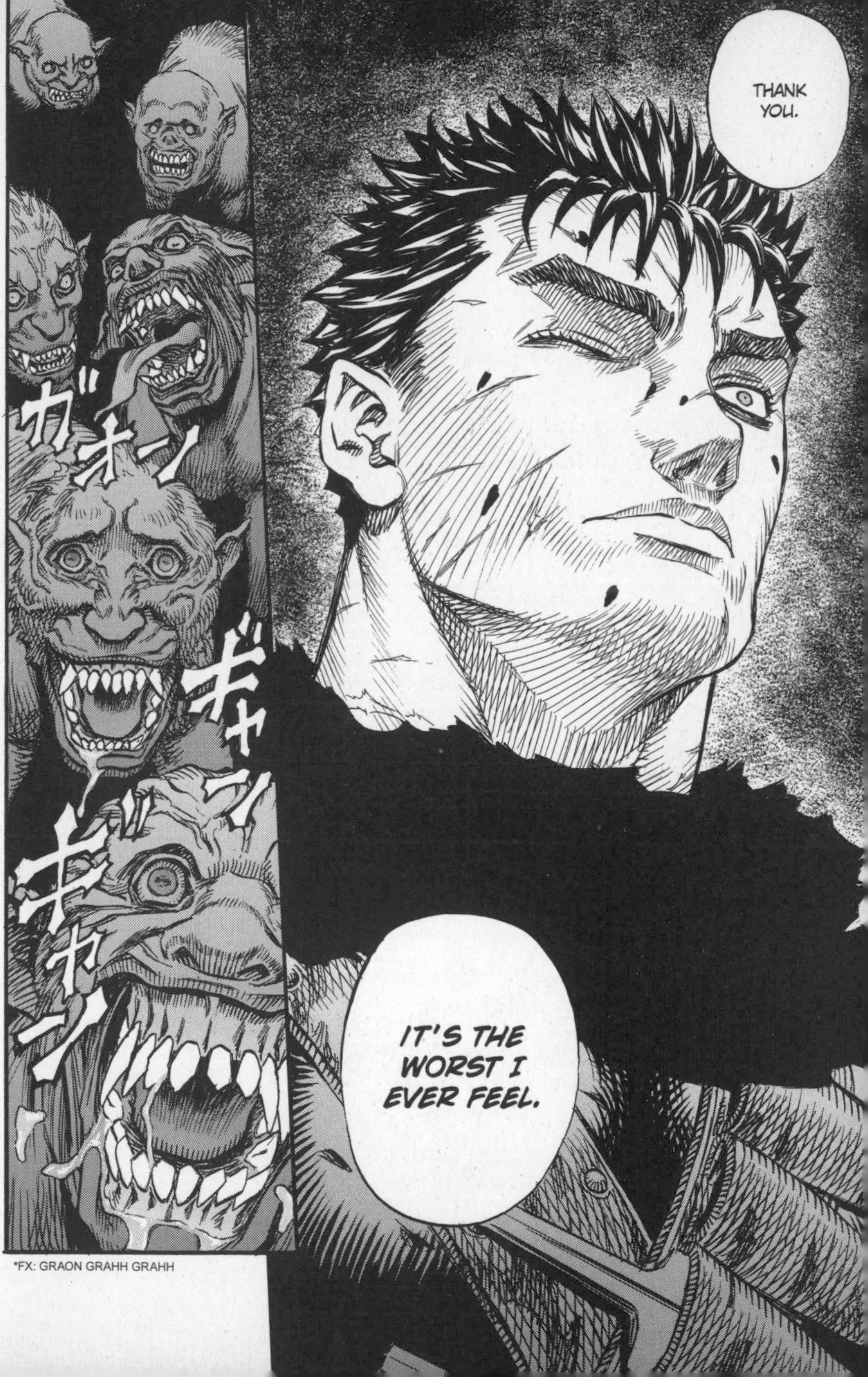
THANK YOU.
IT'S THE WORST I EVER FEEL.
ガオーン
ギャーン
ギャーン
*FX: GRAON GRAHH GRAHH

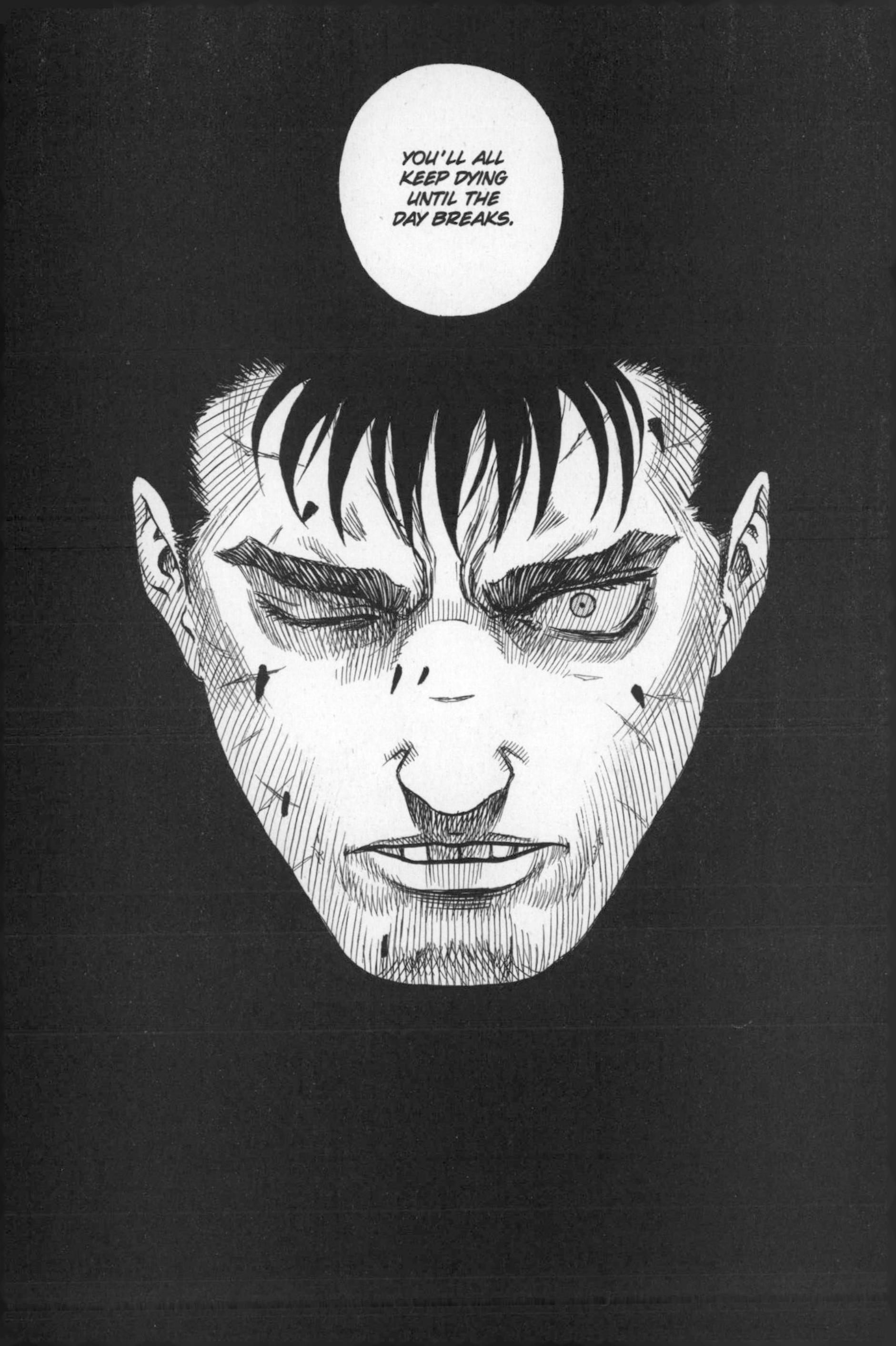
YOU'LL ALL KEEP DYING UNTIL THE DAY BREAKS.

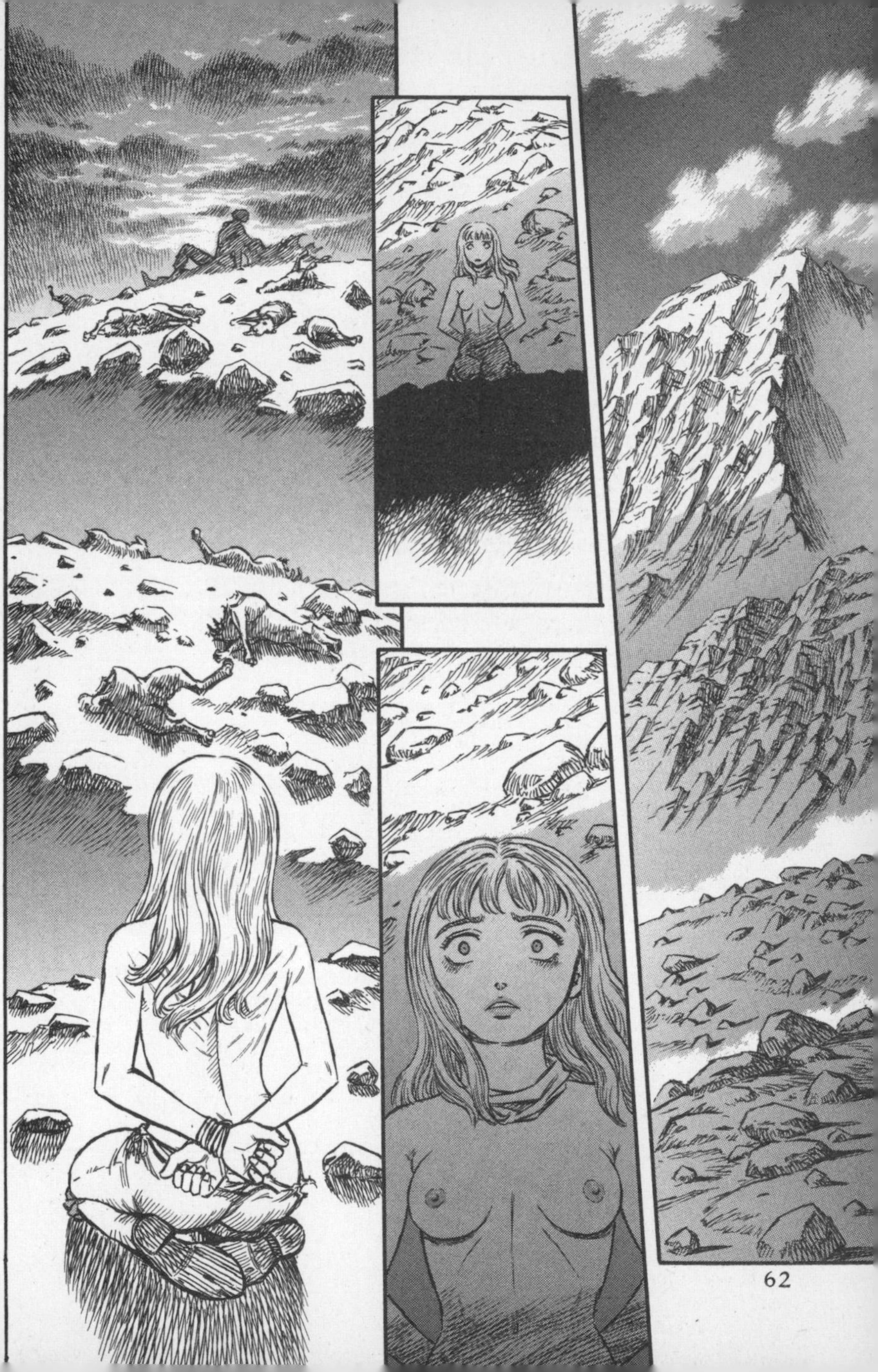

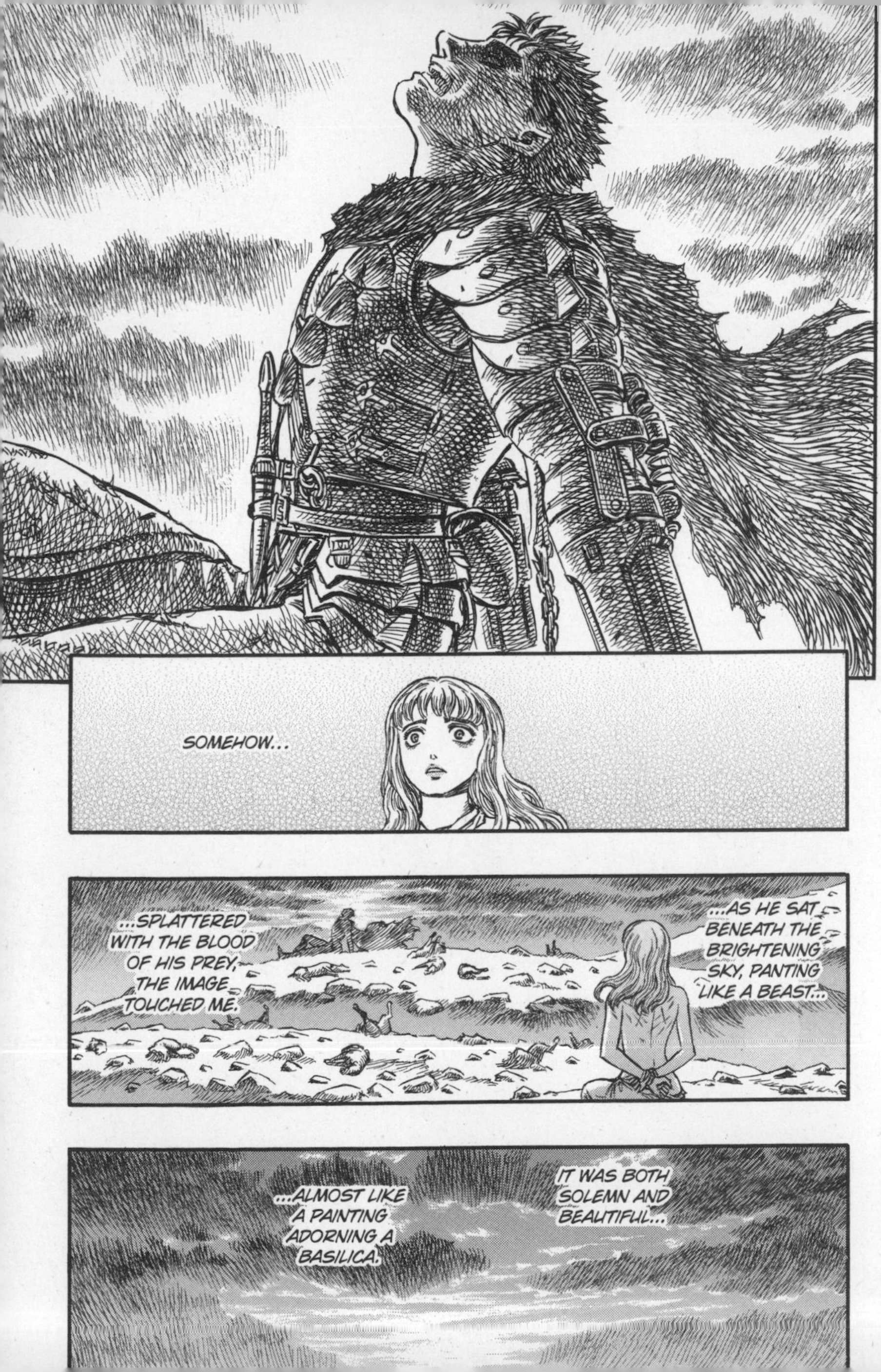
SOMEHOW...
...AS HE SAT BENEATH THE BRIGHTENING SKY, PANTING LIKE A BEAST...
...SPLATTERED WITH THE BLOOD OF HIS PREY, THE IMAGE TOUCHED ME.
IT WAS BOTH SOLEMN AND BEAUTIFUL...
...ALMOST LIKE A PAINTING ADORNING A BASILICA.

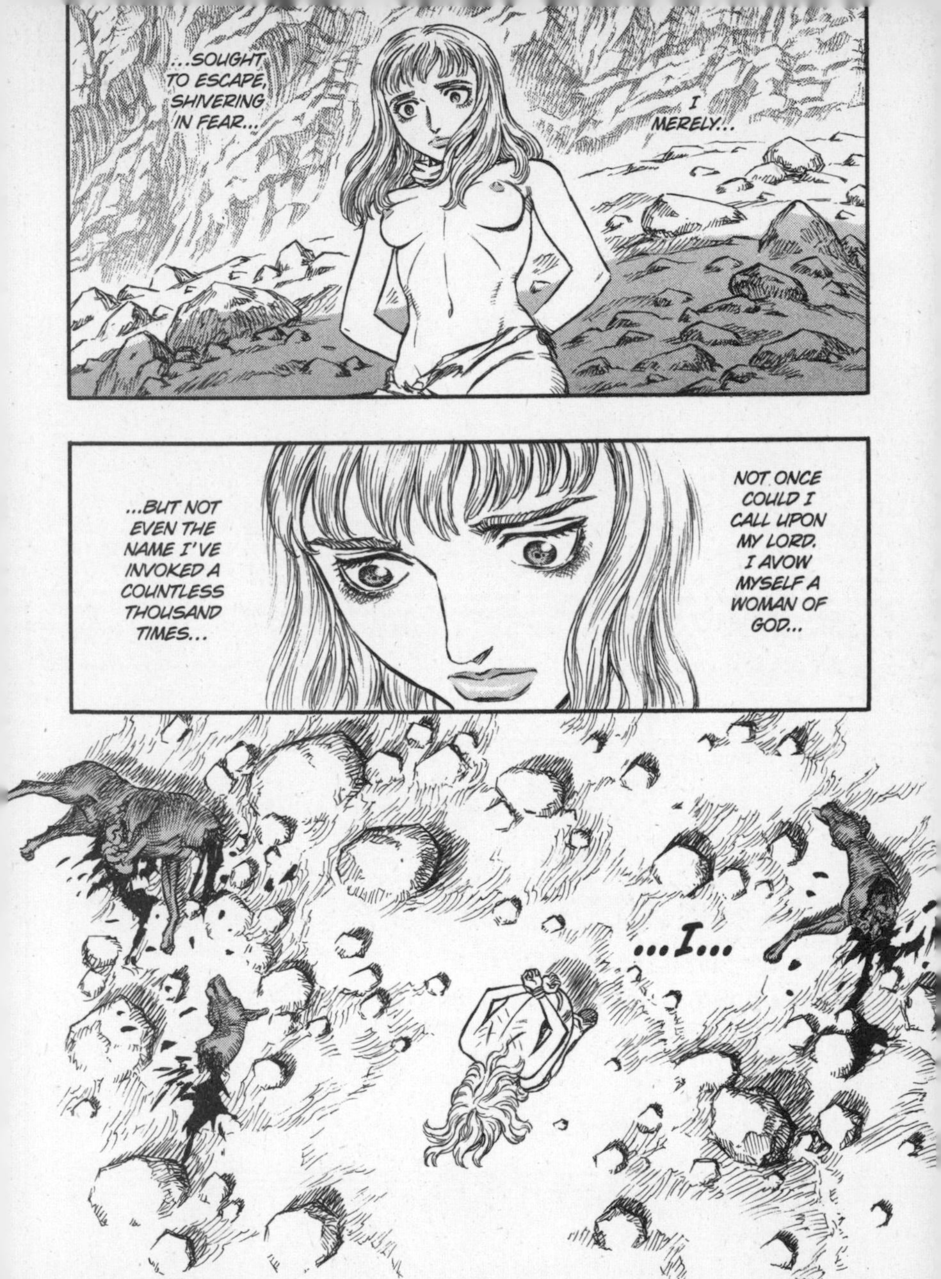
I MERELY...
...SOUGHT TO ESCAPE, SHIVERING IN FEAR...
NOT ONCE COULD I CALL UPON MY LORD. I AVOW MYSELF A WOMAN OF GOD...
...BUT NOT EVEN THE NAME I'VE INVOKED A COUNTLESS THOUSAND TIMES...
...I...

ONVICTION ARC
NDING CHAIN CHAPTER
AST AND FUTURE: END

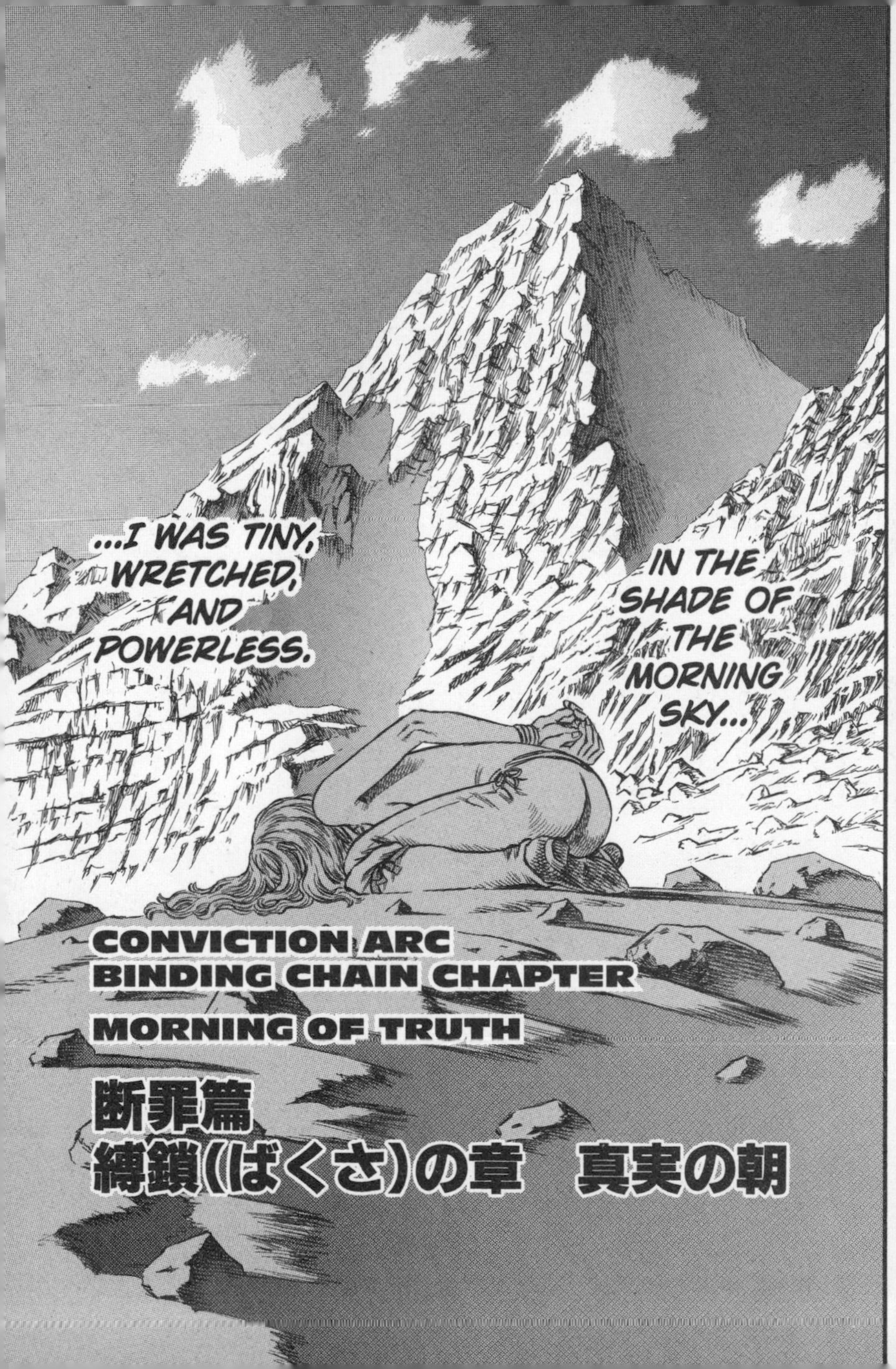
IN THE SHADE OF THE MORNING SKY...
...I WAS TINY, WRETCHED, AND POWERLESS.

CONVICTION ARC
BINDING CHAIN CHAPTER
MORNING OF TRUTH

断罪篇
縛鎖(ばくさ)の章　真実の朝

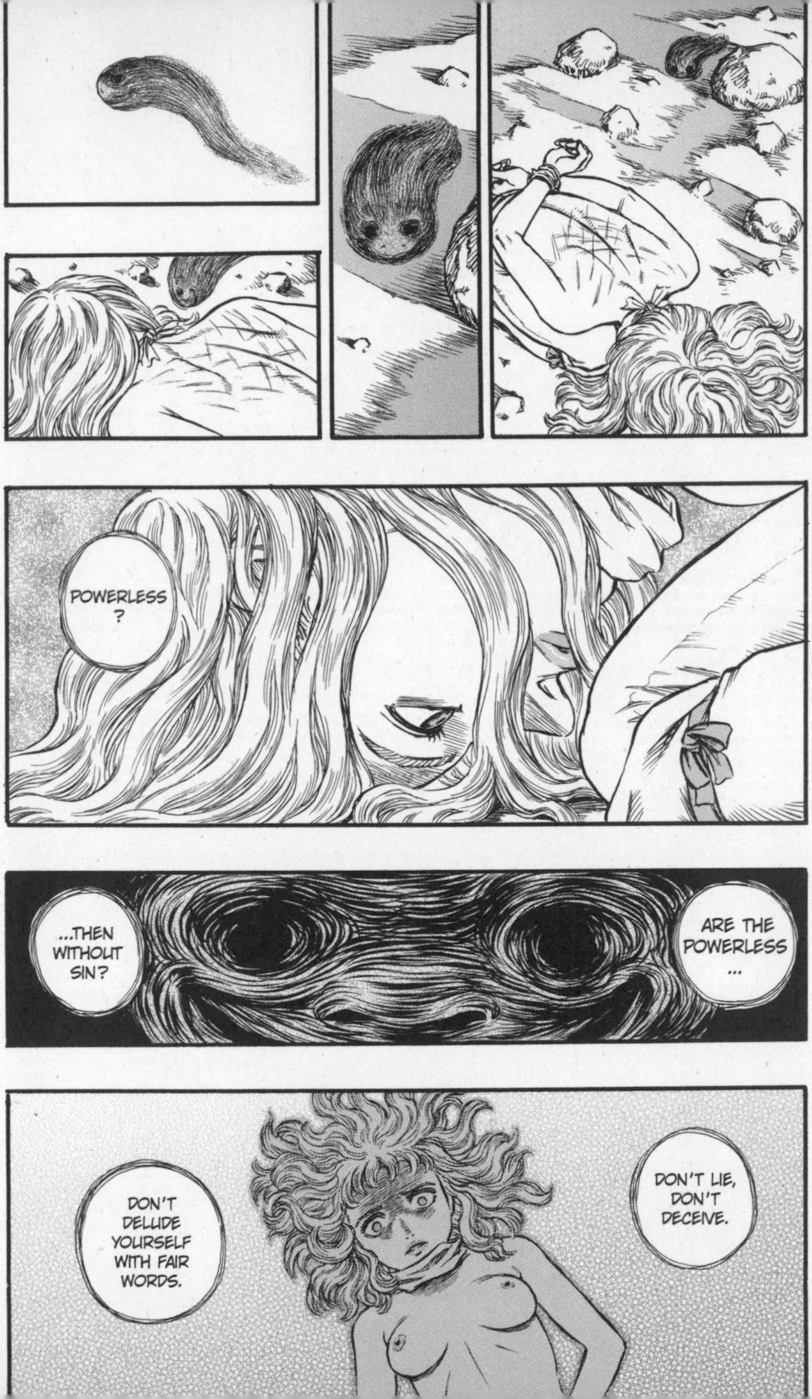
POWERLESS ?
ARE THE POWERLESS ...
...THEN WITHOUT SIN?
DON'T LIE, DON'T DECEIVE.
DON'T DELUDE YOURSELF WITH FAIR WORDS.

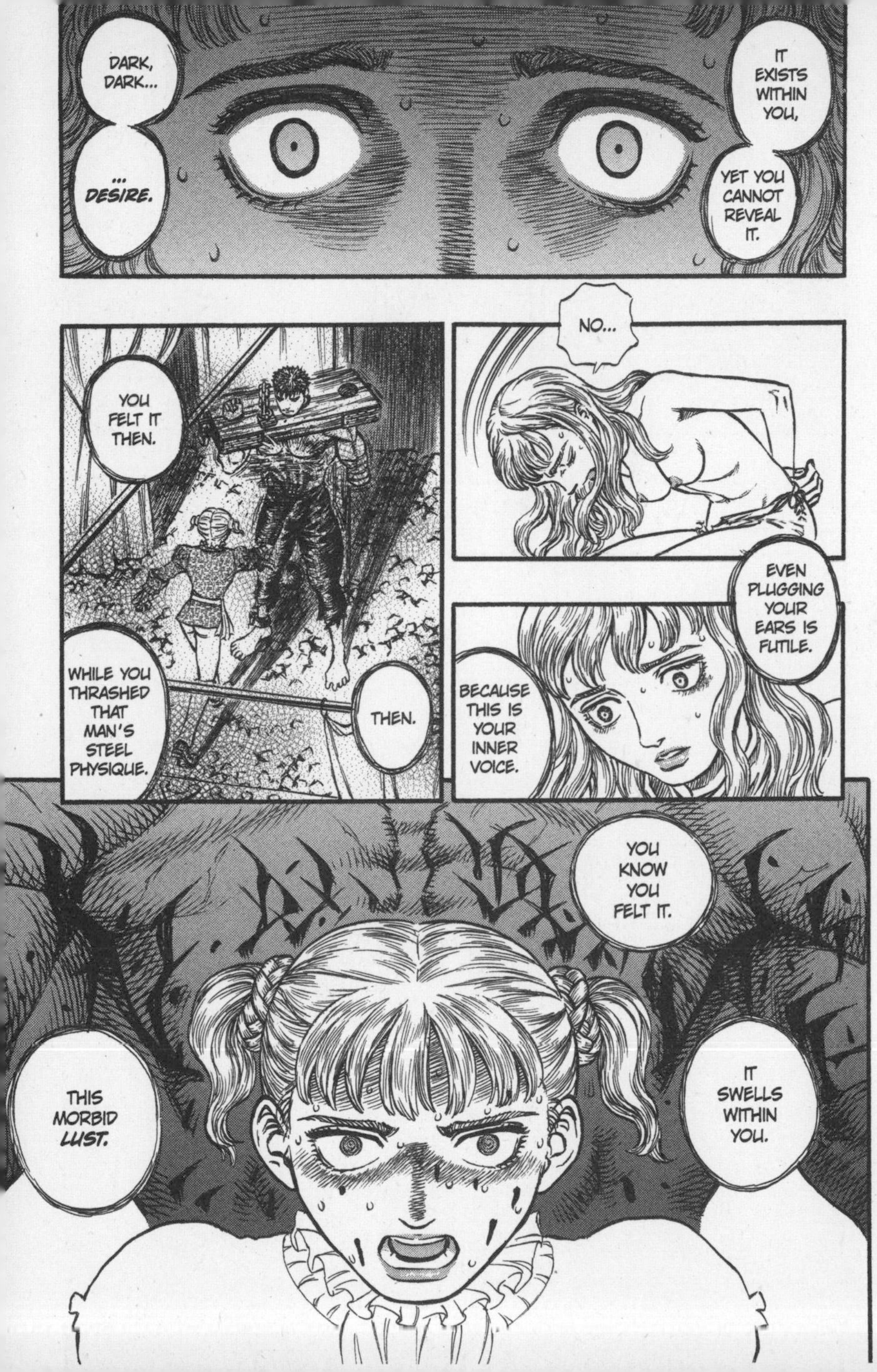
IT EXISTS WITHIN YOU,
YET YOU CANNOT REVEAL IT.
DARK, DARK...
... *DESIRE.*
NO...
EVEN PLUGGING YOUR EARS IS FUTILE.
BECAUSE THIS IS YOUR INNER VOICE.
YOU FELT IT THEN.
THEN.
WHILE YOU THRASHED THAT MAN'S STEEL PHYSIQUE.
YOU KNOW YOU FELT IT.
IT SWELLS WITHIN YOU.
THIS MORBID *LUST.*

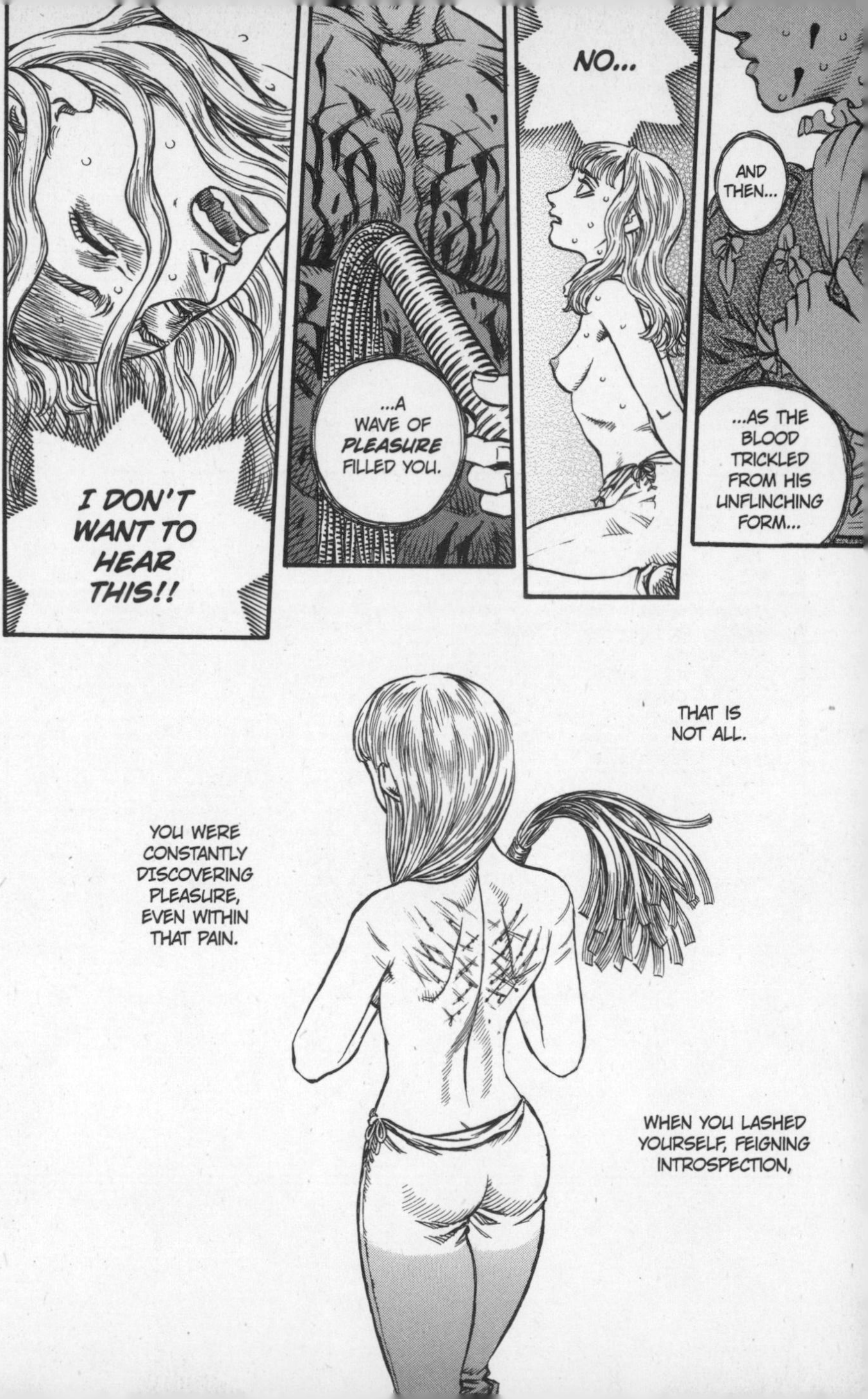
AND THEN...
...AS THE BLOOD TRICKLED FROM HIS UNFLINCHING FORM...
NO...
...A WAVE OF PLEASURE FILLED YOU.
I DON'T WANT TO HEAR THIS!!
THAT IS NOT ALL.
WHEN YOU LASHED YOURSELF, FEIGNING INTROSPECTION,
YOU WERE CONSTANTLY DISCOVERING PLEASURE, EVEN WITHIN THAT PAIN.

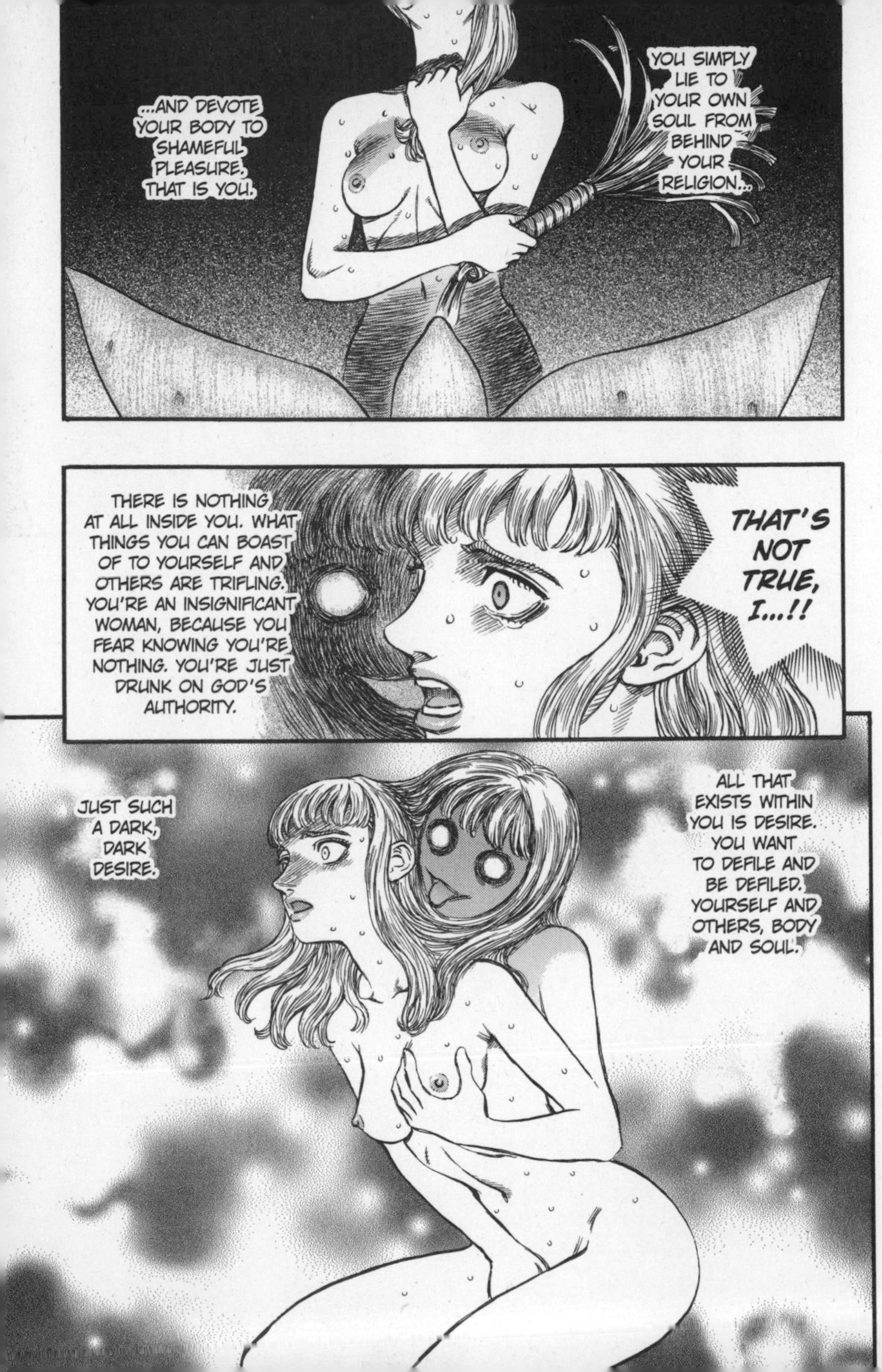
YOU SIMPLY LIE TO YOUR OWN SOUL FROM BEHIND YOUR RELIGION...
...AND DEVOTE YOUR BODY TO SHAMEFUL PLEASURE. THAT IS YOU.
THAT'S NOT TRUE, I...!!
THERE IS NOTHING AT ALL INSIDE YOU. WHAT THINGS YOU CAN BOAST OF TO YOURSELF AND OTHERS ARE TRIFLING. YOU'RE AN INSIGNIFICANT WOMAN, BECAUSE YOU FEAR KNOWING YOU'RE NOTHING. YOU'RE JUST DRUNK ON GOD'S AUTHORITY.
ALL THAT EXISTS WITHIN YOU IS DESIRE. YOU WANT TO DEFILE AND BE DEFILED. YOURSELF AND OTHERS, BODY AND SOUL.
JUST SUCH A DARK, DARK DESIRE.

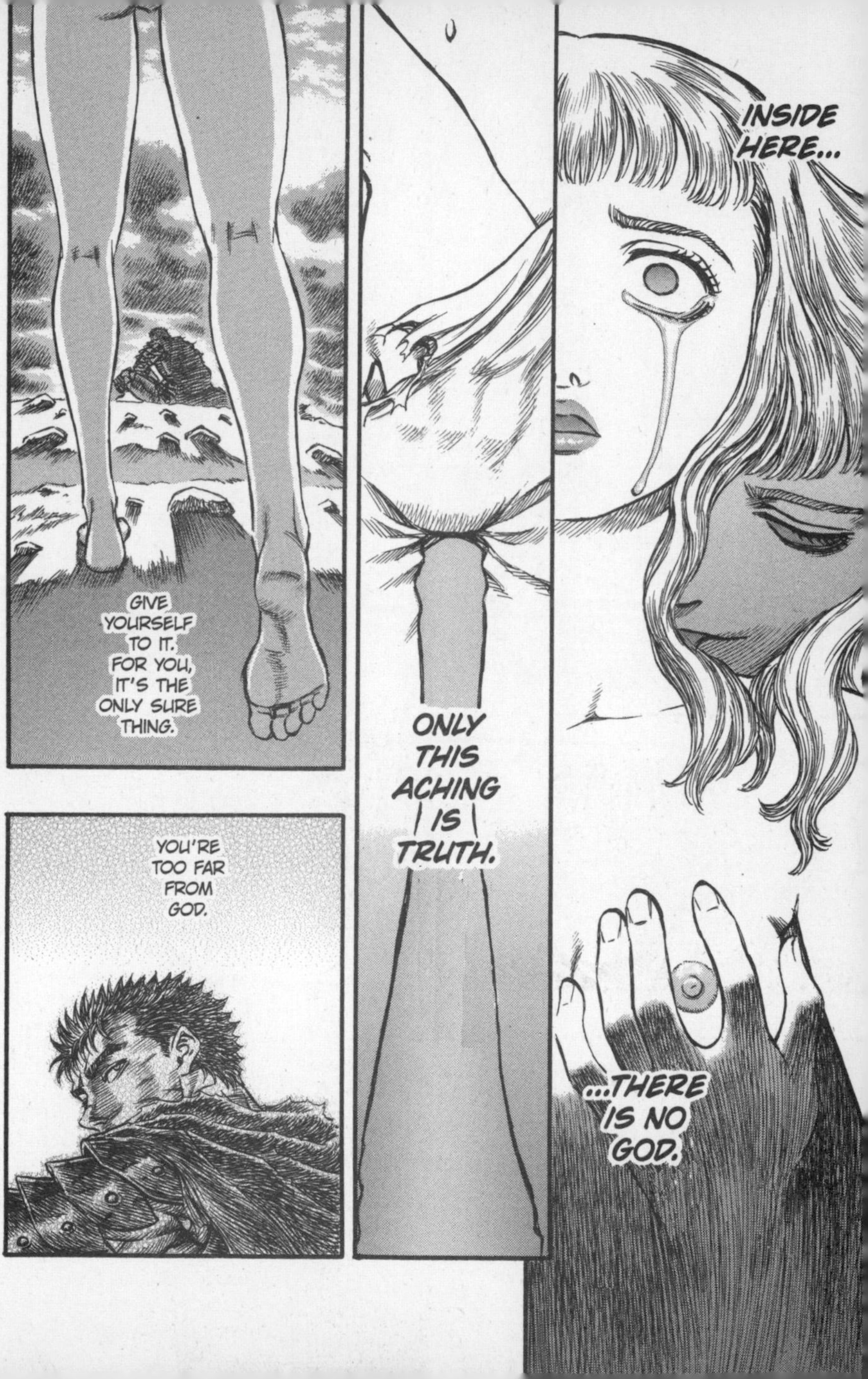
INSIDE HERE...
...THERE IS NO GOD.
ONLY THIS ACHING IS TRUTH.
GIVE YOURSELF TO IT. FOR YOU, IT'S THE ONLY SURE THING.
YOU'RE TOO FAR FROM GOD.

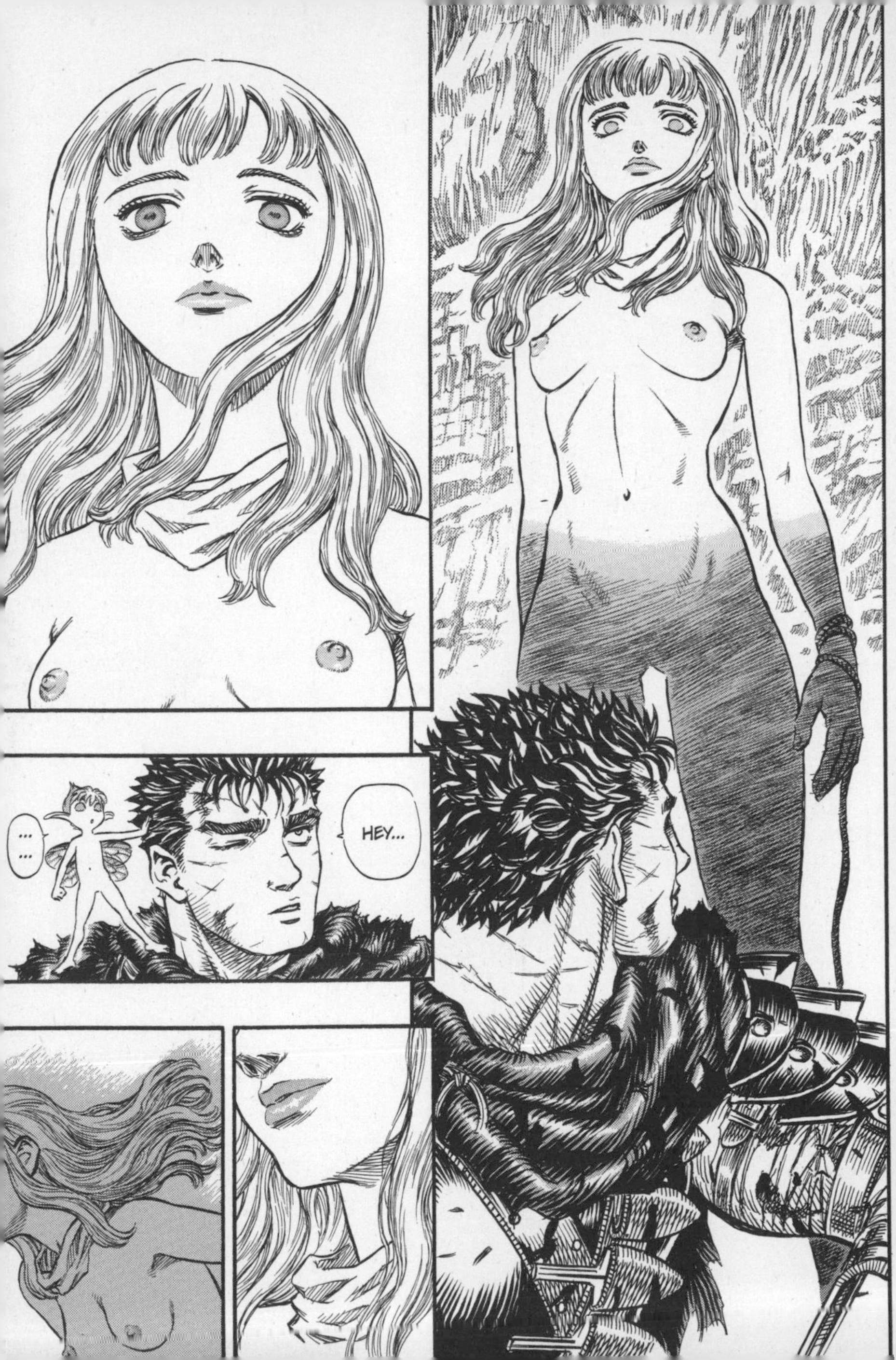
HEY...
......

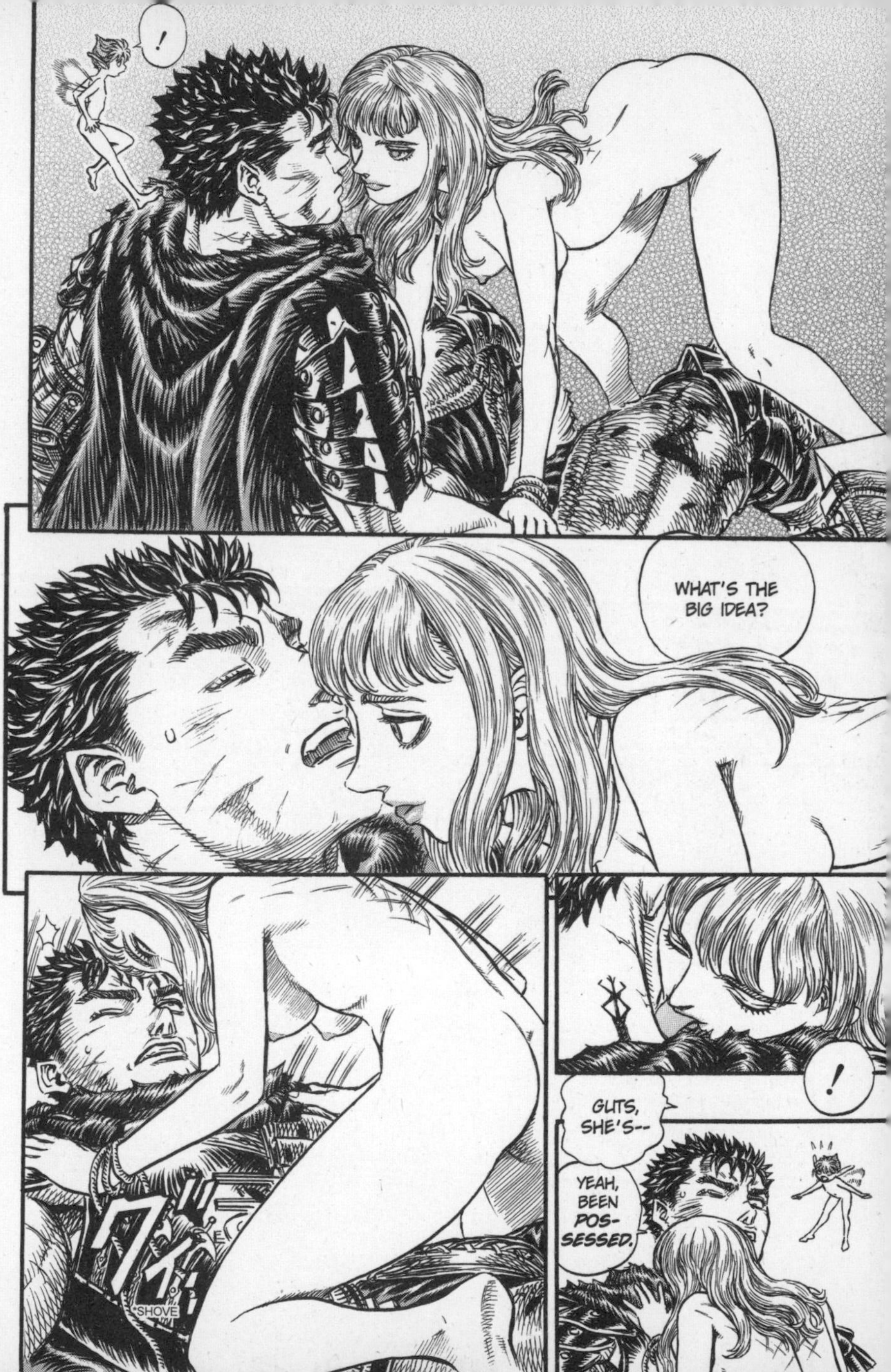
!
WHAT'S THE BIG IDEA?
!
GUTS, SHE'S--
YEAH, BEEN POSSESSED.
SHOVE

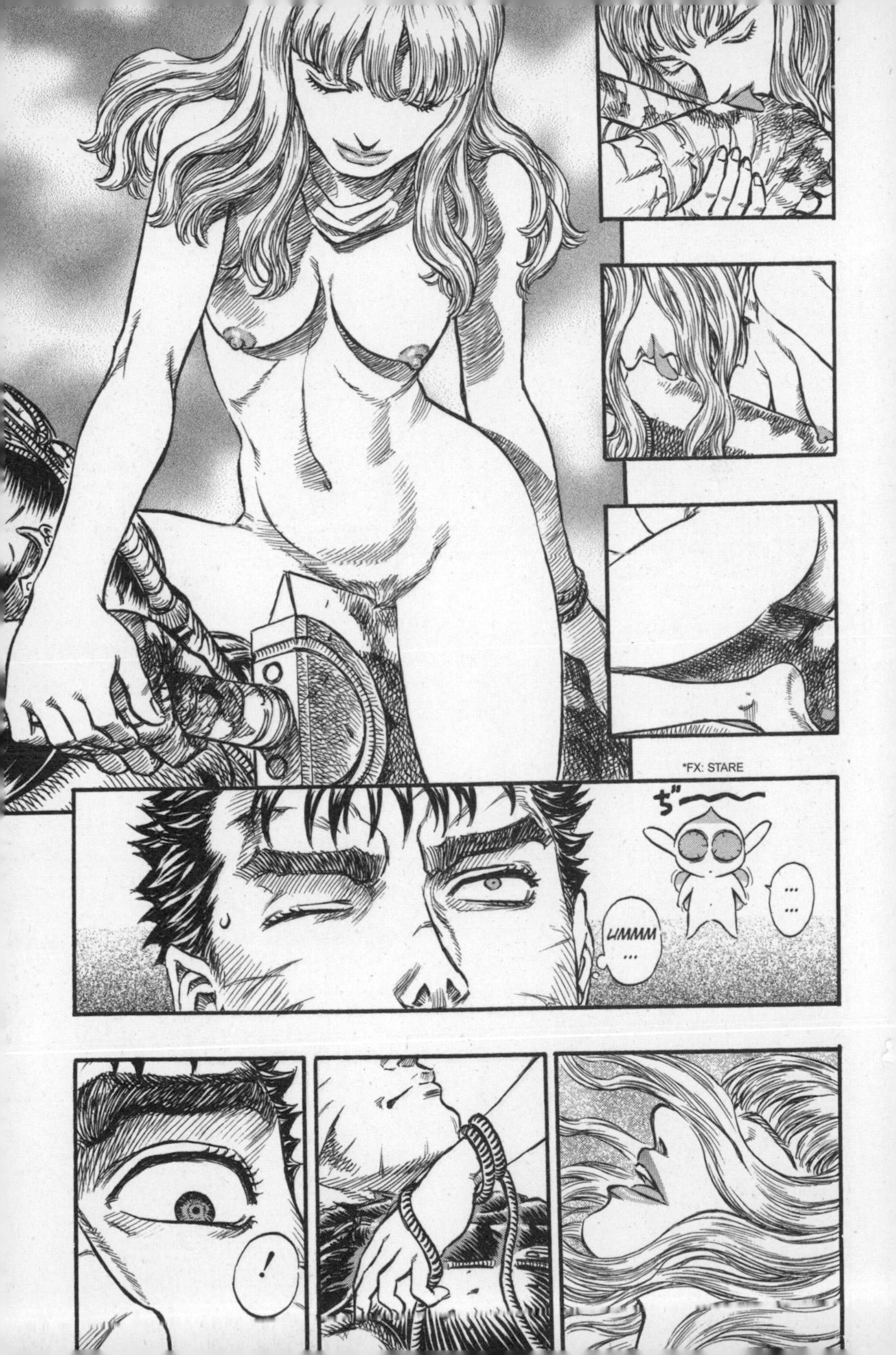

*FX: STARE
ぢ〜〜〜
......
UMMM
...
!

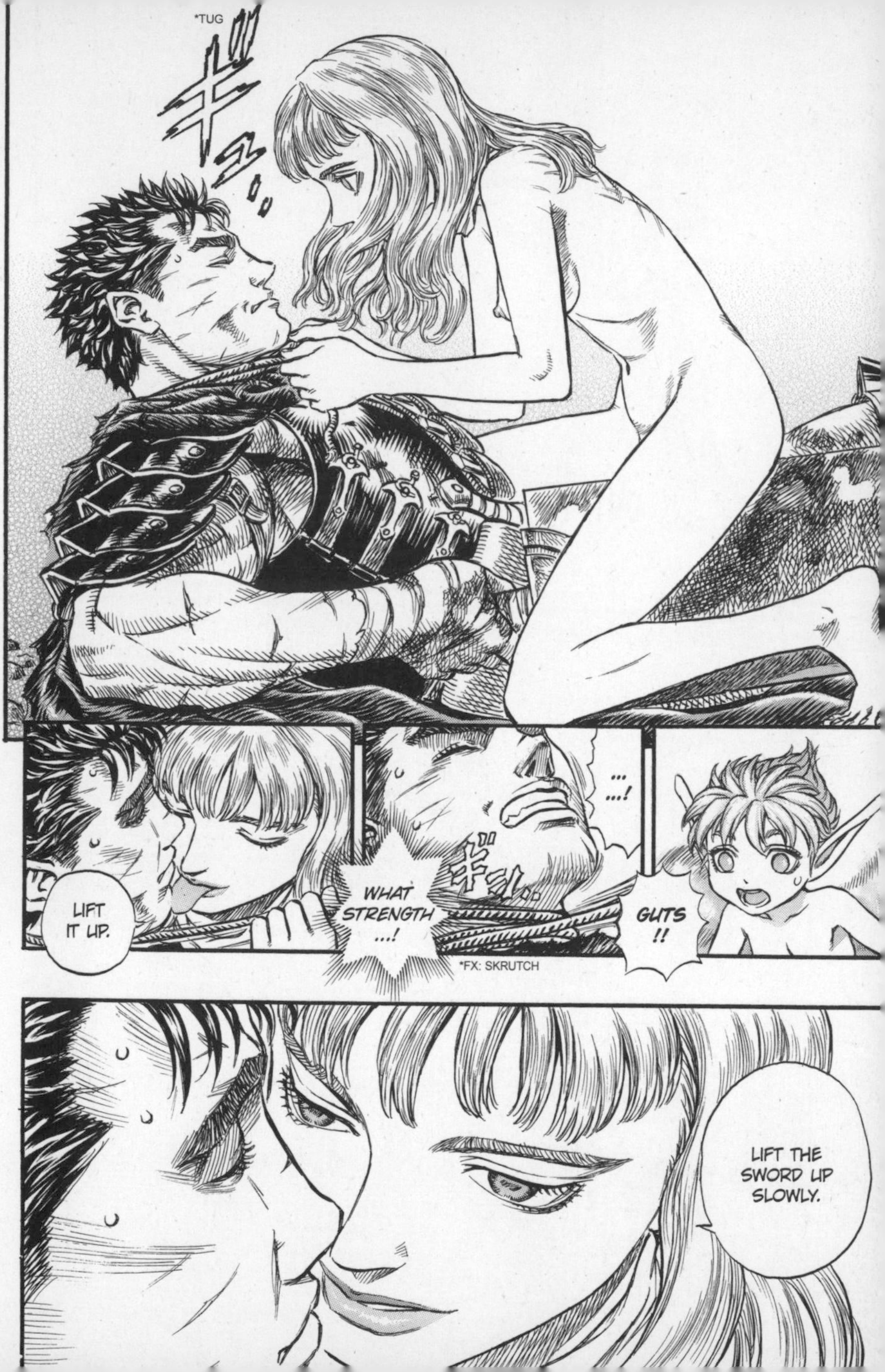
*TUG
GUTS !!
...
...!
WHAT STRENGTH ...!
*FX: SKRUTCH
LIFT IT UP.
LIFT THE SWORD UP SLOWLY.

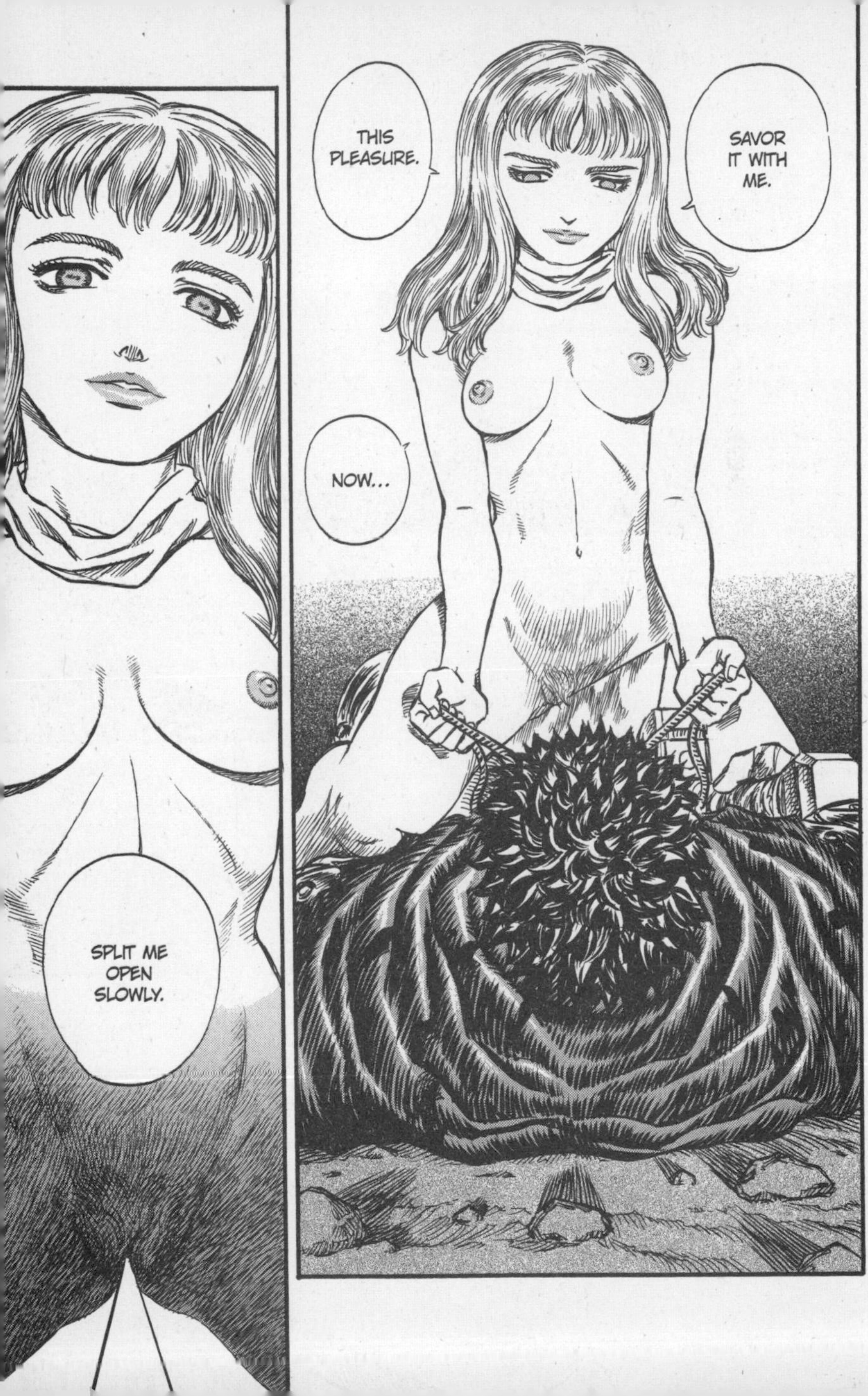
SAVOR IT WITH ME.
THIS PLEASURE.
NOW...
SPLIT ME OPEN SLOWLY.

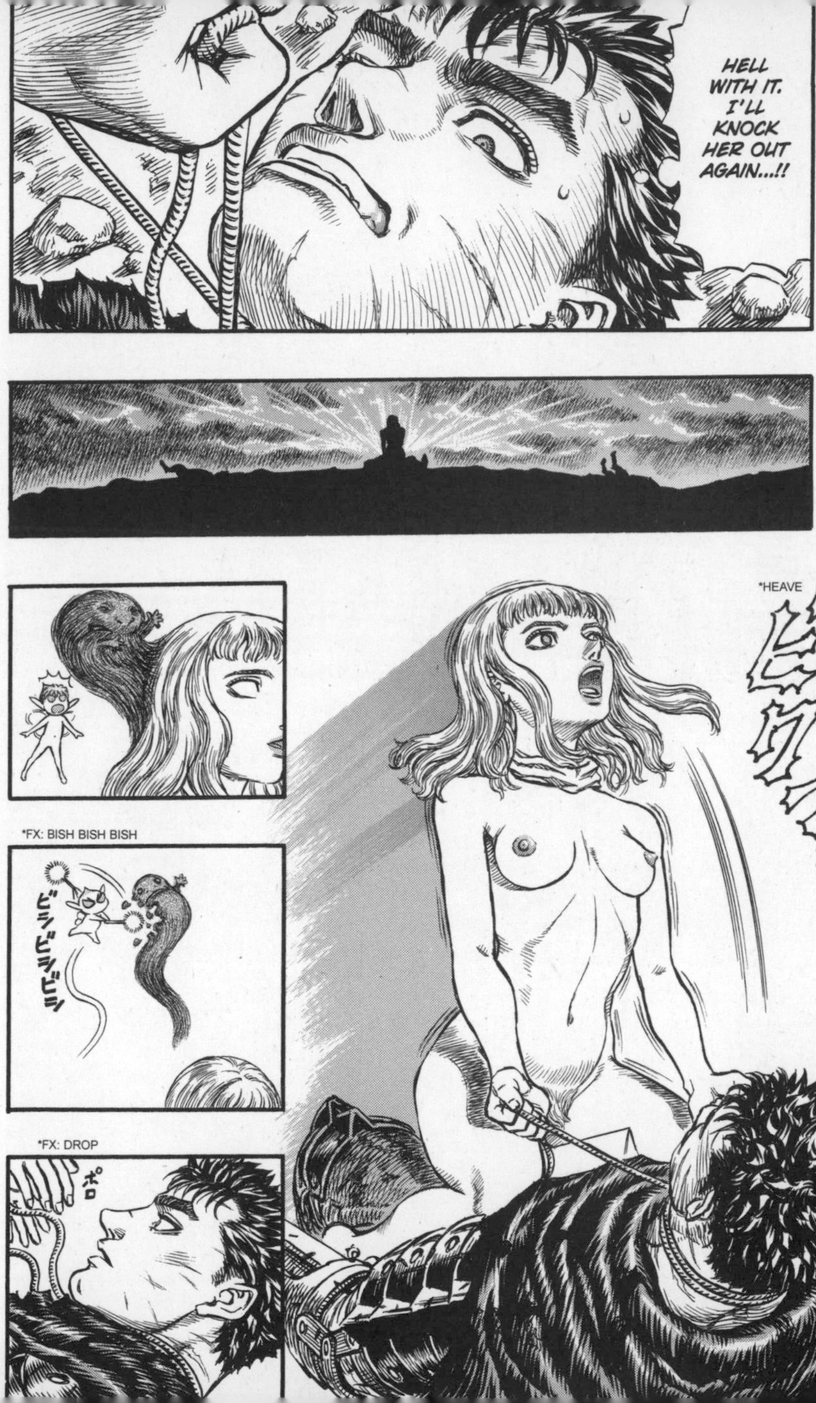
HELL WITH IT. I'LL KNOCK HER OUT AGAIN...!!
*HEAVE
ビクッ
*FX: BISH BISH BISH
ビシビシビシッ
*FX: DROP
ポロ

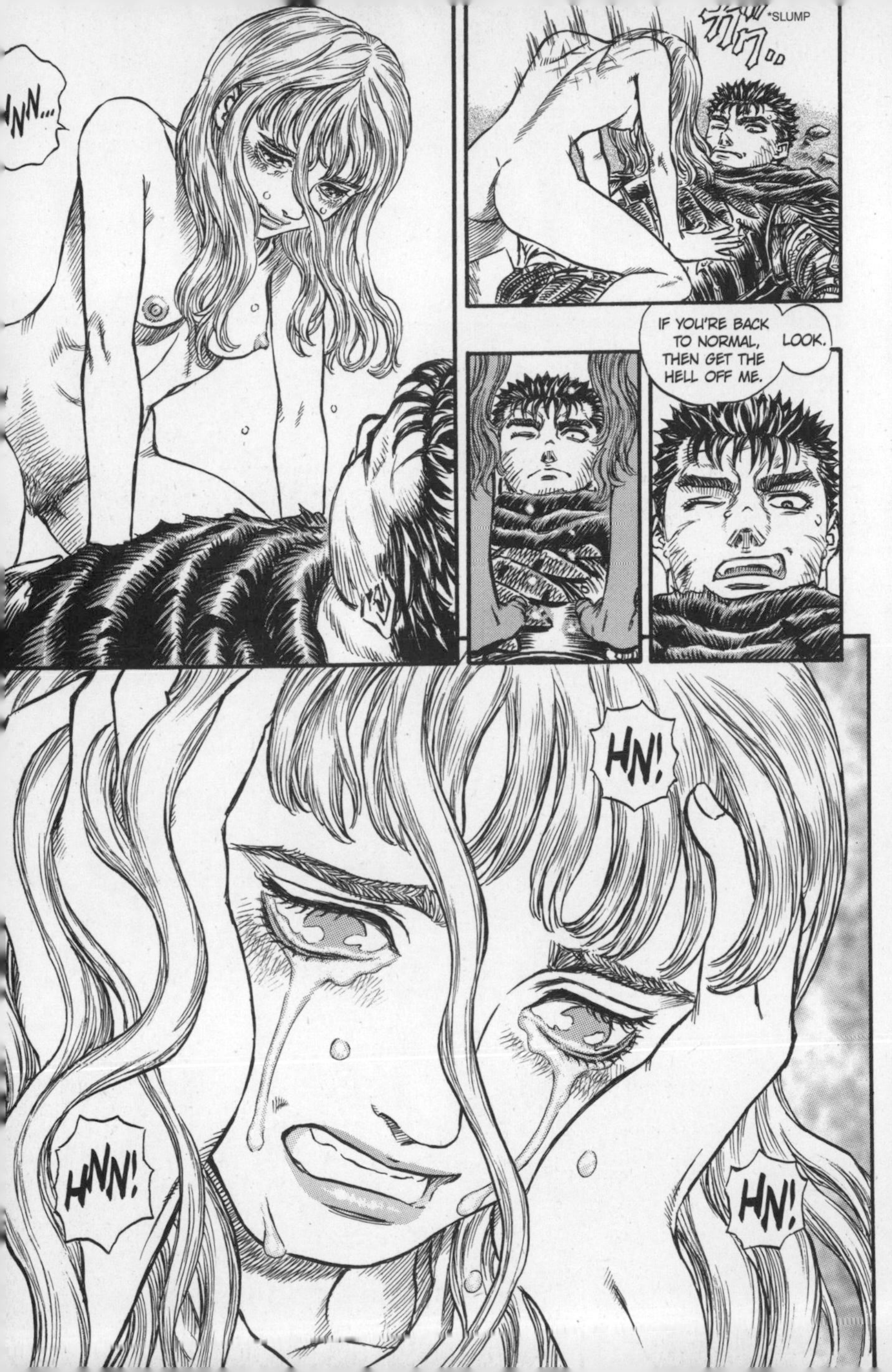
*SLUMP
LOOK.
IF YOU'RE BACK TO NORMAL, THEN GET THE HELL OFF ME.
HNN...
HN!
HN!
HNN!

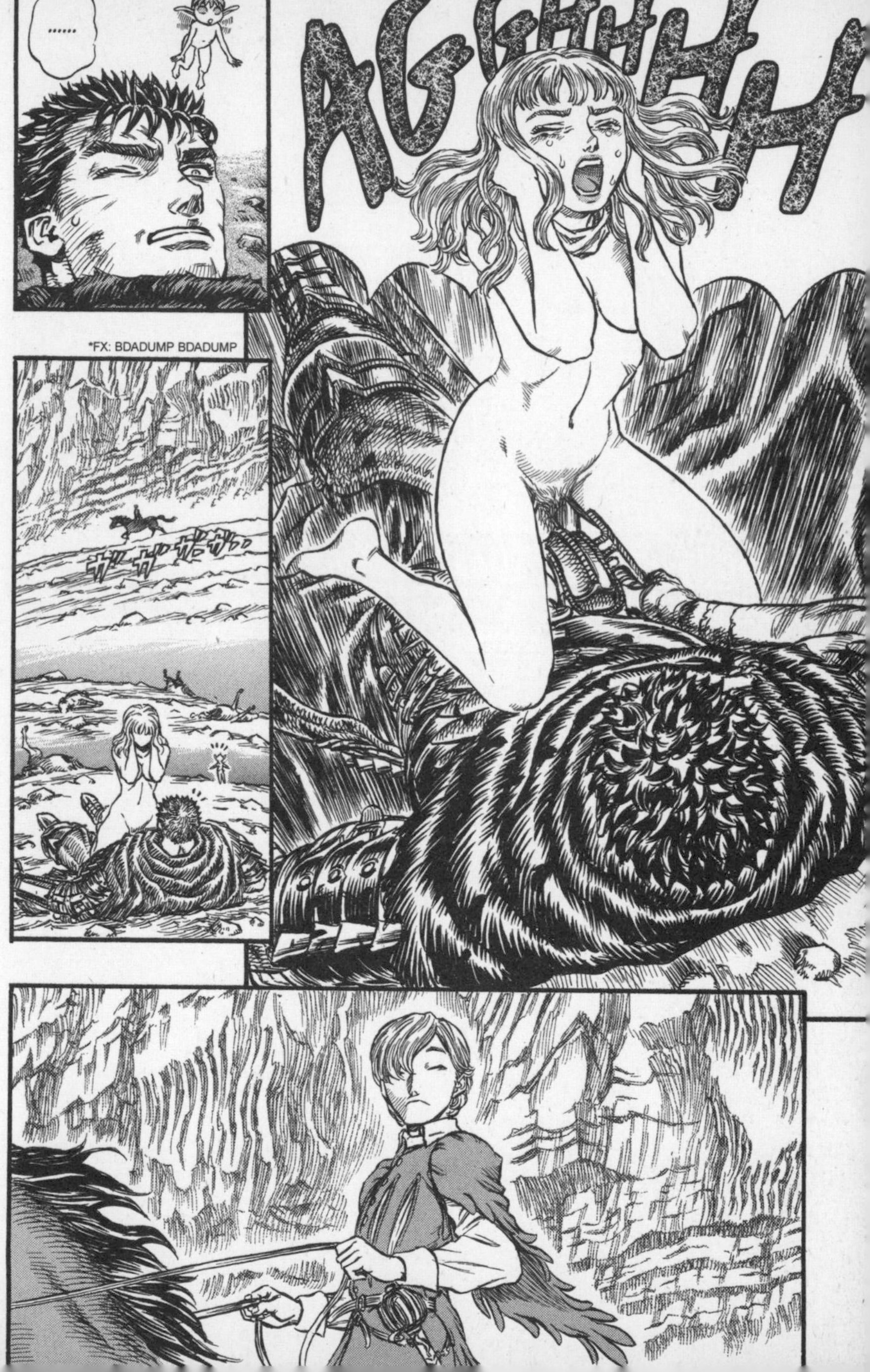
AGGHHHH
......
*FX: BDADUMP BDADUMP

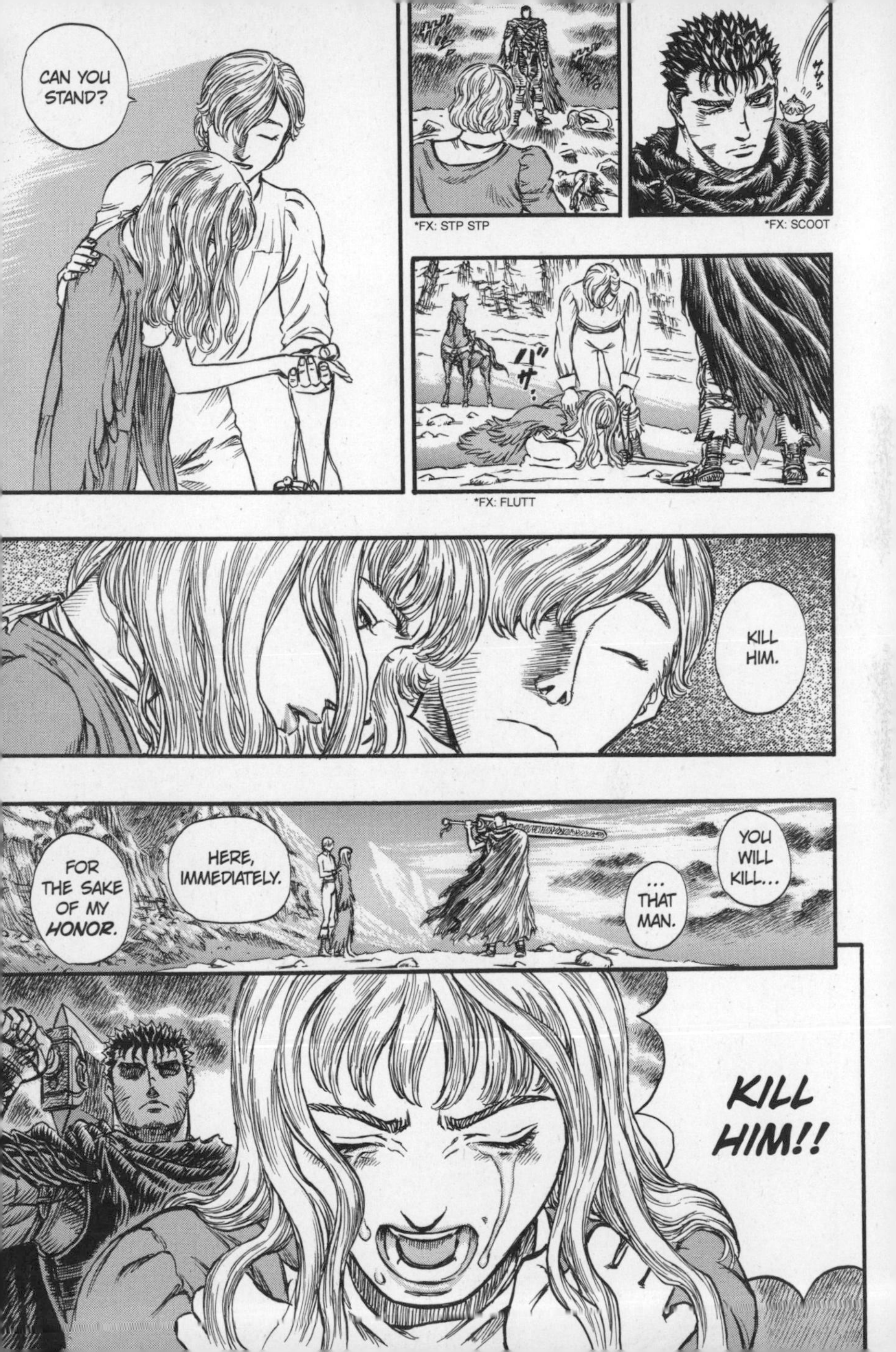
*FX: SCOOT
*FX: STP STP
*FX: FLUTT
CAN YOU STAND?
KILL HIM.
YOU WILL KILL...
... THAT MAN.
HERE, IMMEDIATELY.
FOR THE SAKE OF MY HONOR.
KILL HIM!!

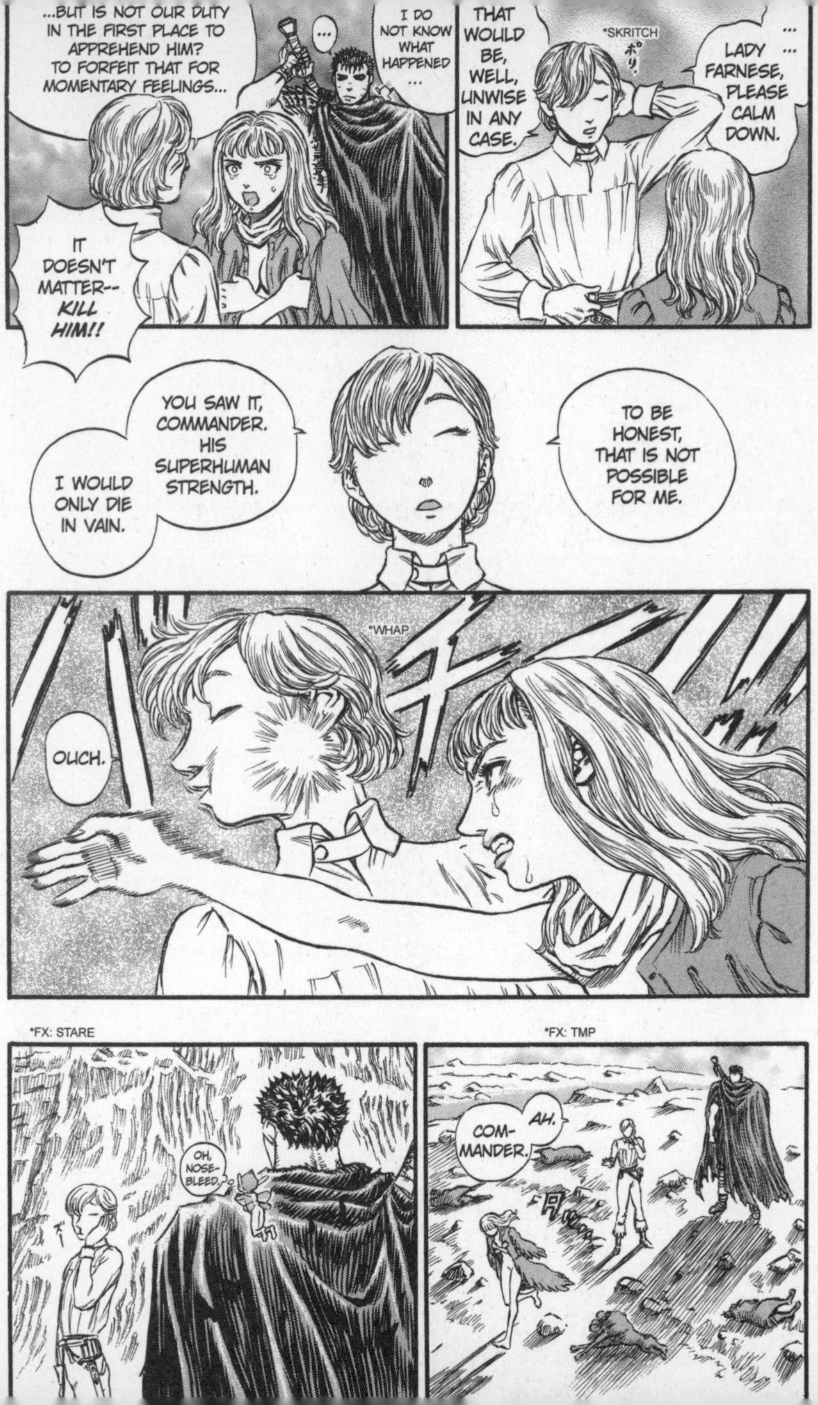
... ...
LADY FARNESE, PLEASE CALM DOWN.
*SKRITCH
ポリ
THAT WOULD BE, WELL, UNWISE IN ANY CASE.
I DO NOT KNOW WHAT HAPPENED ...
...
...BUT IS NOT OUR DUTY IN THE FIRST PLACE TO APPREHEND HIM? TO FORFEIT THAT FOR MOMENTARY FEELINGS...
IT DOESN'T MATTER-- KILL HIM!!
TO BE HONEST, THAT IS NOT POSSIBLE FOR ME.
YOU SAW IT, COMMANDER. HIS SUPERHUMAN STRENGTH.
I WOULD ONLY DIE IN VAIN.
*WHAP
OUCH.
*FX: TMP
AH.
COMMANDER.
*FX: STARE
OH, NOSE-BLEED.

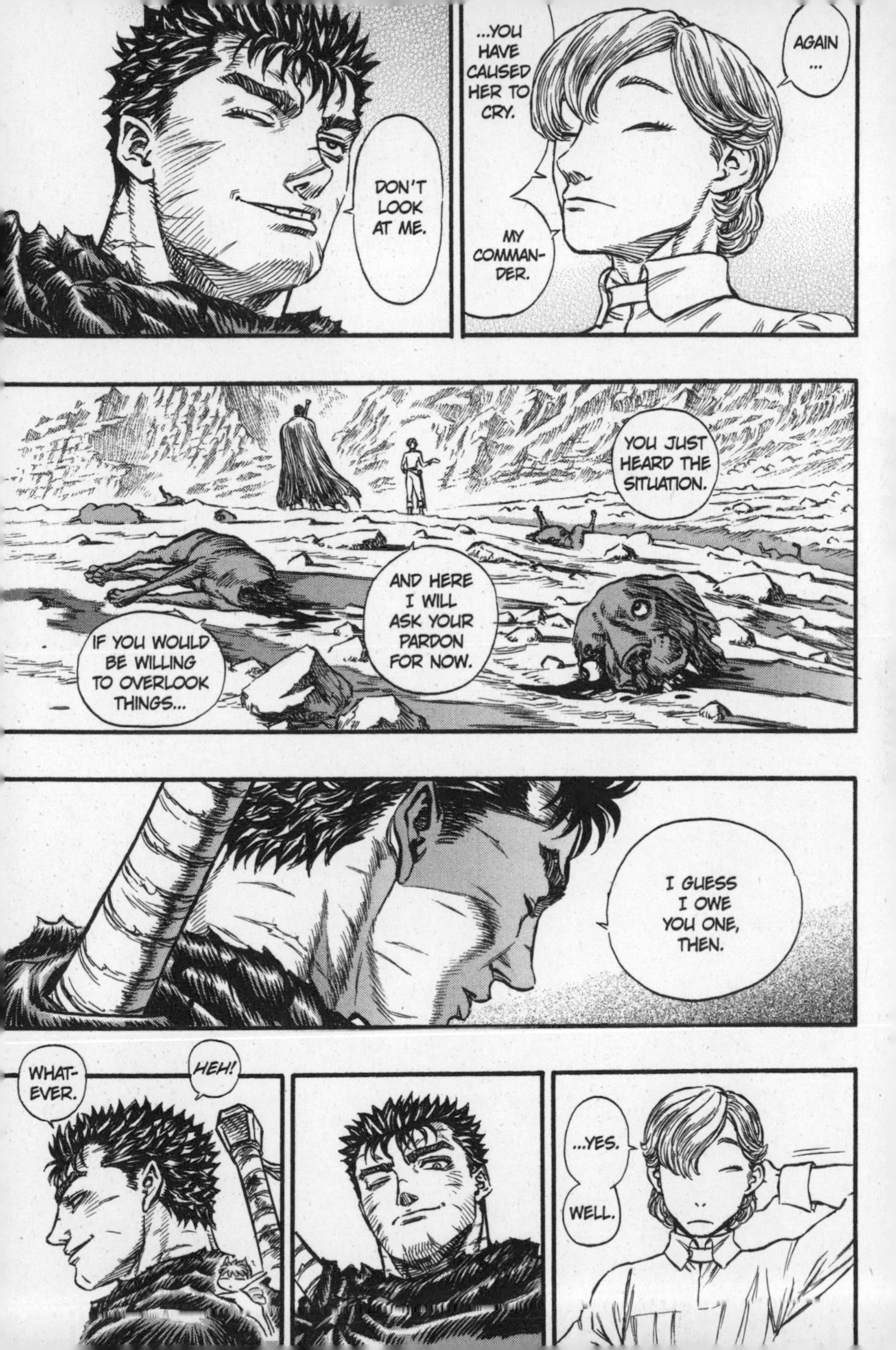
AGAIN...
...YOU HAVE CAUSED HER TO CRY.
MY COMMANDER.
DON'T LOOK AT ME.
YOU JUST HEARD THE SITUATION.
AND HERE I WILL ASK YOUR PARDON FOR NOW.
IF YOU WOULD BE WILLING TO OVERLOOK THINGS...
I GUESS I OWE YOU ONE, THEN.
...YES.
WELL.
HEH!
WHAT-EVER.

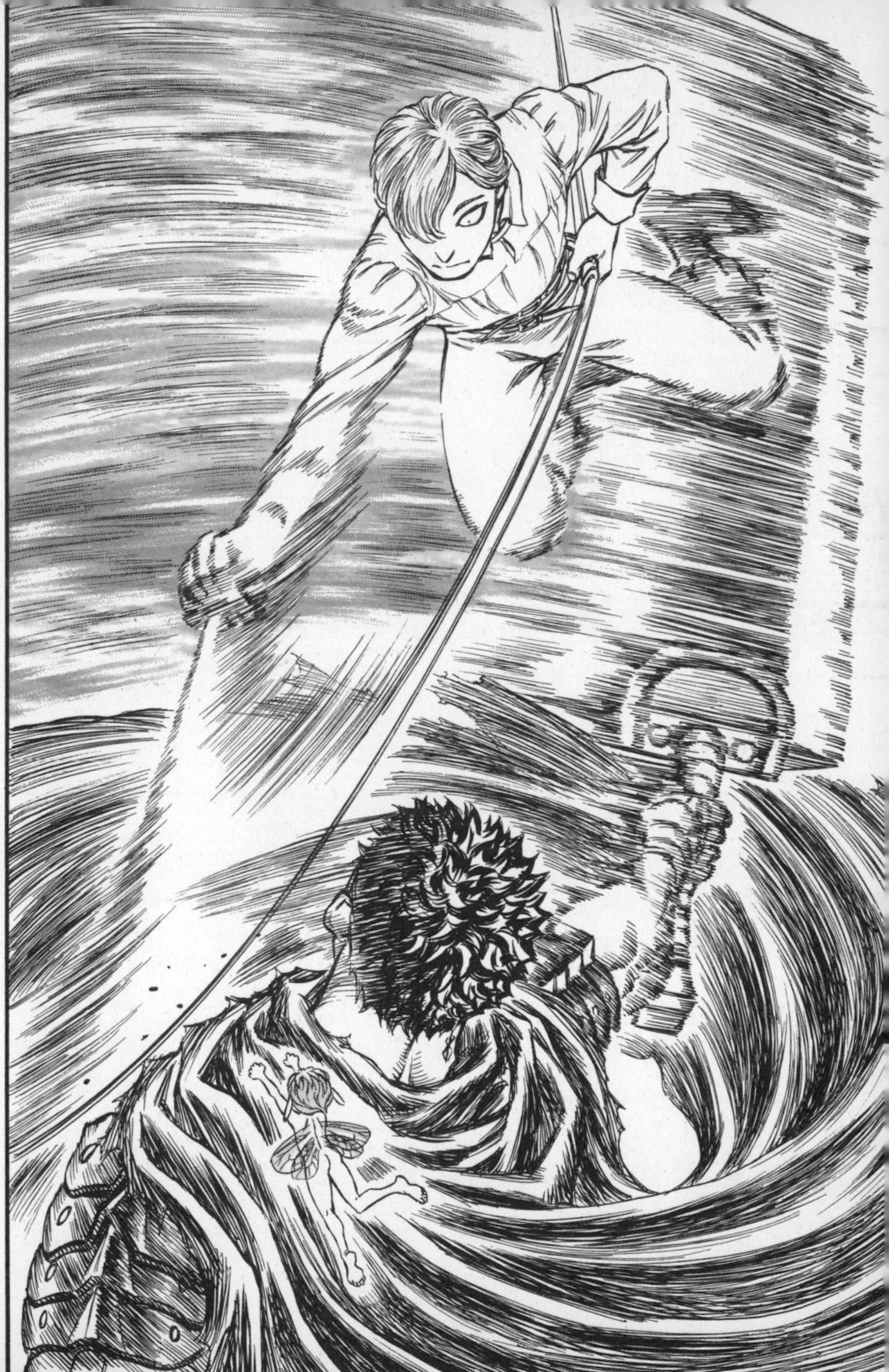

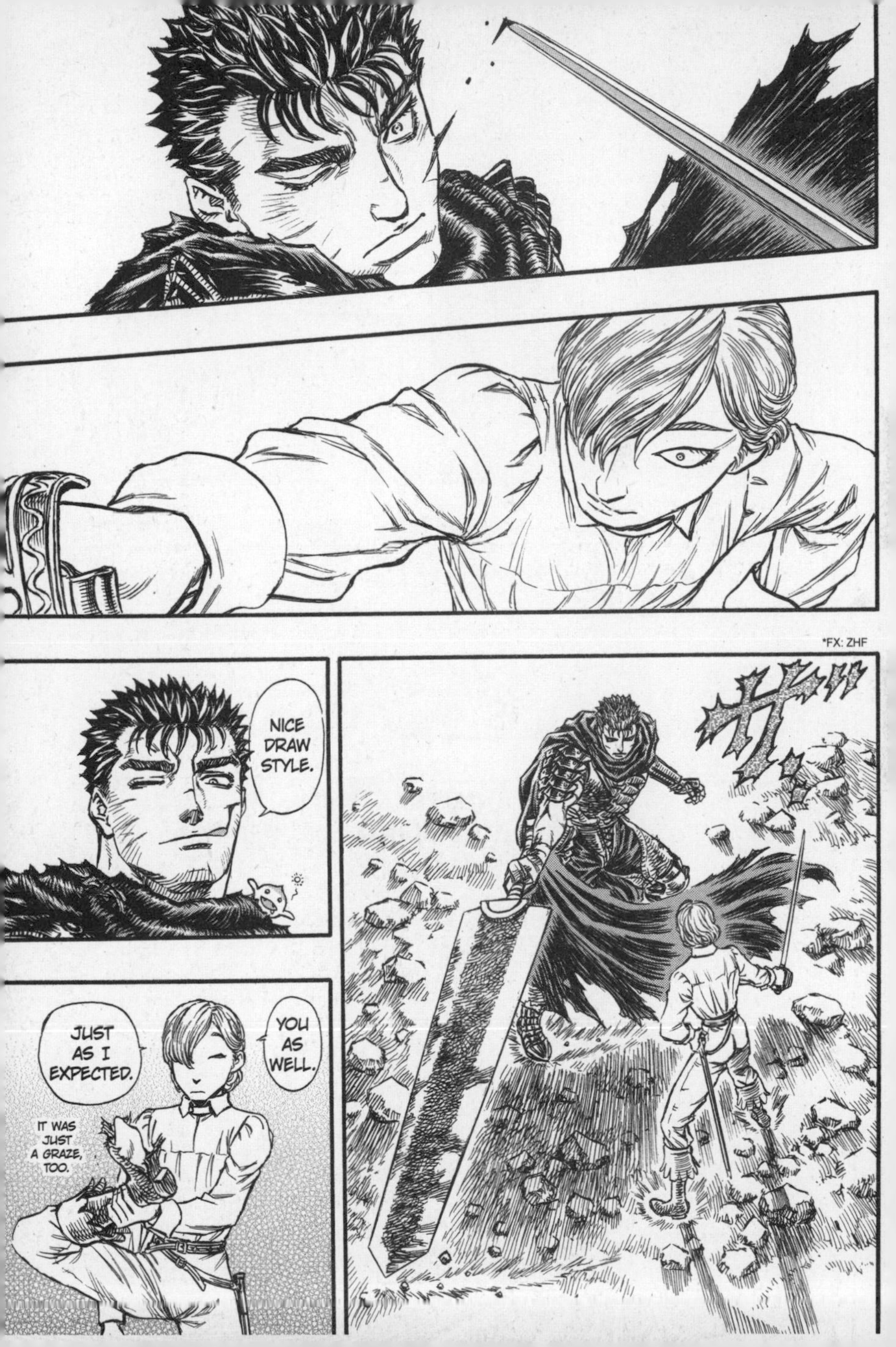
*FX: ZHF
NICE DRAW STYLE.
YOU AS WELL.
JUST AS I EXPECTED.
IT WAS JUST A GRAZE, TOO.

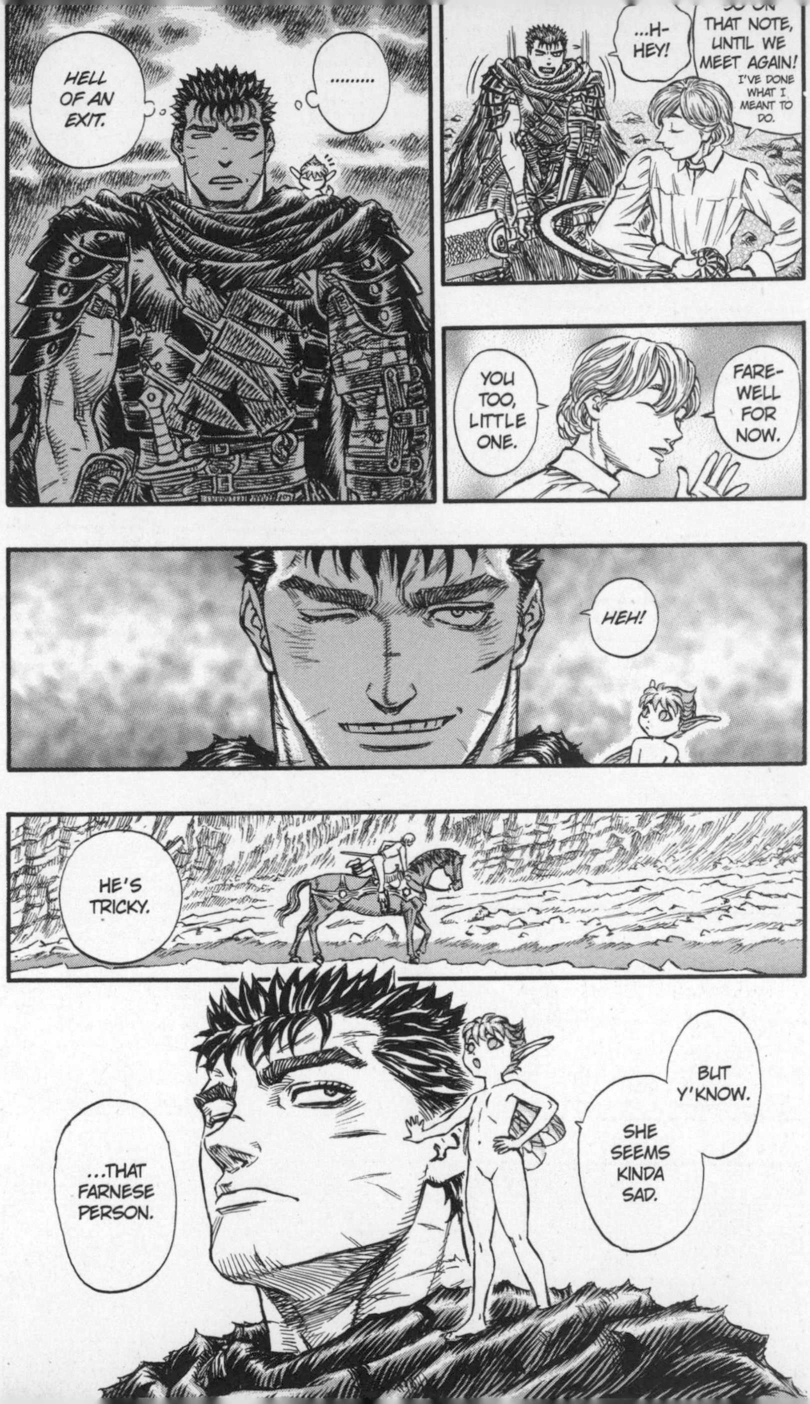
THAT NOTE, UNTIL WE MEET AGAIN!
I'VE DONE WHAT I MEANT TO DO.
...H- HEY!
FARE- WELL FOR NOW.
YOU TOO, LITTLE ONE.
....
HELL OF AN EXIT.
HEH!
HE'S TRICKY.
BUT Y'KNOW.
SHE SEEMS KINDA SAD.
...THAT FARNESE PERSON.

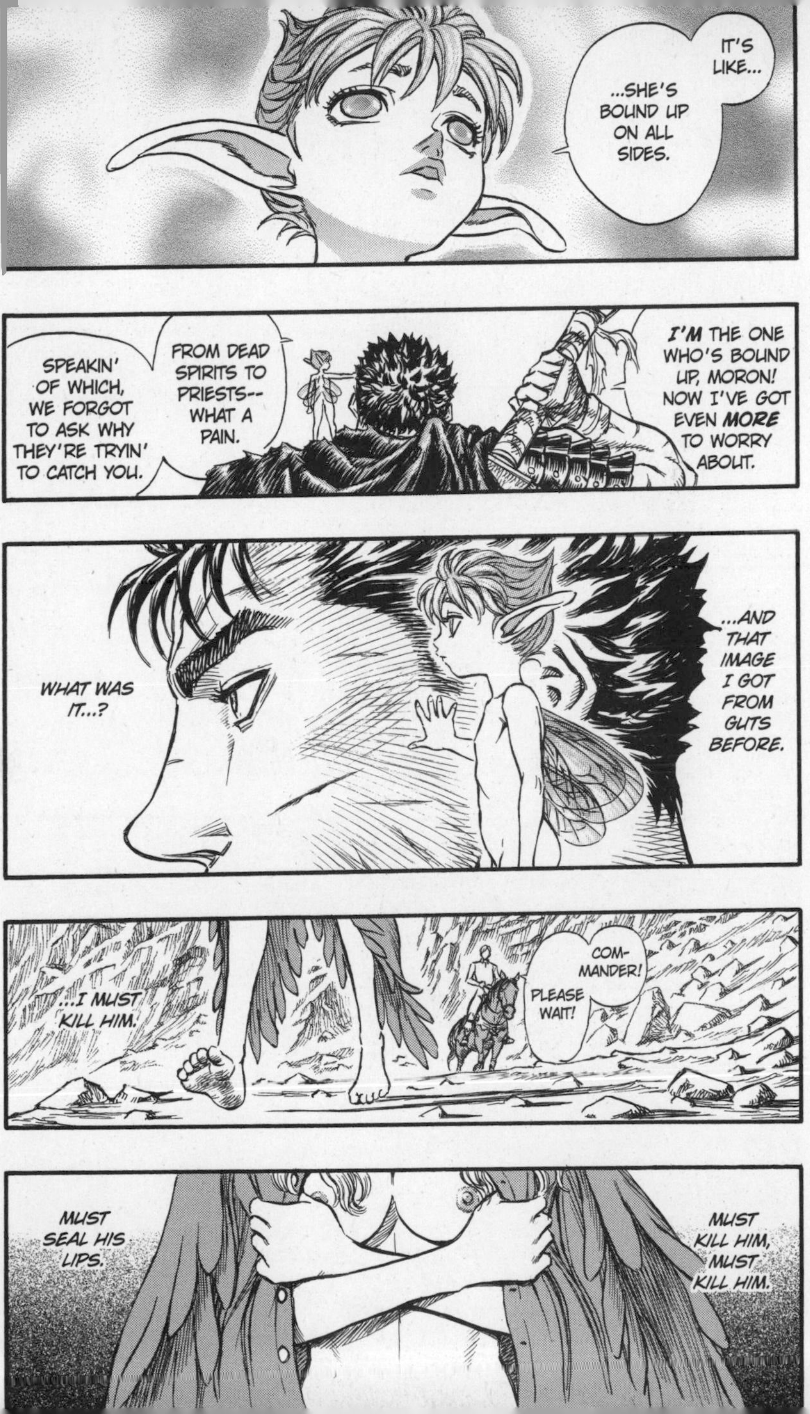
IT'S LIKE...
...SHE'S BOUND UP ON ALL SIDES.
I'M THE ONE WHO'S BOUND UP, MORON! NOW I'VE GOT EVEN MORE TO WORRY ABOUT.
FROM DEAD SPIRITS TO PRIESTS-- WHAT A PAIN.
SPEAKIN' OF WHICH, WE FORGOT TO ASK WHY THEY'RE TRYIN' TO CATCH YOU.
...AND THAT IMAGE I GOT FROM GUTS BEFORE.
WHAT WAS IT...?
COM-MANDER!
PLEASE WAIT!
...I MUST KILL HIM.
MUST KILL HIM, MUST KILL HIM.
MUST SEAL HIS LIPS.

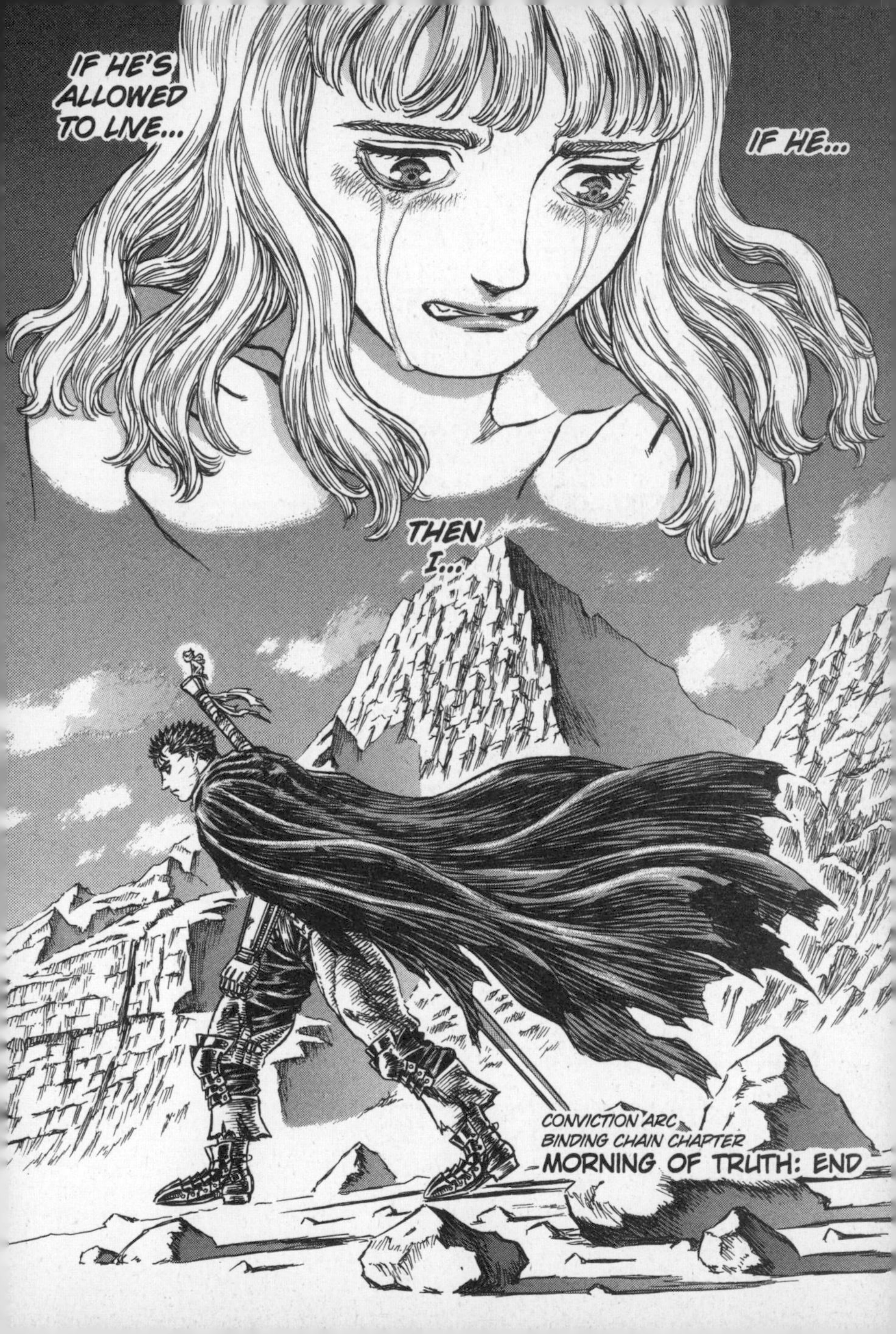
IF HE...
IF HE'S ALLOWED TO LIVE...
THEN I...
CONVICTION ARC
BINDING CHAIN CHAPTER
MORNING OF TRUTH: END

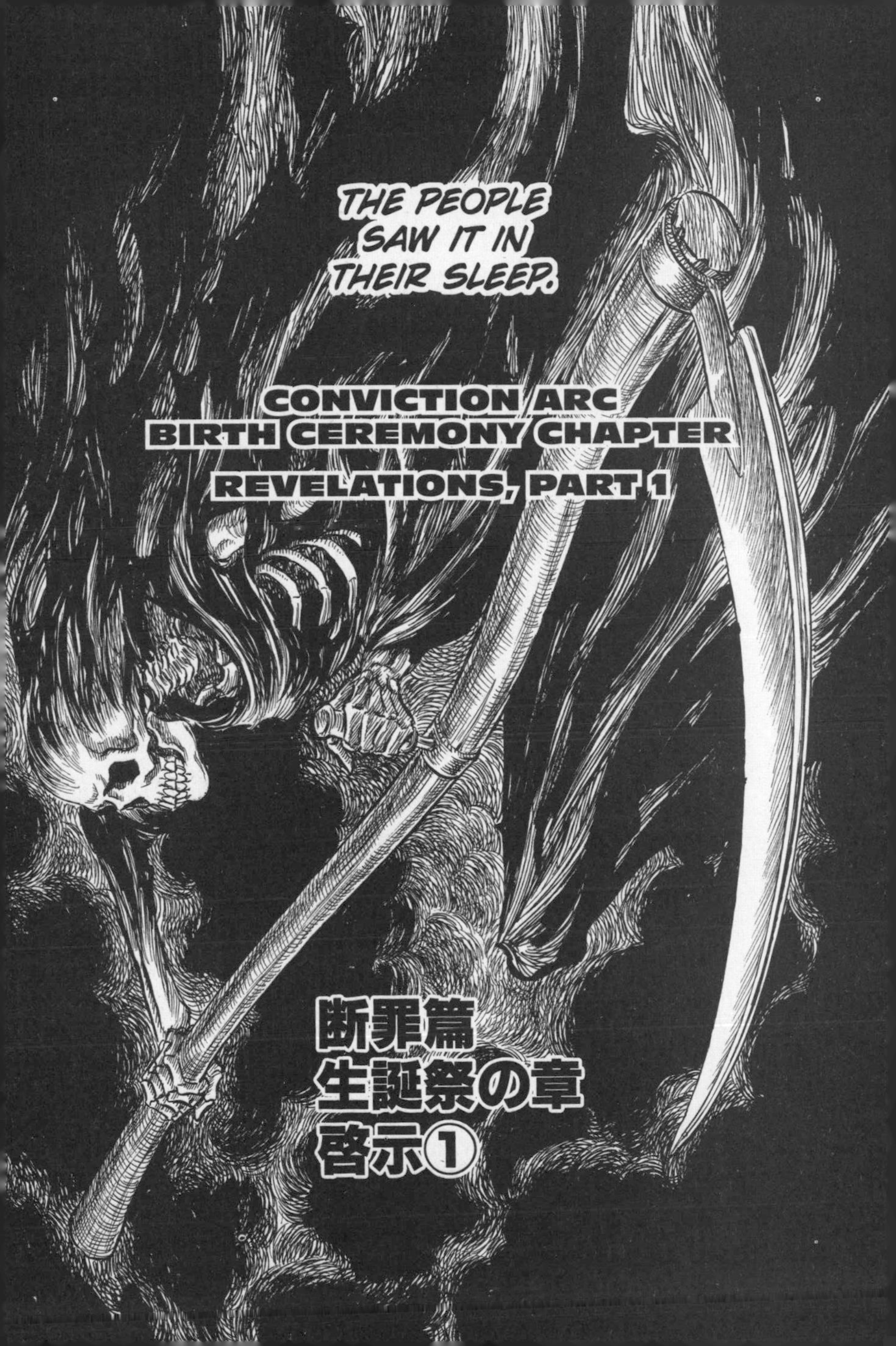
THE PEOPLE SAW IT IN THEIR SLEEP.
CONVICTION ARC
BIRTH CEREMONY CHAPTER
REVELATIONS, PART 1
断罪篇
生誕祭の章
啓示①

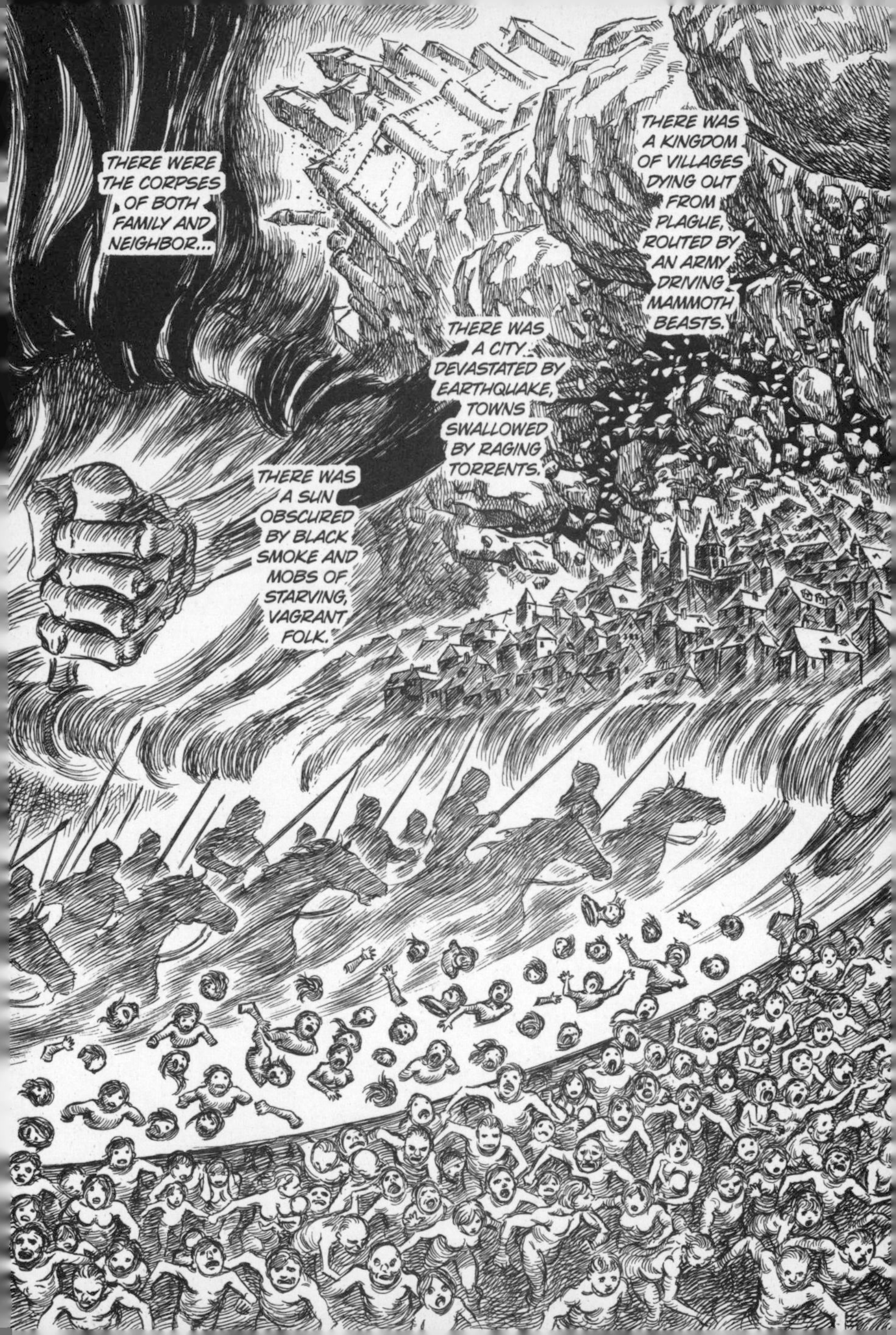
THERE WAS A KINGDOM OF VILLAGES DYING OUT FROM PLAGUE, ROUTED BY AN ARMY DRIVING MAMMOTH BEASTS.
THERE WERE THE CORPSES OF BOTH FAMILY AND NEIGHBOR...
THERE WAS A CITY DEVASTATED BY EARTHQUAKE, TOWNS SWALLOWED BY RAGING TORRENTS.
THERE WAS A SUN OBSCURED BY BLACK SMOKE AND MOBS OF STARVING, VAGRANT FOLK.

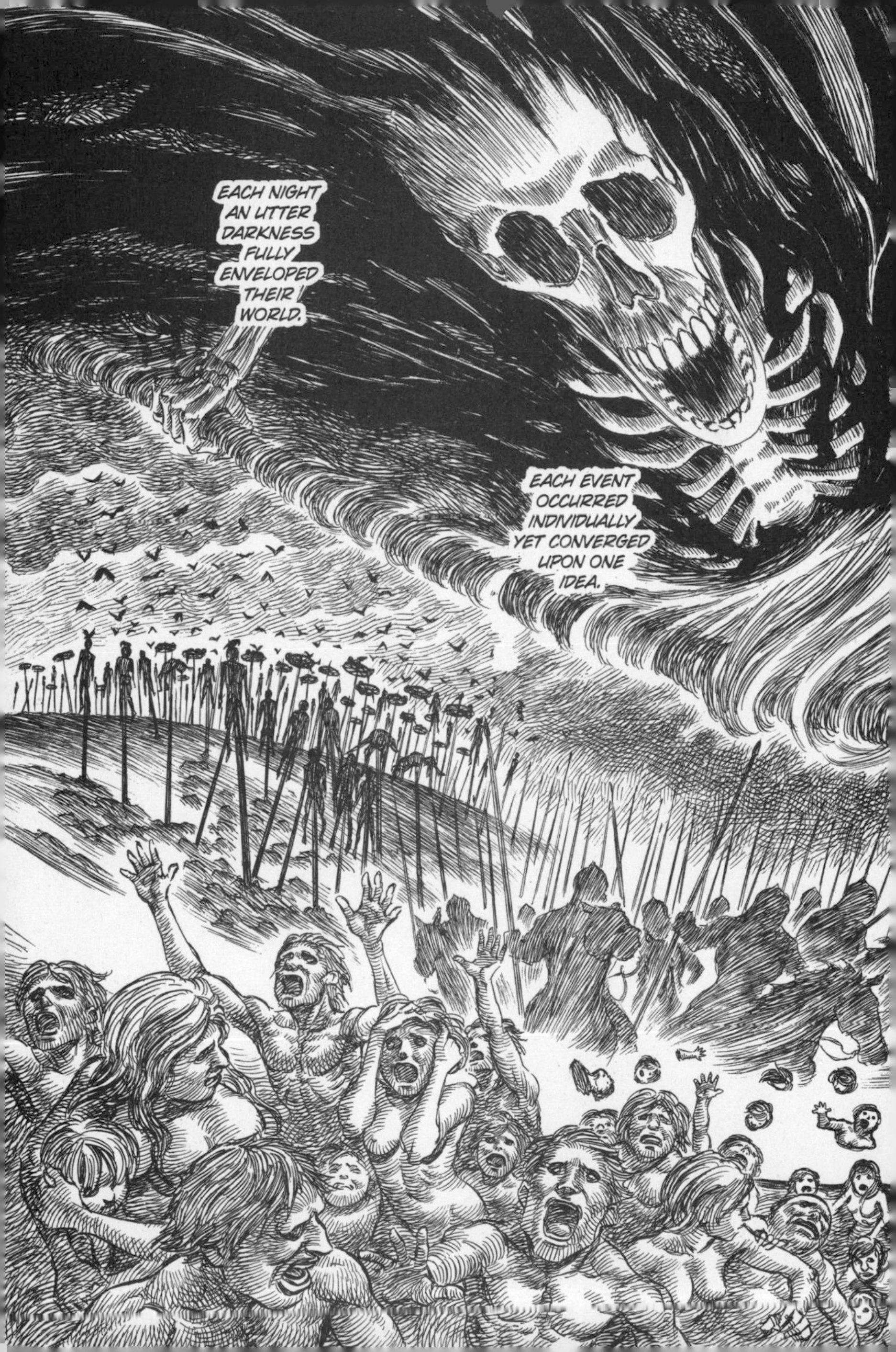
EACH NIGHT AN UTTER DARKNESS FULLY ENVELOPED THEIR WORLD.
EACH EVENT OCCURRED INDIVIDUALLY YET CONVERGED UPON ONE IDEA.

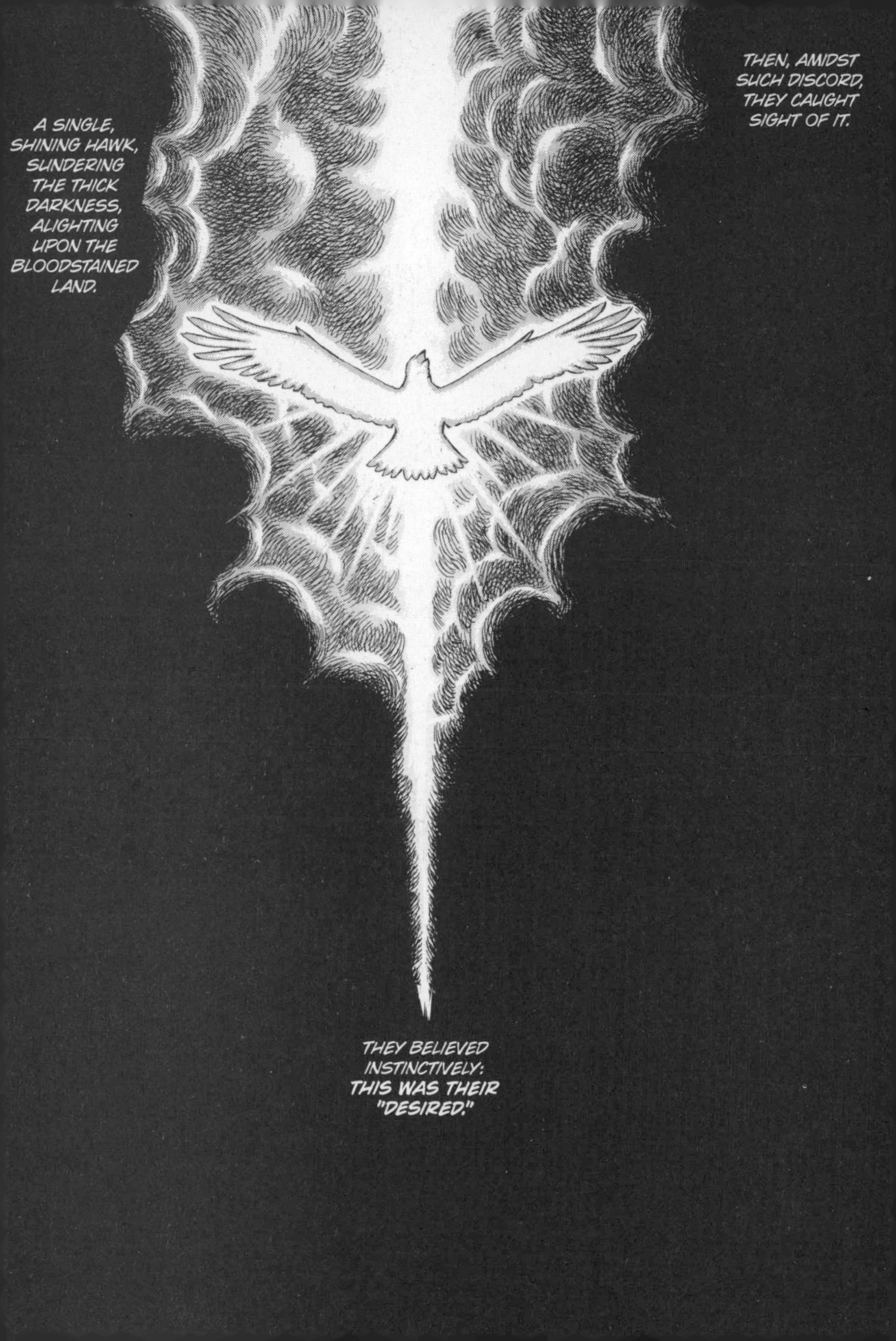
THEN, AMIDST SUCH DISCORD, THEY CAUGHT SIGHT OF IT.
A SINGLE, SHINING HAWK, SUNDERING THE THICK DARKNESS, ALIGHTING UPON THE BLOODSTAINED LAND.
THEY BELIEVED INSTINCTIVELY: THIS WAS THEIR "DESIRED."

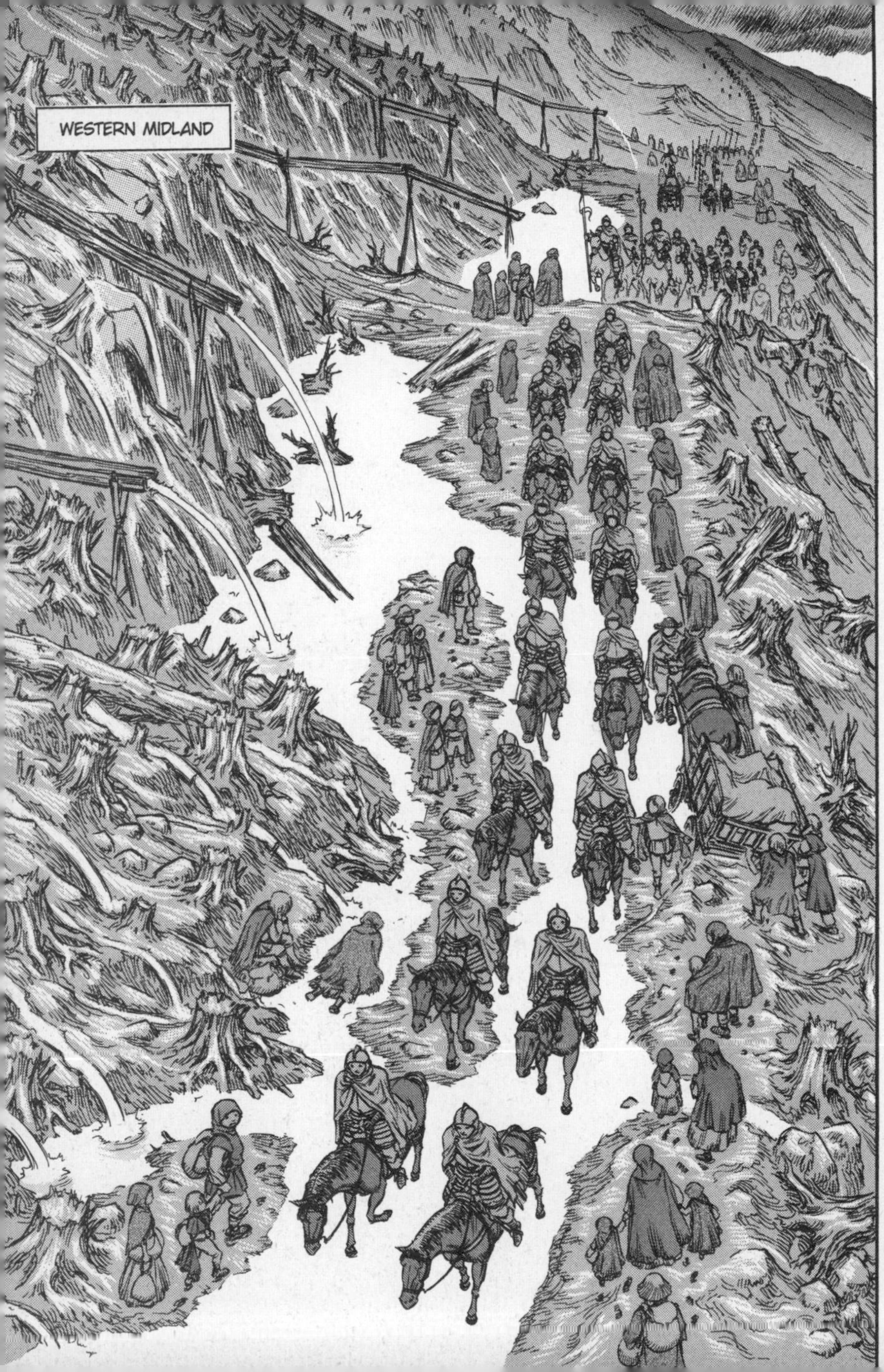
WESTERN MIDLAND

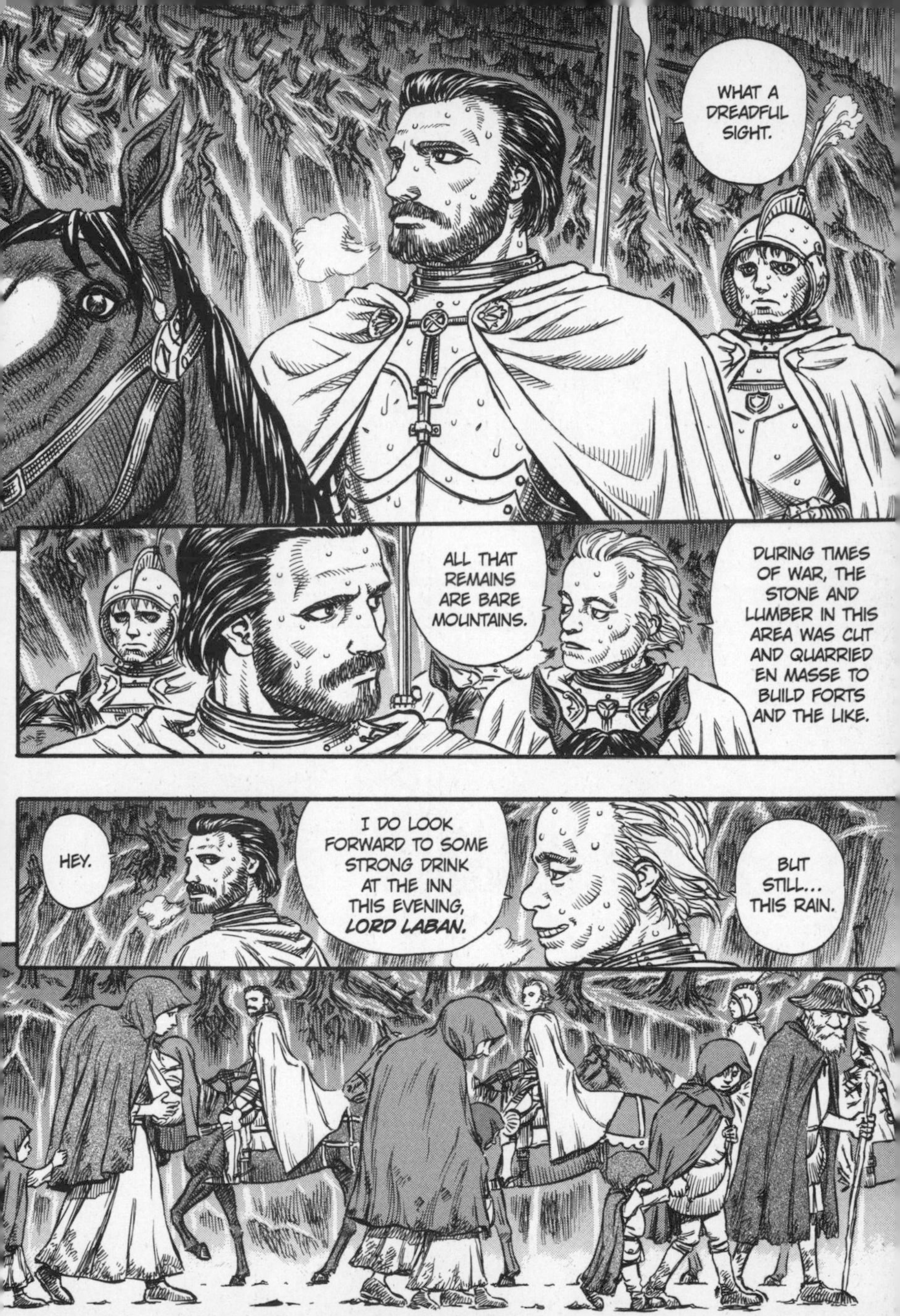
WHAT A DREADFUL SIGHT.
DURING TIMES OF WAR, THE STONE AND LUMBER IN THIS AREA WAS CUT AND QUARRIED EN MASSE TO BUILD FORTS AND THE LIKE.
ALL THAT REMAINS ARE BARE MOUNTAINS.
BUT STILL... THIS RAIN.
I DO LOOK FORWARD TO SOME STRONG DRINK AT THE INN THIS EVENING, LORD LABAN.
HEY.

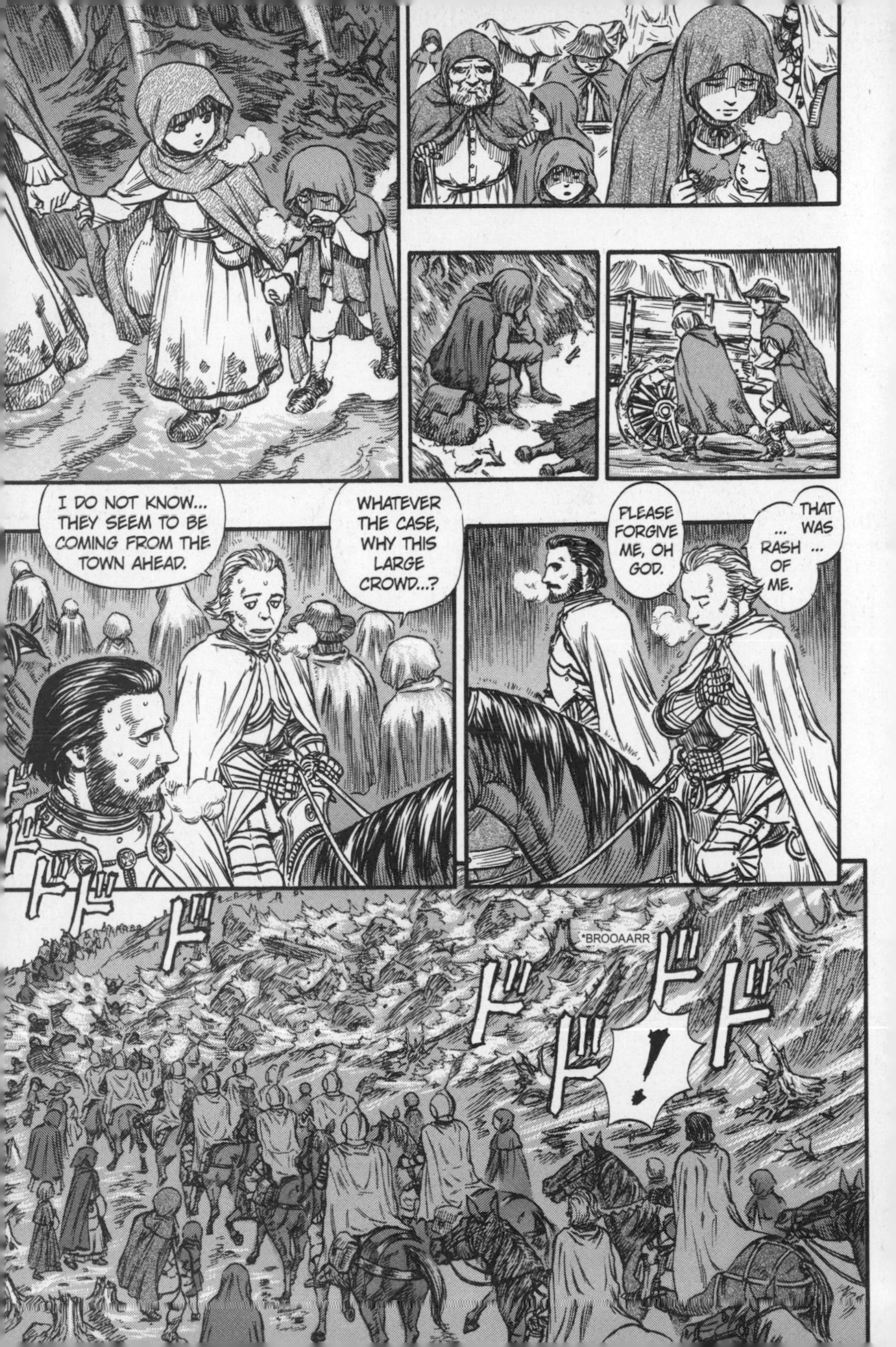

... THAT WAS RASH ... OF ME.
PLEASE FORGIVE ME, OH GOD.
WHATEVER THE CASE, WHY THIS LARGE CROWD...?
I DO NOT KNOW... THEY SEEM TO BE COMING FROM THE TOWN AHEAD.
*BROOAARR

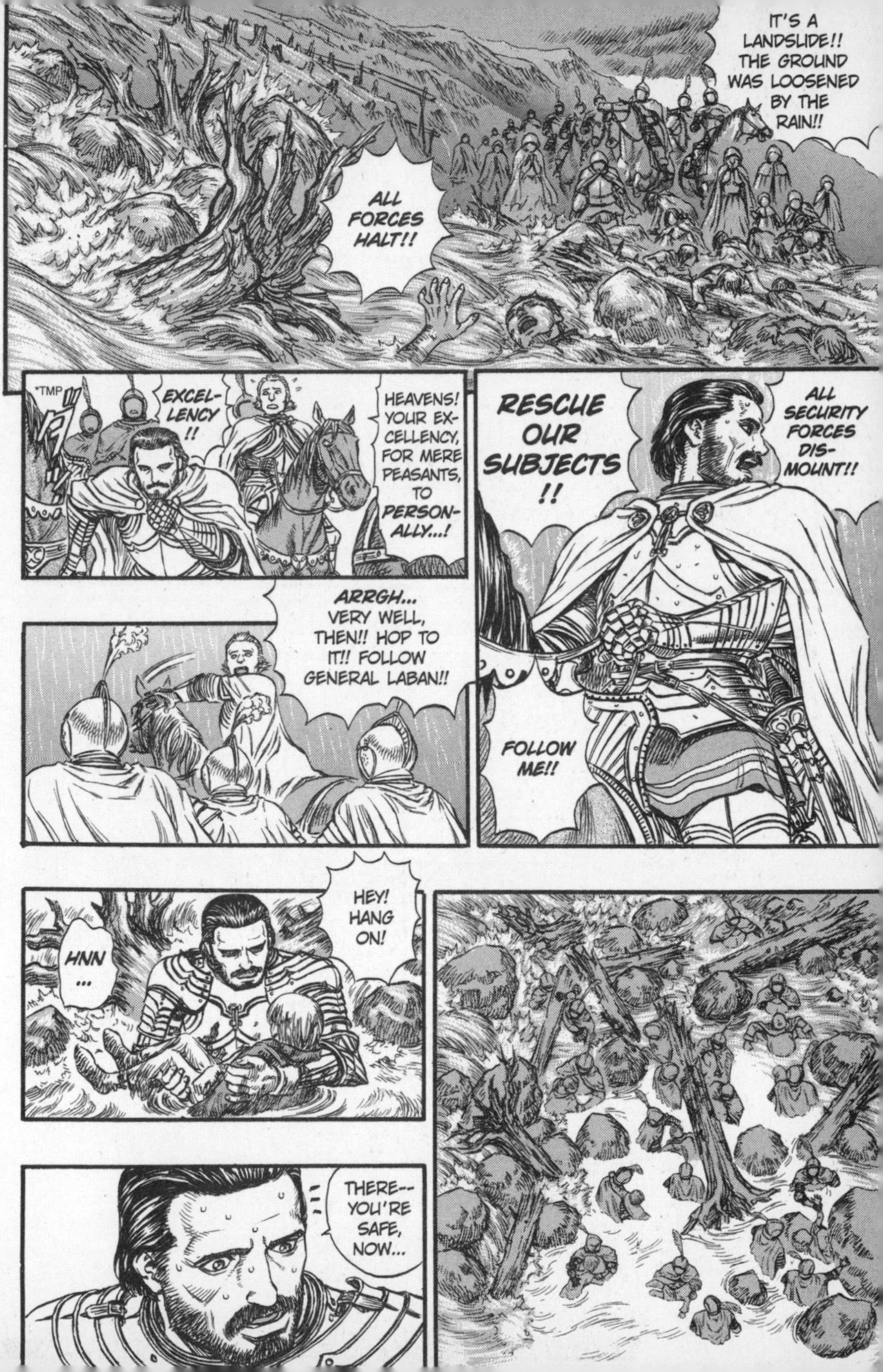
IT'S A LANDSLIDE!! THE GROUND WAS LOOSENED BY THE RAIN!!
ALL FORCES HALT!!
ALL SECURITY FORCES DIS-MOUNT!!
RESCUE OUR SUBJECTS !!
FOLLOW ME!!
HEAVENS! YOUR EX-CELLENCY, FOR MERE PEASANTS, TO PERSON-ALLY...!
EXCEL-LENCY !!
*TMP
ARRGH... VERY WELL, THEN!! HOP TO IT!! FOLLOW GENERAL LABAN!!
HEY! HANG ON!
HNN ...
THERE-- YOU'RE SAFE, NOW...

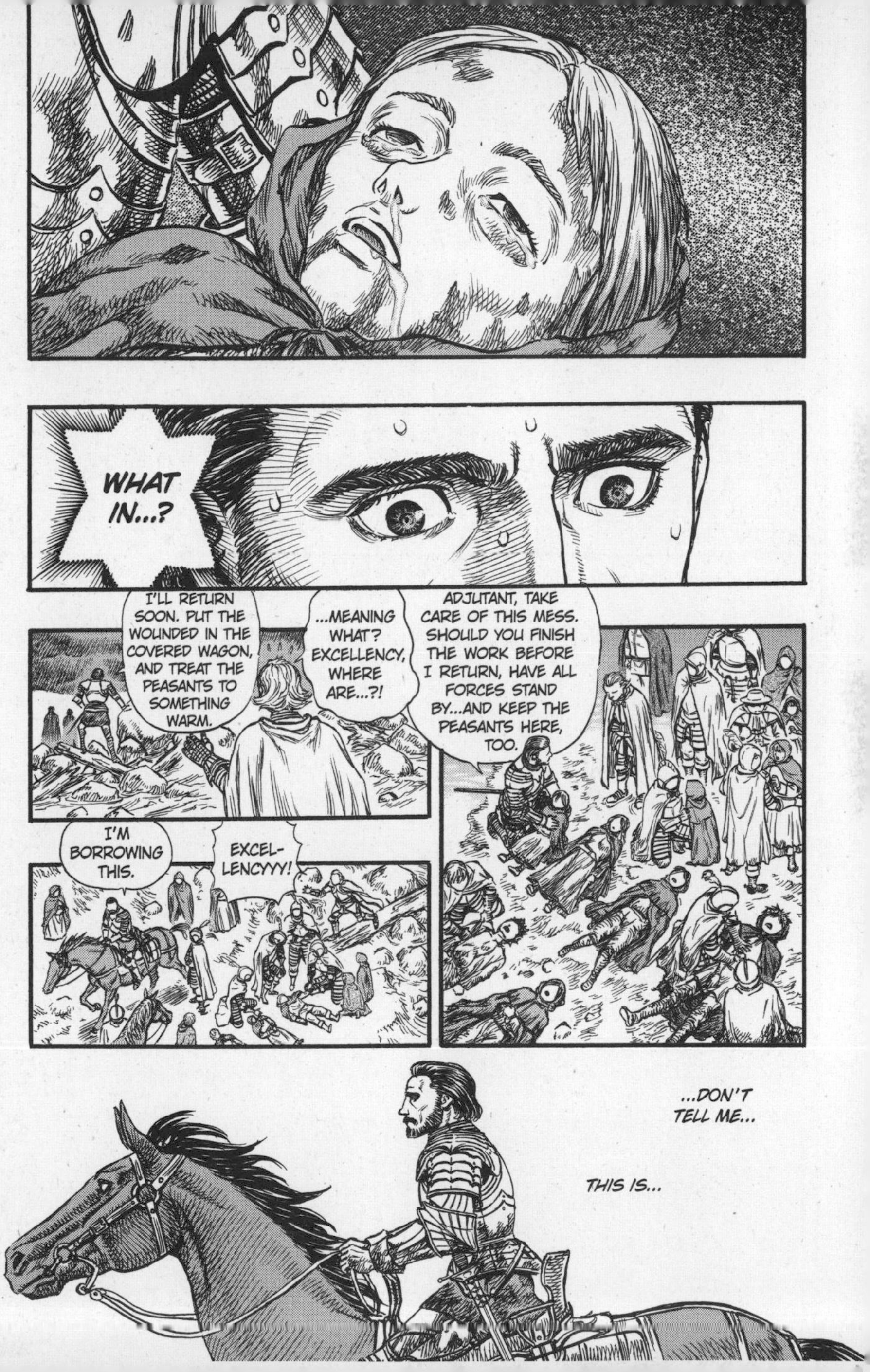

WHAT IN...?
ADJUTANT, TAKE CARE OF THIS MESS. SHOULD YOU FINISH THE WORK BEFORE I RETURN, HAVE ALL FORCES STAND BY...AND KEEP THE PEASANTS HERE, TOO.
...MEANING WHAT? EXCELLENCY, WHERE ARE...?!
I'LL RETURN SOON. PUT THE WOUNDED IN THE COVERED WAGON, AND TREAT THE PEASANTS TO SOMETHING WARM.
EXCEL-LENCYYY!
I'M BORROWING THIS.
...DON'T TELL ME...
THIS IS...

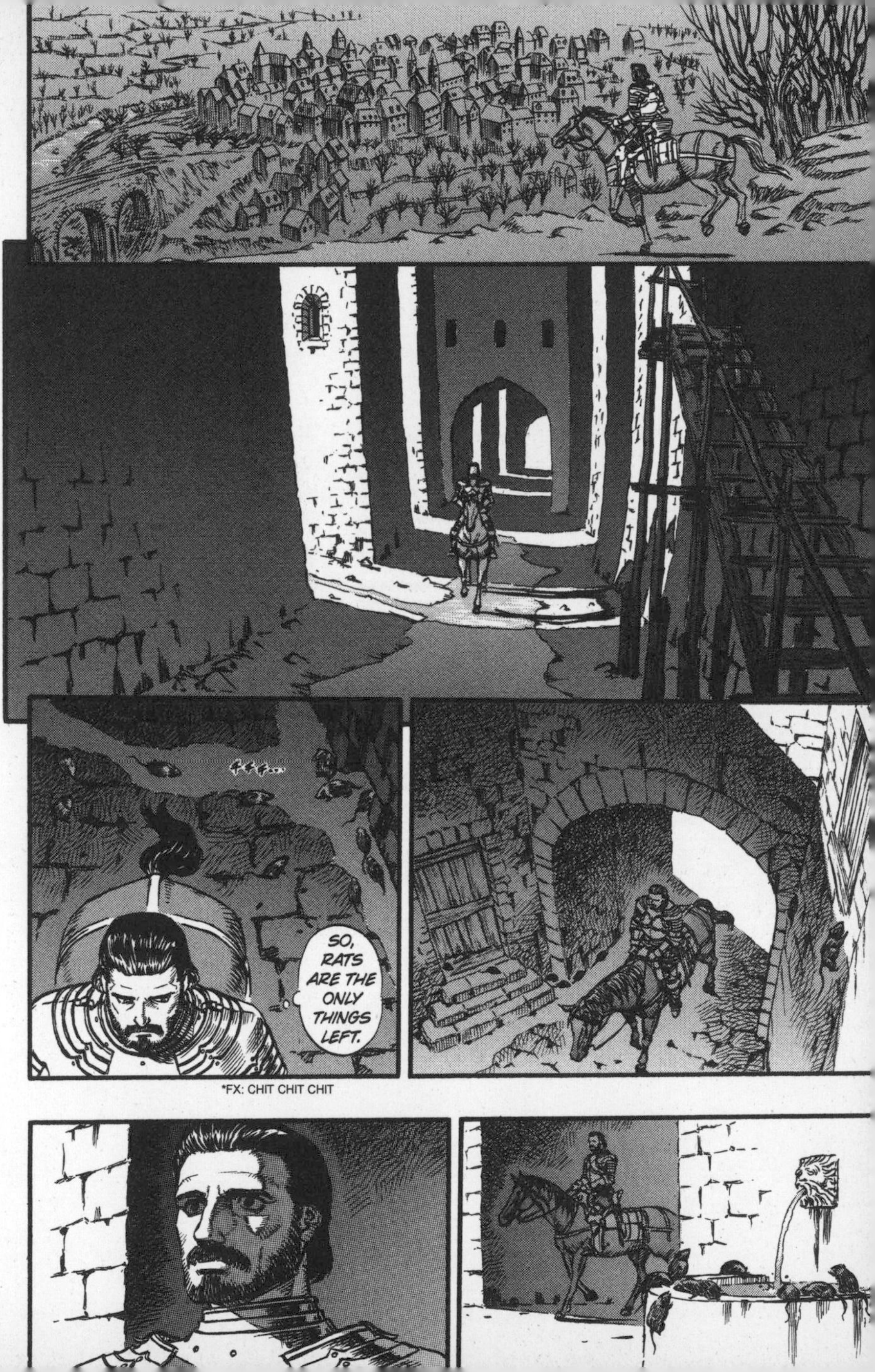
SO, RATS ARE THE ONLY THINGS LEFT.
*FX: CHIT CHIT CHIT

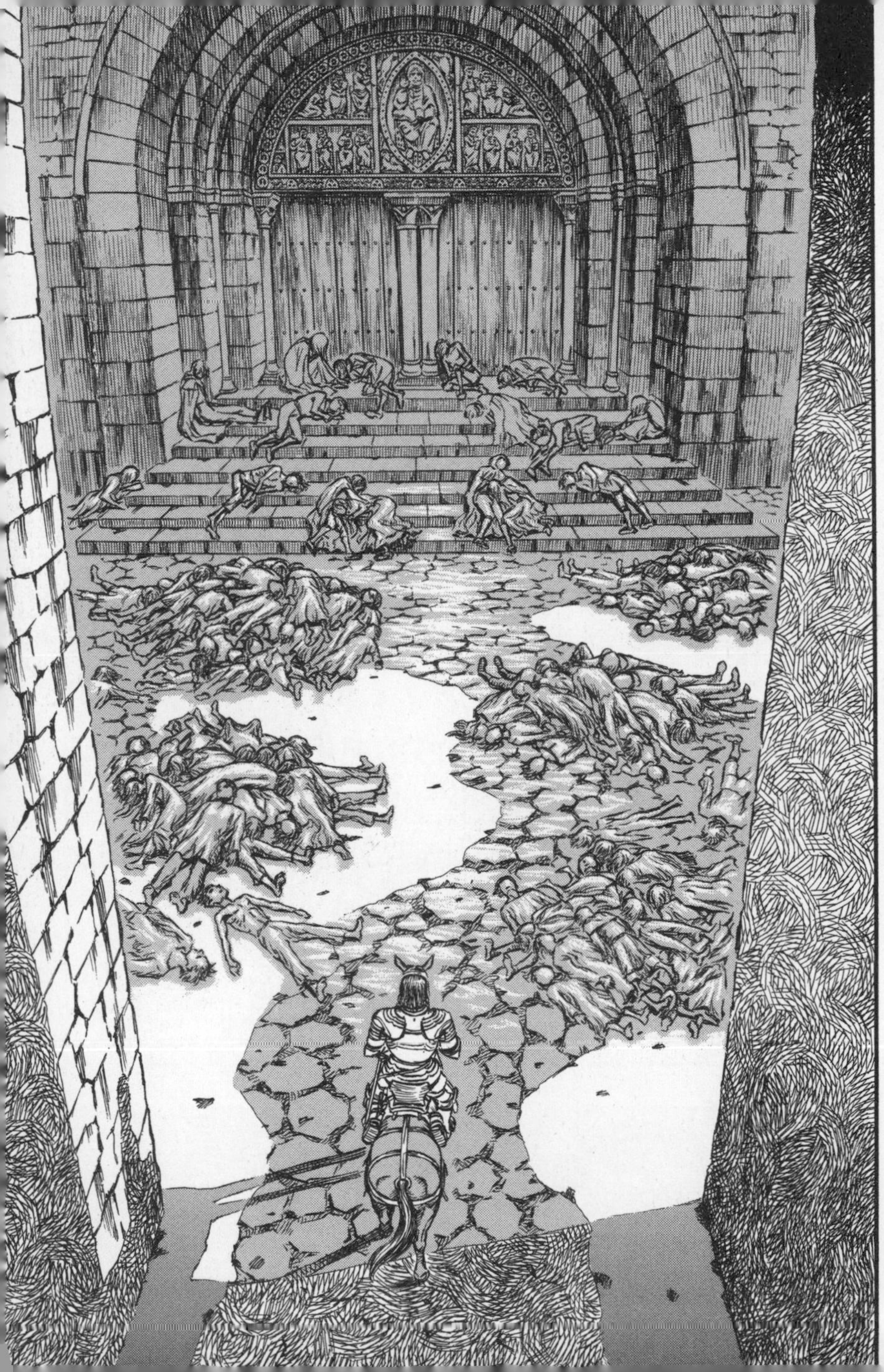

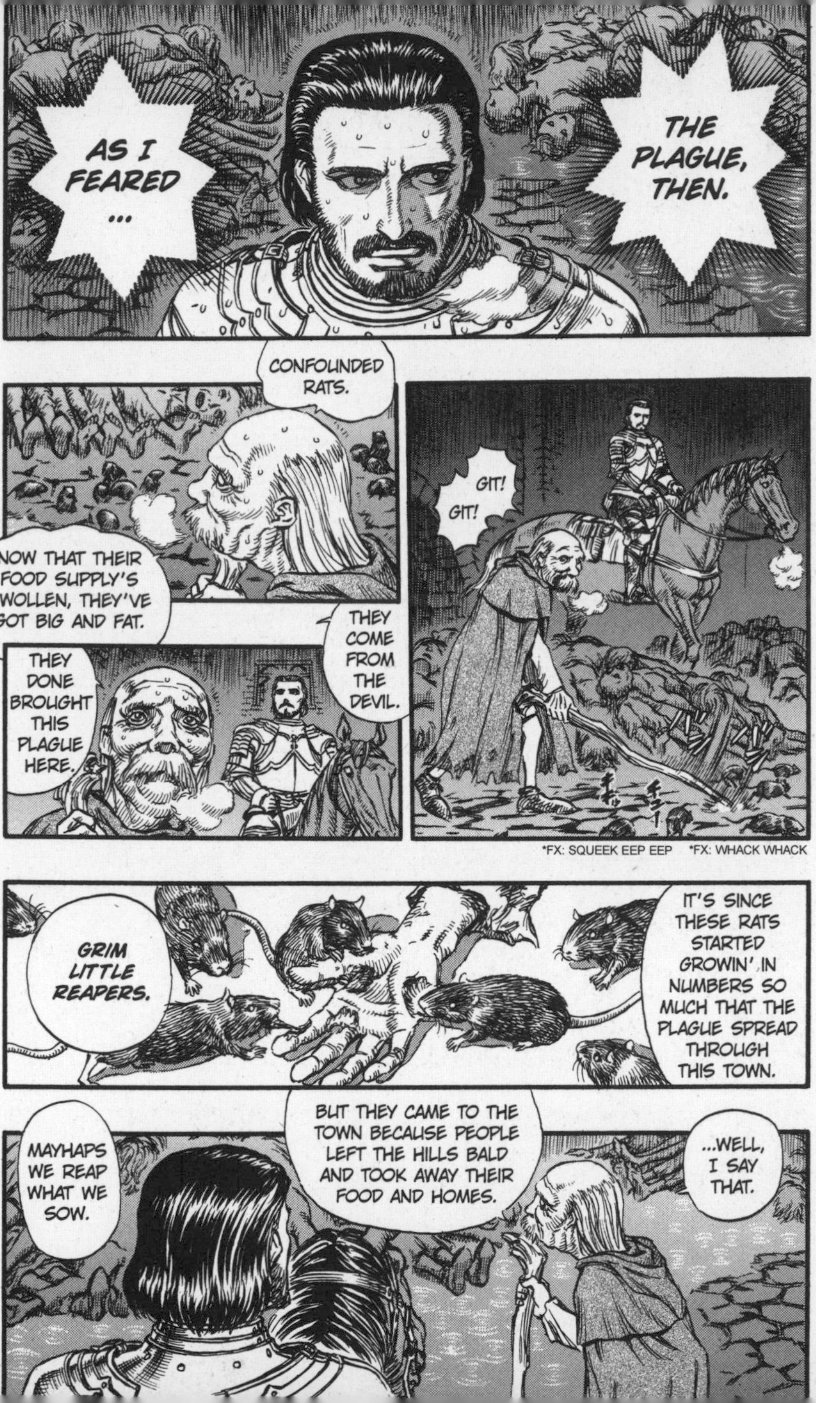
THE PLAGUE, THEN.
AS I FEARED ...
GIT! GIT!
CONFOUNDED RATS.
NOW THAT THEIR FOOD SUPPLY'S SWOLLEN, THEY'VE GOT BIG AND FAT.
THEY COME FROM THE DEVIL.
THEY DONE BROUGHT THIS PLAGUE HERE.
IT'S SINCE THESE RATS STARTED GROWIN' IN NUMBERS SO MUCH THAT THE PLAGUE SPREAD THROUGH THIS TOWN.
GRIM LITTLE REAPERS.
...WELL, I SAY THAT.
BUT THEY CAME TO THE TOWN BECAUSE PEOPLE LEFT THE HILLS BALD AND TOOK AWAY THEIR FOOD AND HOMES.
MAYHAPS WE REAP WHAT WE SOW.
*FX: SQUEEK EEP EEP *FX: WHACK WHACK

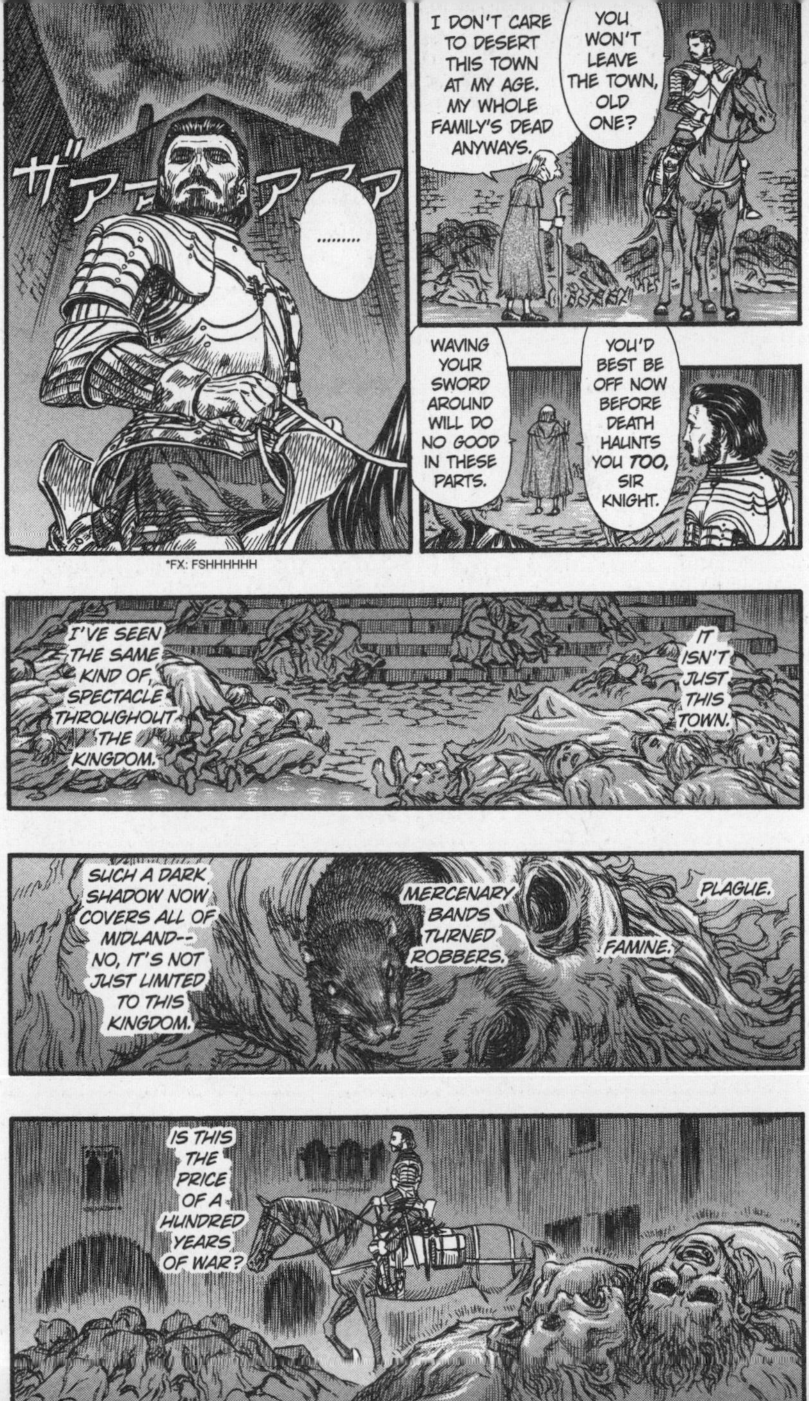
YOU WON'T LEAVE THE TOWN, OLD ONE?
I DON'T CARE TO DESERT THIS TOWN AT MY AGE. MY WHOLE FAMILY'S DEAD ANYWAYS.
YOU'D BEST BE OFF NOW BEFORE DEATH HAUNTS YOU *TOO*, SIR KNIGHT.
WAVING YOUR SWORD AROUND WILL DO NO GOOD IN THESE PARTS.
....
*FX: FSHHHHHH
IT ISN'T JUST THIS TOWN.
I'VE SEEN THE SAME KIND OF SPECTACLE THROUGHOUT THE KINGDOM.
PLAGUE.
FAMINE.
MERCENARY BANDS TURNED ROBBERS.
SUCH A DARK SHADOW NOW COVERS ALL OF MIDLAND-- NO, IT'S NOT JUST LIMITED TO THIS KINGDOM.
IS THIS THE PRICE OF A HUNDRED YEARS OF WAR?

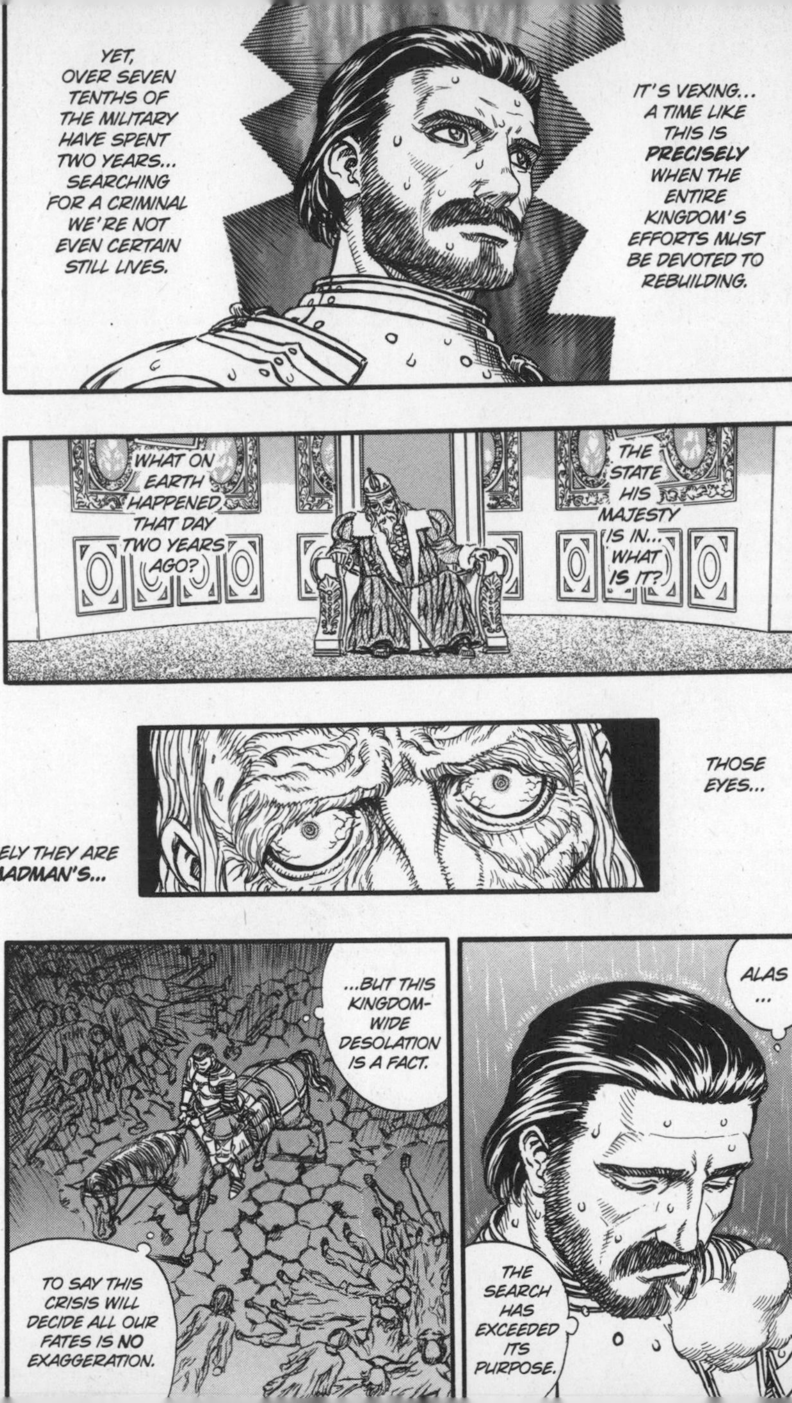
IT'S VEXING... A TIME LIKE THIS IS PRECISELY WHEN THE ENTIRE KINGDOM'S EFFORTS MUST BE DEVOTED TO REBUILDING.
YET, OVER SEVEN TENTHS OF THE MILITARY HAVE SPENT TWO YEARS... SEARCHING FOR A CRIMINAL WE'RE NOT EVEN CERTAIN STILL LIVES.
THE STATE HIS MAJESTY IS IN... WHAT IS IT?
WHAT ON EARTH HAPPENED THAT DAY TWO YEARS AGO?
THOSE EYES...
SURELY THEY ARE A MADMAN'S...
ALAS...
THE SEARCH HAS EXCEEDED ITS PURPOSE.
...BUT THIS KINGDOM-WIDE DESOLATION IS A FACT.
TO SAY THIS CRISIS WILL DECIDE ALL OUR FATES IS NO EXAGGERATION.

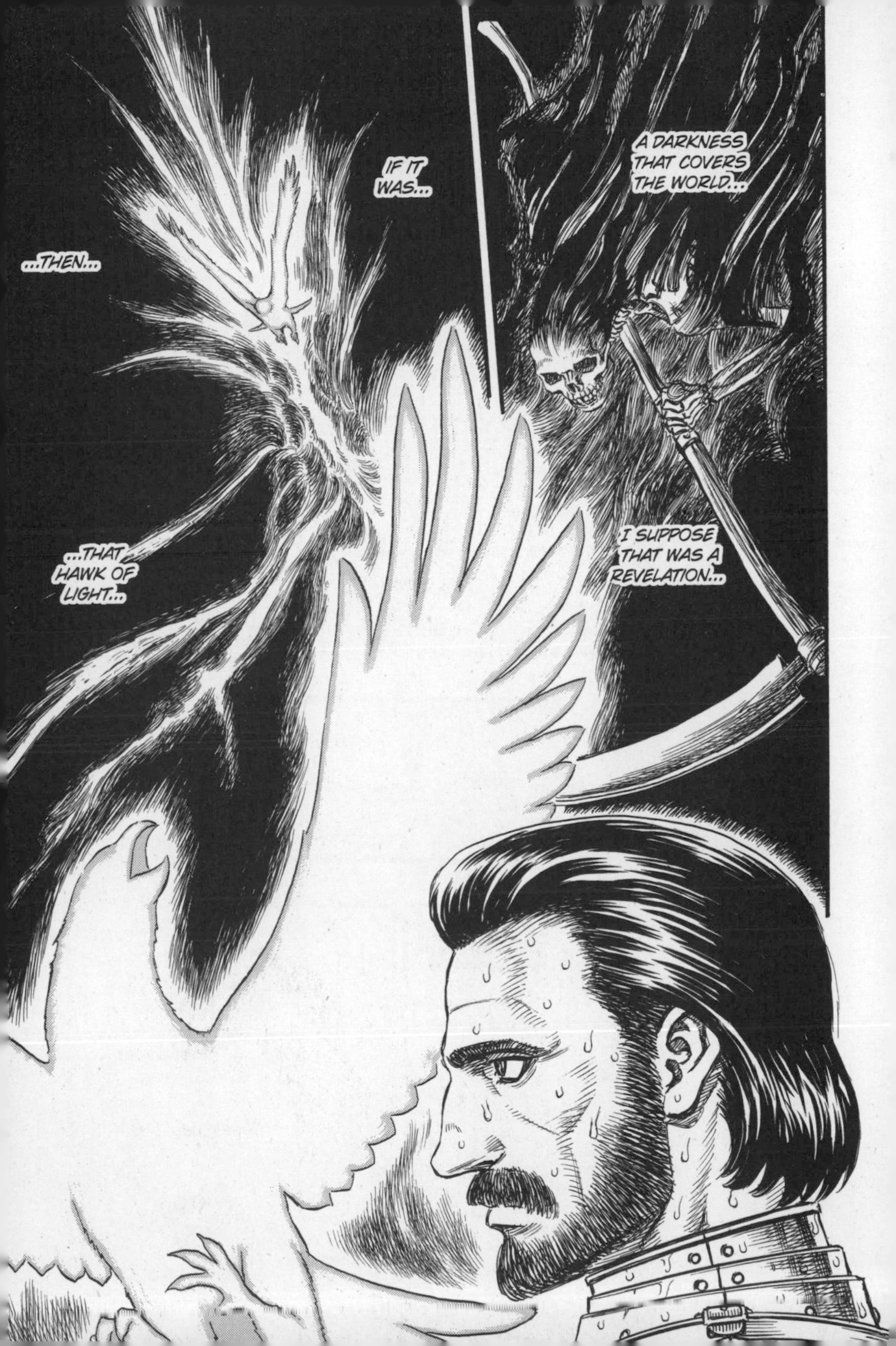
A DARKNESS THAT COVERS THE WORLD...
I SUPPOSE THAT WAS A REVELATION...
IF IT WAS...
...THEN...
...THAT HAWK OF LIGHT...

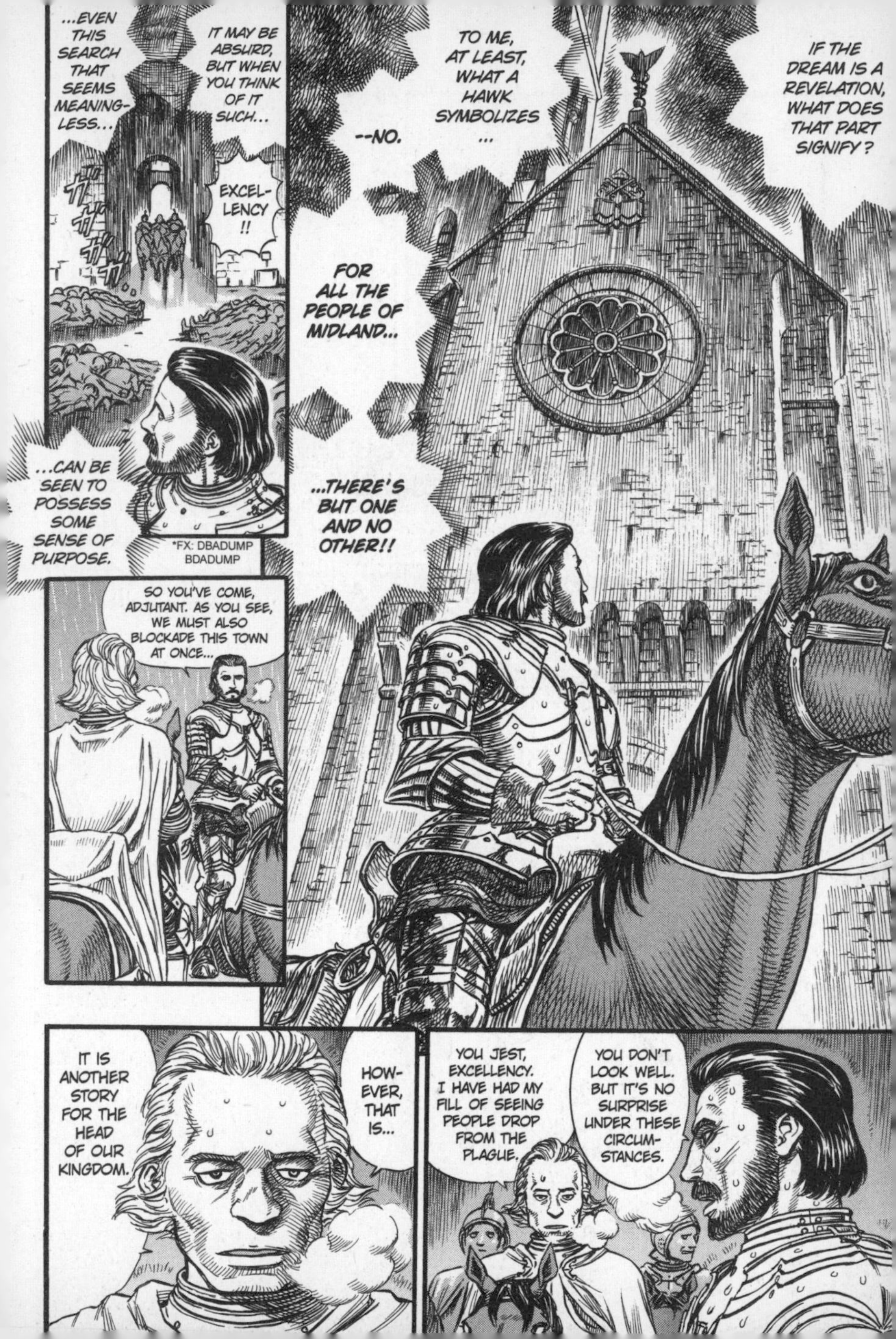
IF THE DREAM IS A REVELATION, WHAT DOES THAT PART SIGNIFY?
TO ME, AT LEAST, WHAT A HAWK SYMBOLIZES...
--NO.
FOR ALL THE PEOPLE OF MIDLAND...
...THERE'S BUT ONE AND NO OTHER!!
IT MAY BE ABSURD, BUT WHEN YOU THINK OF IT SUCH...
...EVEN THIS SEARCH THAT SEEMS MEANING-LESS...
EXCEL-LENCY !!
...CAN BE SEEN TO POSSESS SOME SENSE OF PURPOSE.
*FX: DBADUMP BDADUMP
SO YOU'VE COME, ADJUTANT. AS YOU SEE, WE MUST ALSO BLOCKADE THIS TOWN AT ONCE...
YOU DON'T LOOK WELL. BUT IT'S NO SURPRISE UNDER THESE CIRCUM-STANCES.
YOU JEST, EXCELLENCY. I HAVE HAD MY FILL OF SEEING PEOPLE DROP FROM THE PLAGUE.
HOW-EVER, THAT IS...
IT IS ANOTHER STORY FOR THE HEAD OF OUR KINGDOM.

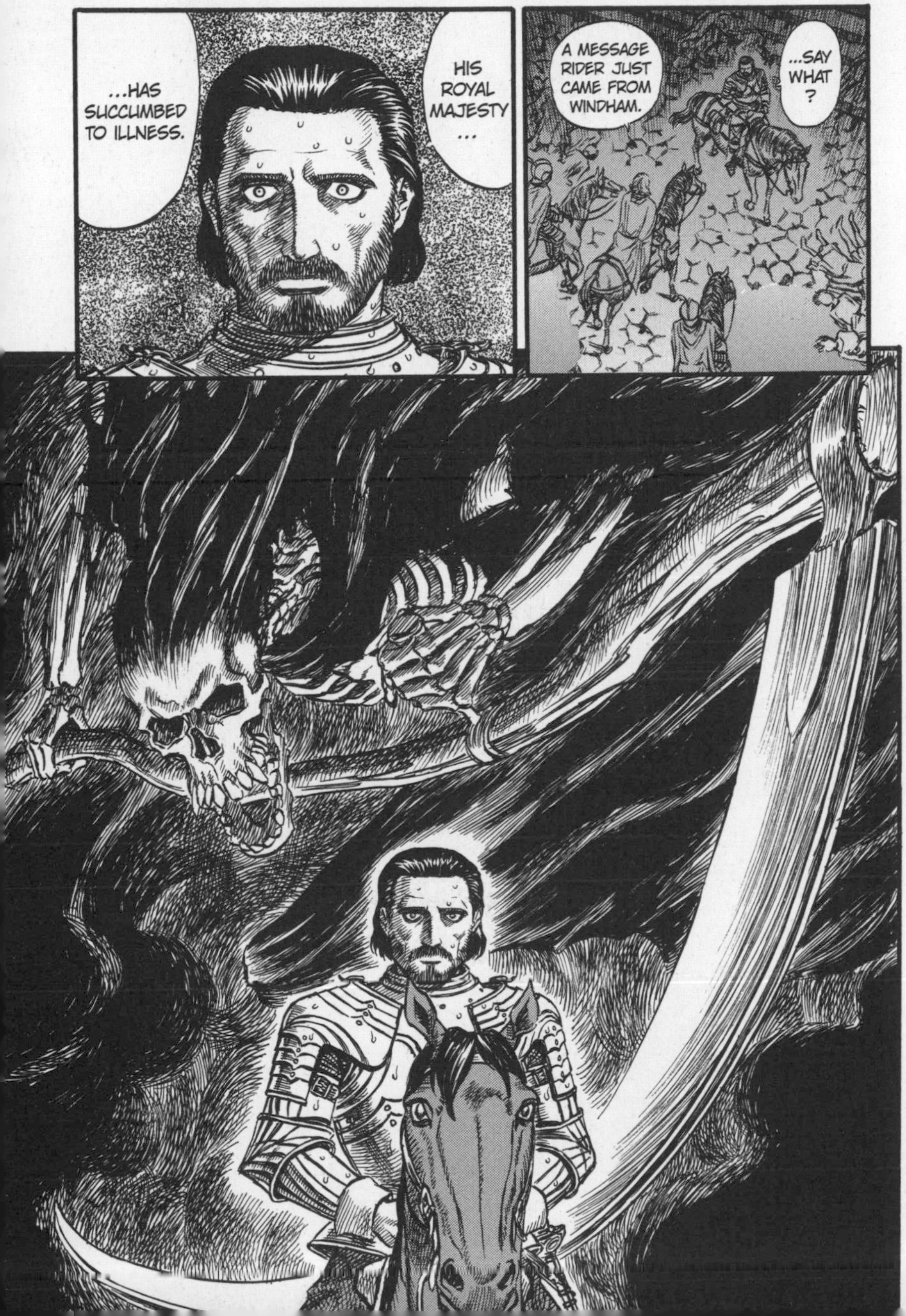
...SAY WHAT ?
A MESSAGE RIDER JUST CAME FROM WINDHAM.
HIS ROYAL MAJESTY ...
...HAS SUCCUMBED TO ILLNESS.

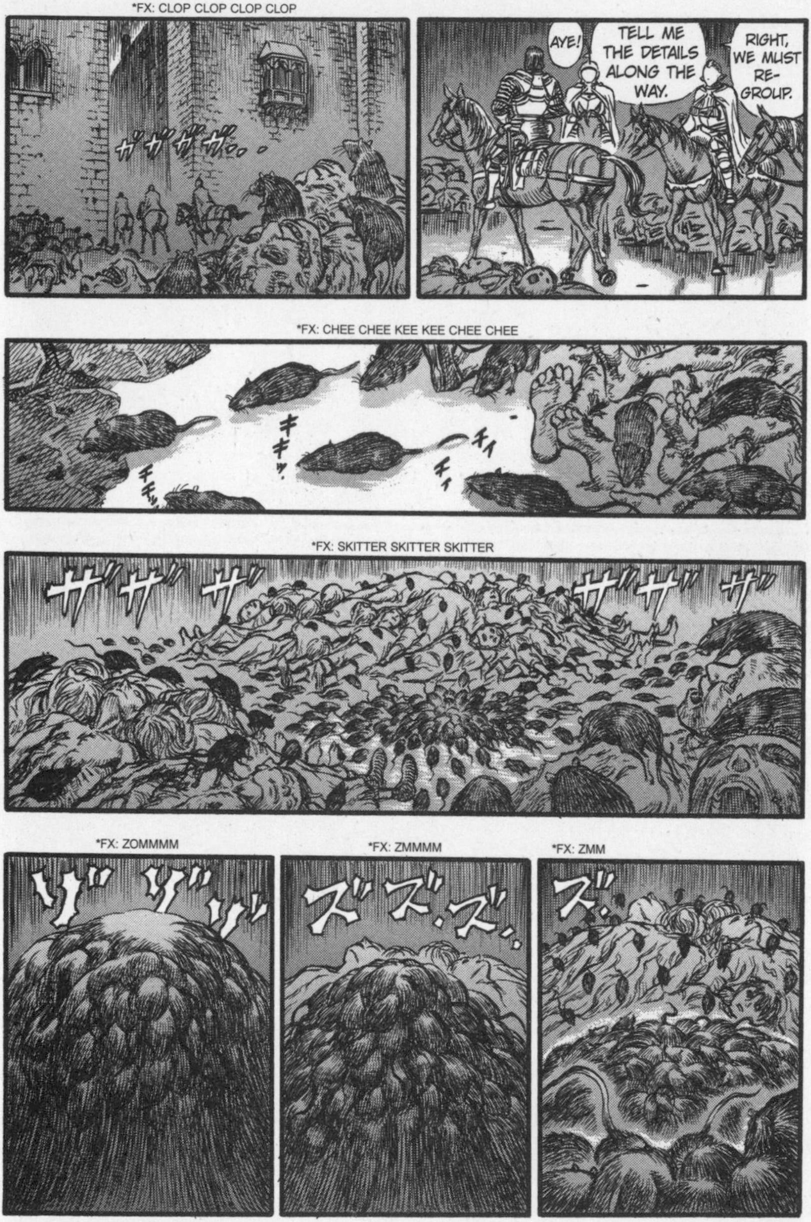
RIGHT, WE MUST RE-GROUP.
TELL ME THE DETAILS ALONG THE WAY.
AYE!
*FX: CLOP CLOP CLOP CLOP
*FX: CHEE CHEE KEE KEE CHEE CHEE
*FX: SKITTER SKITTER SKITTER
*FX: ZMM
*FX: ZMMMM
*FX: ZOMMMM

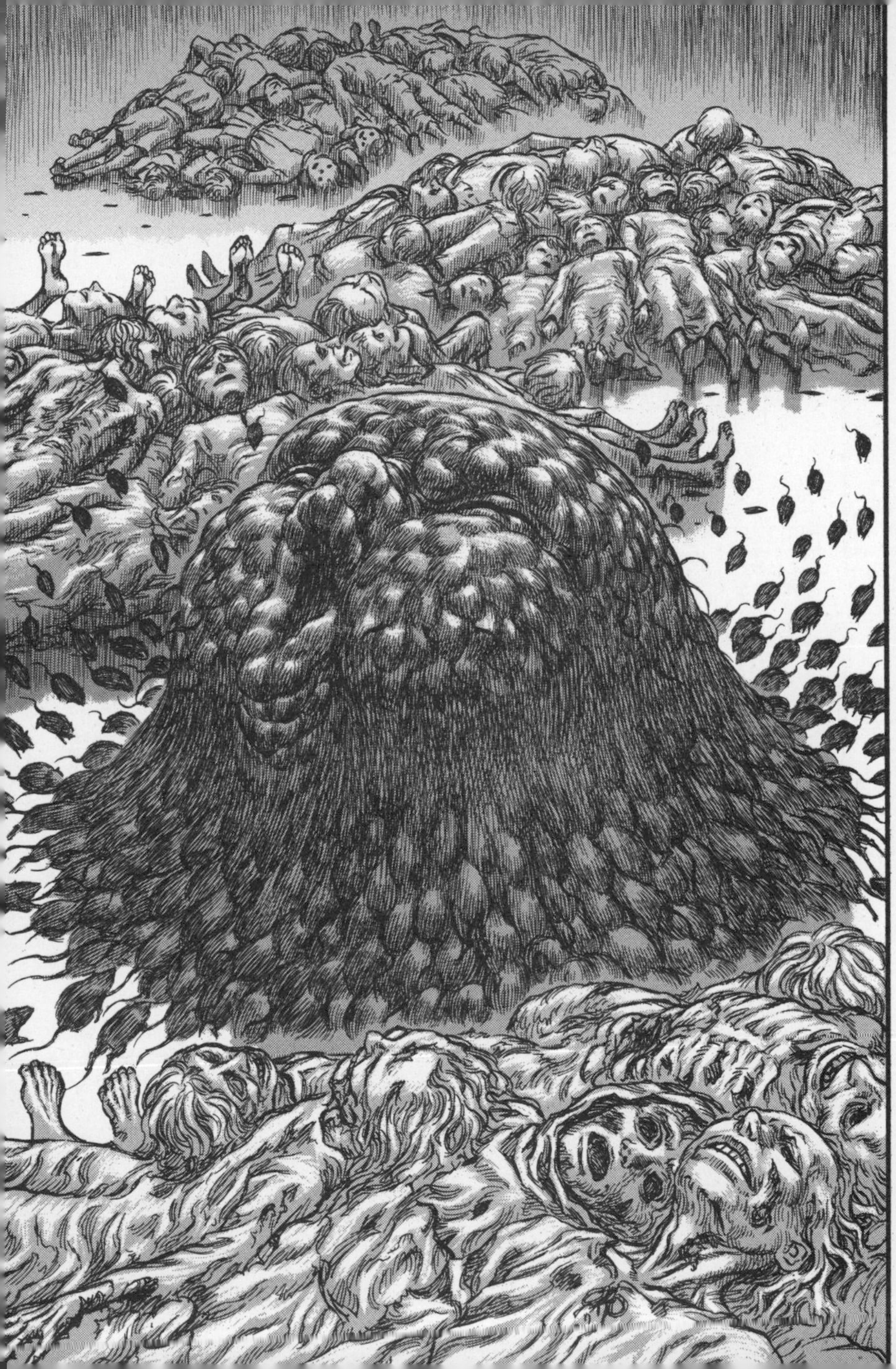

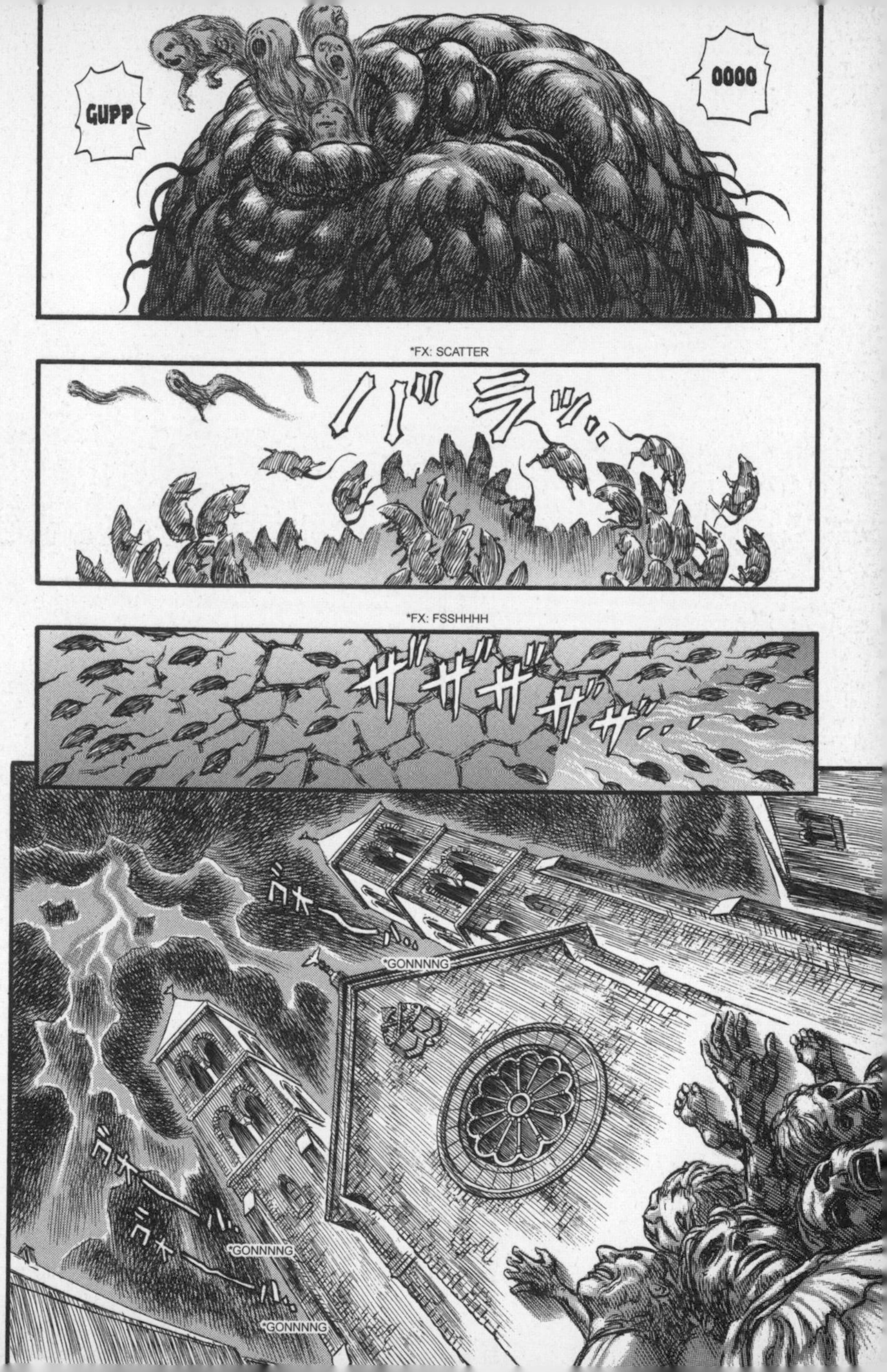
OOOO
GUPP
*FX: SCATTER
*FX: FSSHHHH
*GONNNNG
*GONNNNG
*GONNNNG

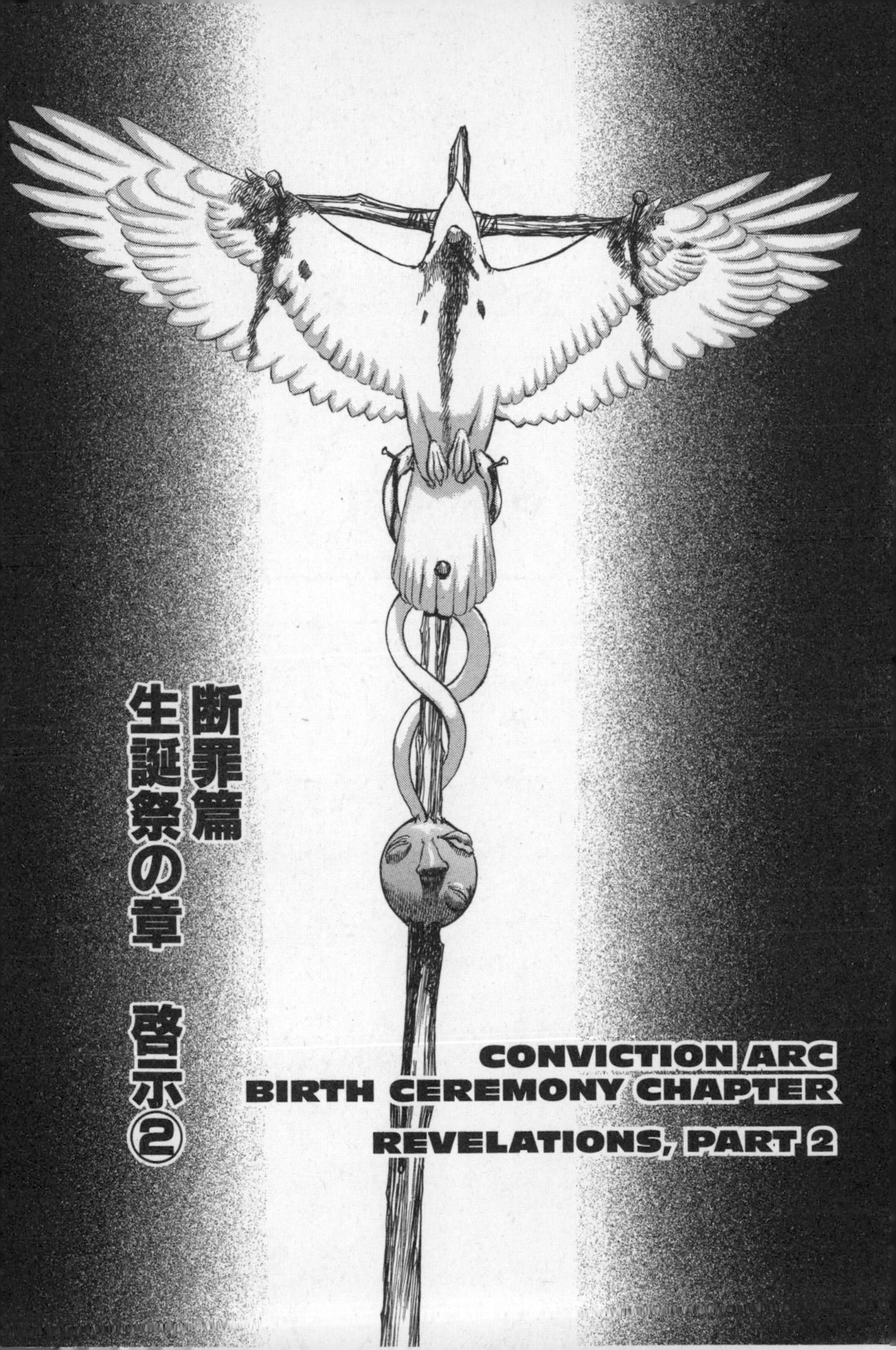
断罪篇
生誕祭の章　啓示②
CONVICTION ARC
BIRTH CEREMONY CHAPTER
REVELATIONS, PART 2

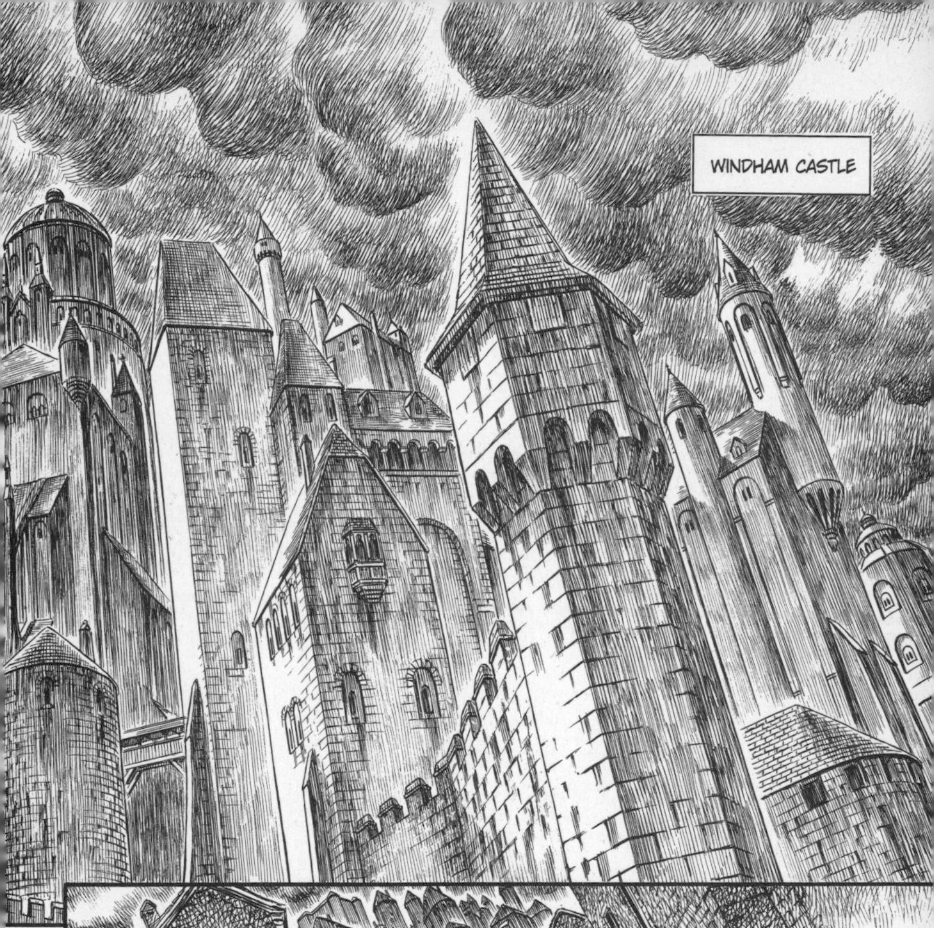
WINDHAM CASTLE
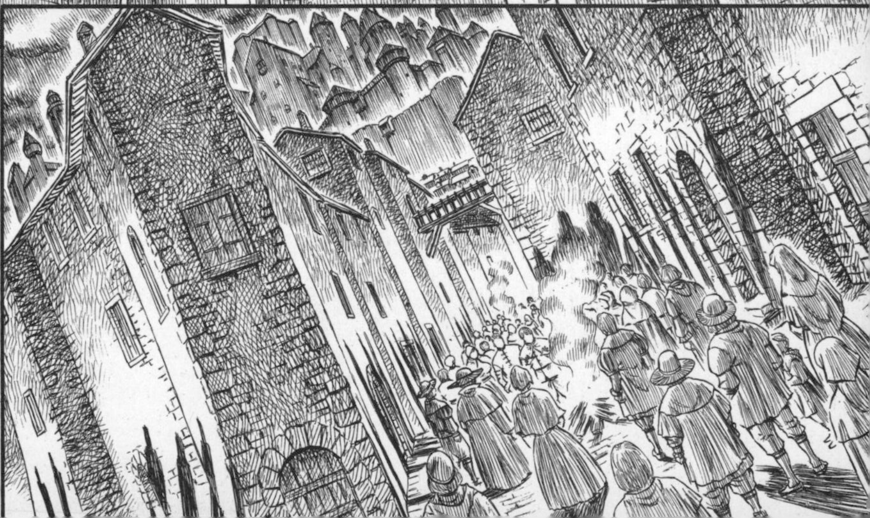

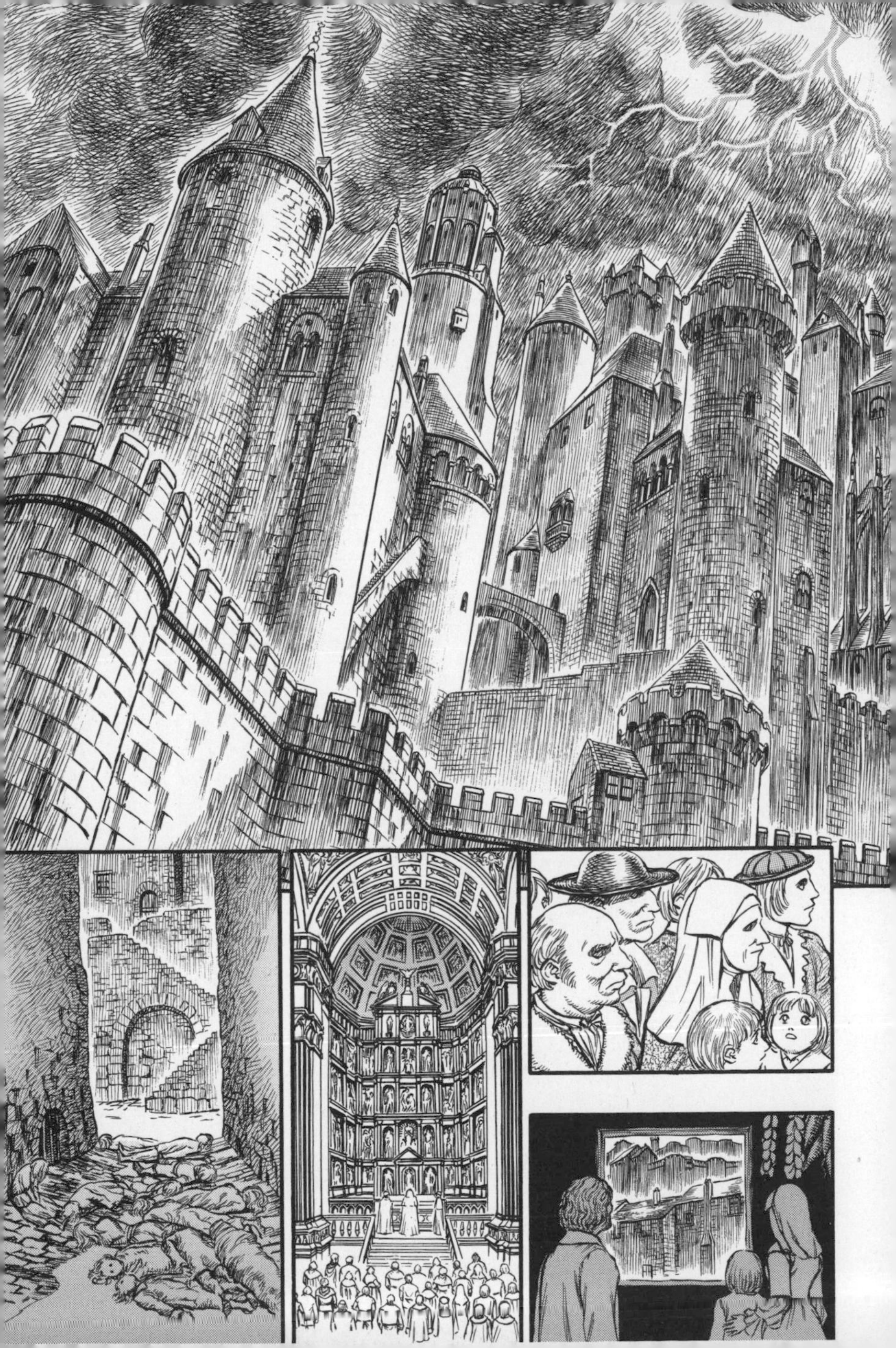

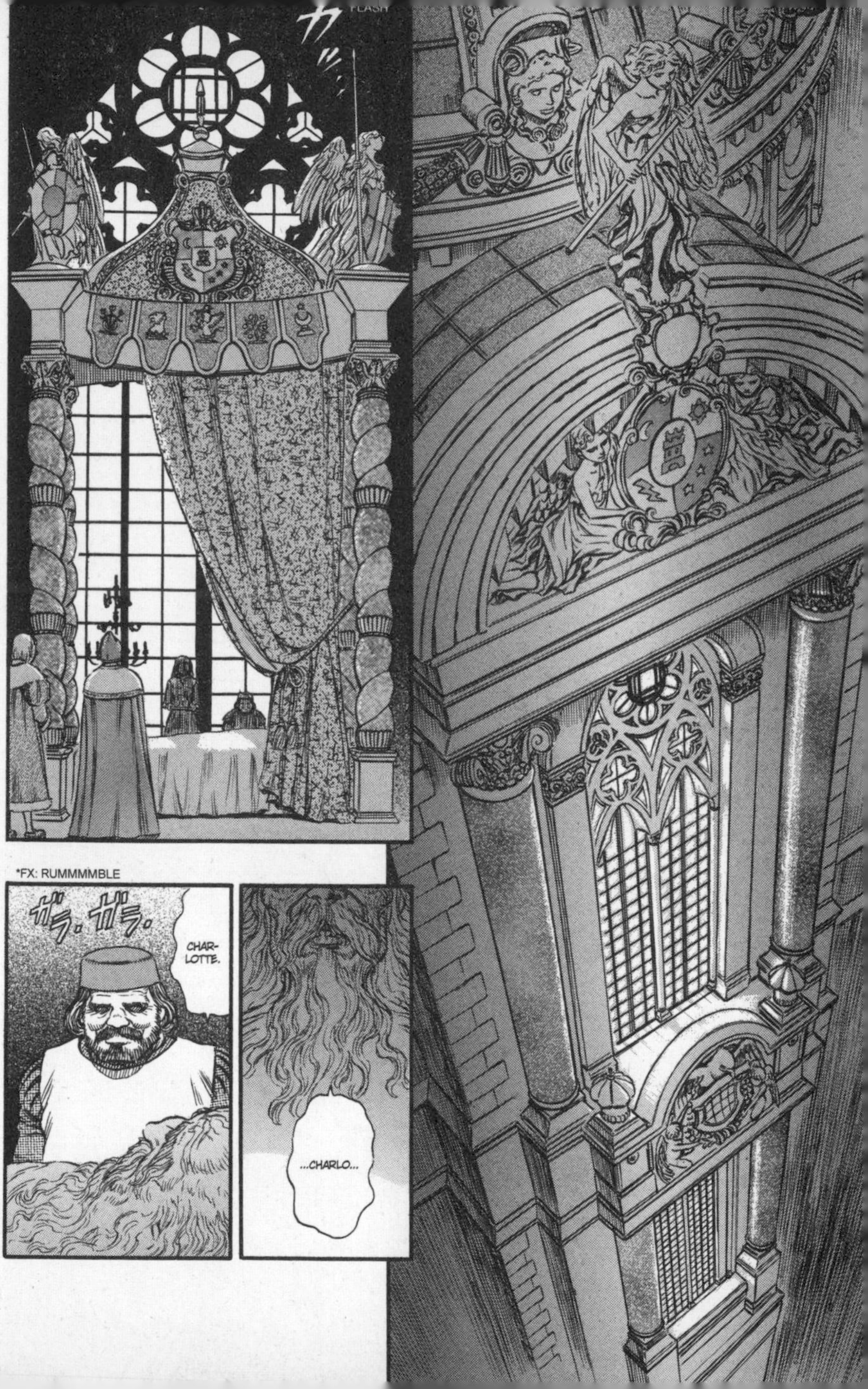
FLASH
カッ
FLASH
*FX: RUMMMMBLE
...CHARLO...
ガラ。ガラ。
CHAR-
LOTTE.

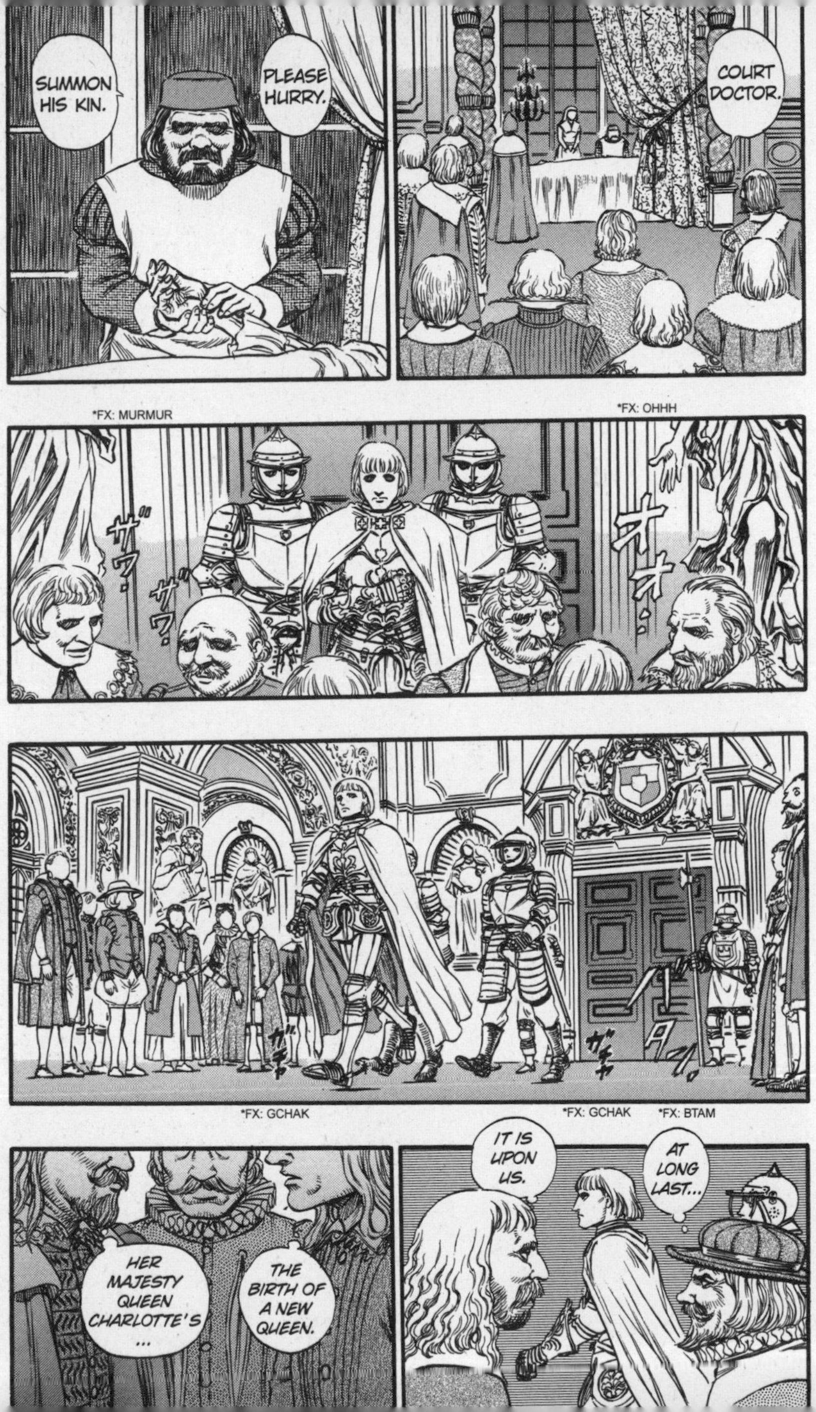
COURT DOCTOR.
PLEASE HURRY.
SUMMON HIS KIN.
*FX: OHHH
*FX: MURMUR
*FX: BTAM
*FX: GCHAK
*FX: GCHAK
AT LONG LAST...
IT IS UPON US.
THE BIRTH OF A NEW QUEEN.
HER MAJESTY QUEEN CHARLOTTE'S ...

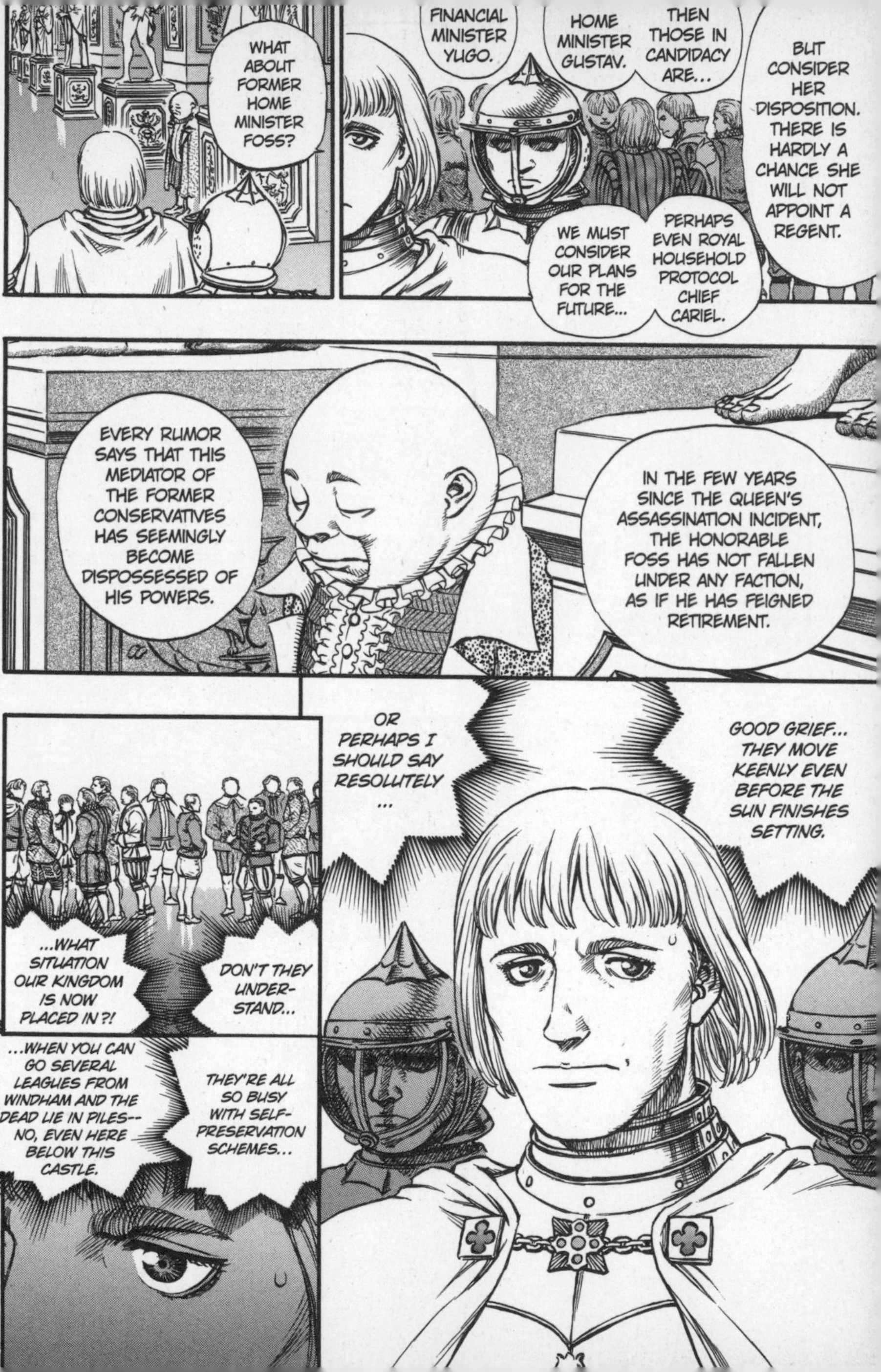
BUT CONSIDER HER DISPOSITION. THERE IS HARDLY A CHANCE SHE WILL NOT APPOINT A REGENT.
THEN THOSE IN CANDIDACY ARE...
HOME MINISTER GUSTAV.
FINANCIAL MINISTER YUGO.
PERHAPS EVEN ROYAL HOUSEHOLD PROTOCOL CHIEF CARIEL.
WE MUST CONSIDER OUR PLANS FOR THE FUTURE...
WHAT ABOUT FORMER HOME MINISTER FOSS?
EVERY RUMOR SAYS THAT THIS MEDIATOR OF THE FORMER CONSERVATIVES HAS SEEMINGLY BECOME DISPOSSESSED OF HIS POWERS.
IN THE FEW YEARS SINCE THE QUEEN'S ASSASSINATION INCIDENT, THE HONORABLE FOSS HAS NOT FALLEN UNDER ANY FACTION, AS IF HE HAS FEIGNED RETIREMENT.
GOOD GRIEF... THEY MOVE KEENLY EVEN BEFORE THE SUN FINISHES SETTING.
OR PERHAPS I SHOULD SAY RESOLUTELY...
DON'T THEY UNDER-STAND...
...WHAT SITUATION OUR KINGDOM IS NOW PLACED IN?!
THEY'RE ALL SO BUSY WITH SELF-PRESERVATION SCHEMES...
...WHEN YOU CAN GO SEVERAL LEAGUES FROM WINDHAM AND THE DEAD LIE IN PILES-- NO, EVEN HERE BELOW THIS CASTLE.

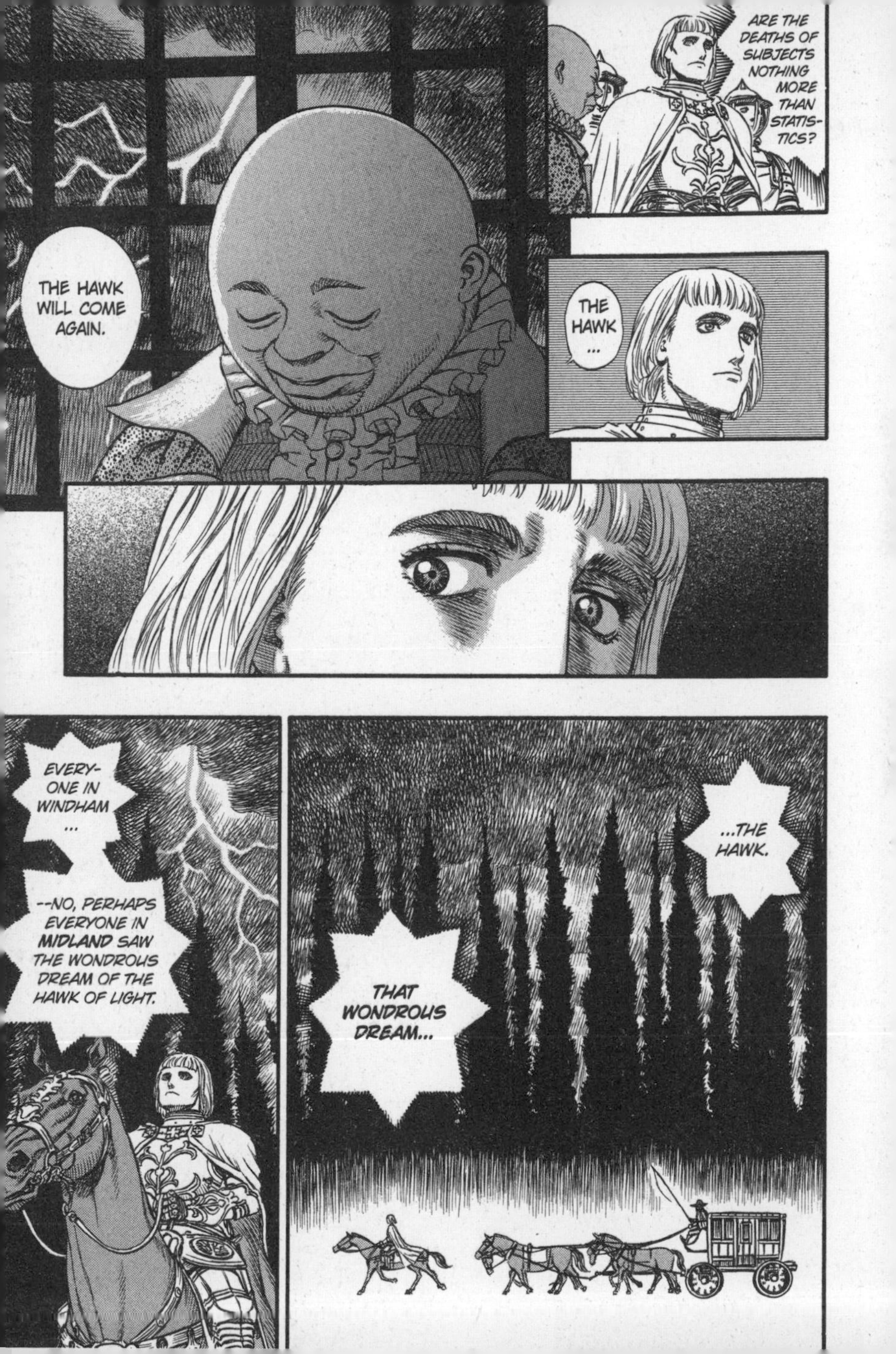

ARE THE DEATHS OF SUBJECTS NOTHING MORE THAN STATISTICS?
THE HAWK ...
THE HAWK WILL COME AGAIN.
...THE HAWK.
THAT WONDROUS DREAM...
EVERYONE IN WINDHAM ...
--NO, PERHAPS EVERYONE IN MIDLAND SAW THE WONDROUS DREAM OF THE HAWK OF LIGHT.

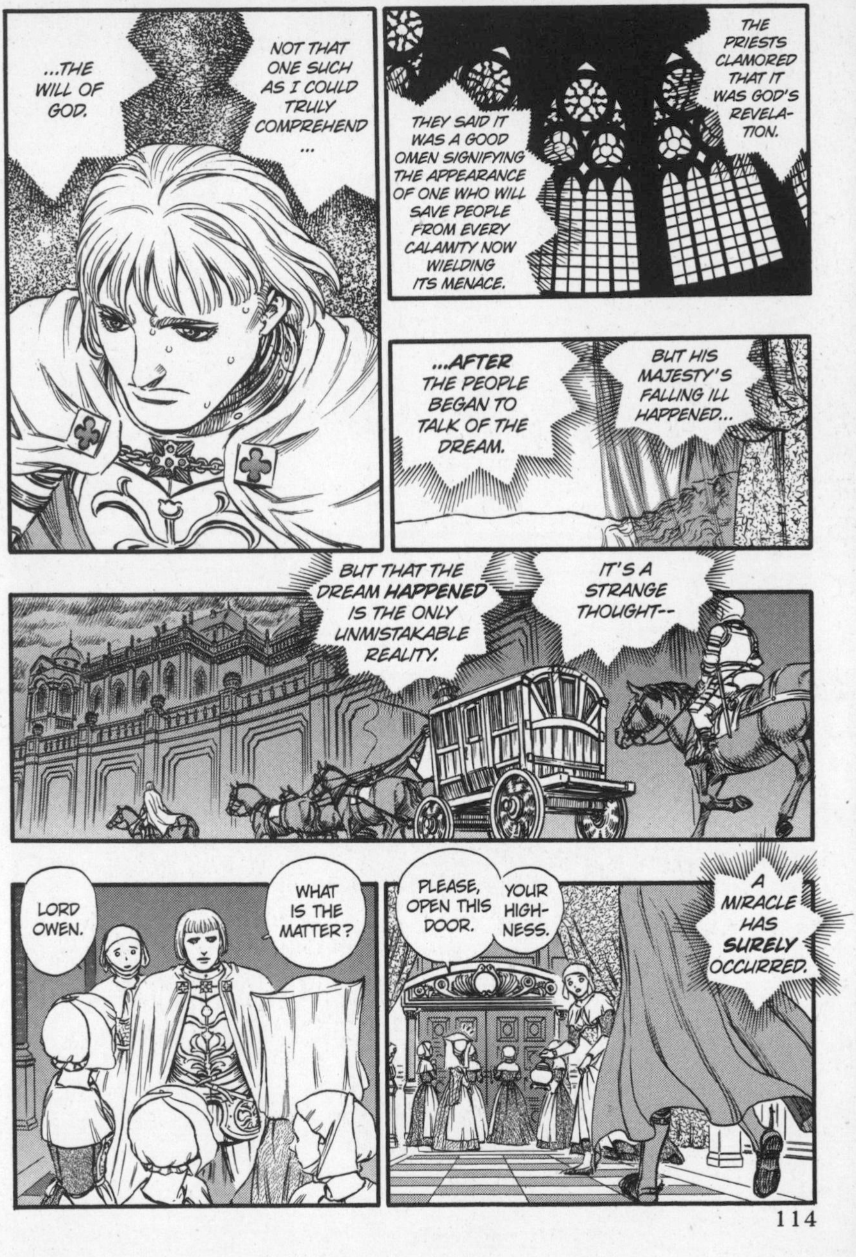
THE PRIESTS CLAMORED THAT IT WAS GOD'S REVELATION.
THEY SAID IT WAS A GOOD OMEN SIGNIFYING THE APPEARANCE OF ONE WHO WILL SAVE PEOPLE FROM EVERY CALAMITY NOW WIELDING ITS MENACE.
BUT HIS MAJESTY'S FALLING ILL HAPPENED...
...**AFTER** THE PEOPLE BEGAN TO TALK OF THE DREAM.
NOT THAT ONE SUCH AS I COULD TRULY COMPREHEND ...
...THE WILL OF GOD.
IT'S A STRANGE THOUGHT--
BUT THAT THE DREAM **HAPPENED** IS THE ONLY UNMISTAKABLE REALITY.
A MIRACLE HAS **SURELY** OCCURRED.
YOUR HIGHNESS.
PLEASE, OPEN THIS DOOR.
WHAT IS THE MATTER?
LORD OWEN.

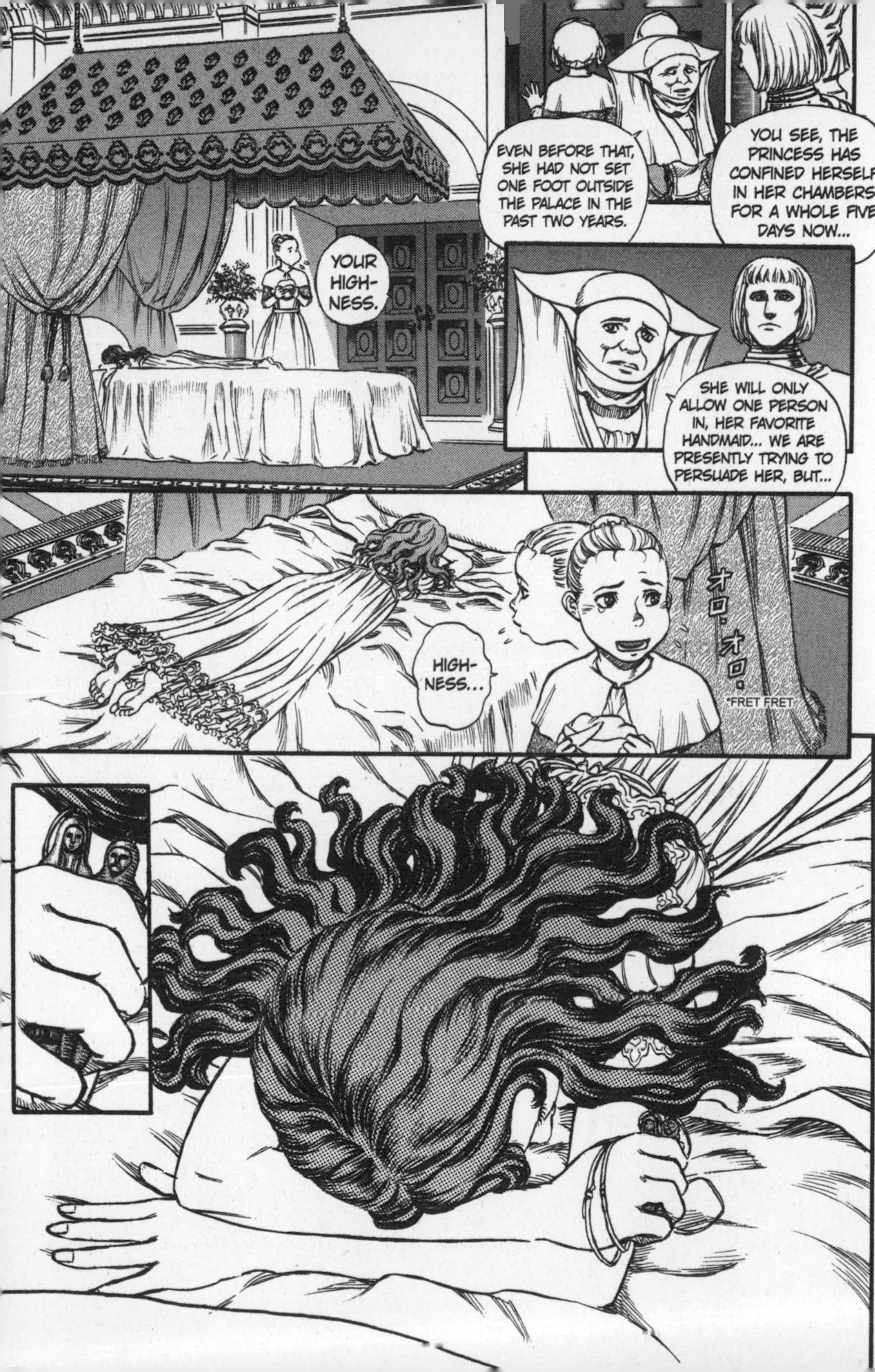
YOU SEE, THE PRINCESS HAS CONFINED HERSELF IN HER CHAMBERS FOR A WHOLE FIVE DAYS NOW...
EVEN BEFORE THAT, SHE HAD NOT SET ONE FOOT OUTSIDE THE PALACE IN THE PAST TWO YEARS.
SHE WILL ONLY ALLOW ONE PERSON IN, HER FAVORITE HANDMAID... WE ARE PRESENTLY TRYING TO PERSUADE HER, BUT...
YOUR HIGH-NESS.
オロ。オロ。
*FRET FRET
HIGH-NESS...

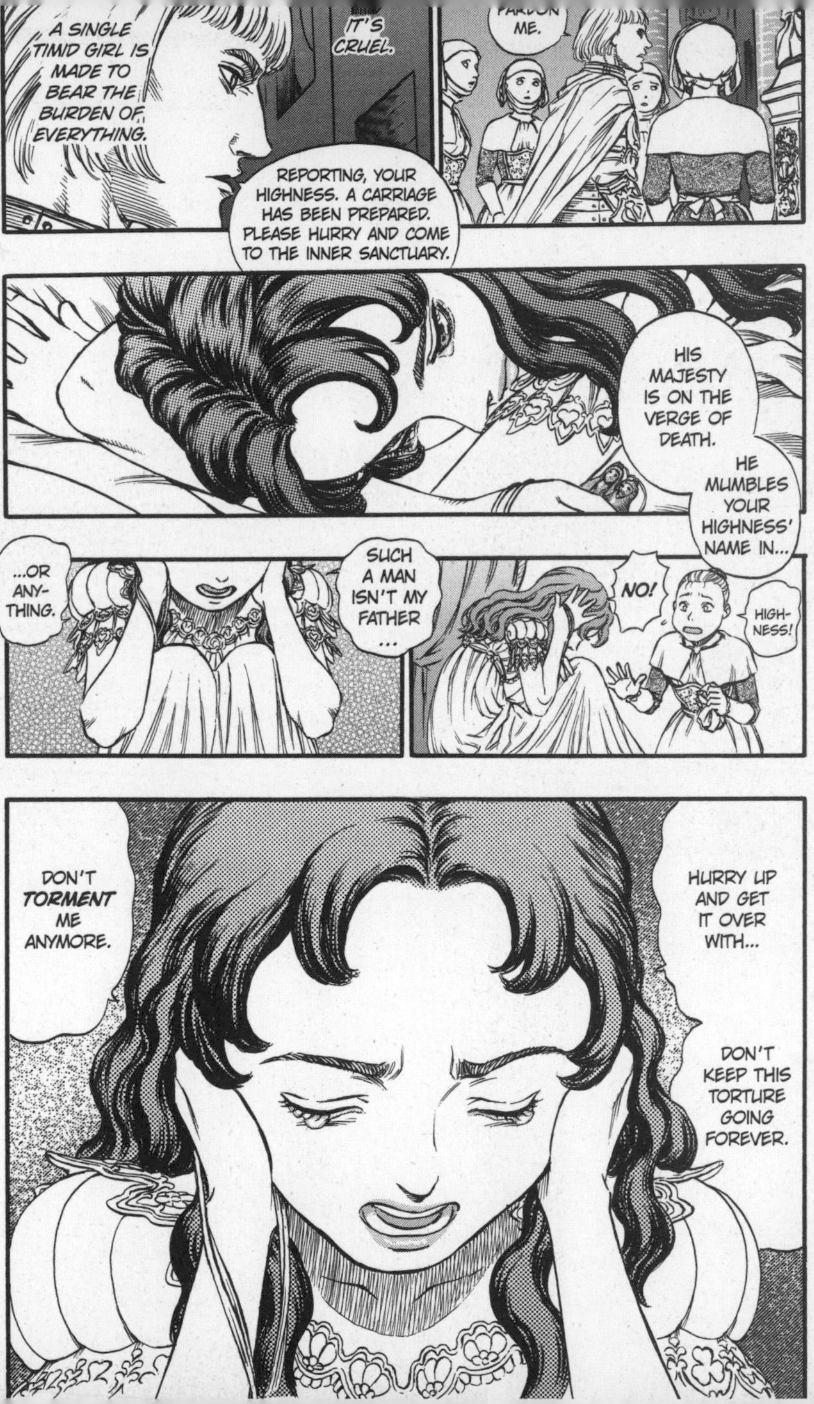
PARDON ME.
IT'S CRUEL.
A SINGLE TIMID GIRL IS MADE TO BEAR THE BURDEN OF EVERYTHING.
REPORTING, YOUR HIGHNESS. A CARRIAGE HAS BEEN PREPARED. PLEASE HURRY AND COME TO THE INNER SANCTUARY.
HIS MAJESTY IS ON THE VERGE OF DEATH.
HE MUMBLES YOUR HIGHNESS' NAME IN...
NO!
HIGH-NESS!
SUCH A MAN ISN'T MY FATHER ...
...OR ANY-THING.
HURRY UP AND GET IT OVER WITH...
DON'T *TORMENT* ME ANYMORE.
DON'T KEEP THIS TORTURE GOING FOREVER.

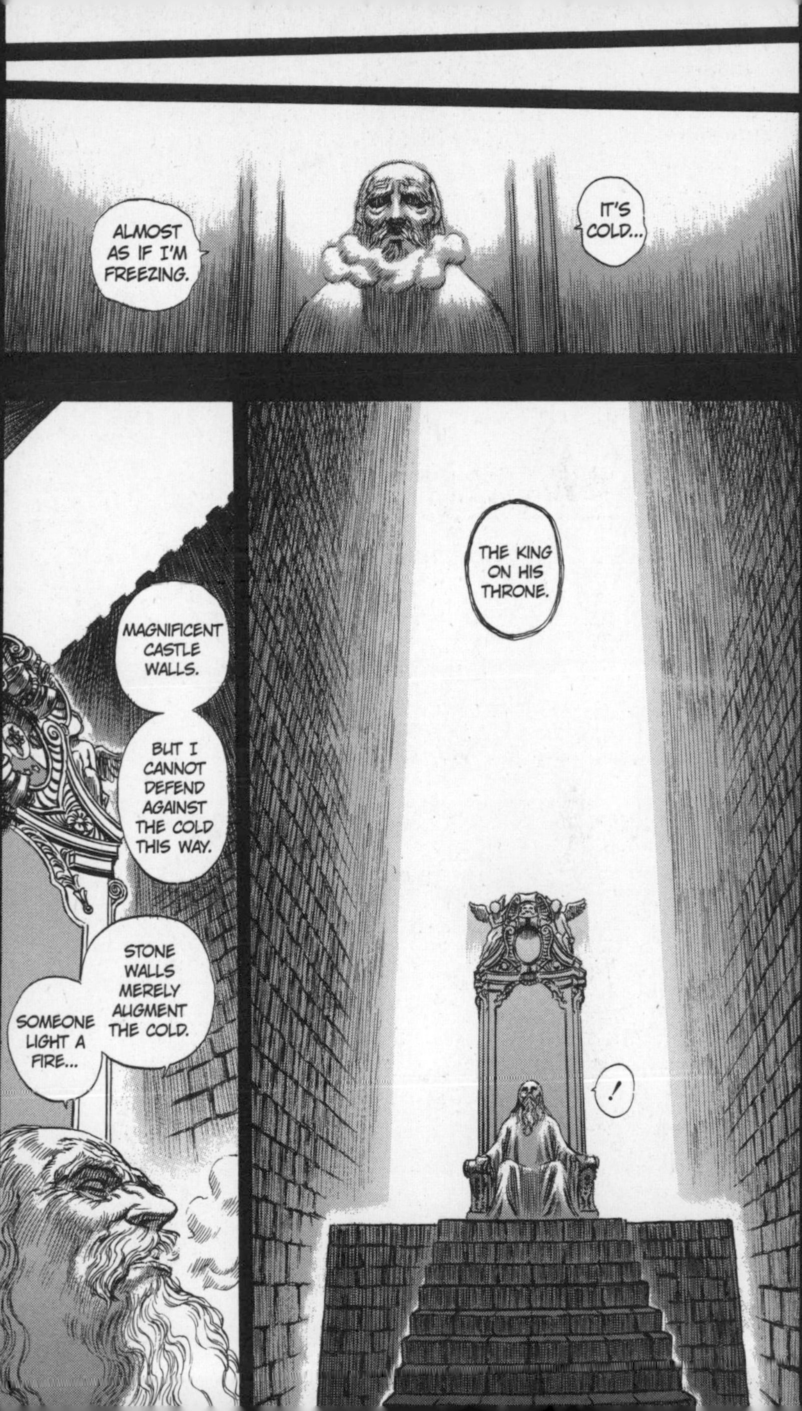
IT'S COLD...
ALMOST AS IF I'M FREEZING.
THE KING ON HIS THRONE.
!
MAGNIFICENT CASTLE WALLS.
BUT I CANNOT DEFEND AGAINST THE COLD THIS WAY.
STONE WALLS MERELY AUGMENT THE COLD.
SOMEONE LIGHT A FIRE...

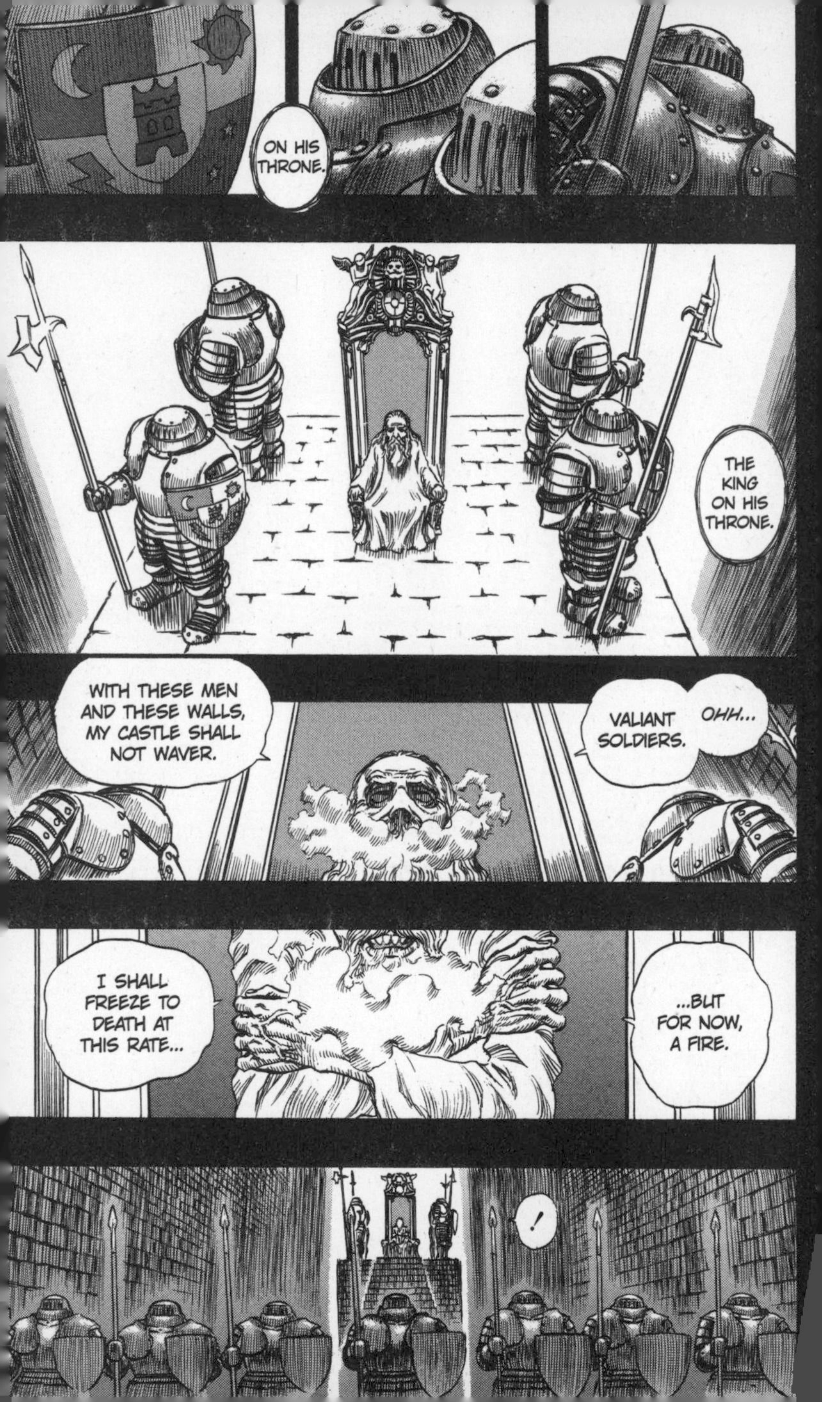
ON HIS THRONE.
THE KING ON HIS THRONE.
OHH...
VALIANT SOLDIERS.
WITH THESE MEN AND THESE WALLS, MY CASTLE SHALL NOT WAVER.
...BUT FOR NOW, A FIRE.
I SHALL FREEZE TO DEATH AT THIS RATE...
!

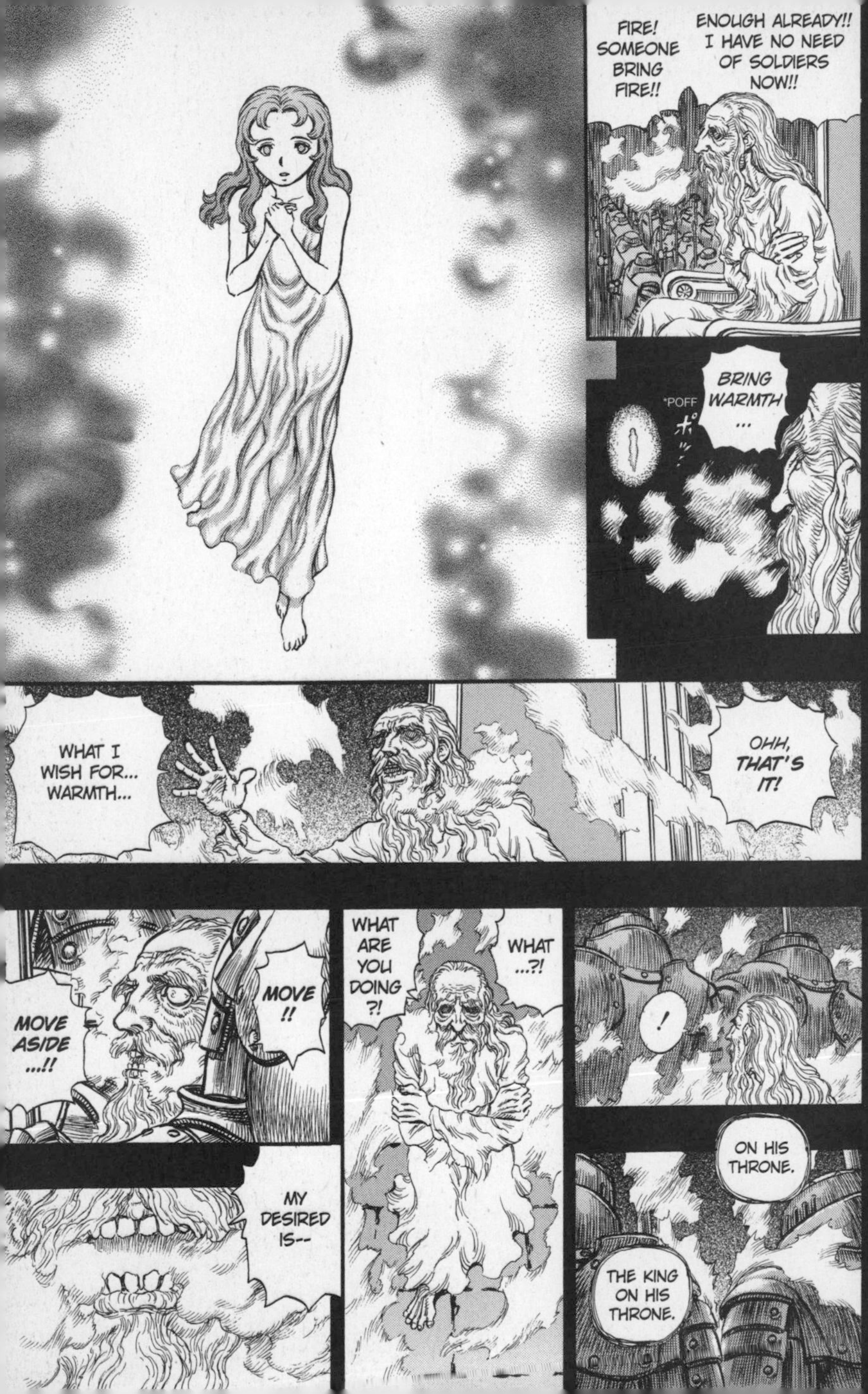

ENOUGH ALREADY!! I HAVE NO NEED OF SOLDIERS NOW!!
FIRE! SOMEONE BRING FIRE!!
BRING WARMTH ...
*POFF
ポッ
OHH, THAT'S IT!
WHAT I WISH FOR... WARMTH...
!
ON HIS THRONE.
THE KING ON HIS THRONE.
WHAT ...?!
WHAT ARE YOU DOING ?!
MOVE !!
MOVE ASIDE ...!!
MY DESIRED IS--

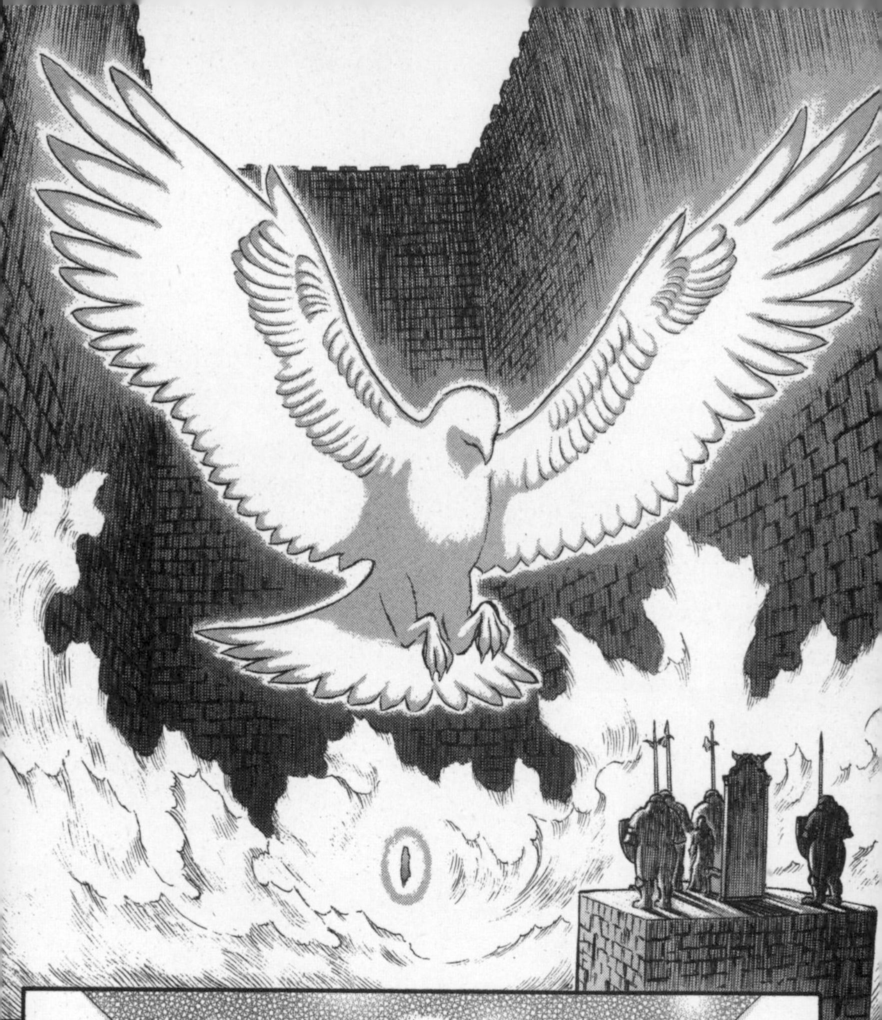
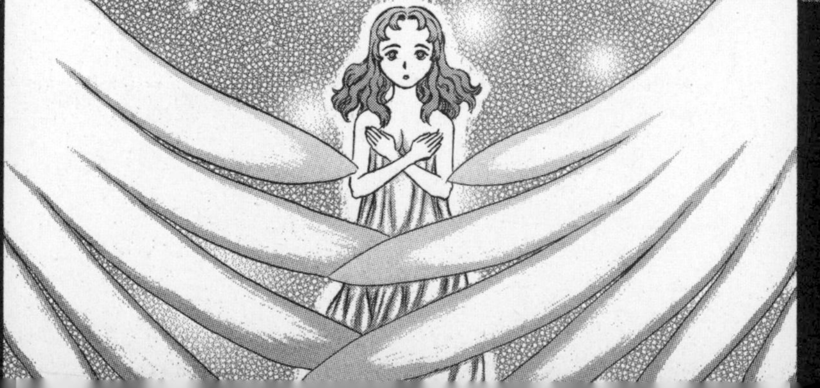

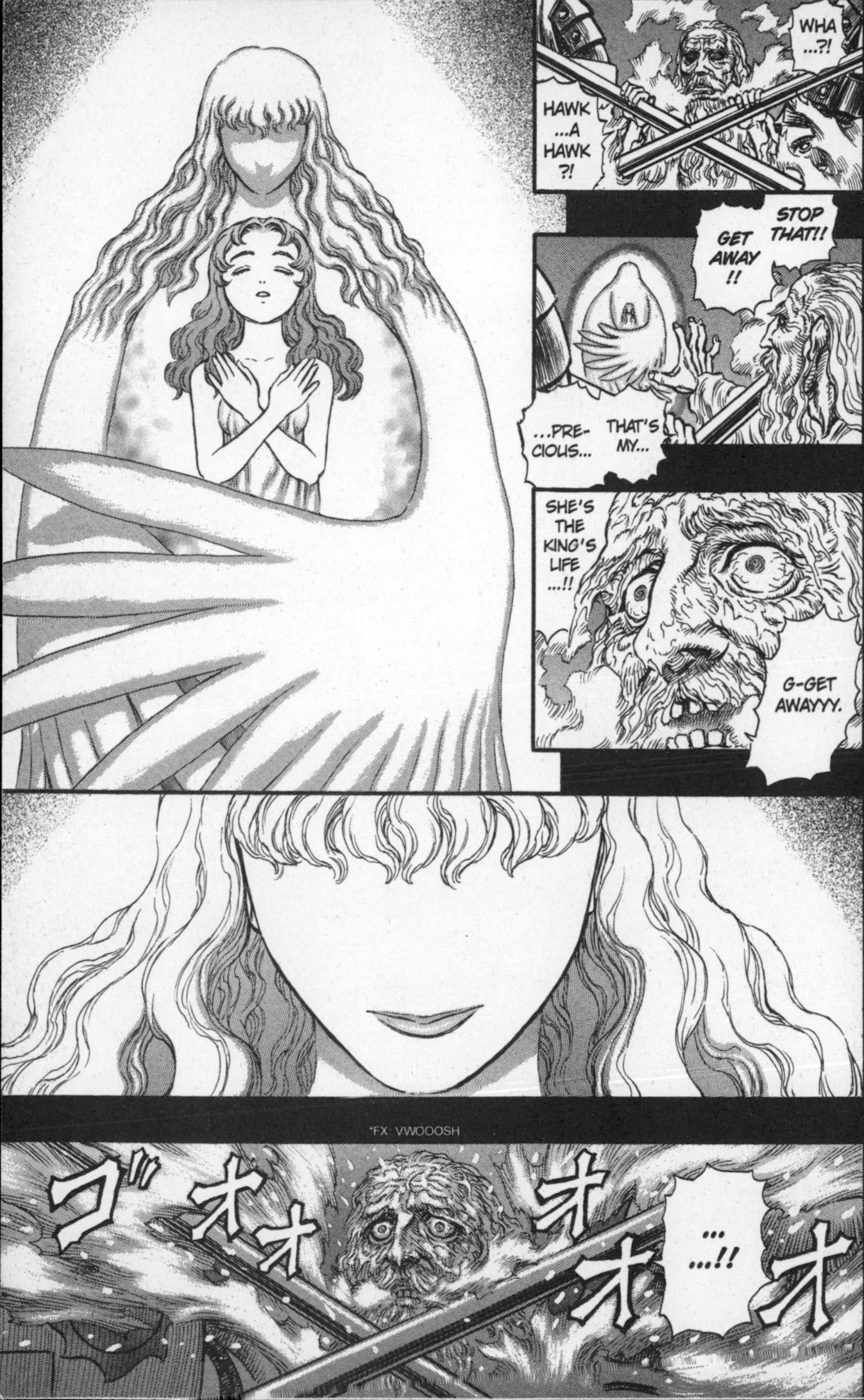
WHA ...?!
HAWK ...A HAWK ?!
STOP THAT!!
GET AWAY !!
THAT'S MY...
...PRE-CIOUS...
SHE'S THE KING'S LIFE ...!!
G-GET AWAYYY.
*FX: VWOOOSH
ゴオオオオオ
... ...!!

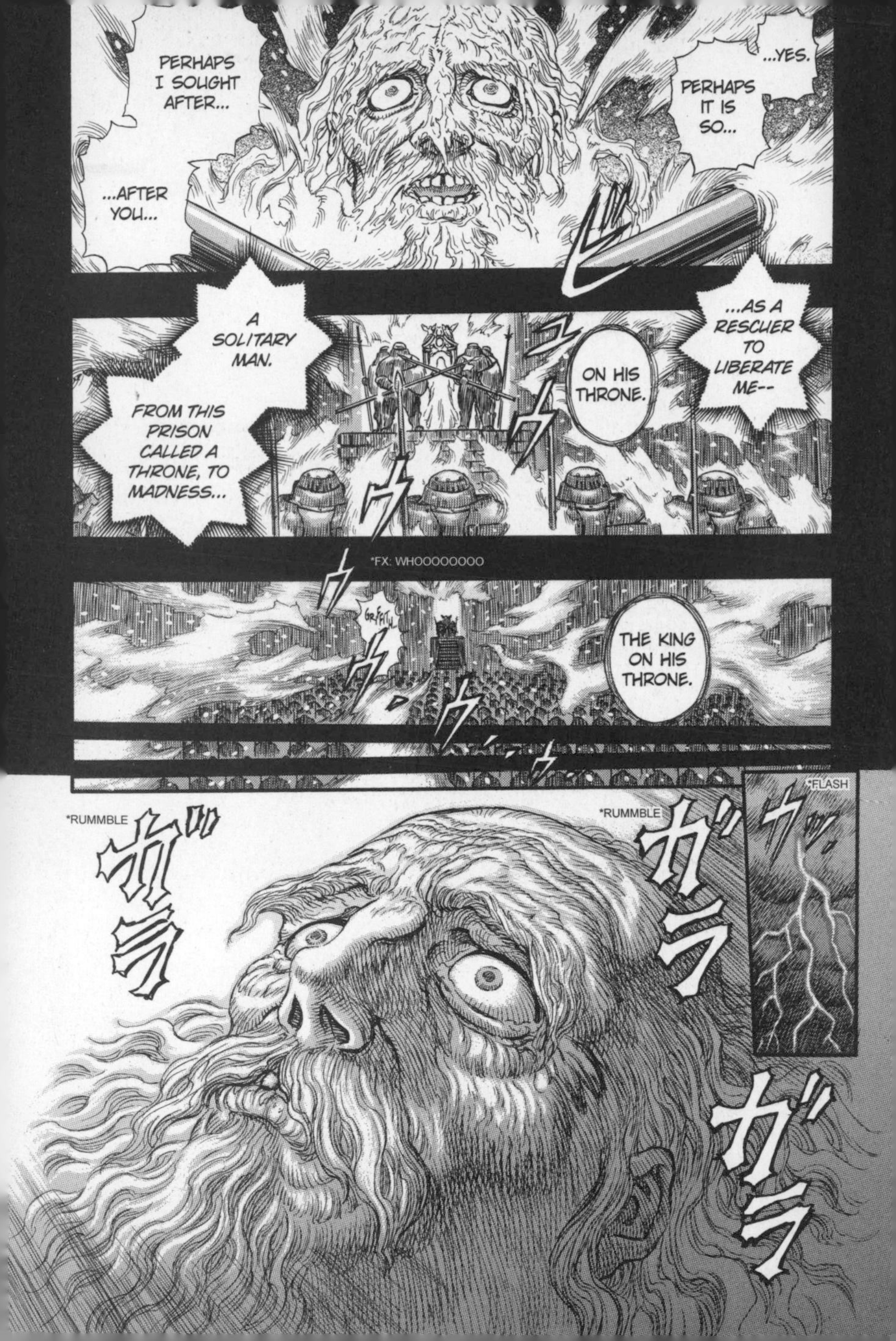
...YES.
PERHAPS IT IS SO...
PERHAPS I SOUGHT AFTER...
...AFTER YOU...
...AS A RESCUER TO LIBERATE ME--
ON HIS THRONE.
A SOLITARY MAN.
FROM THIS PRISON CALLED A THRONE, TO MADNESS...
*FX: WHOOOOOOOO
THE KING ON HIS THRONE.
*FLASH
*RUMMBLE
*RUMMBLE

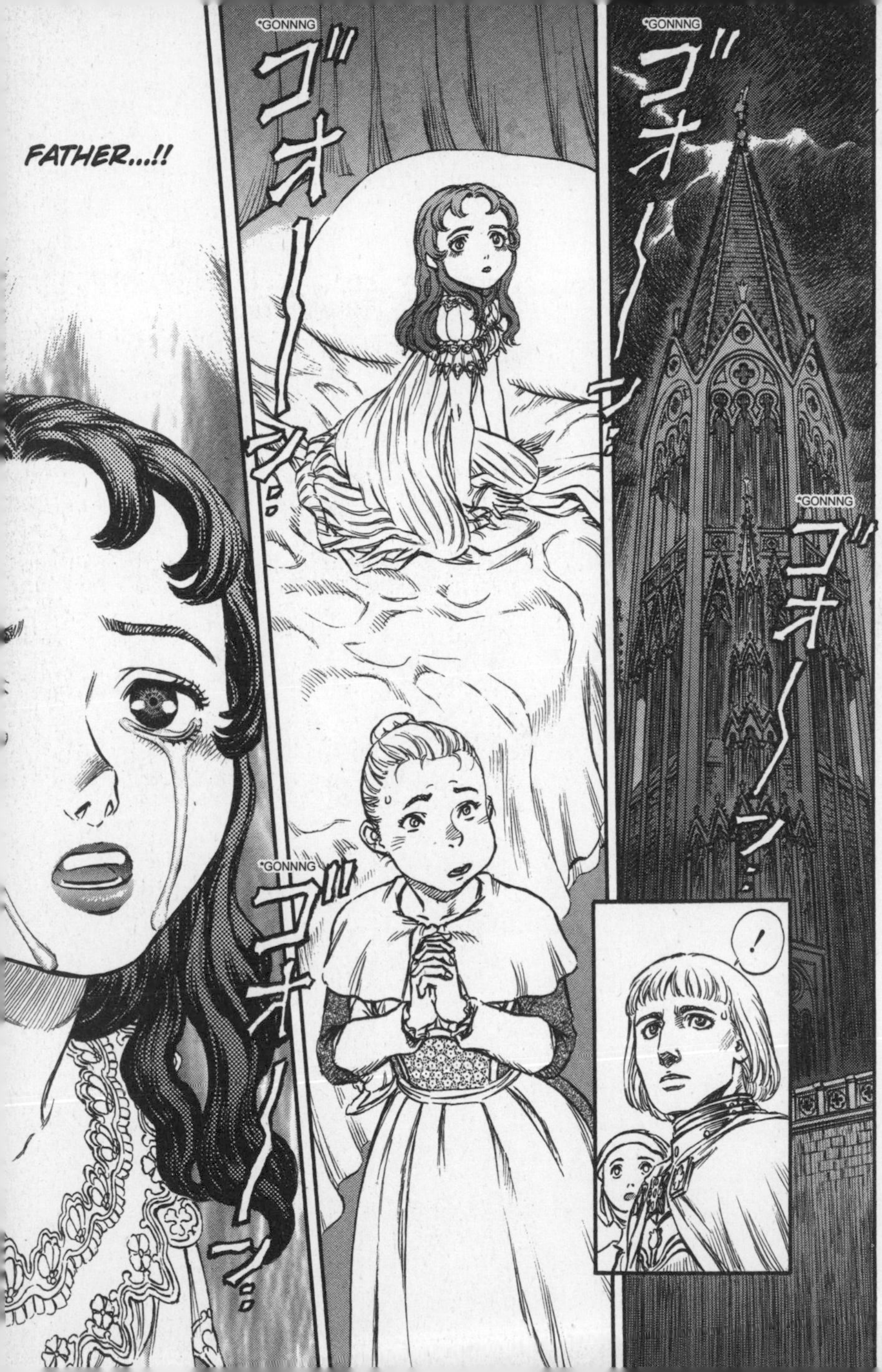
*GONNNG
ゴォーン
*GONNNG
ゴォーン
!
*GONNNG
ゴォーン
*GONNNG
ゴォーン
FATHER...!!

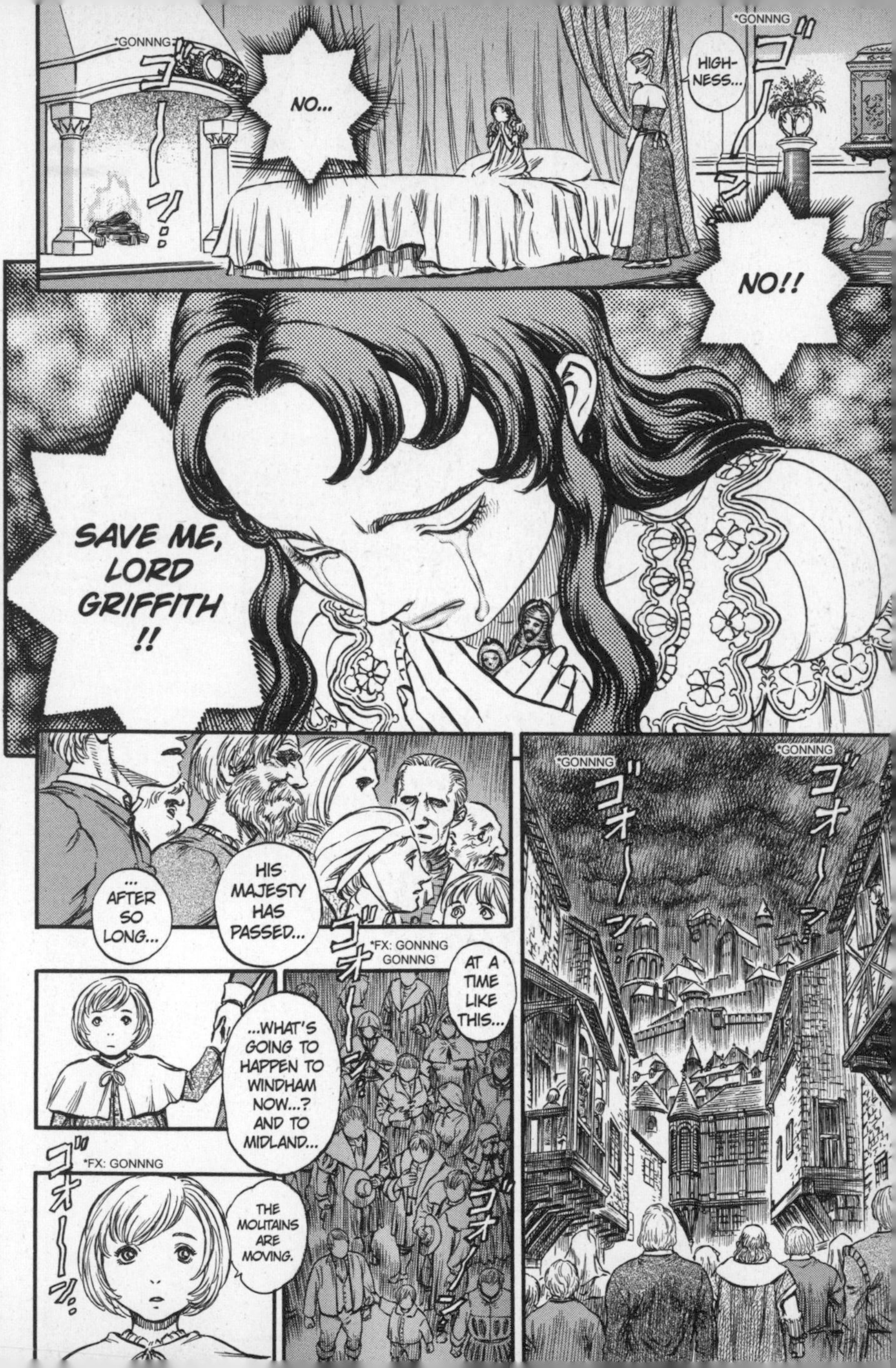
*GONNNG
HIGH-NESS...
NO...
*GONNNG
NO!!
SAVE ME, LORD GRIFFITH!!
*GONNNG
*GONNNG
HIS MAJESTY HAS PASSED...
... AFTER SO LONG...
*FX: GONNNG GONNNG
AT A TIME LIKE THIS...
...WHAT'S GOING TO HAPPEN TO WINDHAM NOW...? AND TO MIDLAND...
*FX: GONNNG
THE MOLTAINS ARE MOVING.

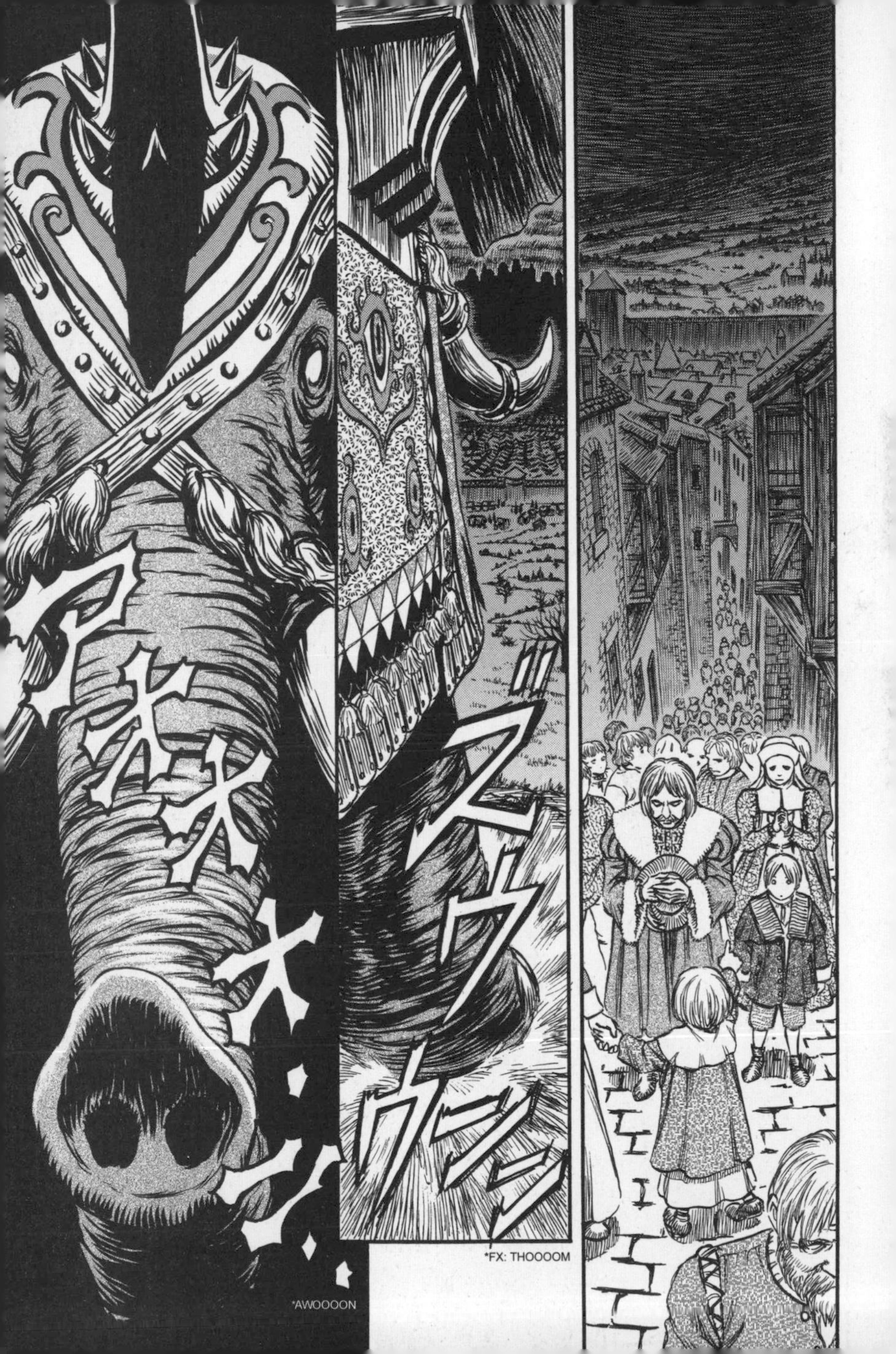
*FX: THOOOM
*AWOOOON

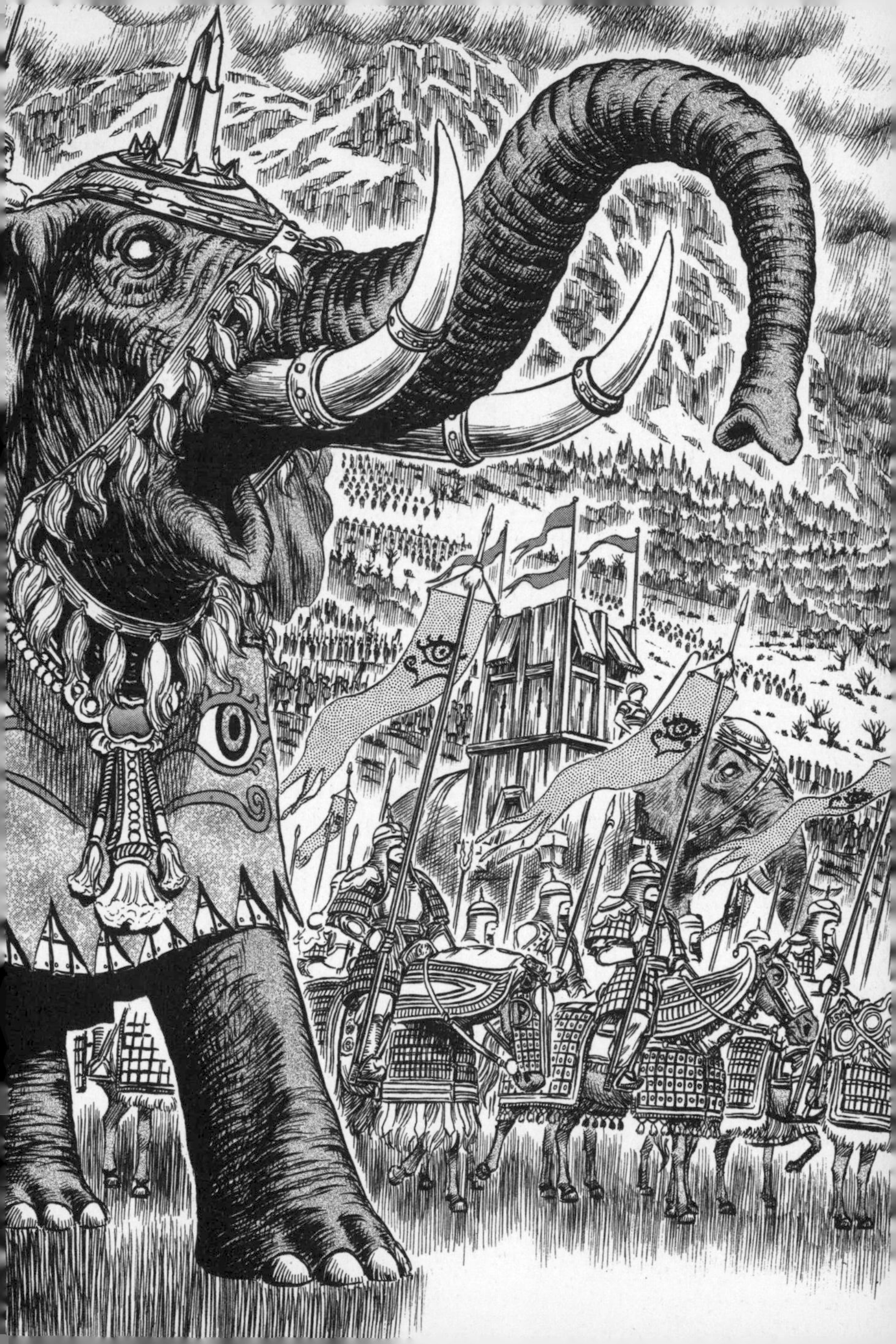

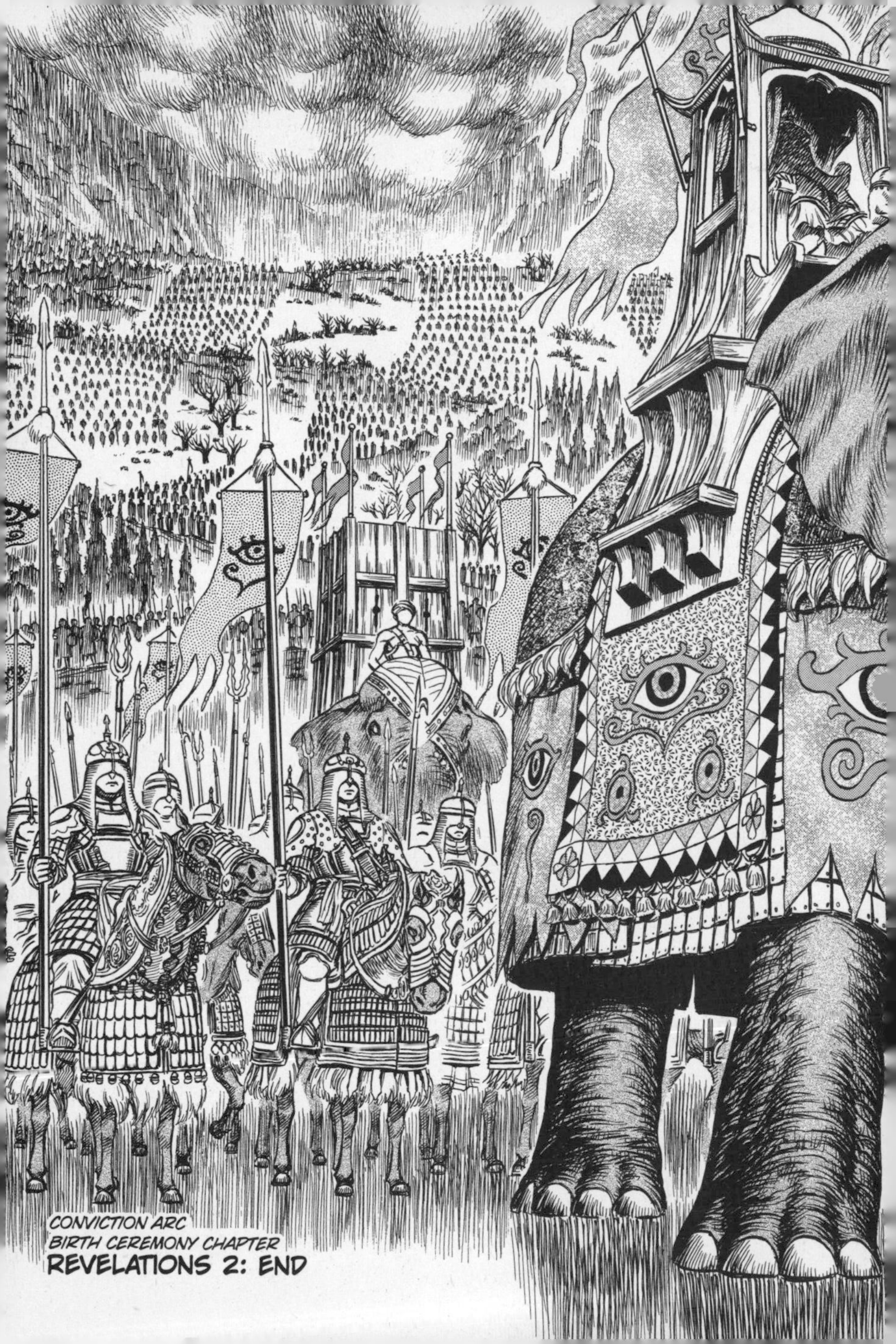
CONVICTION ARC
BIRTH CEREMONY CHAPTER
REVELATIONS 2: END

BERSERK

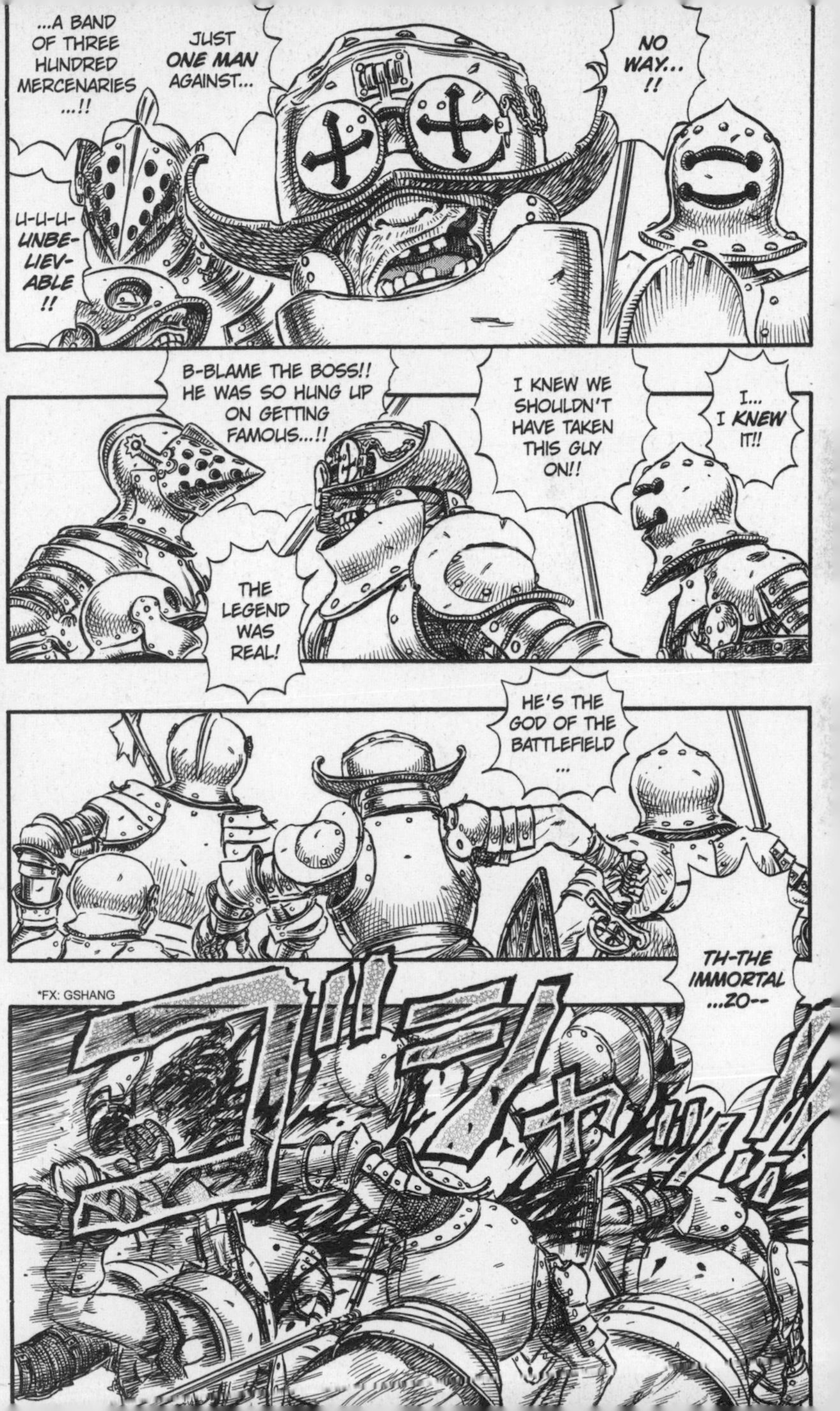
NO WAY... !!
JUST ONE MAN AGAINST...
...A BAND OF THREE HUNDRED MERCENARIES ...!!
U-U-U-UNBE-LIEV-ABLE !!
I... I KNEW IT!!
I KNEW WE SHOULDN'T HAVE TAKEN THIS GUY ON!!
B-BLAME THE BOSS!! HE WAS SO HUNG UP ON GETTING FAMOUS...!!
THE LEGEND WAS REAL!
HE'S THE GOD OF THE BATTLEFIELD ...
TH-THE IMMORTAL ...ZO--
*FX: GSHANG

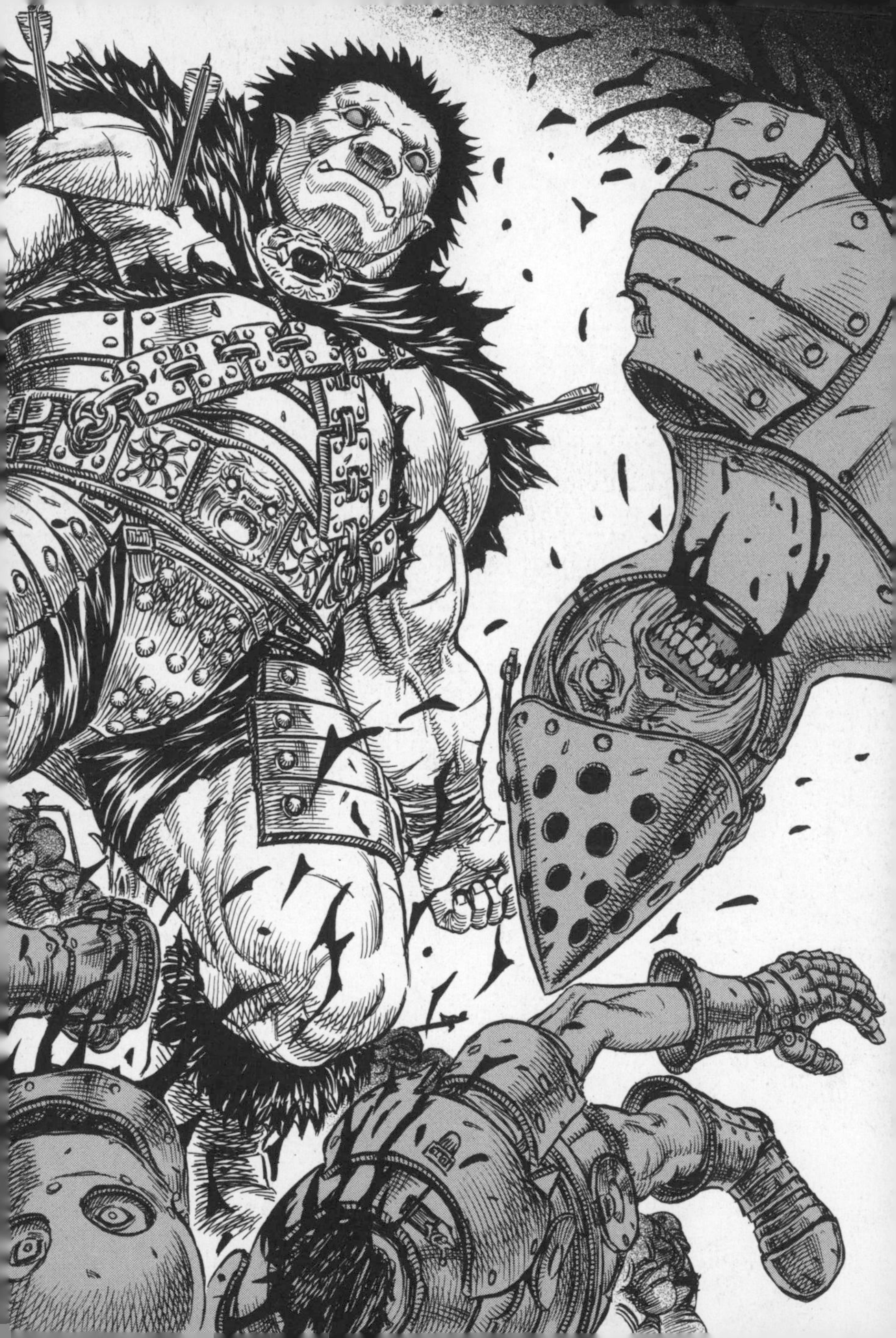

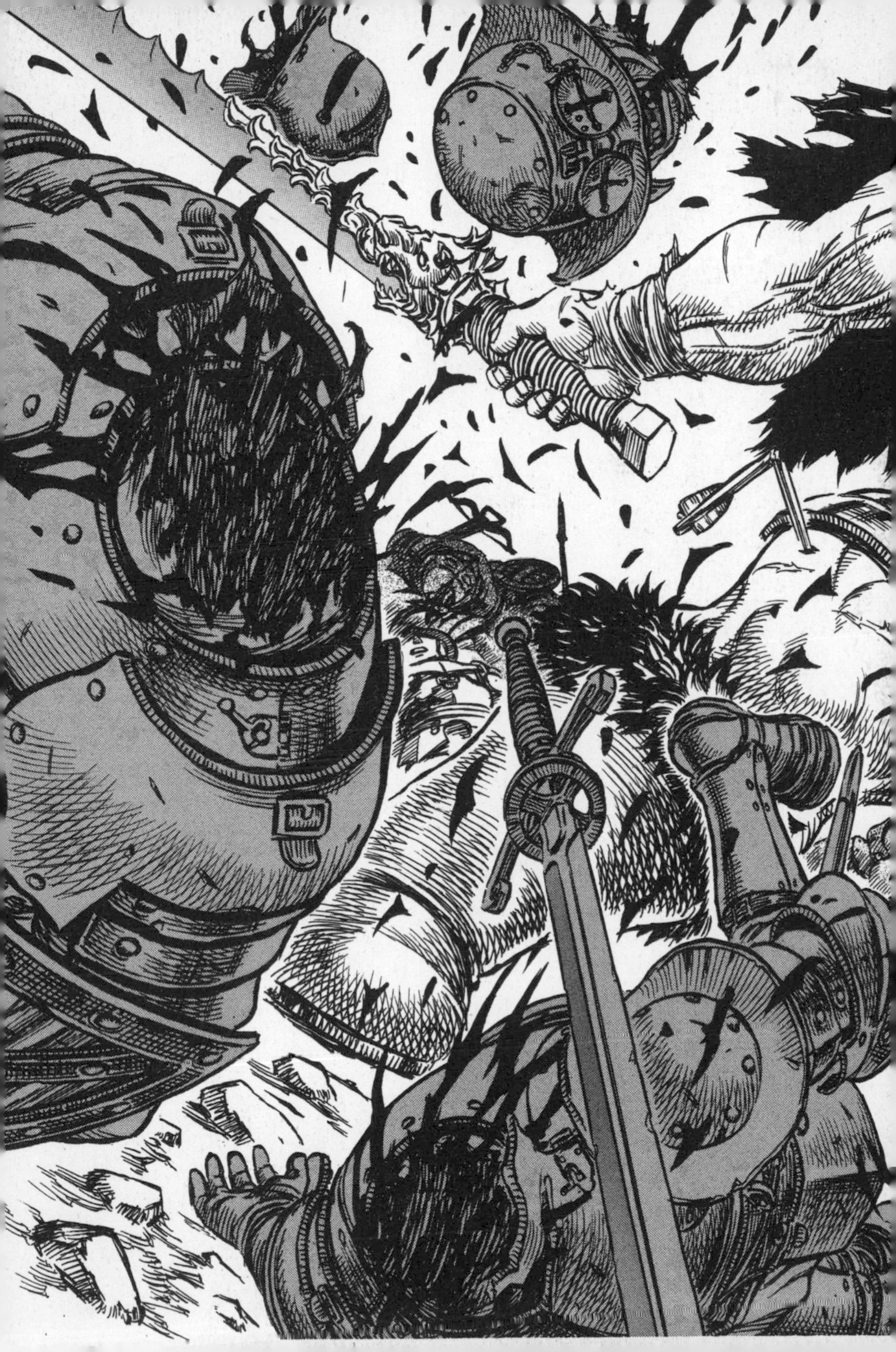

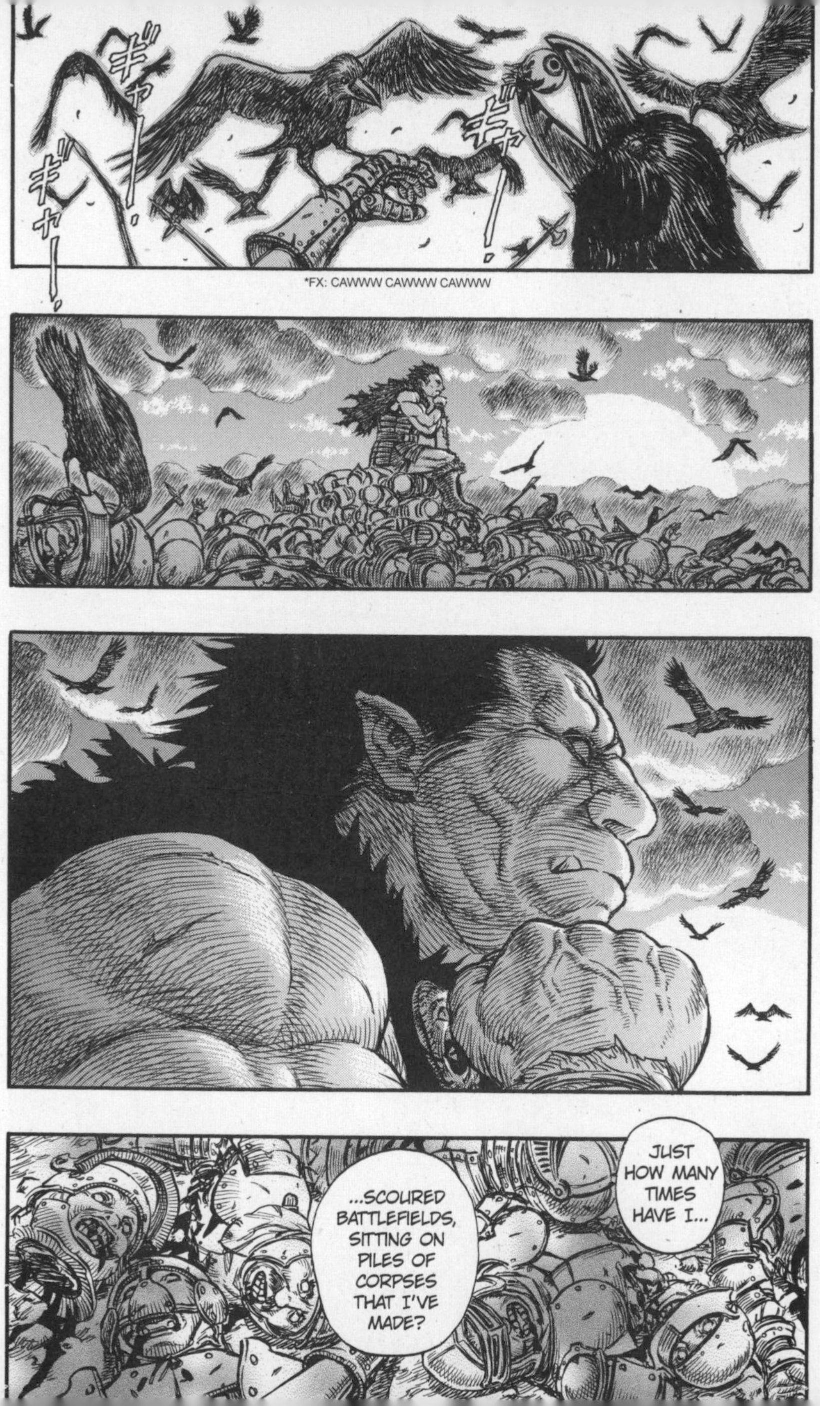
*FX: CAWWW CAWWW CAWWW
JUST HOW MANY TIMES HAVE I...
...SCOURED BATTLEFIELDS, SITTING ON PILES OF CORPSES THAT I'VE MADE?

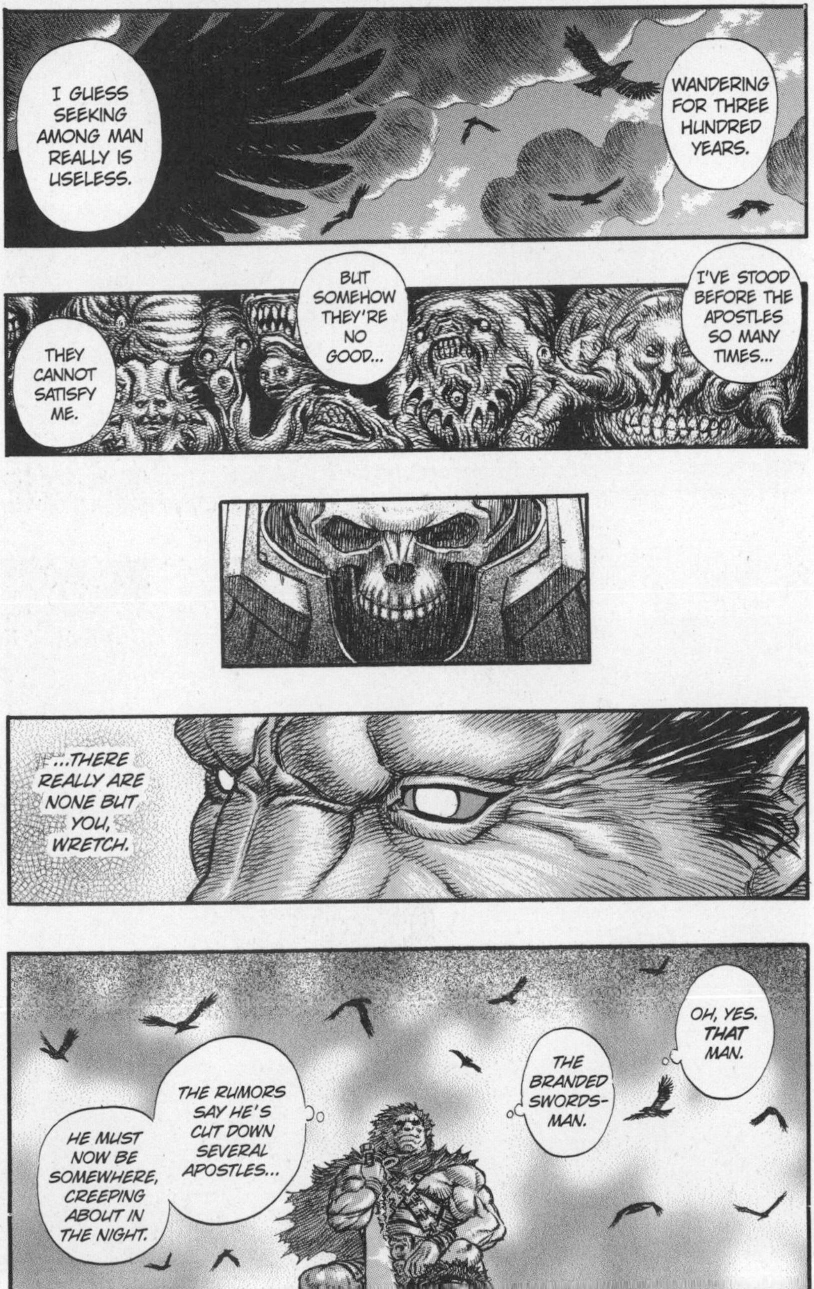
WANDERING FOR THREE HUNDRED YEARS.
I GUESS SEEKING AMONG MAN REALLY IS USELESS.
I'VE STOOD BEFORE THE APOSTLES SO MANY TIMES...
BUT SOMEHOW THEY'RE NO GOOD...
THEY CANNOT SATISFY ME.
...THERE REALLY ARE NONE BUT YOU, WRETCH.
OH, YES. THAT MAN.
THE BRANDED SWORDS-MAN.
THE RUMORS SAY HE'S CUT DOWN SEVERAL APOSTLES...
HE MUST NOW BE SOMEWHERE, CREEPING ABOUT IN THE NIGHT.

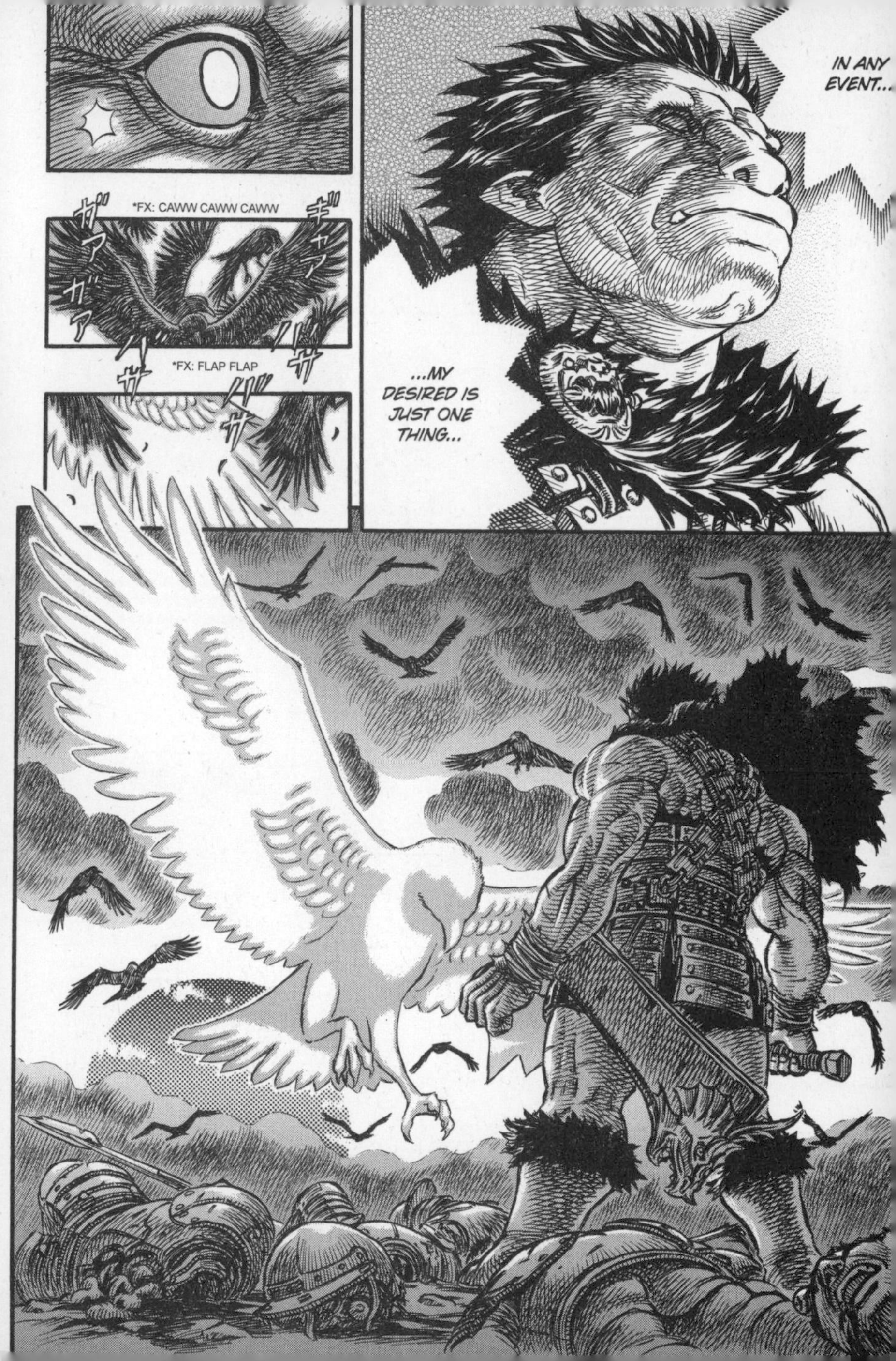
IN ANY EVENT...
...MY DESIRED IS JUST ONE THING...
*FX: CAWW CAWW CAWW
*FX: FLAP FLAP

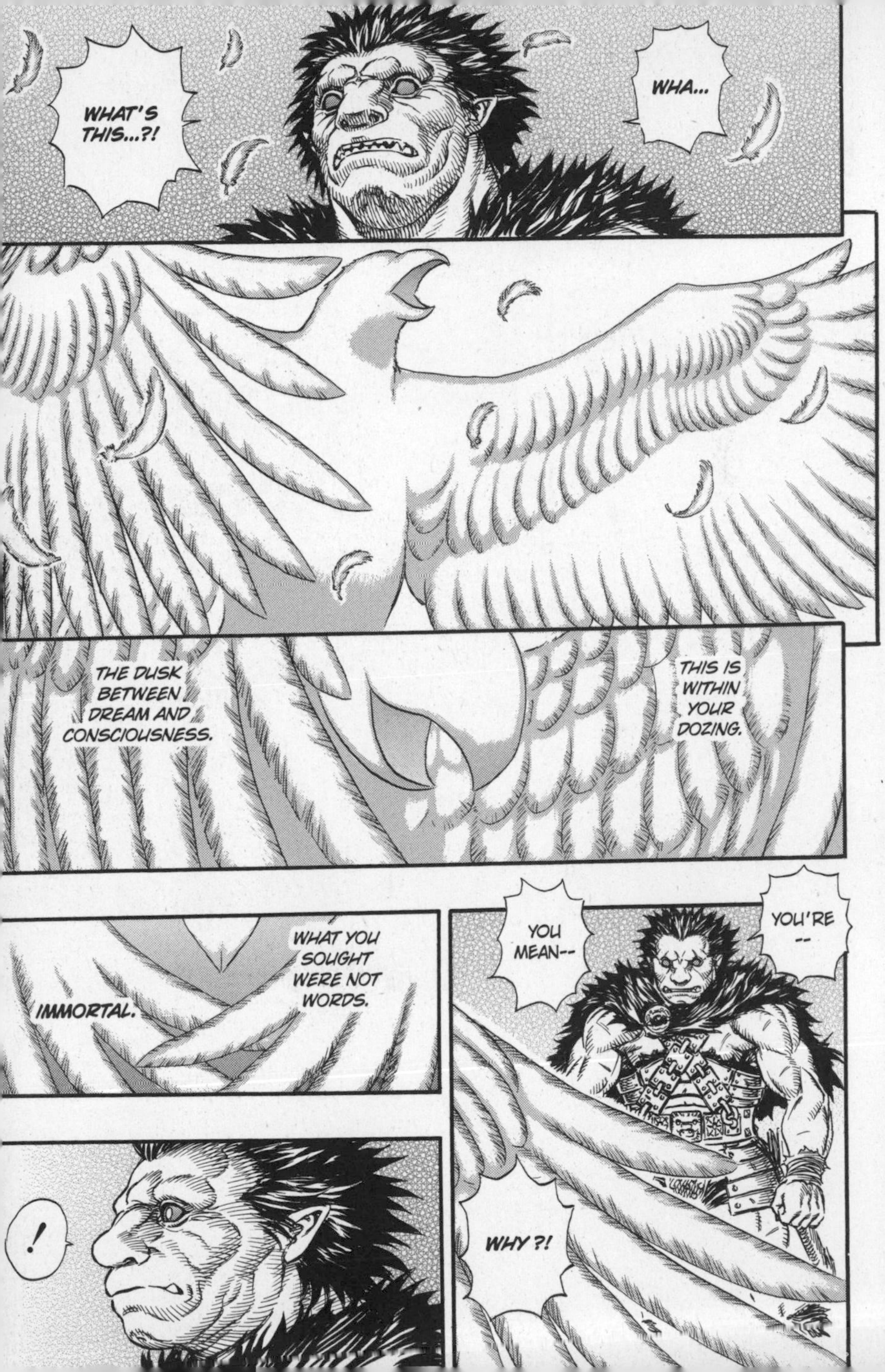
WHA...
WHAT'S THIS...?!
THIS IS WITHIN YOUR DOZING.
THE DUSK BETWEEN DREAM AND CONSCIOUSNESS.
YOU'RE --
YOU MEAN--
WHY ?!
WHAT YOU SOUGHT WERE NOT WORDS.
IMMORTAL.
!

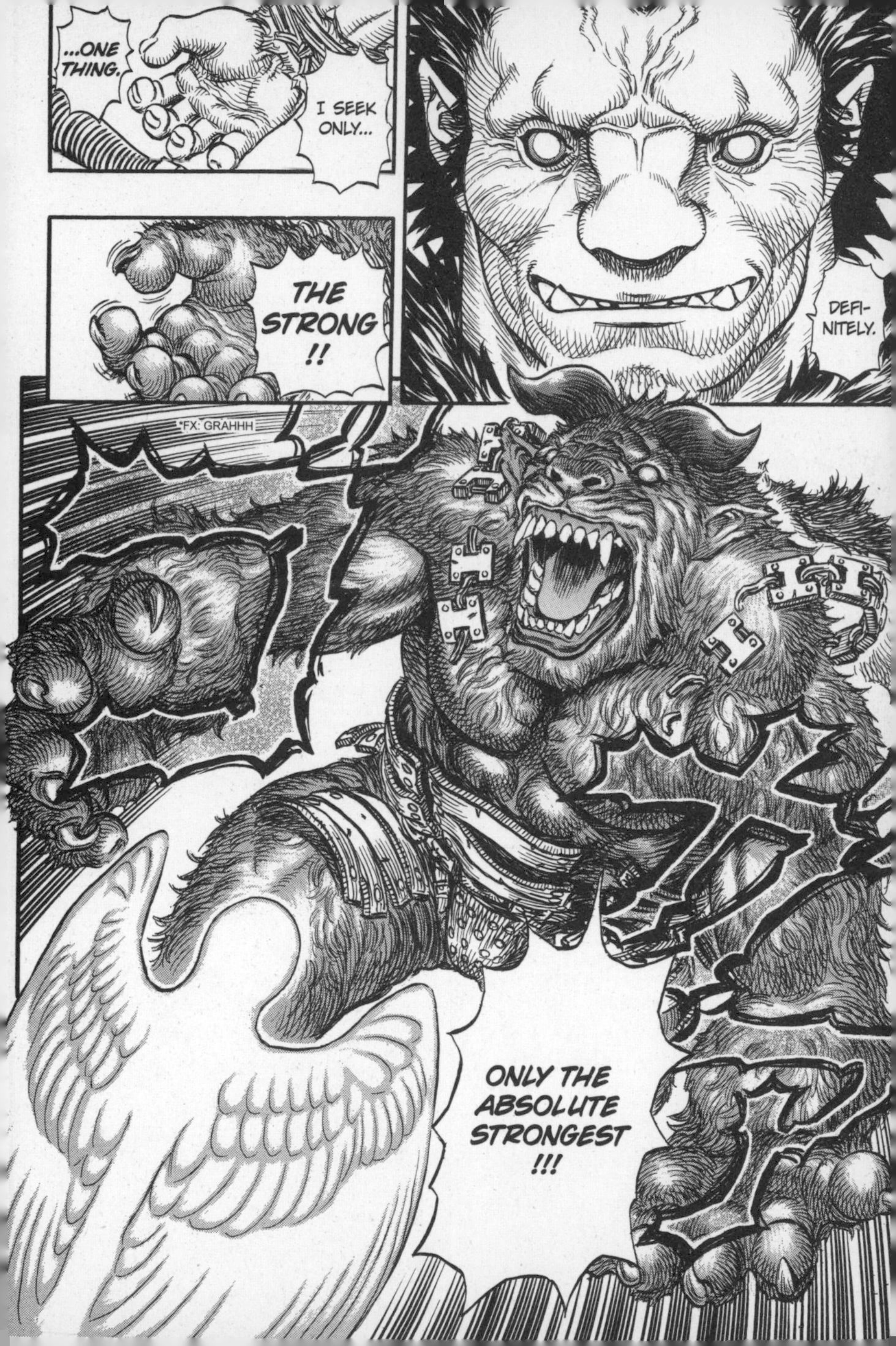
DEFI-
NITELY.
I SEEK ONLY...
...ONE THING.
THE STRONG !!
*FX: GRAHHH
ONLY THE ABSOLUTE STRONGEST !!!

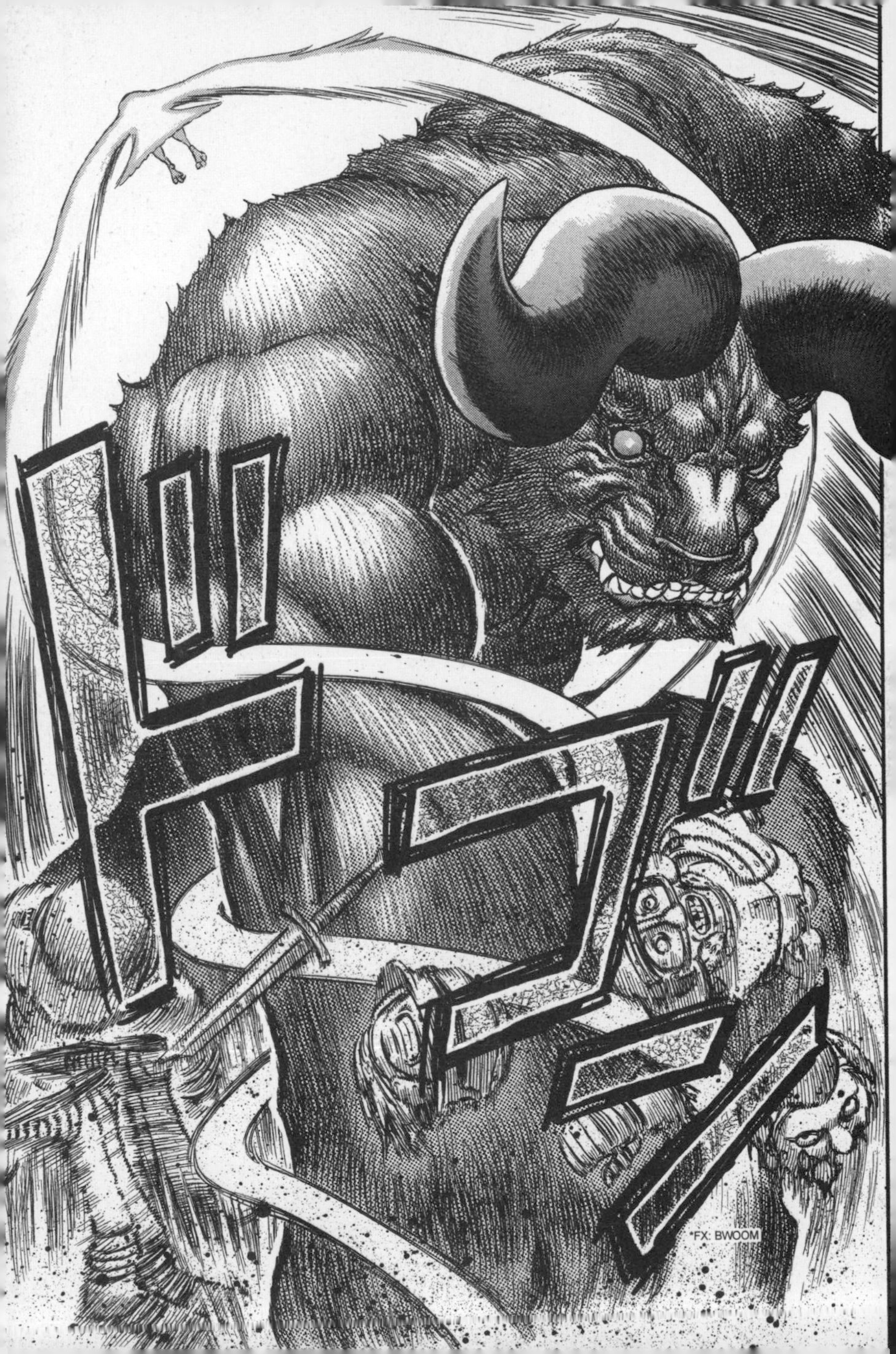
*FX: BWOOM

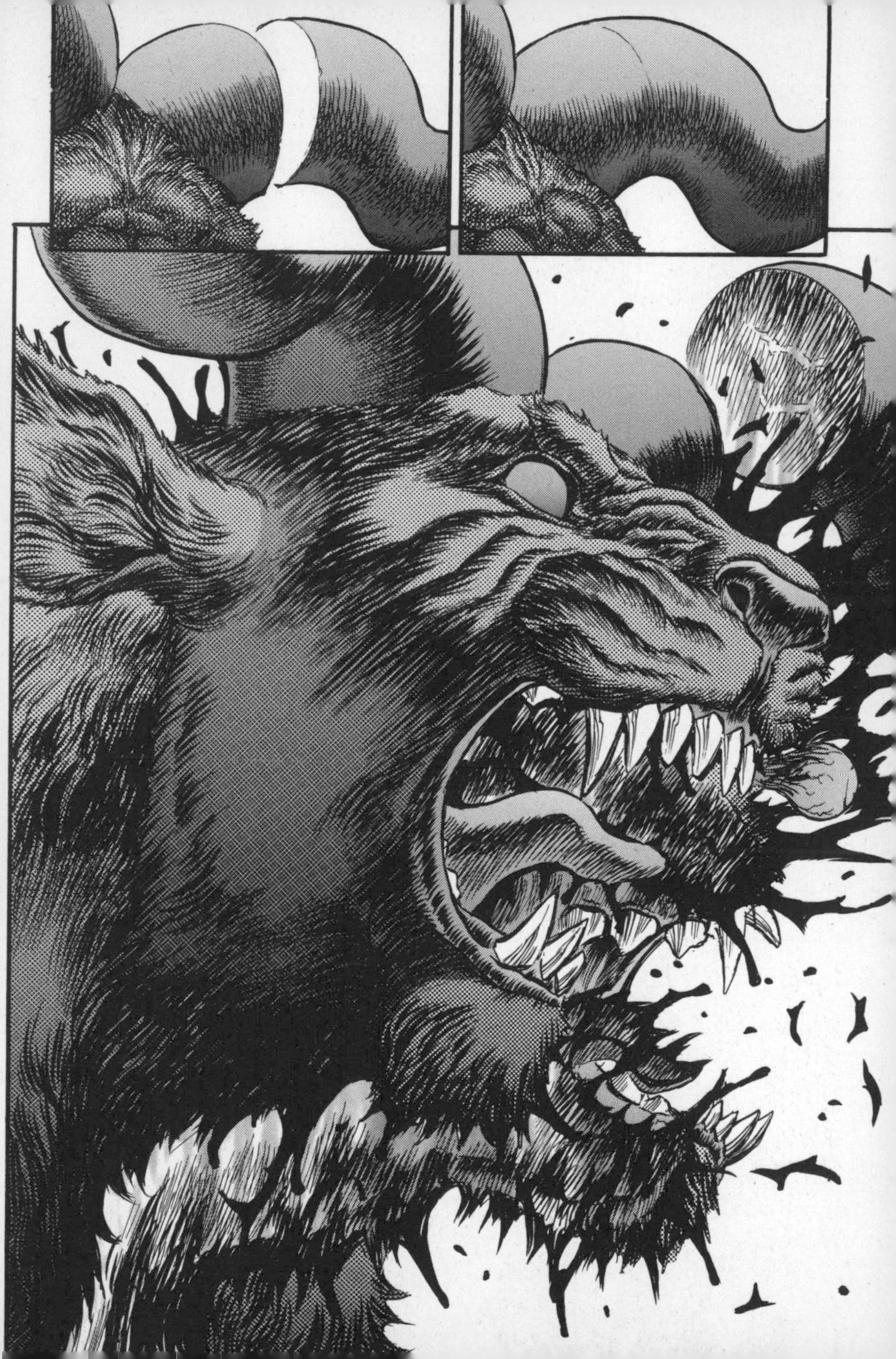

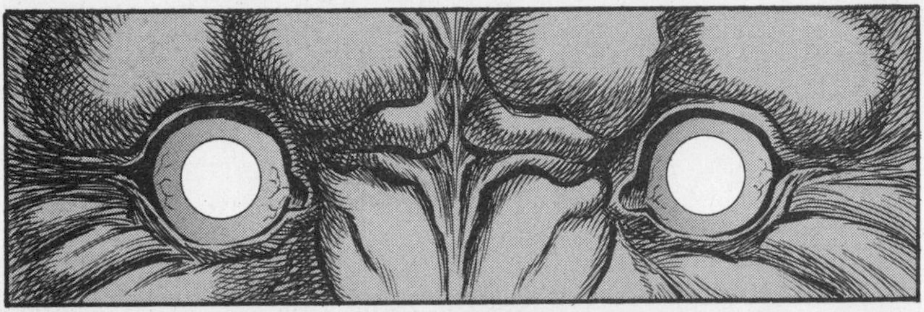

*FX: CAWWW CAWWW CAWWW

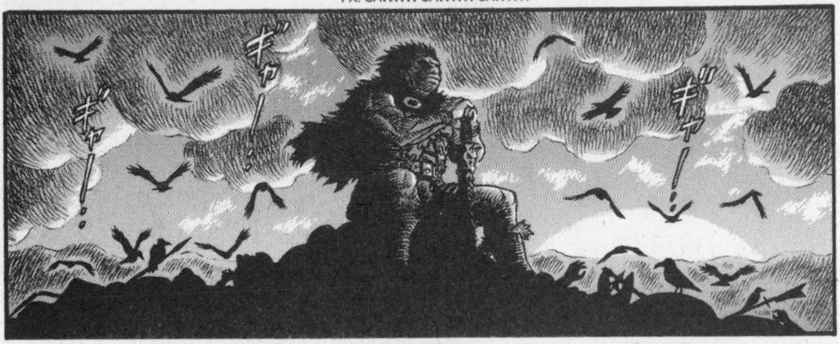

*FX: PULSE

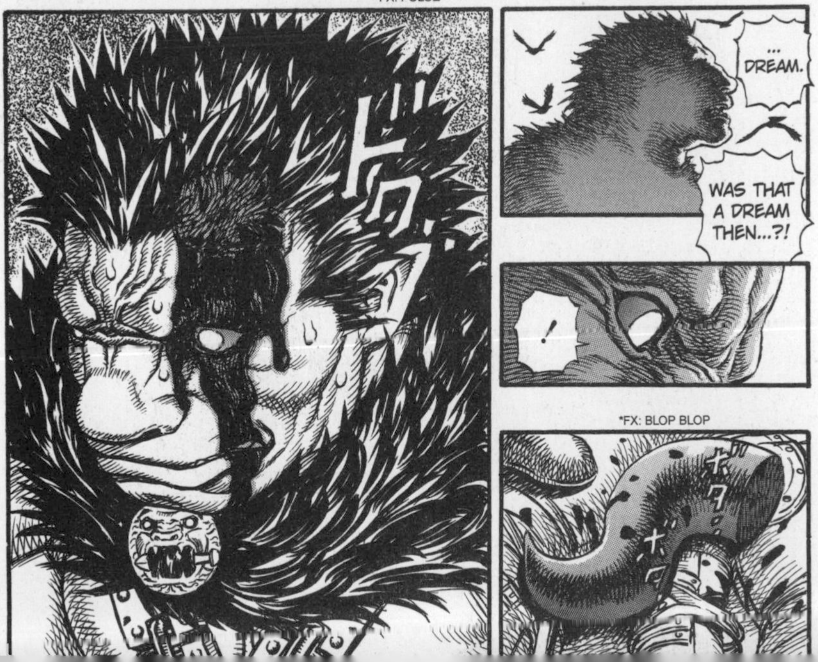
...DREAM.
WAS THAT A DREAM THEN...?!
!
*FX: BLOP BLOP

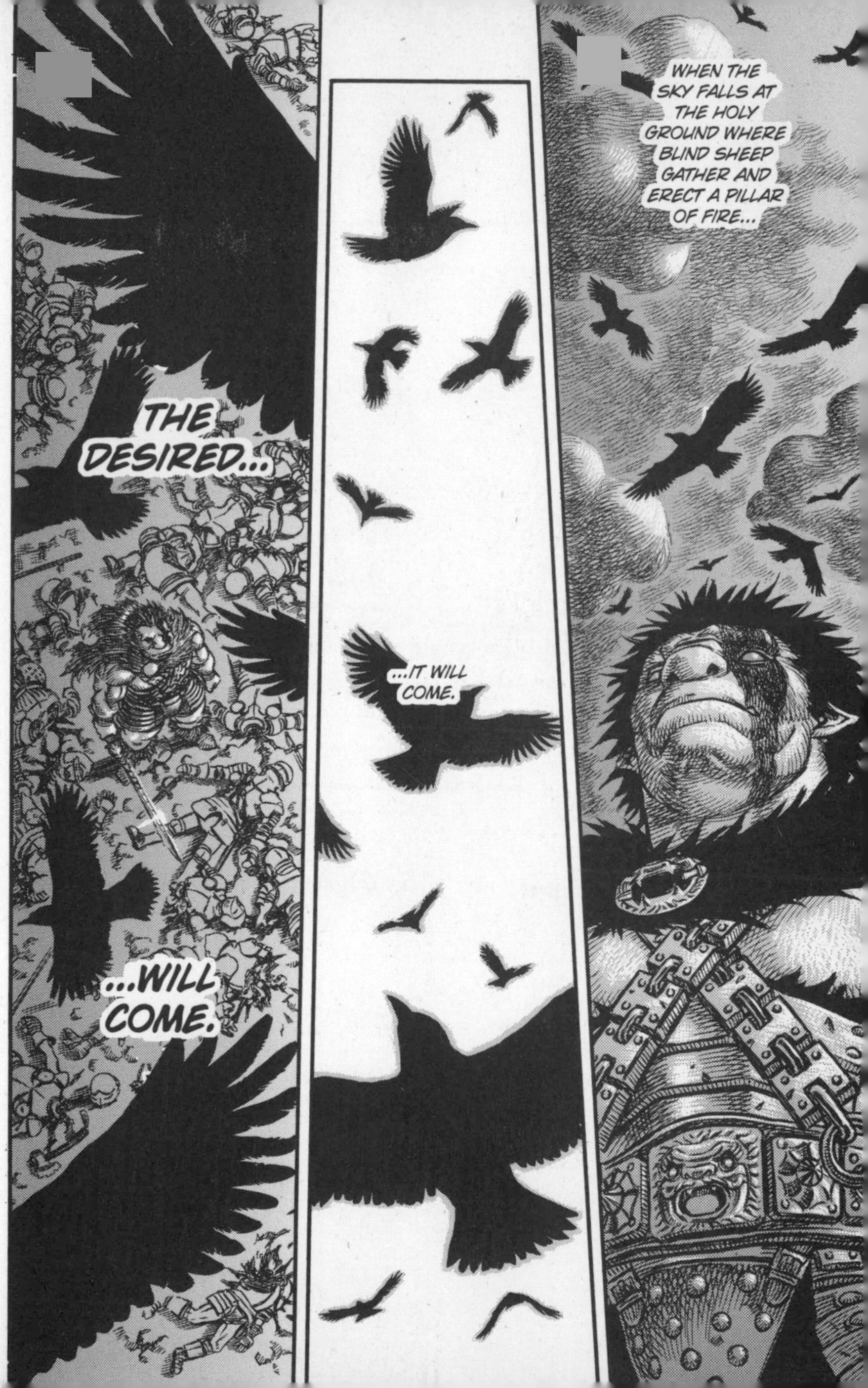
WHEN THE SKY FALLS AT THE HOLY GROUND WHERE BLIND SHEEP GATHER AND ERECT A PILLAR OF FIRE...
...IT WILL COME.
THE DESIRED...
...WILL COME.

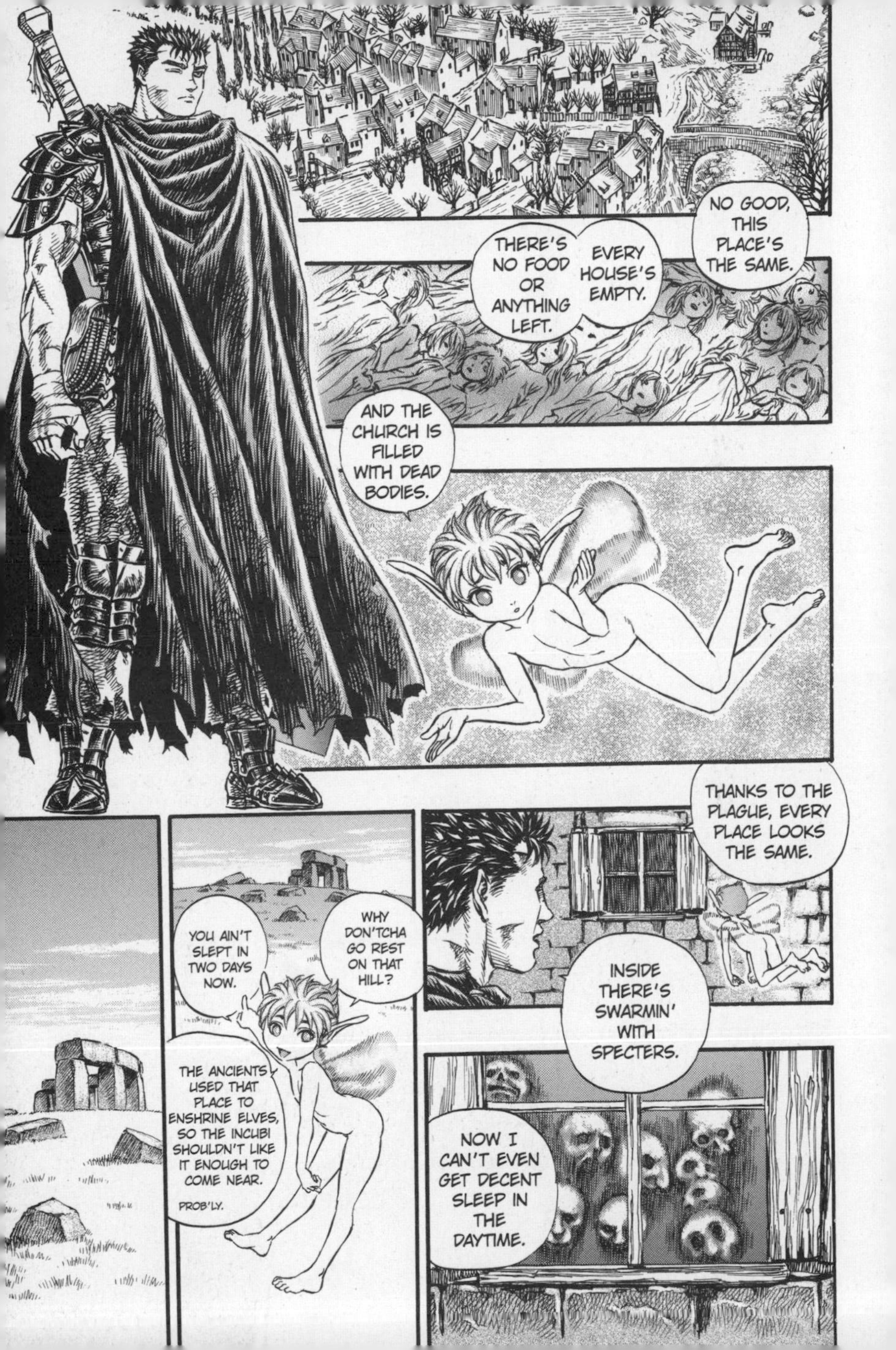
NO GOOD, THIS PLACE'S THE SAME.
EVERY HOUSE'S EMPTY.
THERE'S NO FOOD OR ANYTHING LEFT.
AND THE CHURCH IS FILLED WITH DEAD BODIES.
THANKS TO THE PLAGUE, EVERY PLACE LOOKS THE SAME.
INSIDE THERE'S SWARMIN' WITH SPECTERS.
NOW I CAN'T EVEN GET DECENT SLEEP IN THE DAYTIME.
WHY DON'TCHA GO REST ON THAT HILL?
YOU AIN'T SLEPT IN TWO DAYS NOW.
THE ANCIENTS USED THAT PLACE TO ENSHRINE ELVES, SO THE INCUBI SHOULDN'T LIKE IT ENOUGH TO COME NEAR.
PROB'LY.

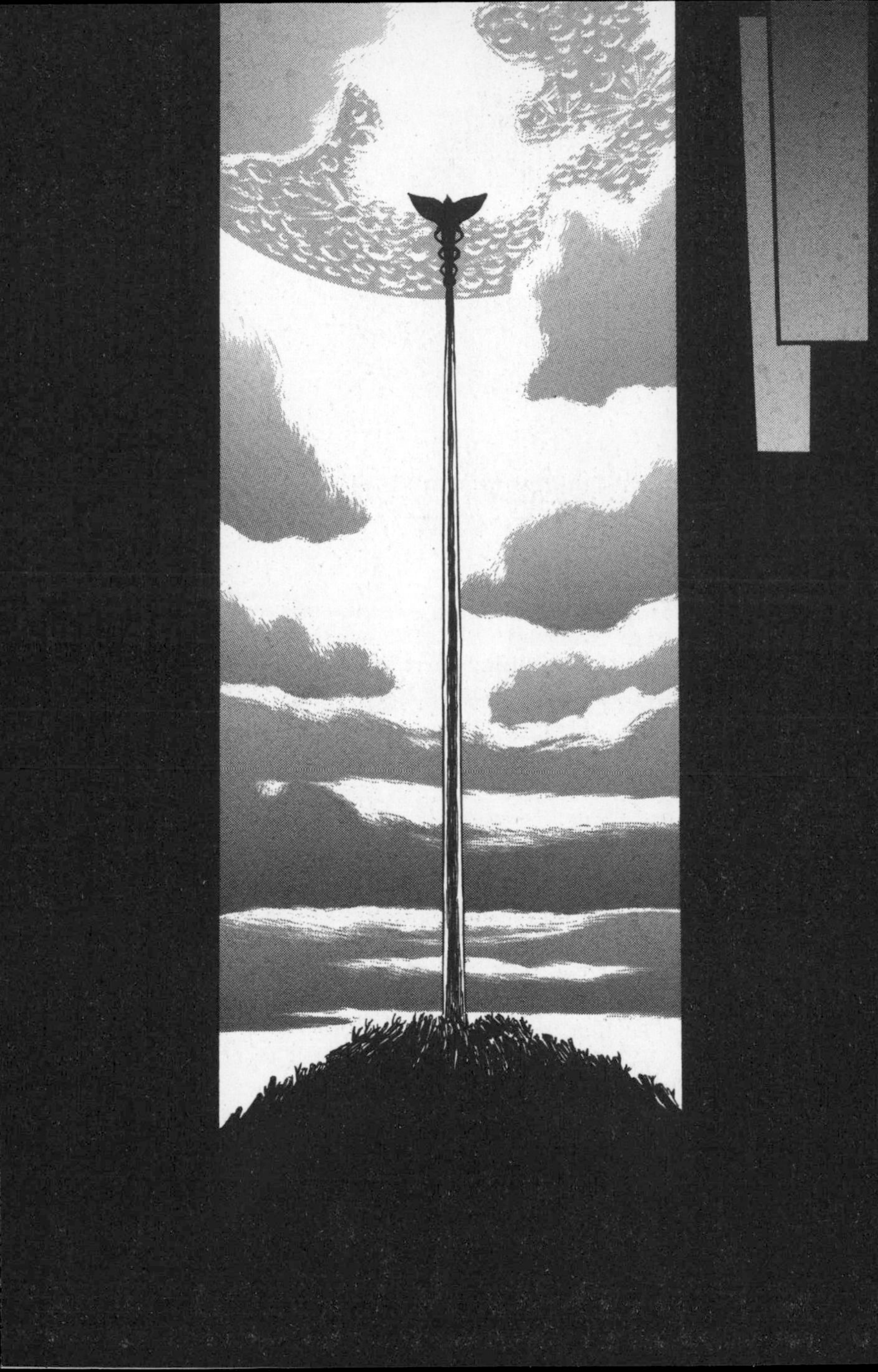

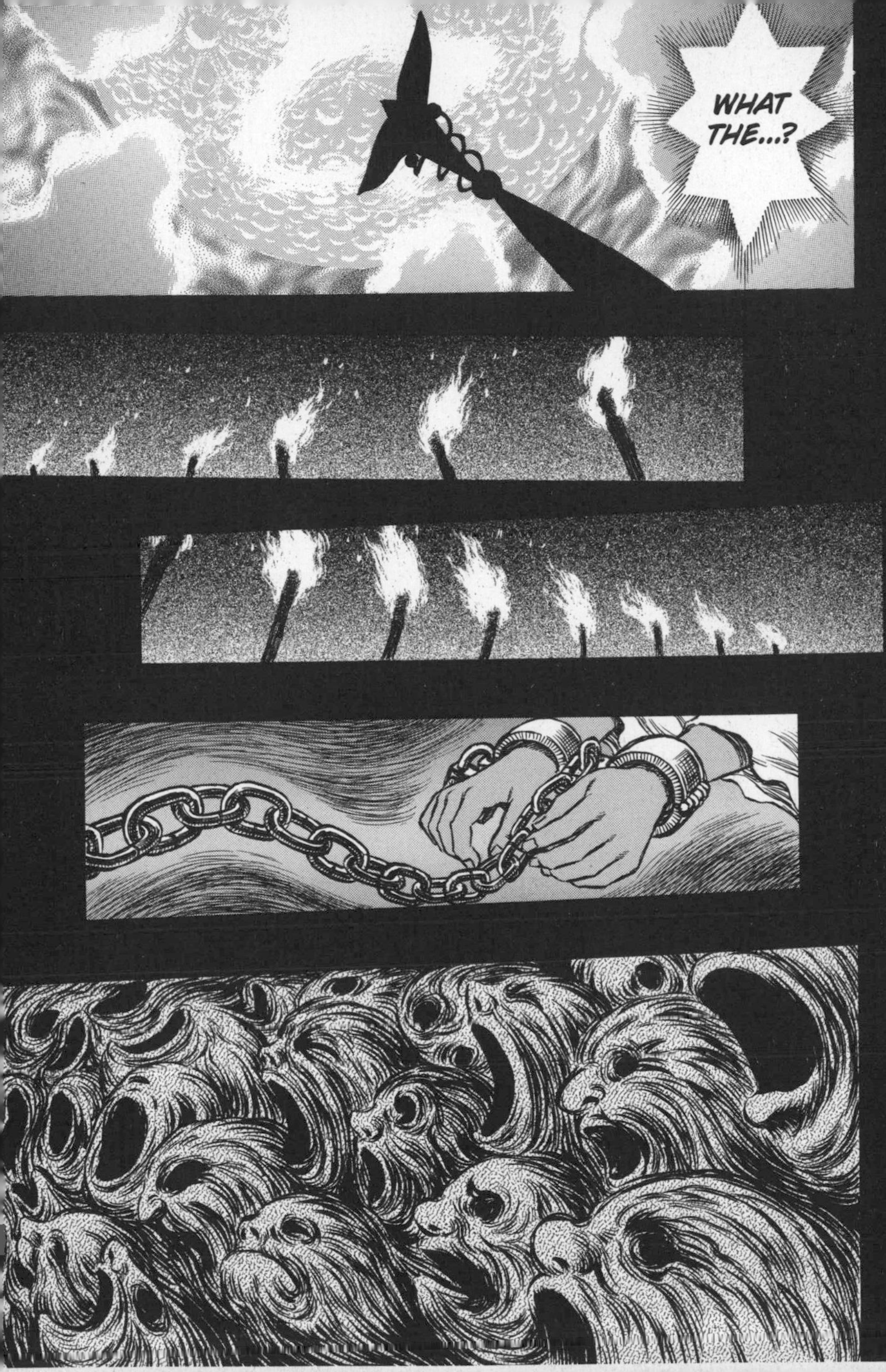
WHAT THE...?

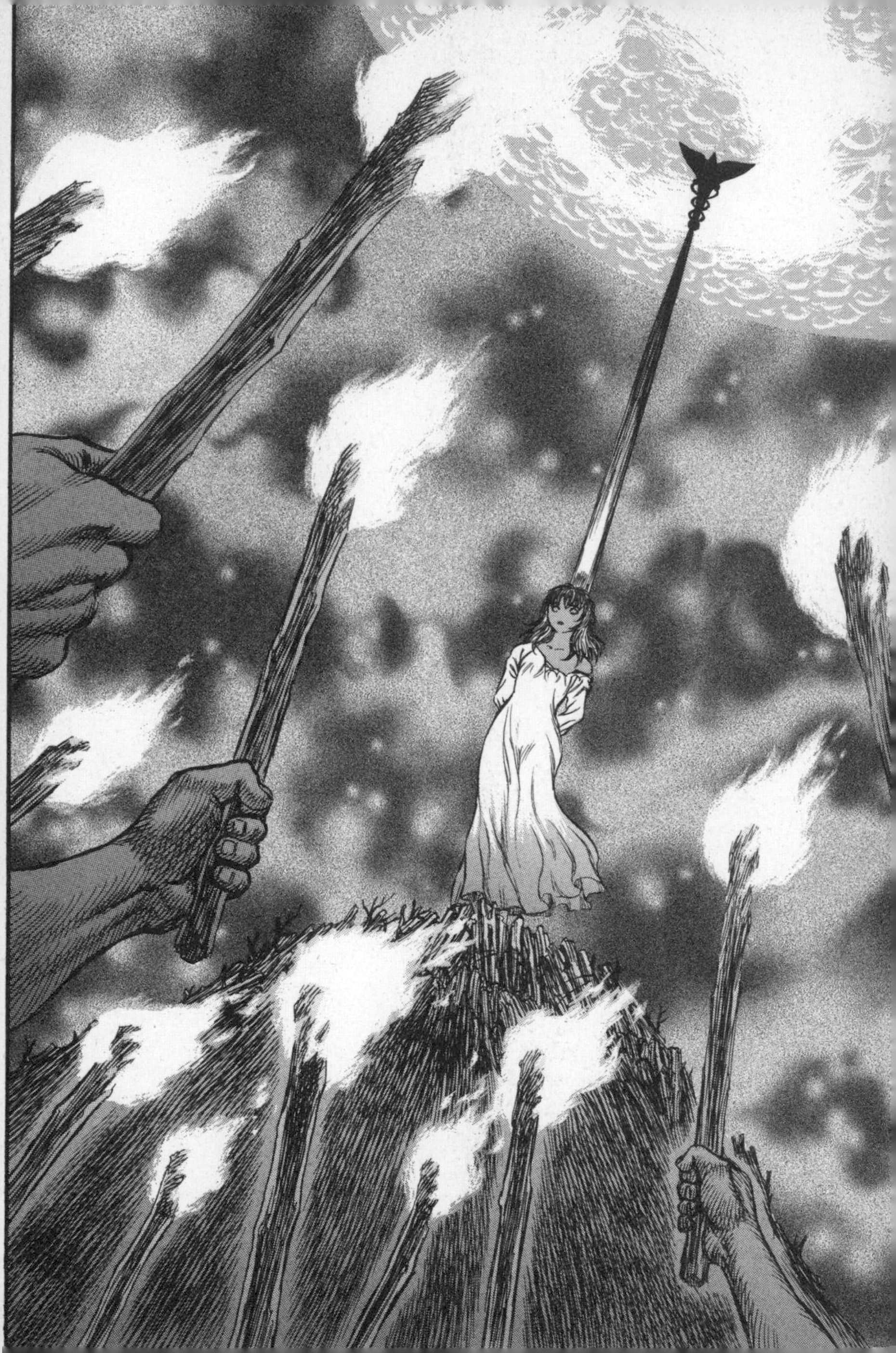

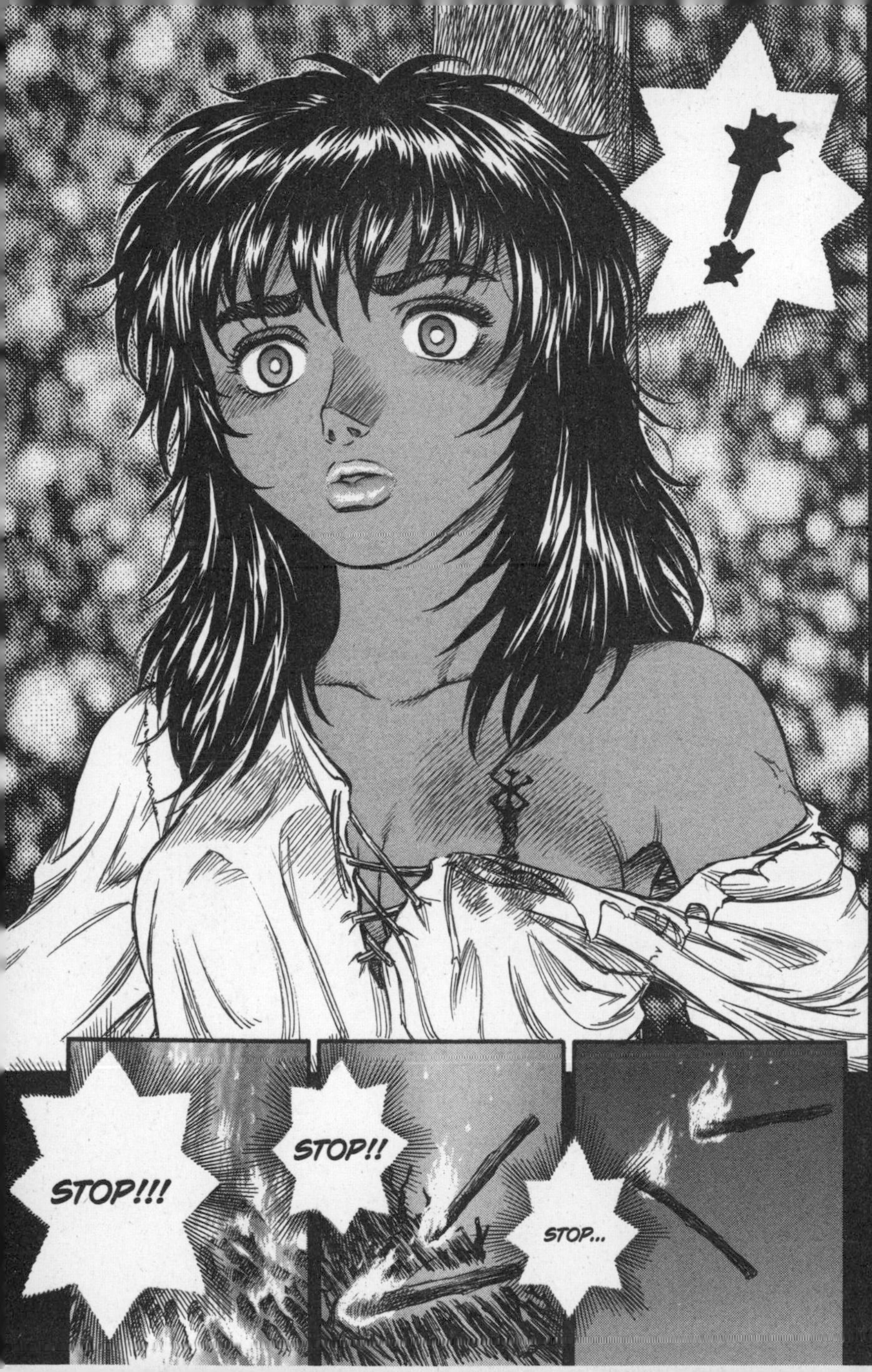
!
STOP...
STOP!!
STOP!!!

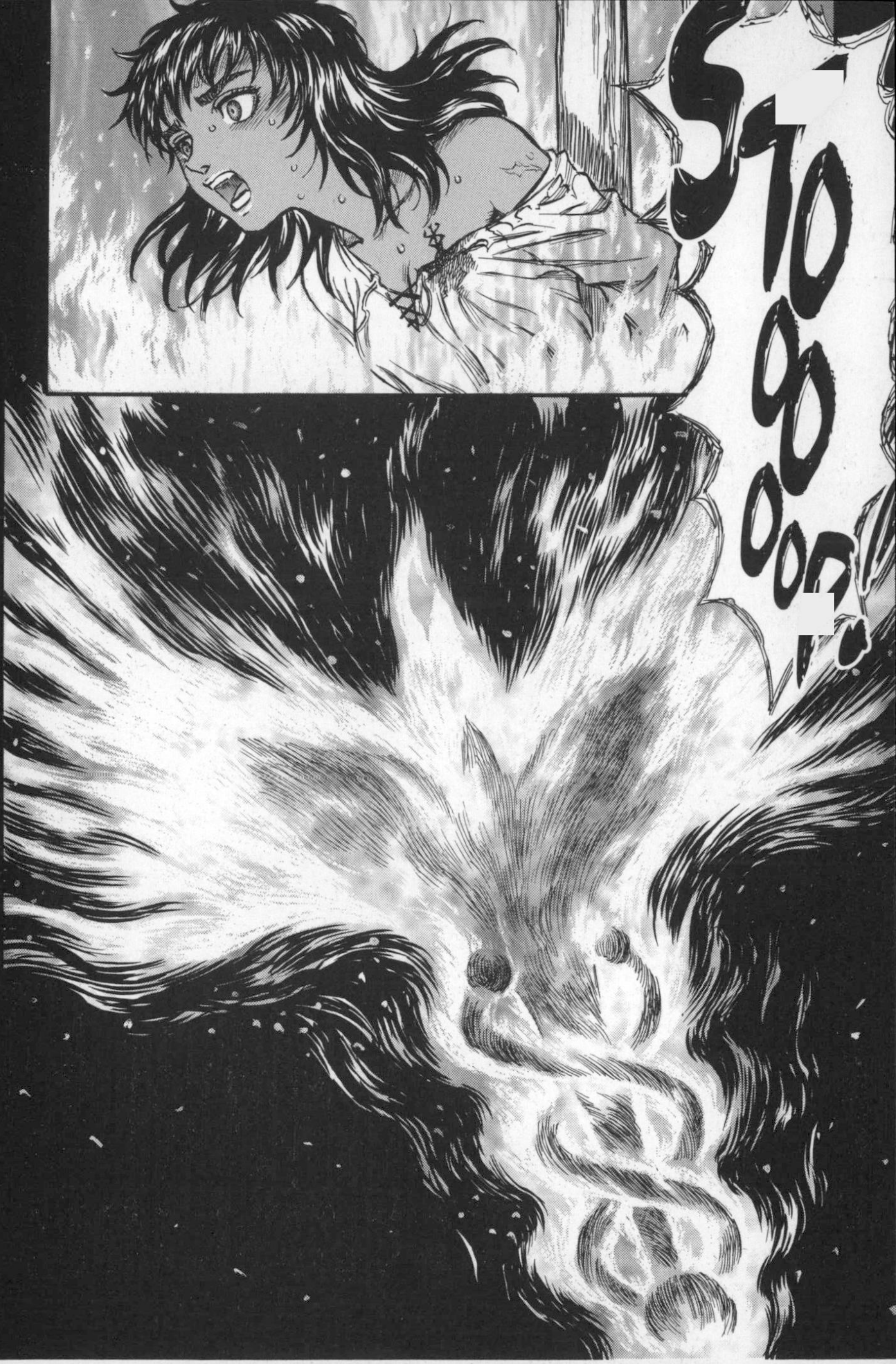
STOOOOOP!!

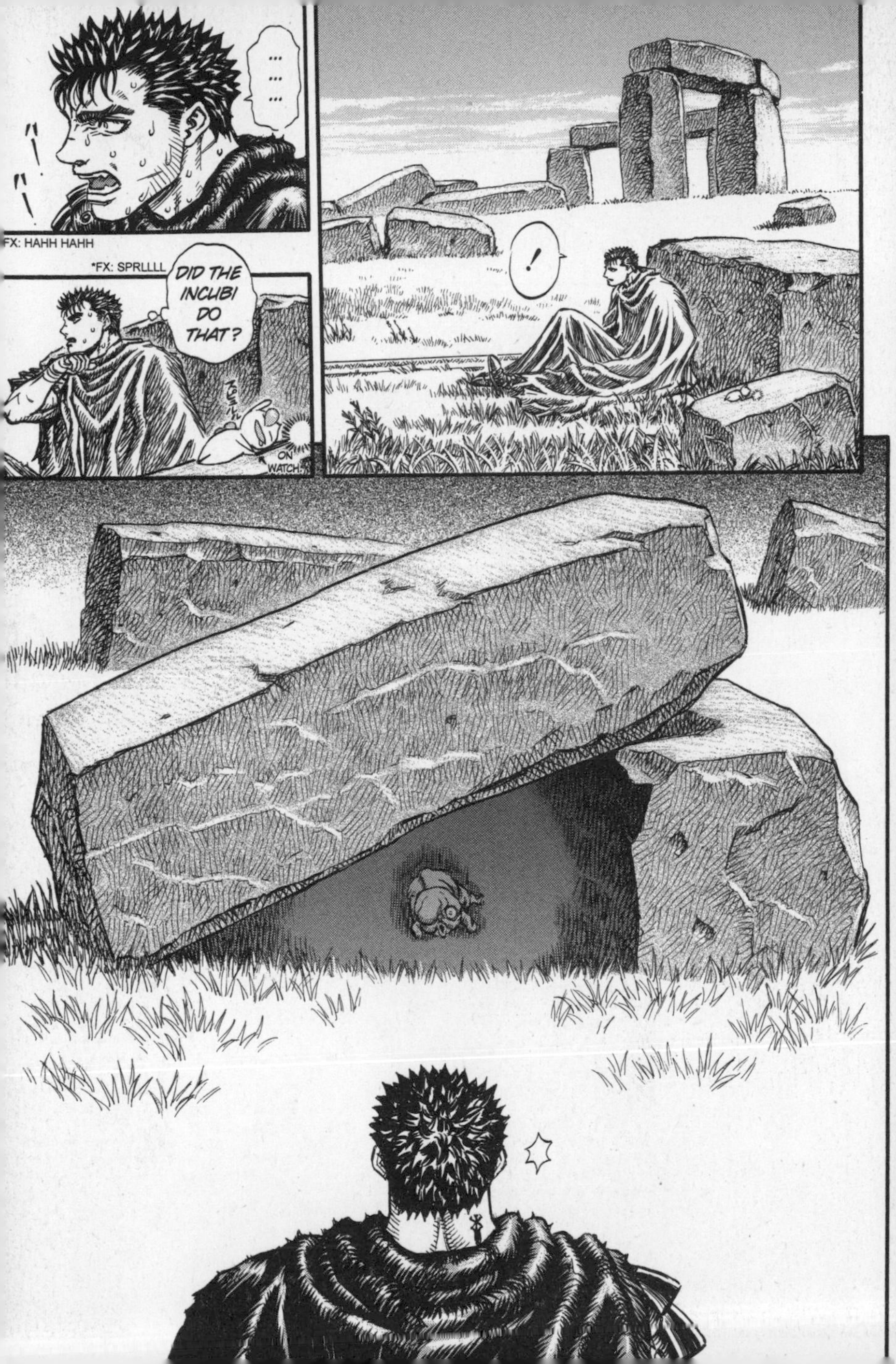
!
...
...
...
FX: HAHH HAHH
DID THE INCUBI DO THAT?
*FX: SPRLLLL
ON WATCH.

YOU DID IT.. JUST NOW.

......

D....

...

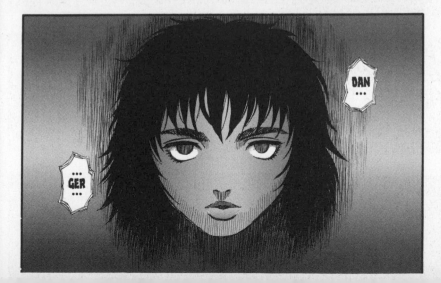

DAN...

...GER...

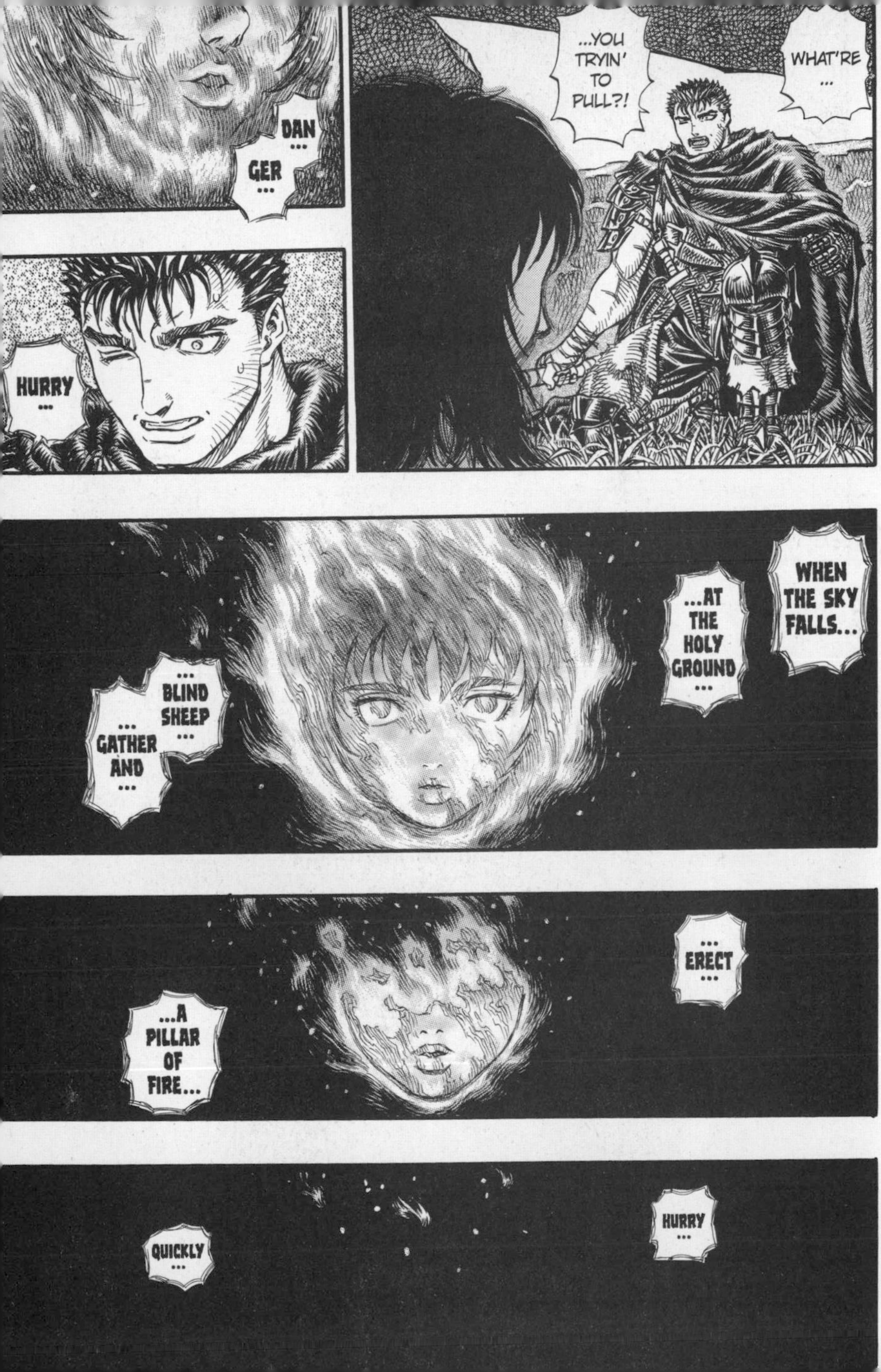
WHAT'RE ...
...YOU TRYIN' TO PULL?!
DAN ... GER ...
HURRY ...
WHEN THE SKY FALLS...
...AT THE HOLY GROUND ...
... BLIND SHEEP ...
... GATHER AND ...
... ERECT ...
...A PILLAR OF FIRE...
HURRY ...
QUICKLY ...

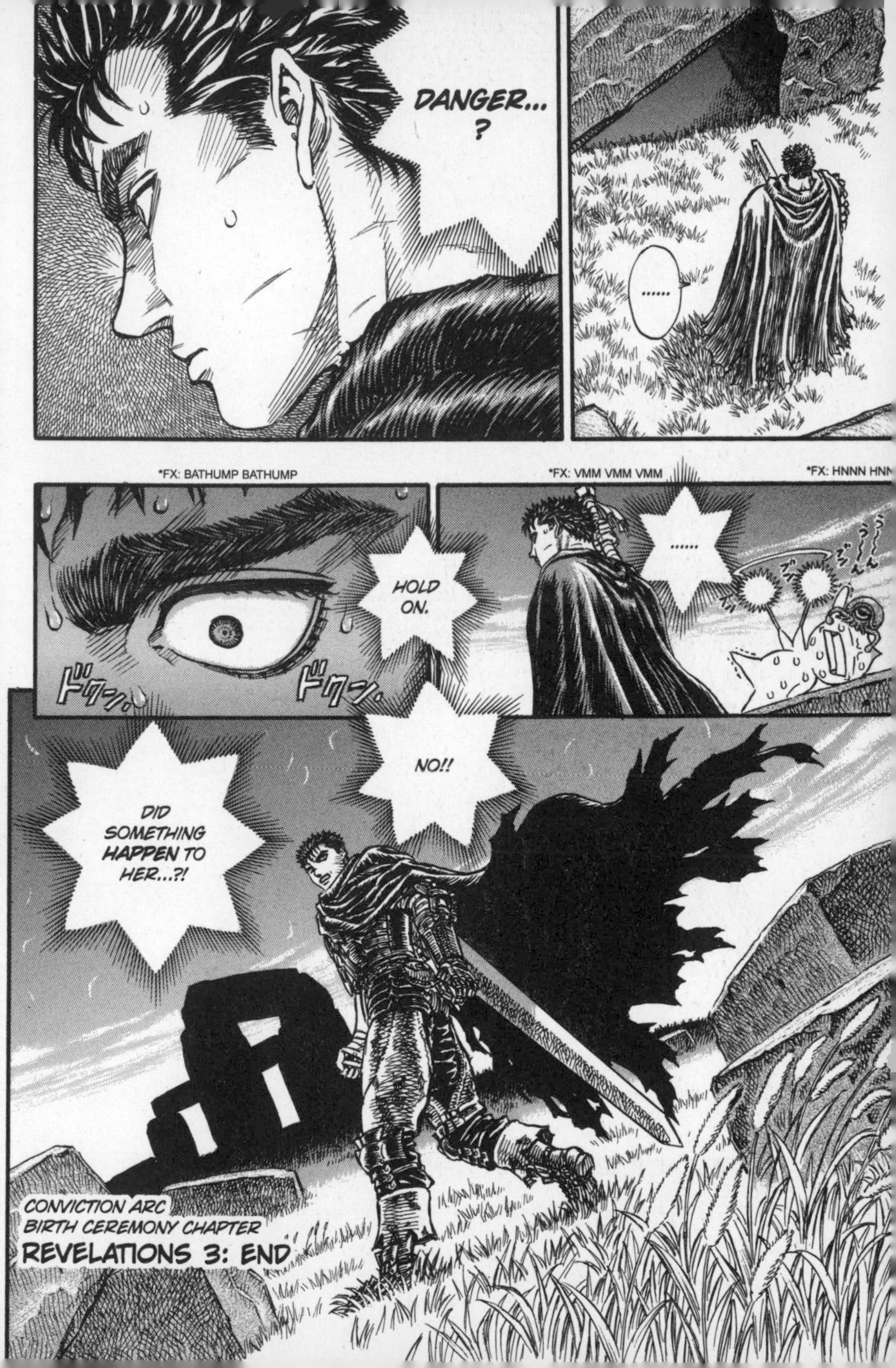
......
DANGER... ?
*FX: HNNN HNN
*FX: VMM VMM VMM
......
*FX: BATHUMP BATHUMP
HOLD ON.
ドクン。ドクン。
NO!!
DID SOMETHING HAPPEN TO HER...?!
CONVICTION ARC
BIRTH CEREMONY CHAPTER
REVELATIONS 3: END

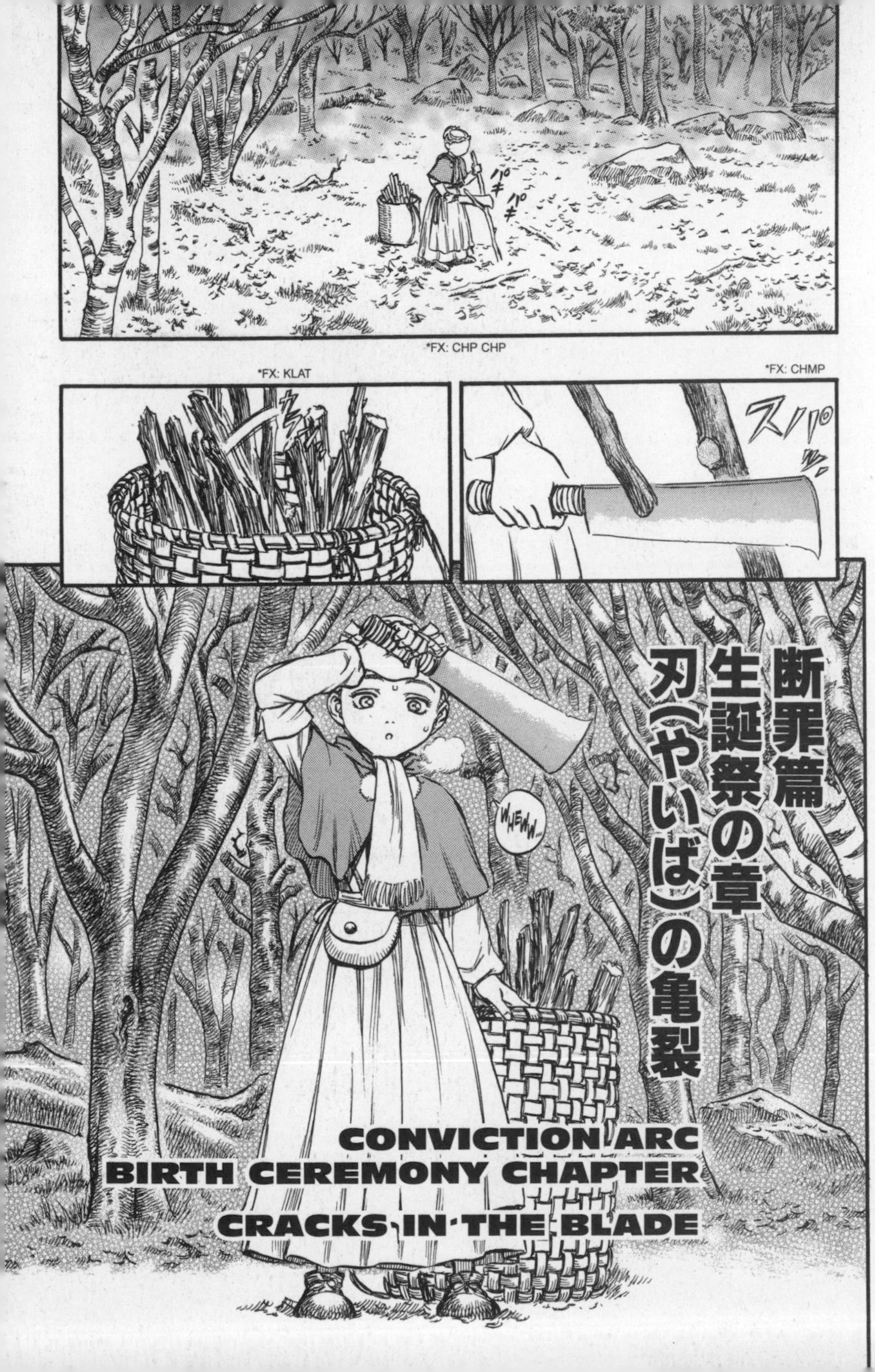
パキ パキ
*FX: CHP CHP
スパ
*FX: CHMP
*FX: KLAT
断罪篇
生誕祭の章
刃(やいば)の亀裂
WHEWW...
CONVICTION ARC
BIRTH CEREMONY CHAPTER
CRACKS IN THE BLADE

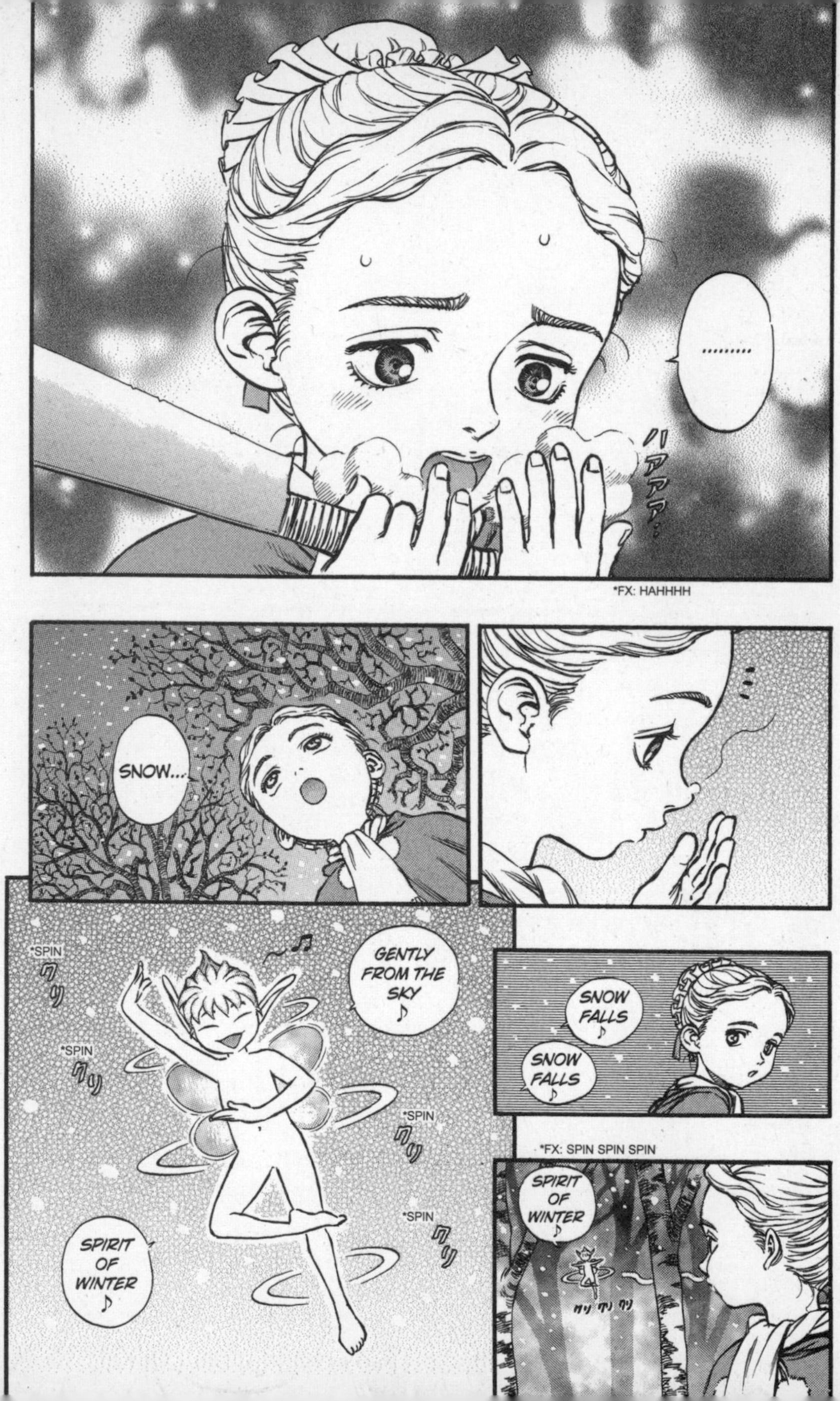

....
*FX: HAHHHH
SNOW...
SNOW FALLS ♪
SNOW FALLS ♪
*FX: SPIN SPIN SPIN
SPIRIT OF WINTER ♪
GENTLY FROM THE SKY ♪
*SPIN
*SPIN
*SPIN
*SPIN
SPIRIT OF WINTER ♪

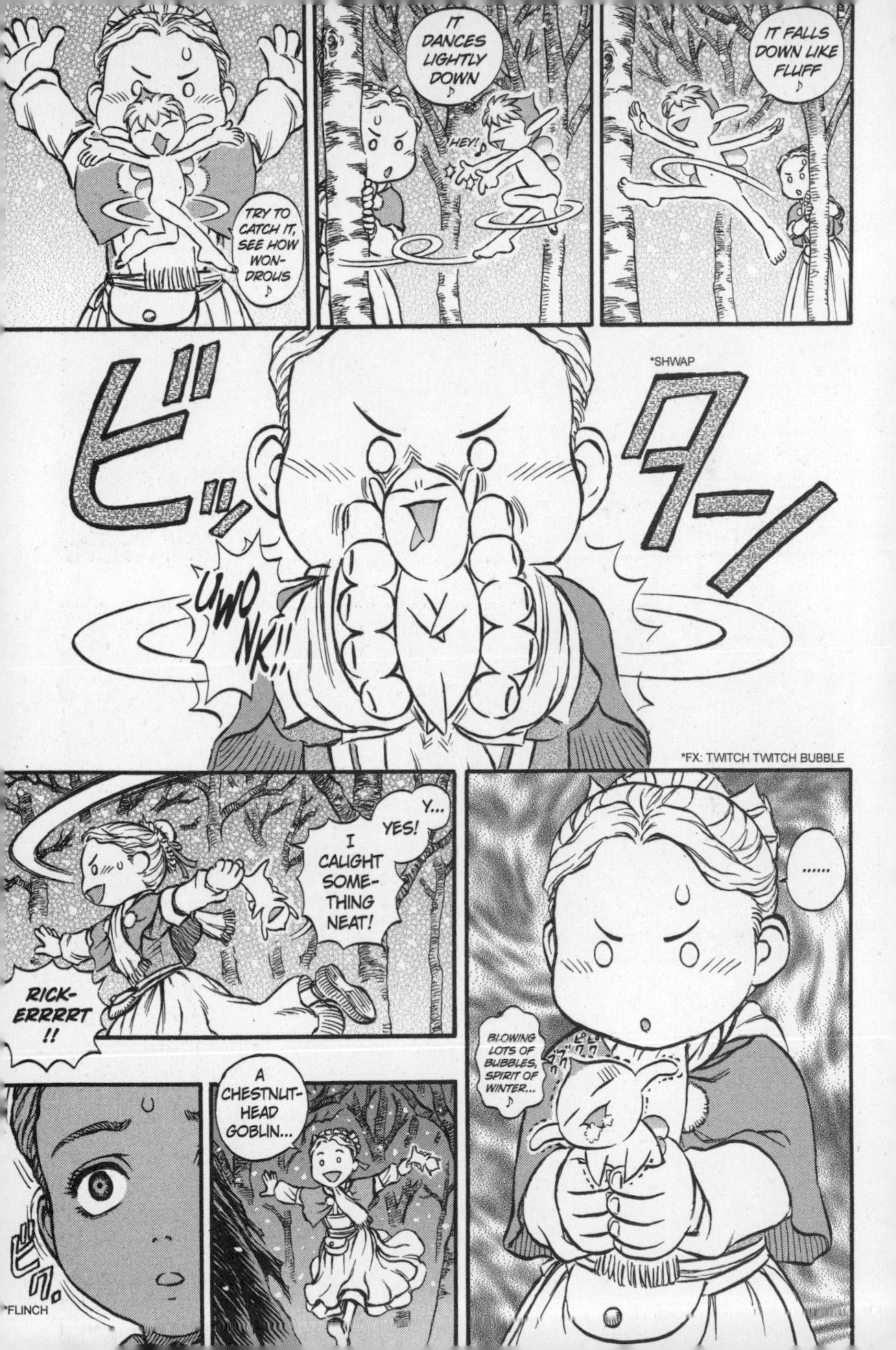
IT FALLS DOWN LIKE FLUFF ♪
IT DANCES LIGHTLY DOWN ♪
HEY! ♪
TRY TO CATCH IT, SEE HOW WONDROUS ♪
*SHWAP
UWONK!!
*FX: TWITCH TWITCH BUBBLE
......
BLOWING LOTS OF BUBBLES, SPIRIT OF WINTER... ♪
Y... YES!
I CAUGHT SOMETHING NEAT!
RICK-ERRRRT!!
A CHESTNUT-HEAD GOBLIN...
*FLINCH

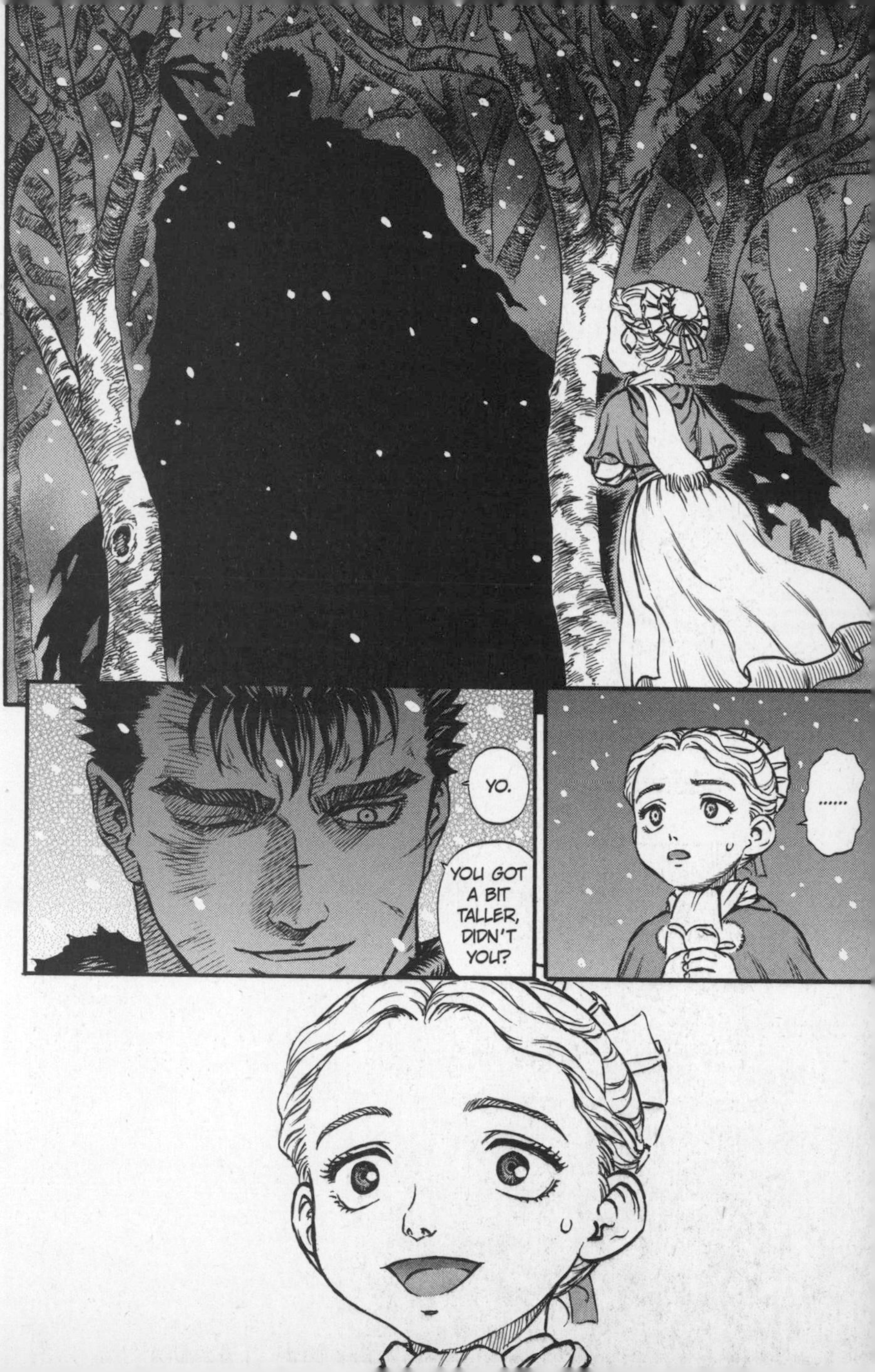
......
YO.
YOU GOT A BIT TALLER, DIDN'T YOU?

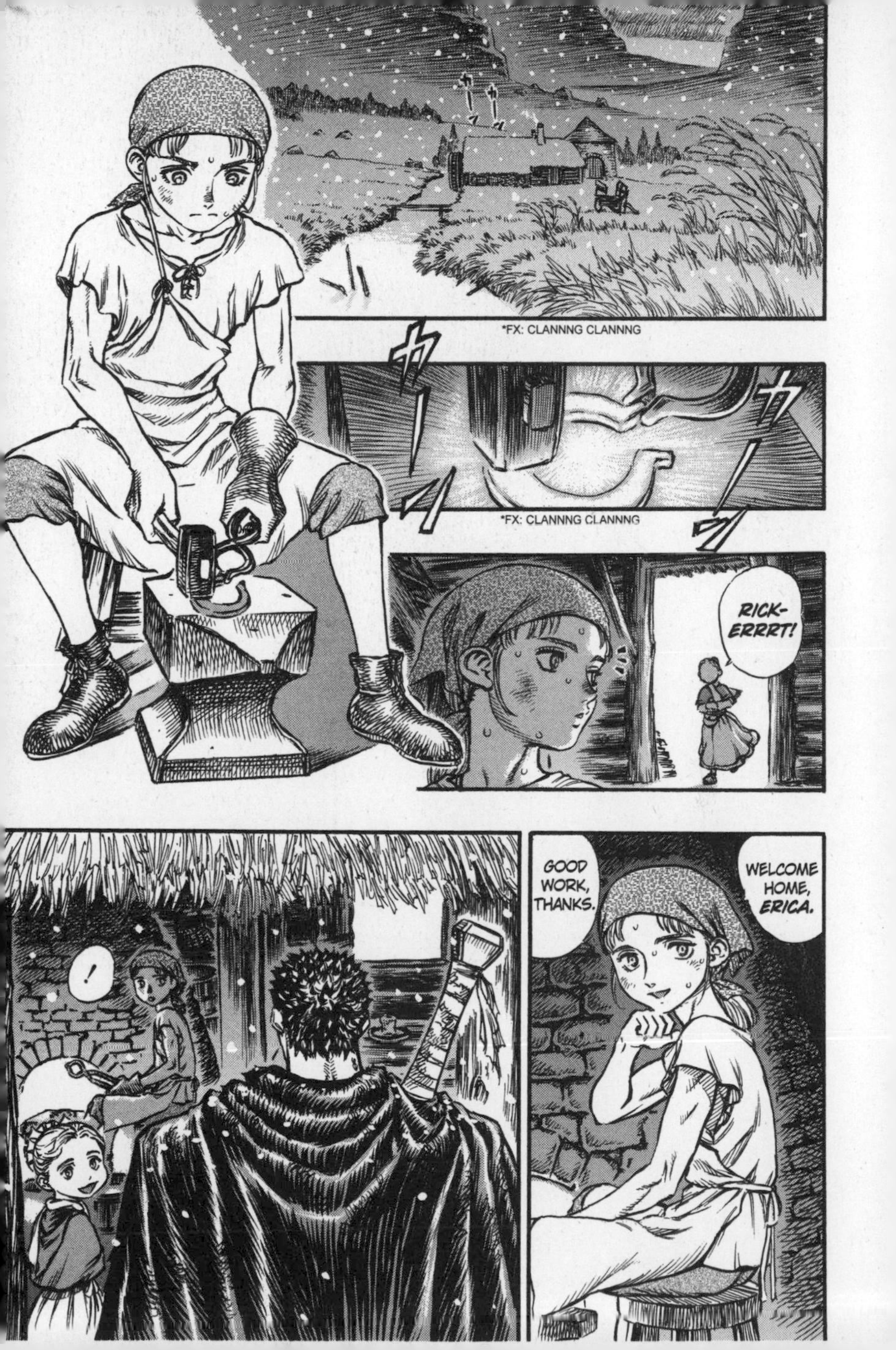
*FX: CLANNNG CLANNNG
*FX: CLANNNG CLANNNG
RICK-ERRRT!
WELCOME HOME, ERICA.
GOOD WORK, THANKS.
!

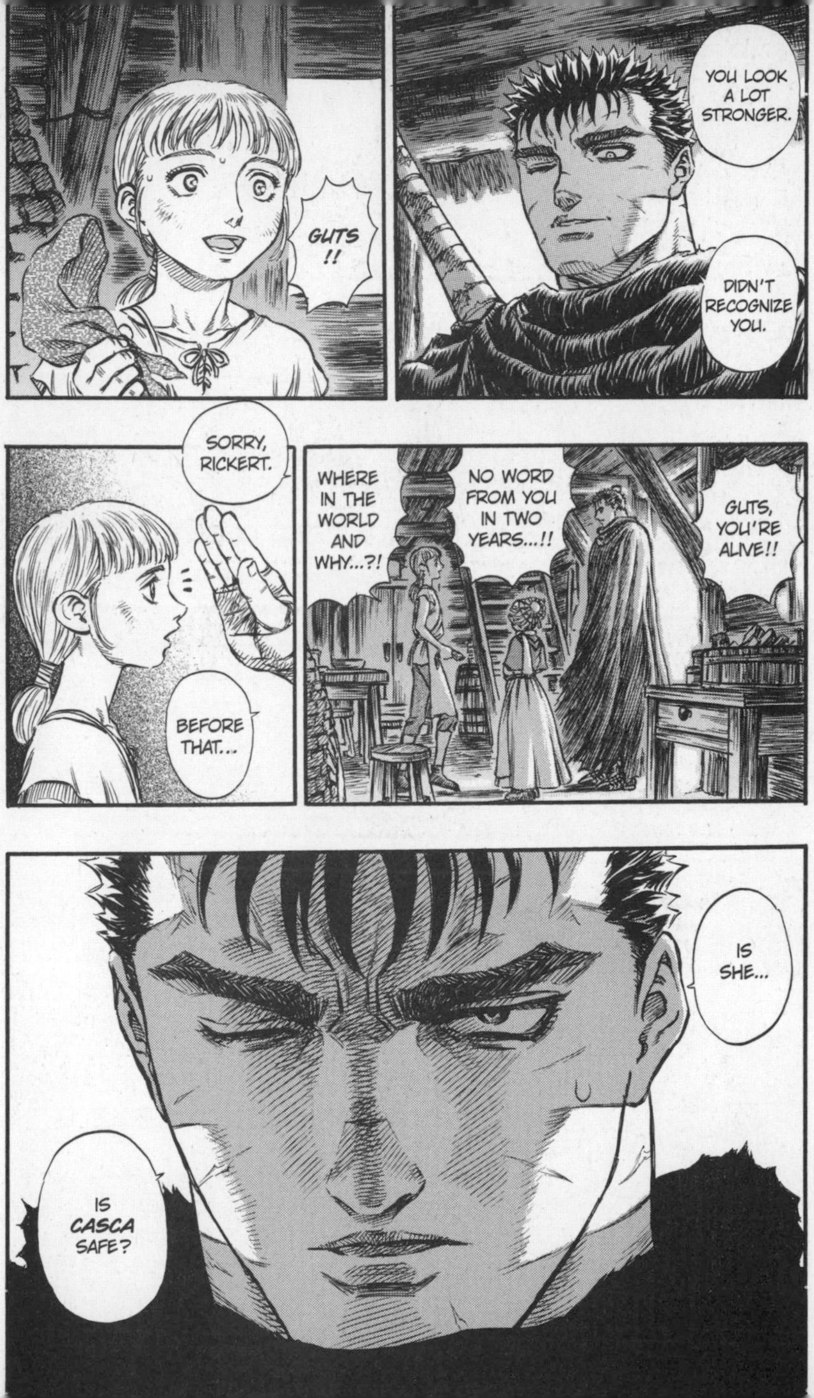
YOU LOOK A LOT STRONGER.
DIDN'T RECOGNIZE YOU.
GUTS!!
GUTS, YOU'RE ALIVE!!
NO WORD FROM YOU IN TWO YEARS...!!
WHERE IN THE WORLD AND WHY...?!
SORRY, RICKERT.
BEFORE THAT...
IS SHE...
IS CASCA SAFE?

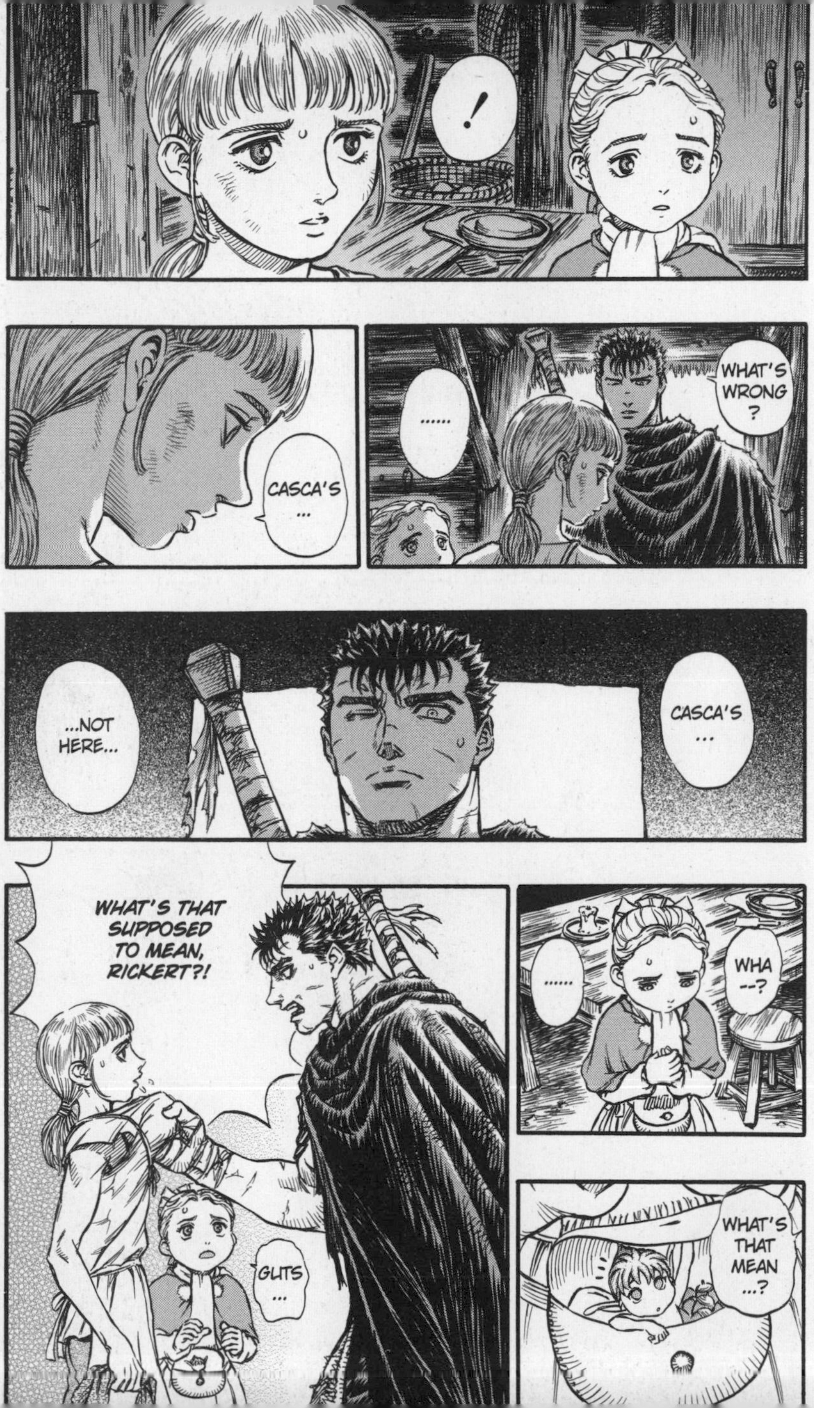
!
WHAT'S WRONG?
......
CASCA'S ...
CASCA'S ...
...NOT HERE...
WHA--?
......
WHAT'S THAT MEAN ...?
WHAT'S THAT SUPPOSED TO MEAN, RICKERT?!
GUTS ...

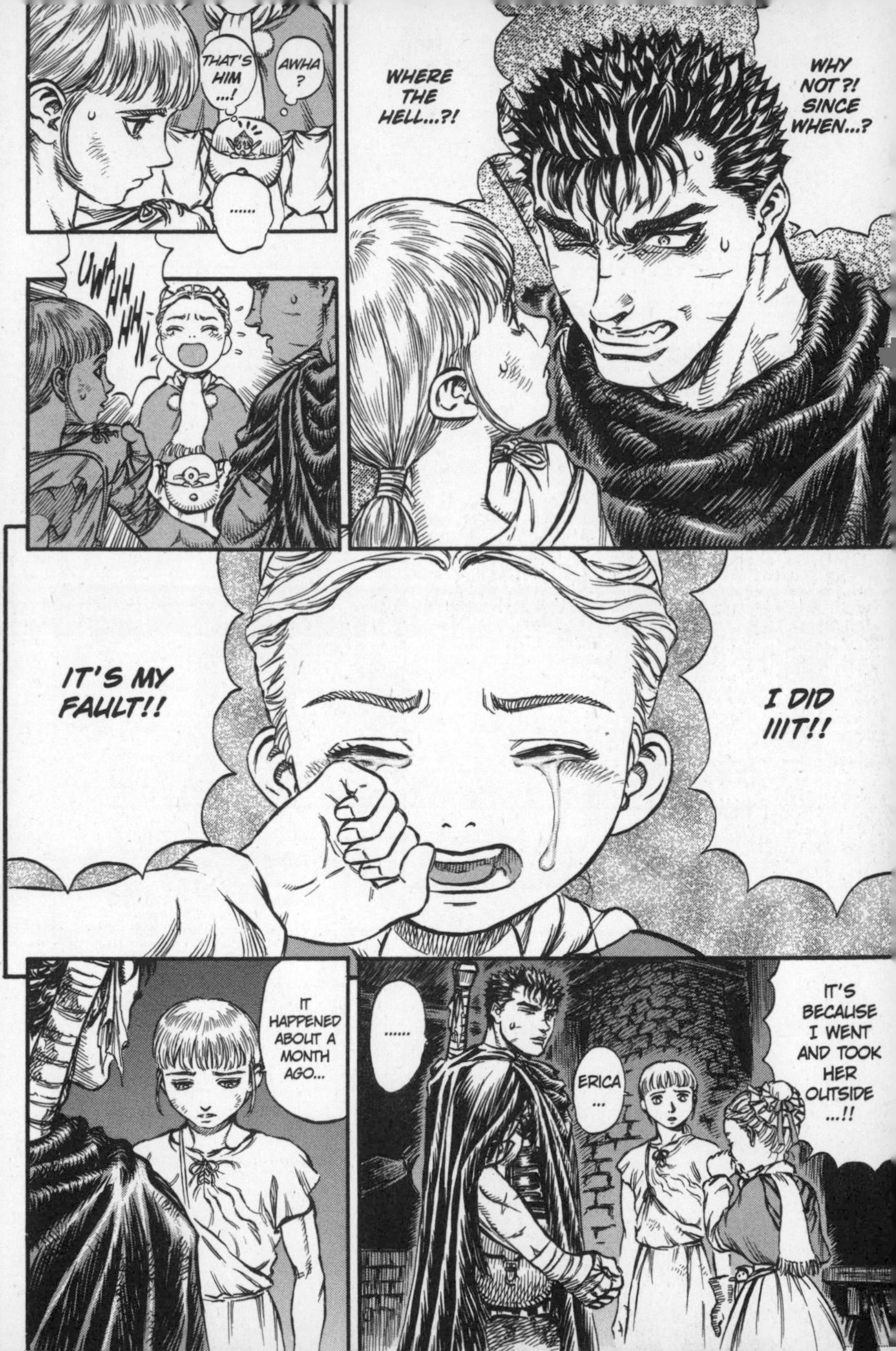
WHY NOT?! SINCE WHEN...?
WHERE THE HELL...?!
AWHA ?
THAT'S HIM ...!
......
UWAHHHHN
I DID IIIT!!
IT'S MY FAULT!!
IT'S BECAUSE I WENT AND TOOK HER OUTSIDE ...!!
ERICA ...
......
IT HAPPENED ABOUT A MONTH AGO...

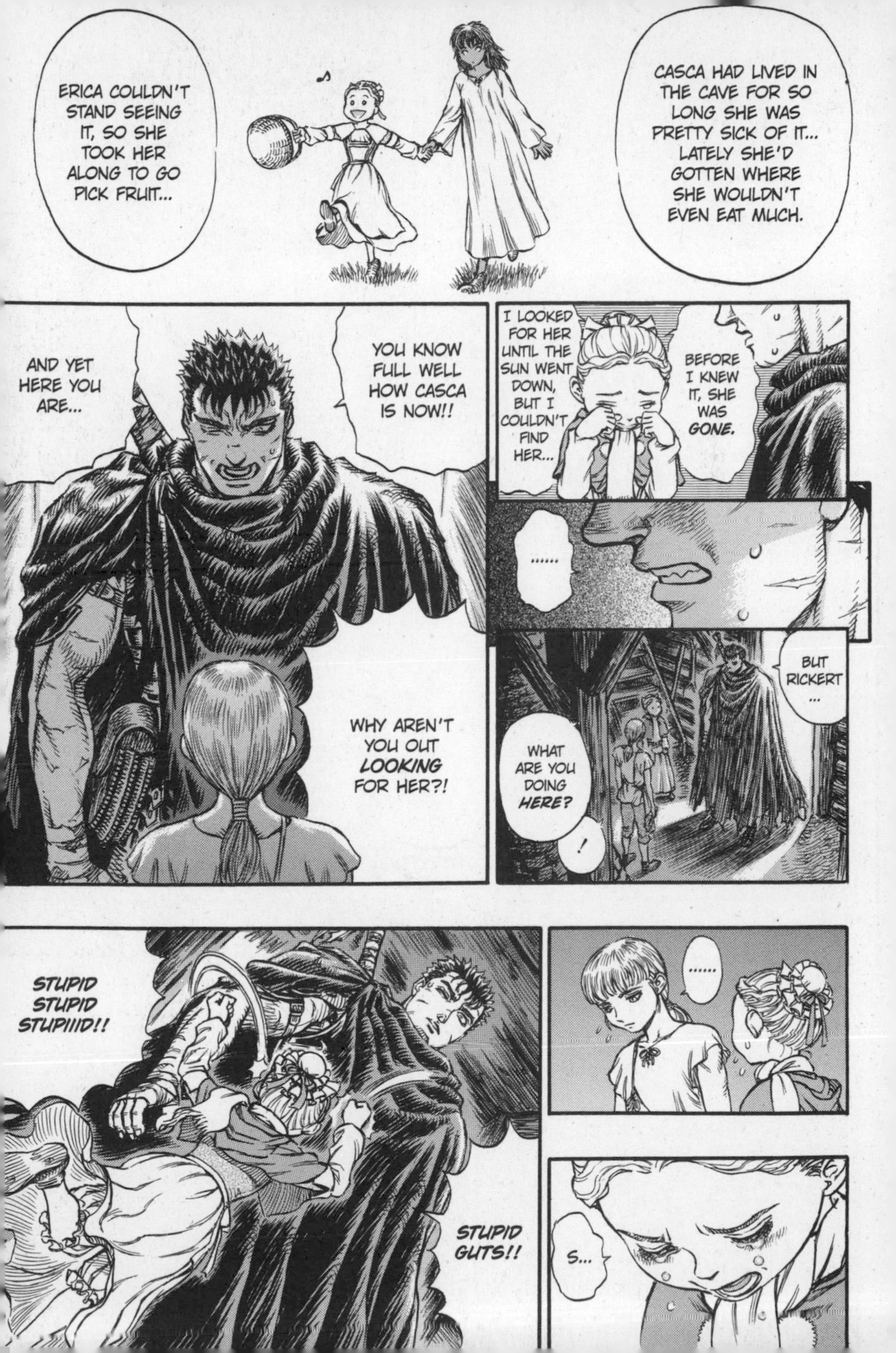
CASCA HAD LIVED IN THE CAVE FOR SO LONG SHE WAS PRETTY SICK OF IT... LATELY SHE'D GOTTEN WHERE SHE WOULDN'T EVEN EAT MUCH.
ERICA COULDN'T STAND SEEING IT, SO SHE TOOK HER ALONG TO GO PICK FRUIT...
BEFORE I KNEW IT, SHE WAS *GONE.*
I LOOKED FOR HER UNTIL THE SUN WENT DOWN, BUT I COULDN'T FIND HER...
......
BUT RICKERT ...
WHAT ARE YOU DOING *HERE?*
!
YOU KNOW FULL WELL HOW CASCA IS NOW!!
AND YET HERE YOU ARE...
WHY AREN'T YOU OUT *LOOKING* FOR HER?!
......
S...
STUPID STUPID STUPIIID!!
STUPID GUTS!!

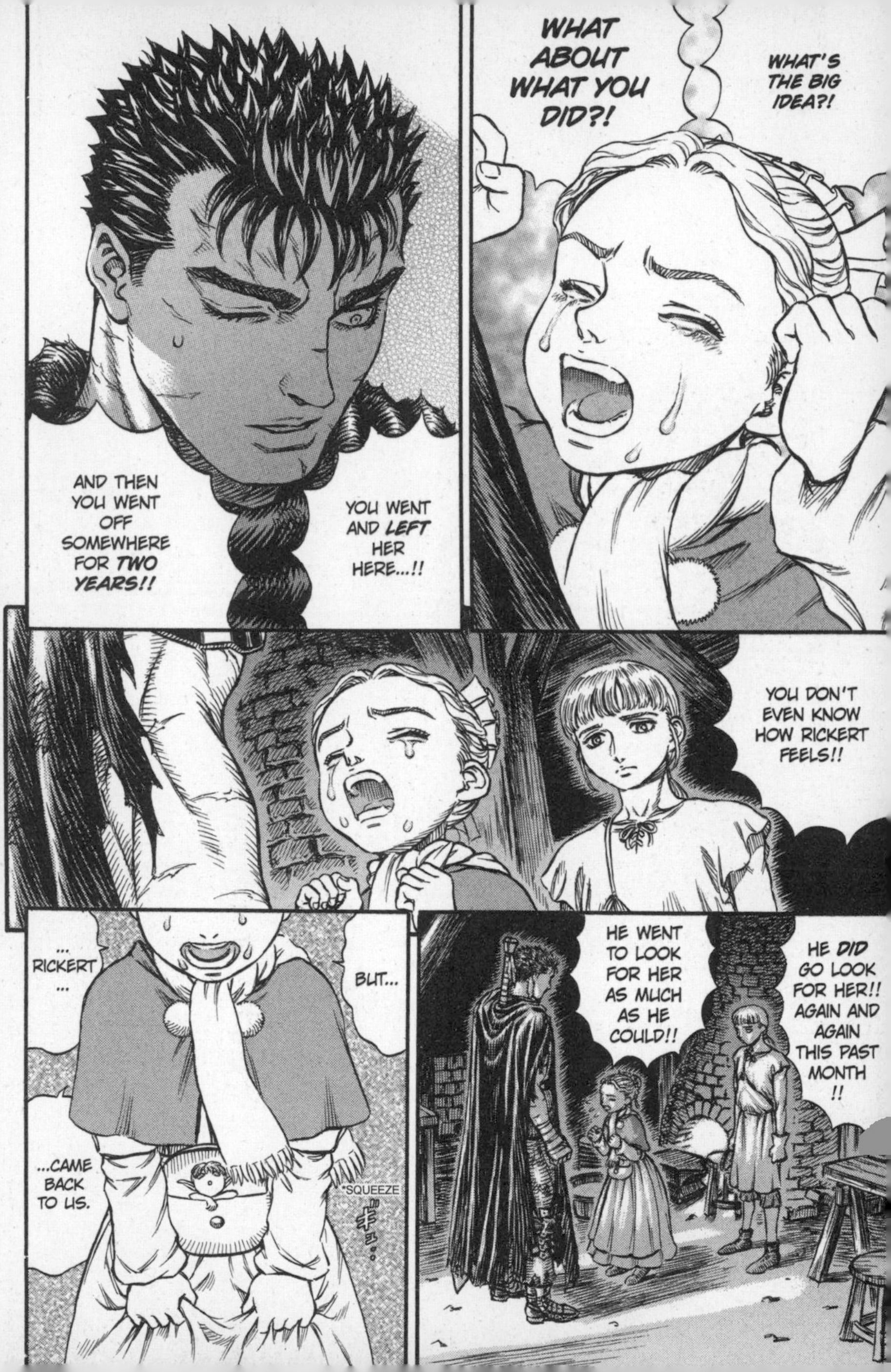
WHAT'S THE BIG IDEA?!
WHAT ABOUT WHAT YOU DID?!
YOU WENT AND LEFT HER HERE...!!
AND THEN YOU WENT OFF SOMEWHERE FOR TWO YEARS!!
YOU DON'T EVEN KNOW HOW RICKERT FEELS!!
HE DID GO LOOK FOR HER!! AGAIN AND AGAIN THIS PAST MONTH !!
HE WENT TO LOOK FOR HER AS MUCH AS HE COULD!!
BUT...
... RICKERT ...
...CAME BACK TO US.
*SQUEEZE

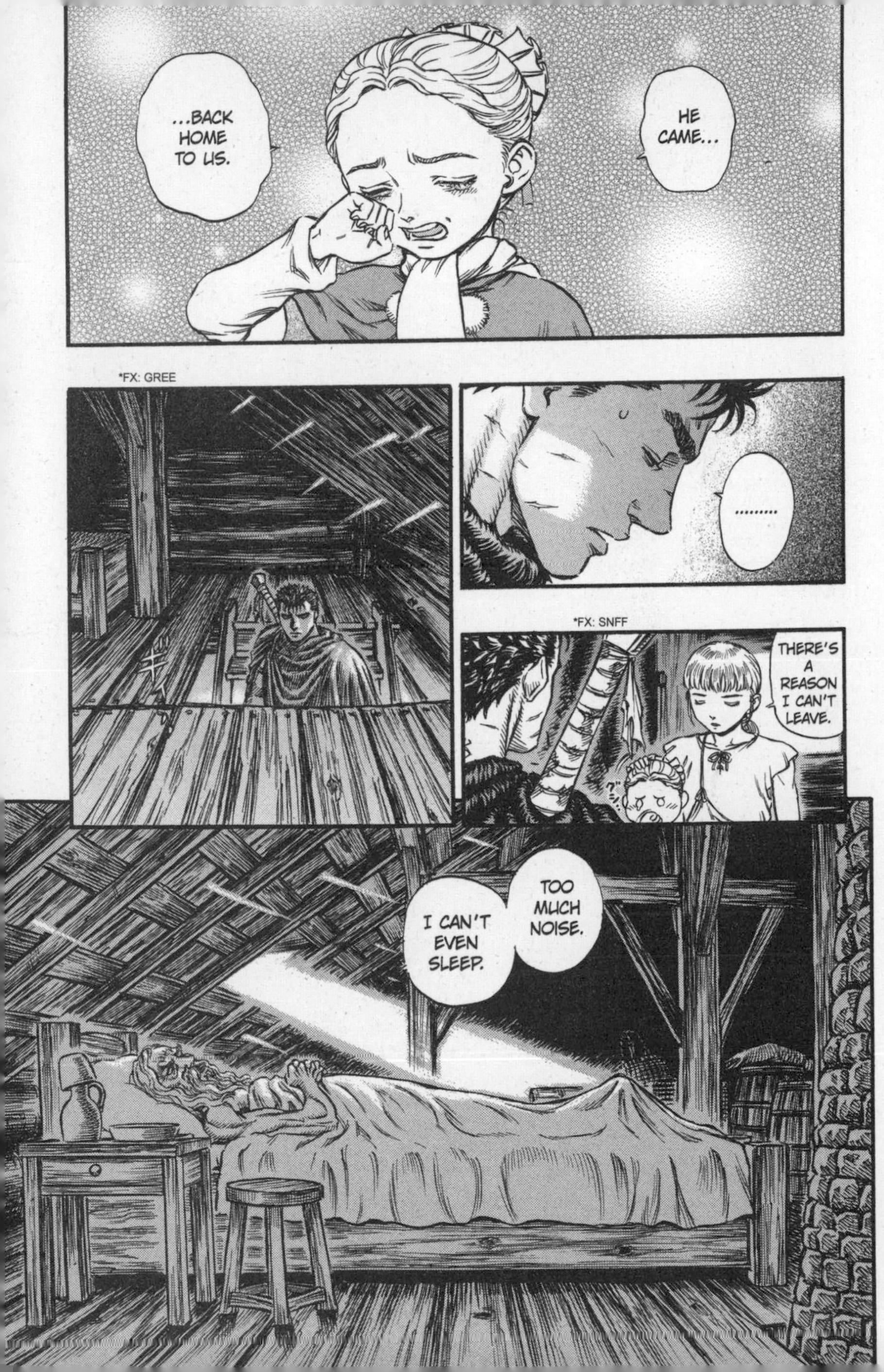

HE CAME...
...BACK HOME TO US.
....
*FX: SNFF
THERE'S A REASON I CAN'T LEAVE.
*FX: GREE
TOO MUCH NOISE.
I CAN'T EVEN SLEEP.

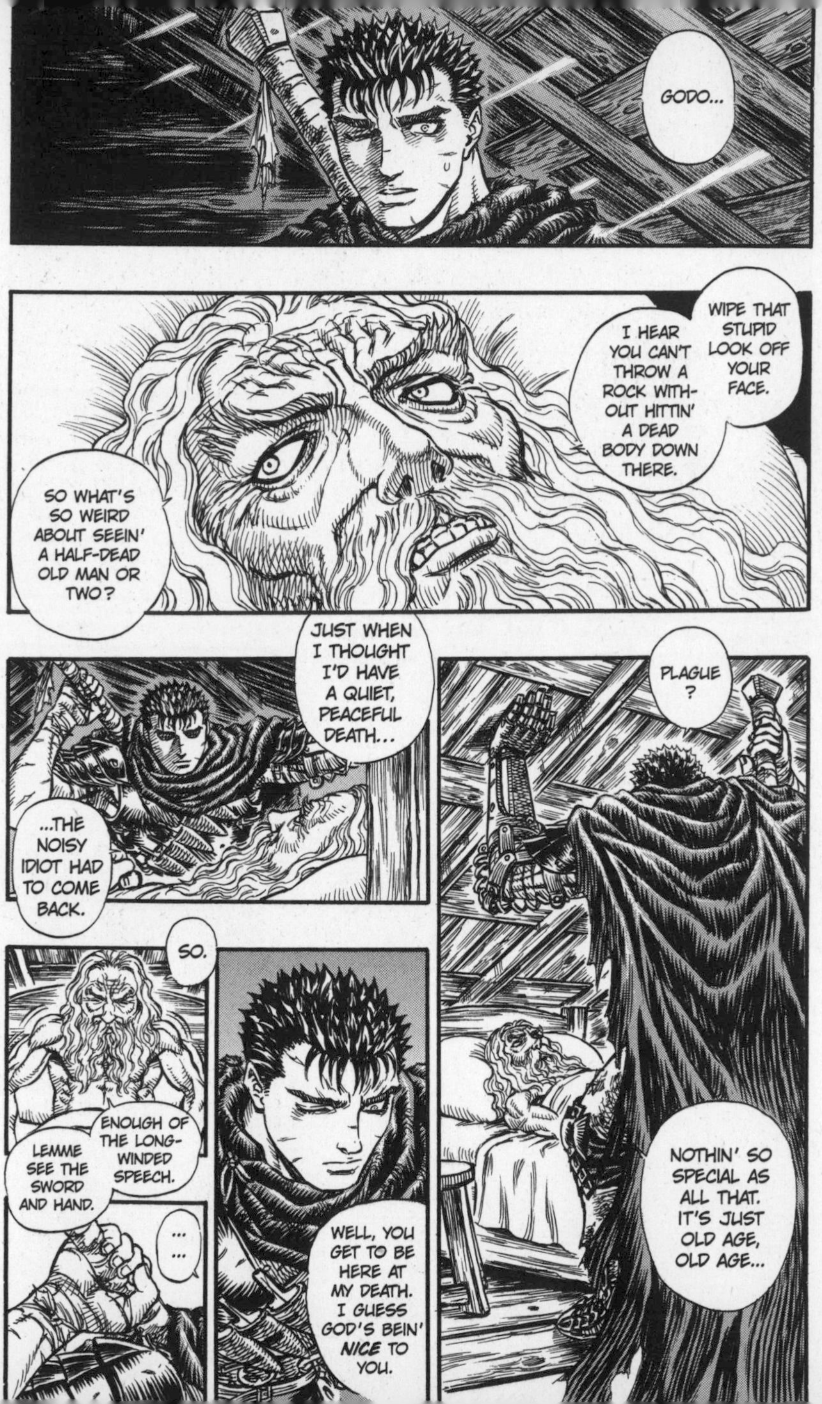
GODO...
WIPE THAT STUPID LOOK OFF YOUR FACE.
I HEAR YOU CAN'T THROW A ROCK WITH-OUT HITTIN' A DEAD BODY DOWN THERE.
SO WHAT'S SO WEIRD ABOUT SEEIN' A HALF-DEAD OLD MAN OR TWO?
PLAGUE?
NOTHIN' SO SPECIAL AS ALL THAT. IT'S JUST OLD AGE, OLD AGE...
JUST WHEN I THOUGHT I'D HAVE A QUIET, PEACEFUL DEATH...
...THE NOISY IDIOT HAD TO COME BACK.
WELL, YOU GET TO BE HERE AT MY DEATH. I GUESS GOD'S BEIN' *NICE* TO YOU.
SO.
ENOUGH OF THE LONG-WINDED SPEECH.
LEMME SEE THE SWORD AND HAND.
... ...

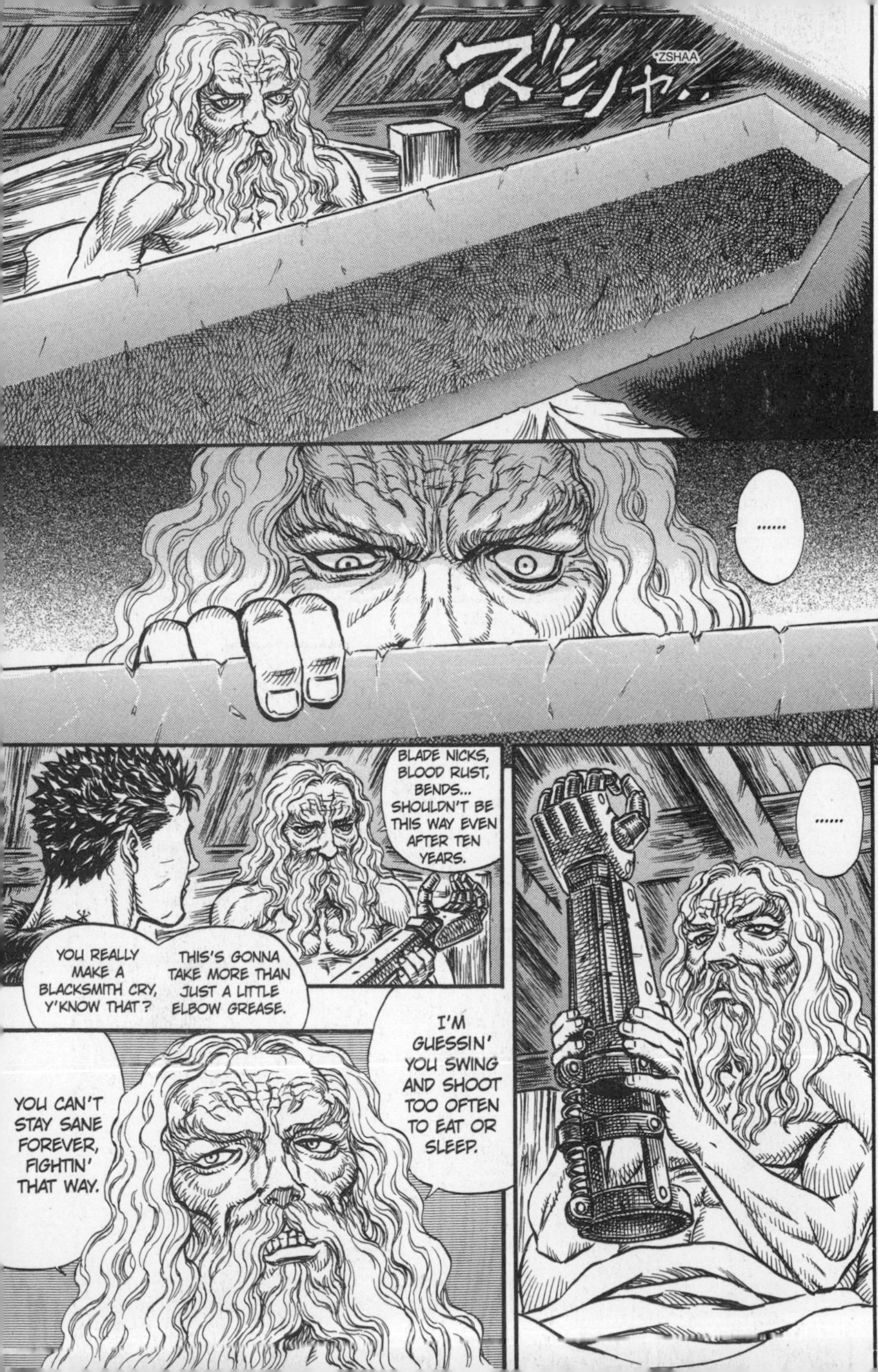
ズシャ
*ZSHAA
......
......
BLADE NICKS, BLOOD RUST, BENDS... SHOULDN'T BE THIS WAY EVEN AFTER TEN YEARS.
YOU REALLY MAKE A BLACKSMITH CRY, Y'KNOW THAT?
THIS'S GONNA TAKE MORE THAN JUST A LITTLE ELBOW GREASE.
I'M GUESSIN' YOU SWING AND SHOOT TOO OFTEN TO EAT OR SLEEP.
YOU CAN'T STAY SANE FOREVER, FIGHTIN' THAT WAY.

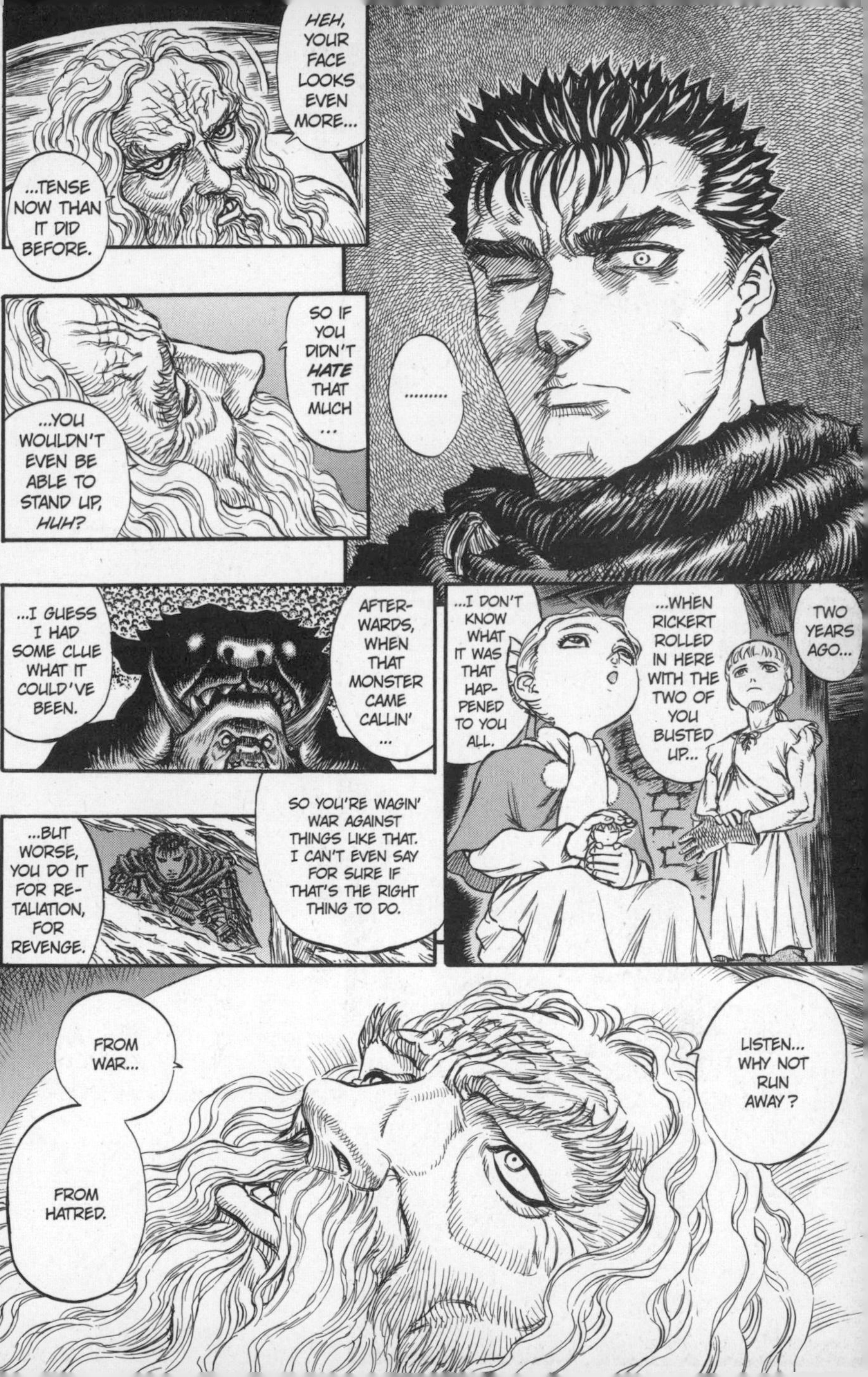
....
HEH, YOUR FACE LOOKS EVEN MORE...
...TENSE NOW THAN IT DID BEFORE.
SO IF YOU DIDN'T *HATE* THAT MUCH ...
...YOU WOULDN'T EVEN BE ABLE TO STAND UP, *HUH*?
TWO YEARS AGO...
...WHEN RICKERT ROLLED IN HERE WITH THE TWO OF YOU BUSTED UP...
...I DON'T KNOW WHAT IT WAS THAT HAPPENED TO YOU ALL.
AFTER-WARDS, WHEN THAT MONSTER CAME CALLIN' ...
...I GUESS I HAD SOME CLUE WHAT IT COULD'VE BEEN.
SO YOU'RE WAGIN' WAR AGAINST THINGS LIKE THAT. I CAN'T EVEN SAY FOR SURE IF THAT'S THE RIGHT THING TO DO.
...BUT WORSE, YOU DO IT FOR RE-TALIATION, FOR REVENGE.
LISTEN... WHY NOT RUN AWAY?
FROM WAR...
FROM HATRED.

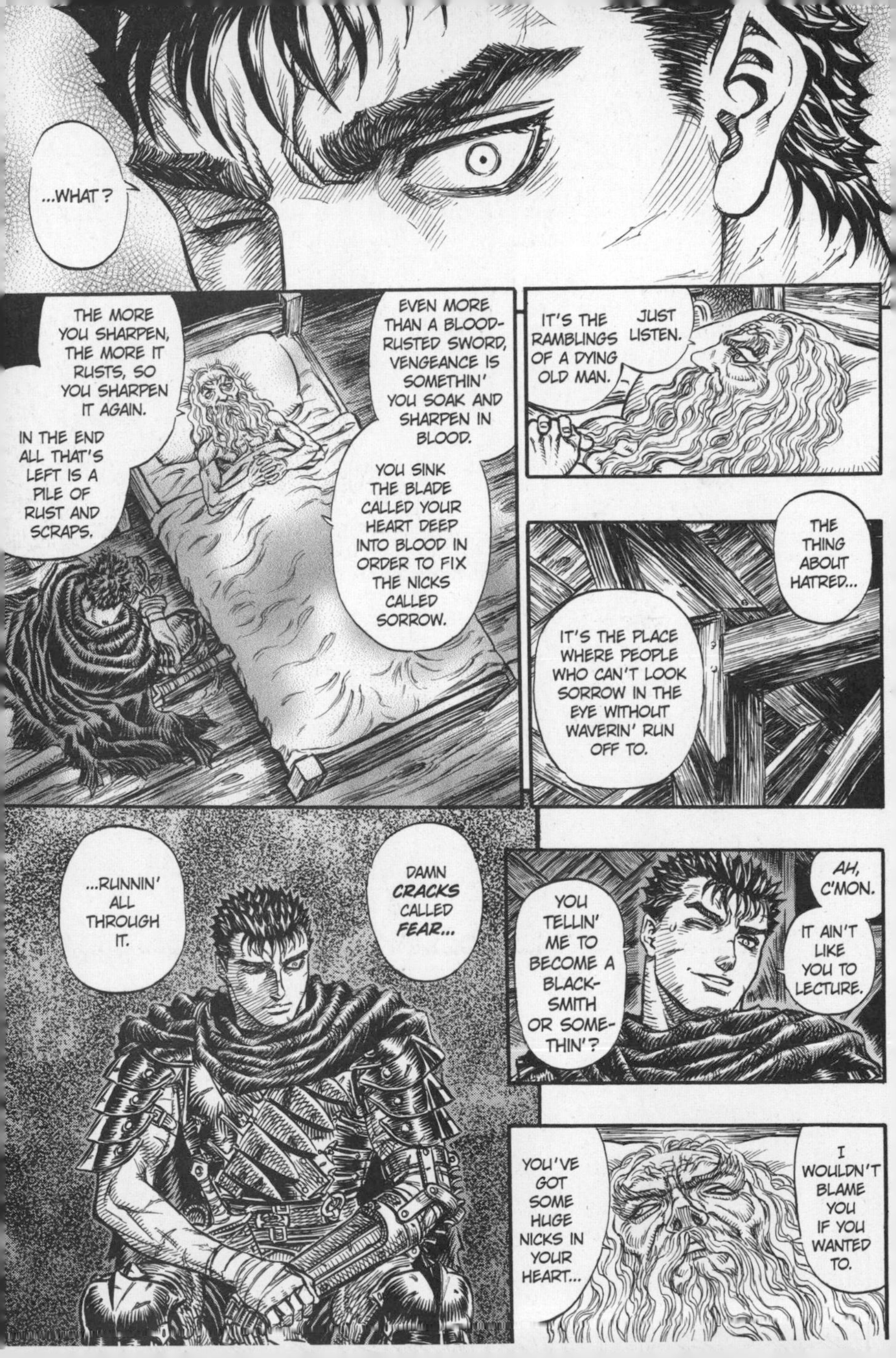

...WHAT?
JUST LISTEN.
IT'S THE RAMBLINGS OF A DYING OLD MAN.
THE THING ABOUT HATRED...
IT'S THE PLACE WHERE PEOPLE WHO CAN'T LOOK SORROW IN THE EYE WITHOUT WAVERIN' RUN OFF TO.
EVEN MORE THAN A BLOOD-RUSTED SWORD, VENGEANCE IS SOMETHIN' YOU SOAK AND SHARPEN IN BLOOD.
YOU SINK THE BLADE CALLED YOUR HEART DEEP INTO BLOOD IN ORDER TO FIX THE NICKS CALLED SORROW.
THE MORE YOU SHARPEN, THE MORE IT RUSTS, SO YOU SHARPEN IT AGAIN.
IN THE END ALL THAT'S LEFT IS A PILE OF RUST AND SCRAPS.
AH, C'MON.
IT AIN'T LIKE YOU TO LECTURE.
YOU TELLIN' ME TO BECOME A BLACK-SMITH OR SOME-THIN'?
I WOULDN'T BLAME YOU IF YOU WANTED TO.
YOU'VE GOT SOME HUGE NICKS IN YOUR HEART...
DAMN ***CRACKS*** CALLED ***FEAR...***
...RUNNIN' ALL THROUGH IT.

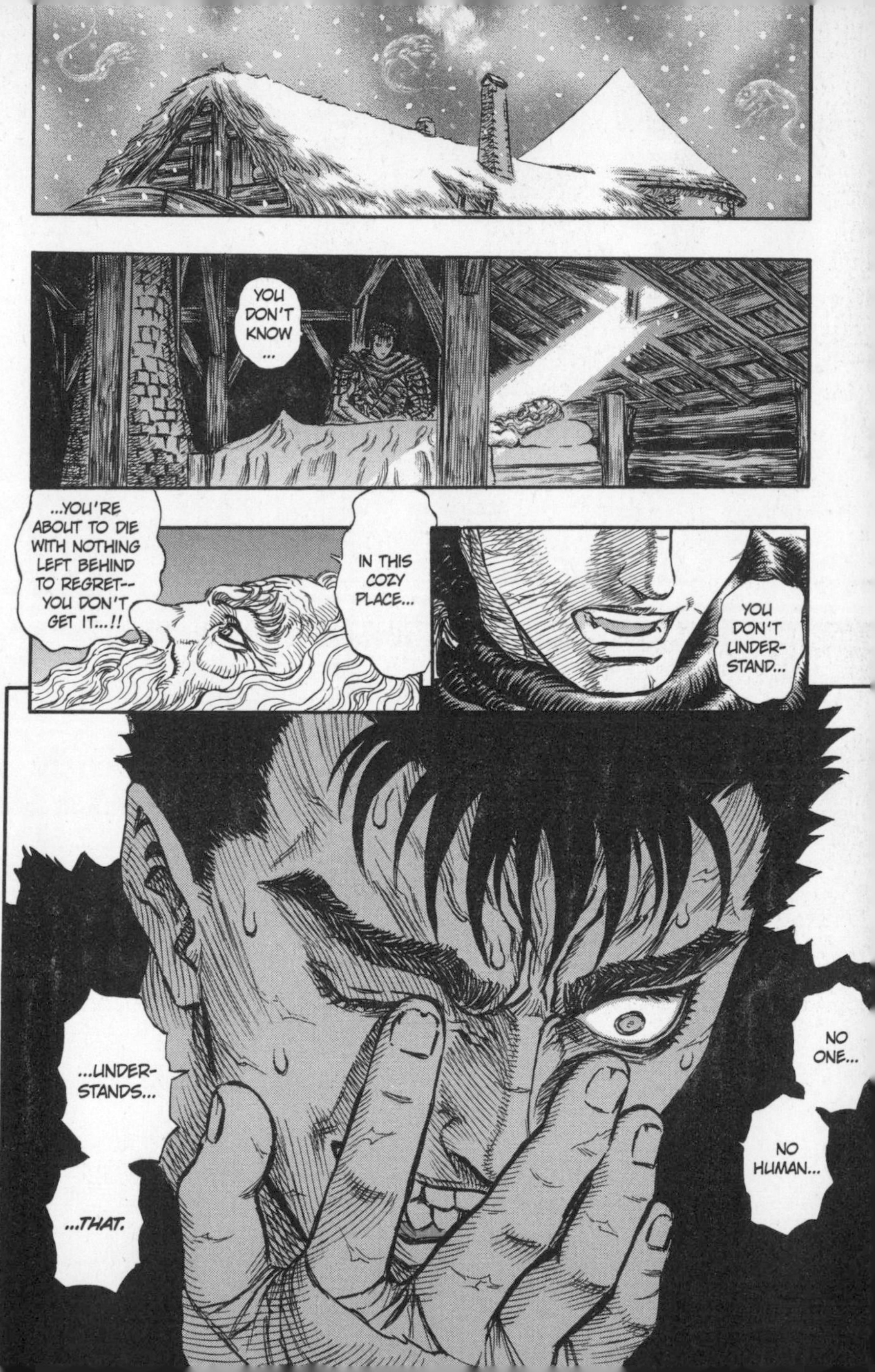

YOU DON'T KNOW ...
YOU DON'T UNDER-STAND...
IN THIS COZY PLACE...
...YOU'RE ABOUT TO DIE WITH NOTHING LEFT BEHIND TO REGRET-- YOU DON'T GET IT...!!
NO ONE...
NO HUMAN...
...UNDER-STANDS...
...THAT.

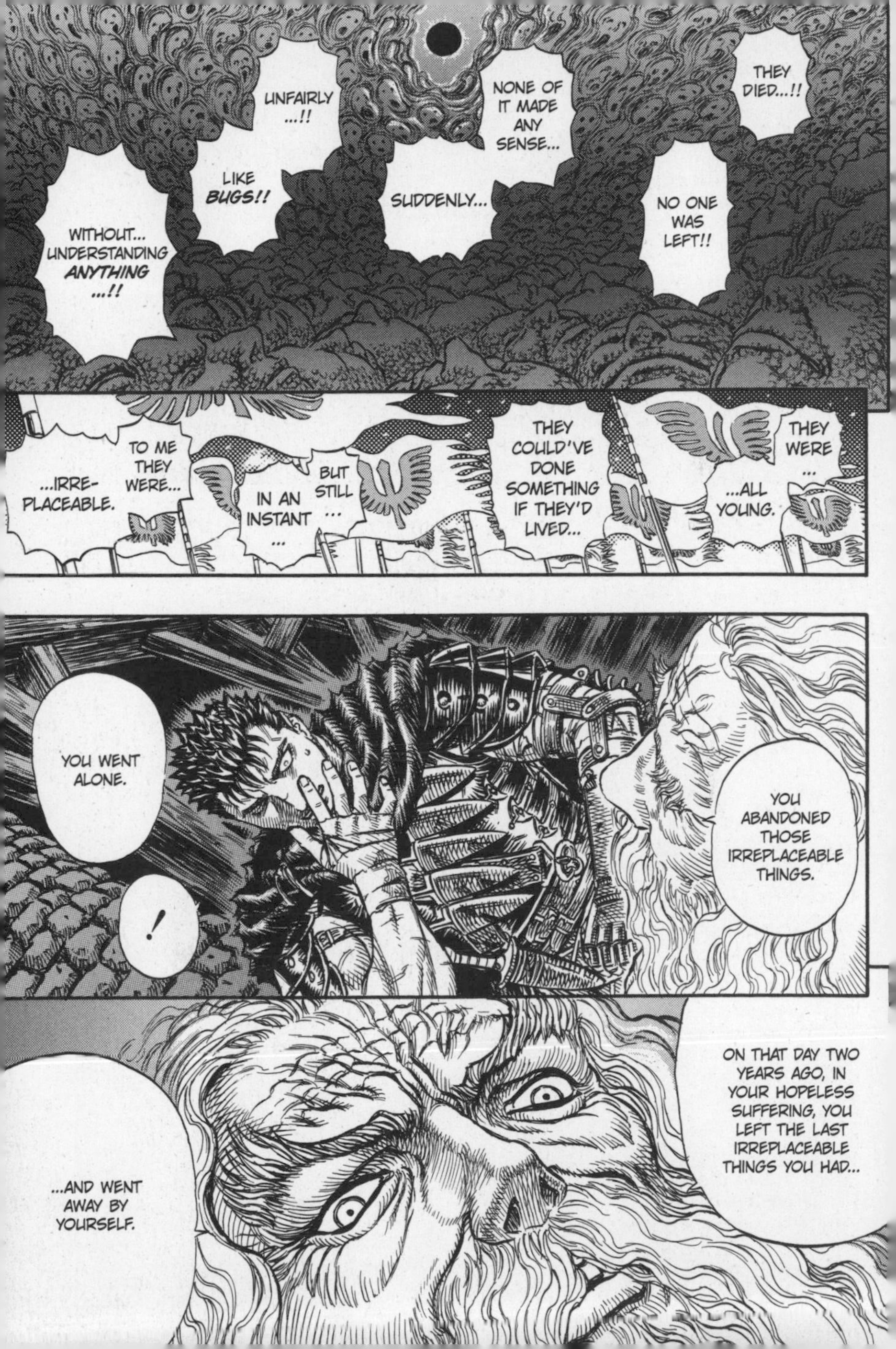
THEY DIED...!!
NO ONE WAS LEFT!!
NONE OF IT MADE ANY SENSE...
SUDDENLY...
UNFAIRLY ...!!
LIKE **BUGS!!**
WITHOUT... UNDERSTANDING **ANYTHING** ...!!
THEY WERE ...
...ALL YOUNG.
THEY COULD'VE DONE SOMETHING IF THEY'D LIVED...
BUT STILL ...
IN AN INSTANT ...
TO ME THEY WERE...
...IRRE-PLACEABLE.
YOU ABANDONED THOSE IRREPLACEABLE THINGS.
YOU WENT ALONE.
!
ON THAT DAY TWO YEARS AGO, IN YOUR HOPELESS SUFFERING, YOU LEFT THE LAST IRREPLACEABLE THINGS YOU HAD...
...AND WENT AWAY BY YOURSELF.

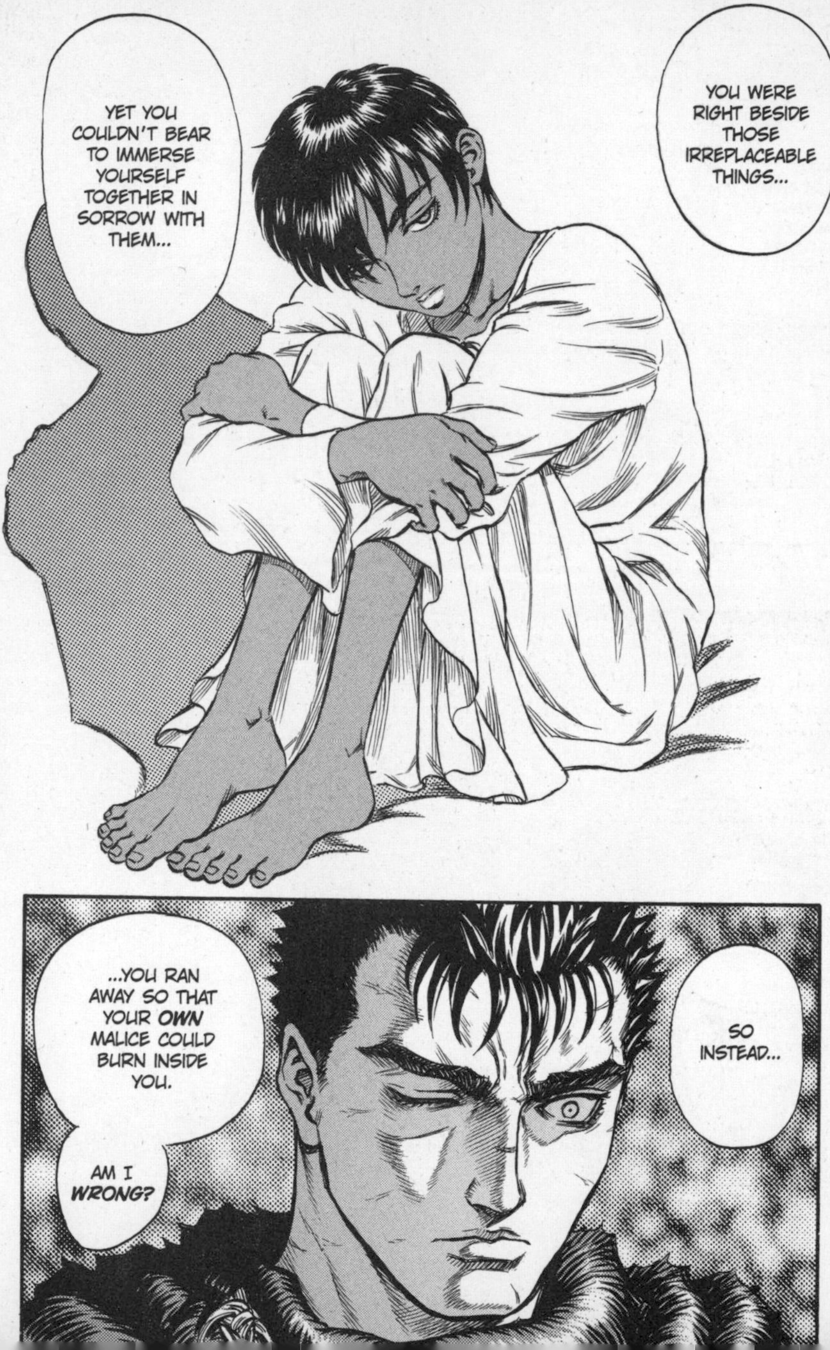
YOU WERE RIGHT BESIDE THOSE IRREPLACEABLE THINGS...
YET YOU COULDN'T BEAR TO IMMERSE YOURSELF TOGETHER IN SORROW WITH THEM...
SO INSTEAD...
...YOU RAN AWAY SO THAT YOUR ***OWN*** MALICE COULD BURN INSIDE YOU.
AM I ***WRONG?***

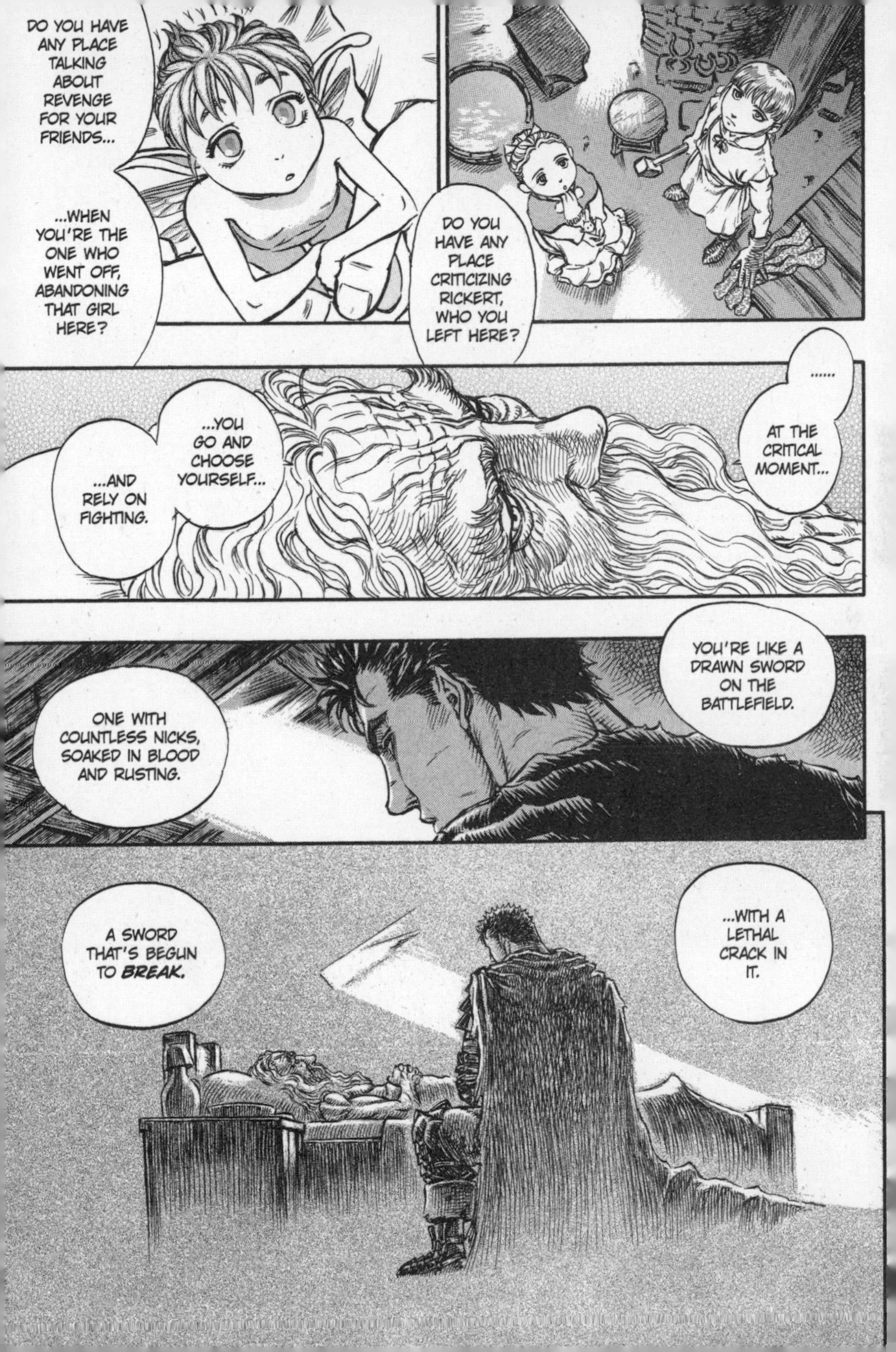
DO YOU HAVE ANY PLACE CRITICIZING RICKERT, WHO YOU LEFT HERE?
DO YOU HAVE ANY PLACE TALKING ABOUT REVENGE FOR YOUR FRIENDS...
...WHEN YOU'RE THE ONE WHO WENT OFF, ABANDONING THAT GIRL HERE?
......
AT THE CRITICAL MOMENT...
...YOU GO AND CHOOSE YOURSELF...
...AND RELY ON FIGHTING.
YOU'RE LIKE A DRAWN SWORD ON THE BATTLEFIELD.
ONE WITH COUNTLESS NICKS, SOAKED IN BLOOD AND RUSTING.
...WITH A LETHAL CRACK IN IT.
A SWORD THAT'S BEGUN TO *BREAK.*

BERSERK

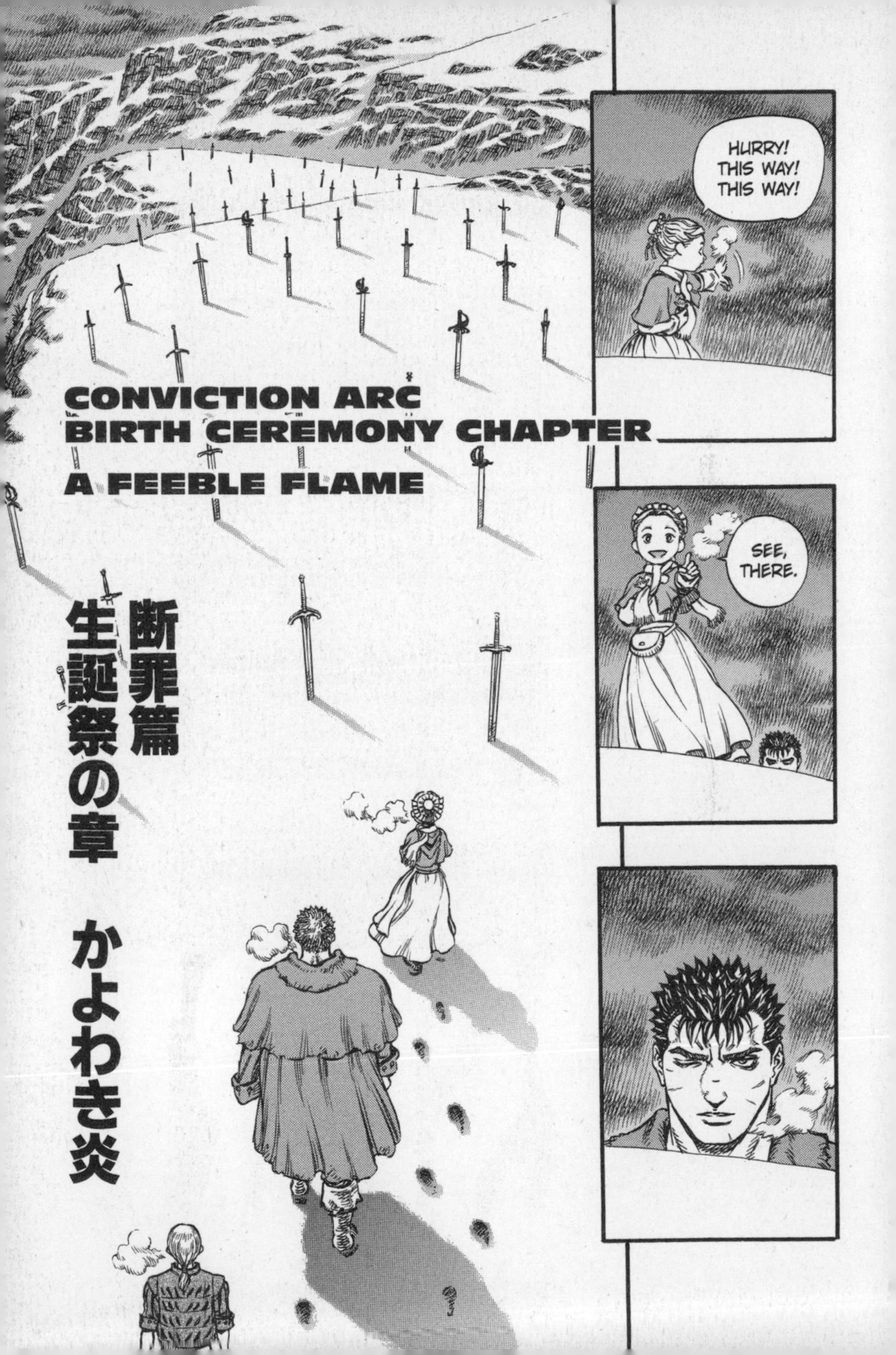
HURRY! THIS WAY! THIS WAY!
SEE, THERE.
CONVICTION ARC
BIRTH CEREMONY CHAPTER
A FEEBLE FLAME
断罪篇
生誕祭の章
かよわき炎

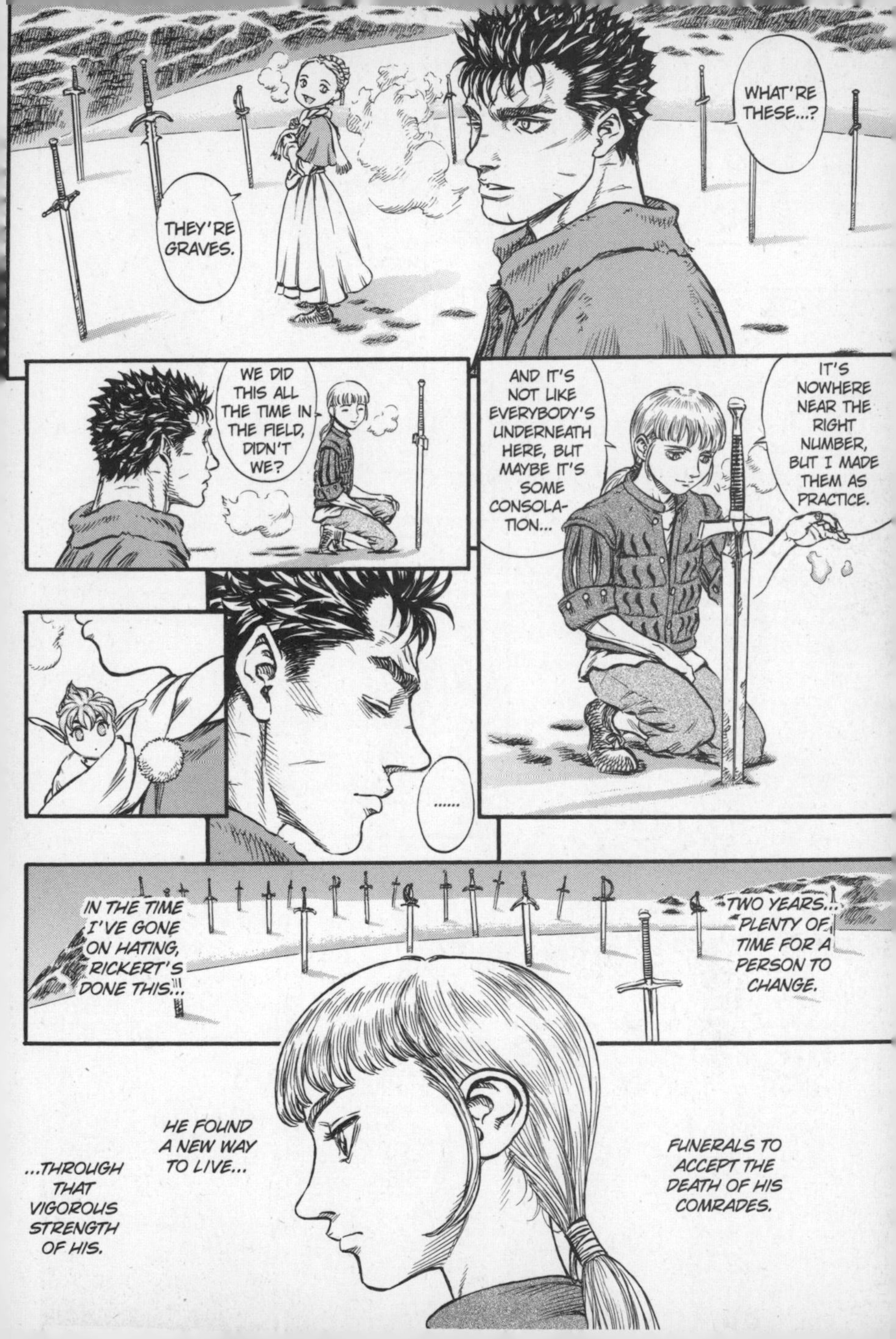
WHAT'RE THESE...?
THEY'RE GRAVES.
IT'S NOWHERE NEAR THE RIGHT NUMBER, BUT I MADE THEM AS PRACTICE.
AND IT'S NOT LIKE EVERYBODY'S UNDERNEATH HERE, BUT MAYBE IT'S SOME CONSOLATION...
WE DID THIS ALL THE TIME IN THE FIELD, DIDN'T WE?
......
TWO YEARS... PLENTY OF TIME FOR A PERSON TO CHANGE.
IN THE TIME I'VE GONE ON HATING, RICKERT'S DONE THIS...
FUNERALS TO ACCEPT THE DEATH OF HIS COMRADES.
HE FOUND A NEW WAY TO LIVE...
...THROUGH THAT VIGOROUS STRENGTH OF HIS.

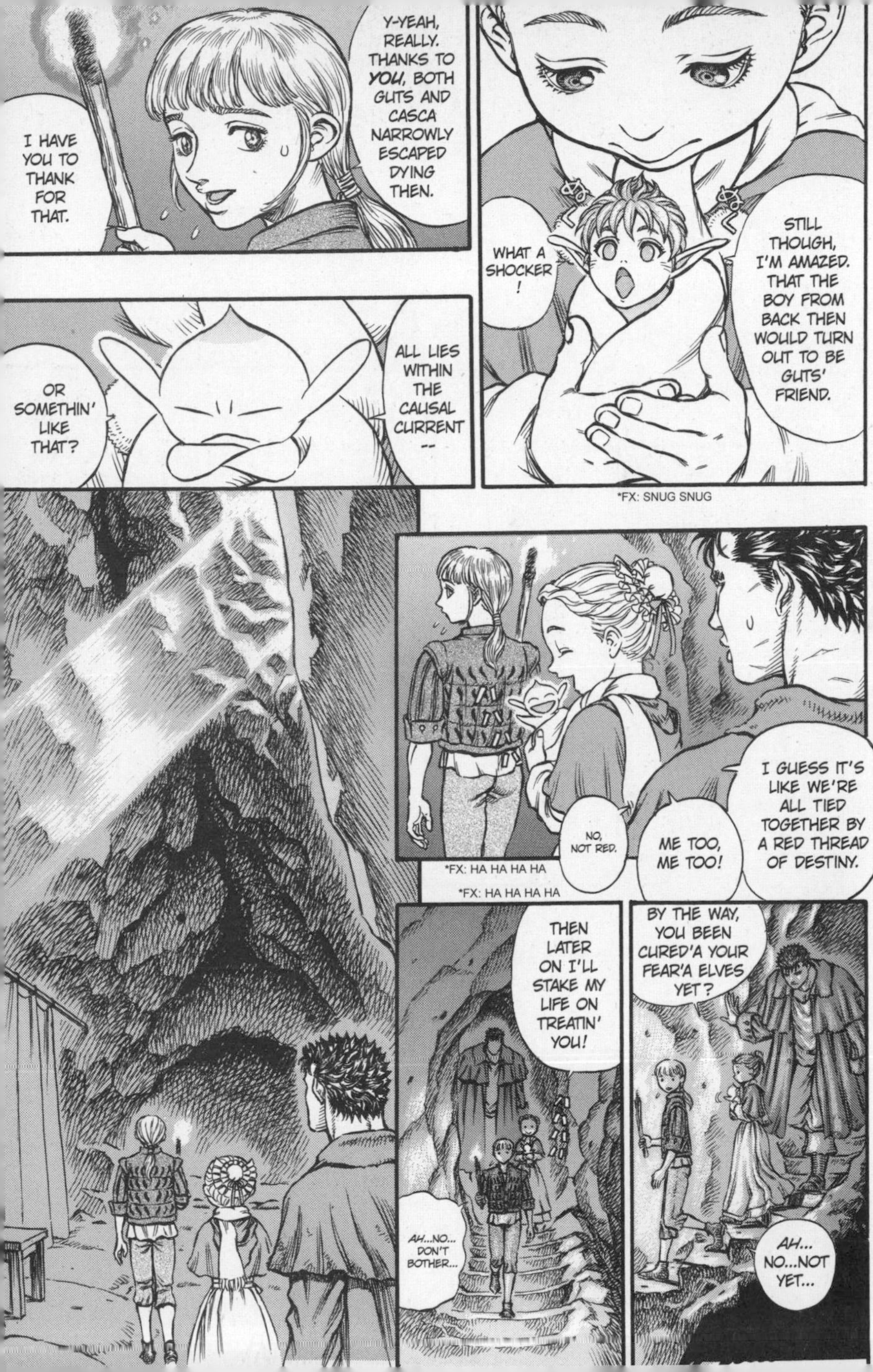
STILL THOUGH, I'M AMAZED. THAT THE BOY FROM BACK THEN WOULD TURN OUT TO BE GUTS' FRIEND.
WHAT A SHOCKER!
Y-YEAH, REALLY. THANKS TO YOU, BOTH GUTS AND CASCA NARROWLY ESCAPED DYING THEN.
I HAVE YOU TO THANK FOR THAT.
ALL LIES WITHIN THE CAUSAL CURRENT --
OR SOMETHIN' LIKE THAT?
*FX: SNUG SNUG
I GUESS IT'S LIKE WE'RE ALL TIED TOGETHER BY A RED THREAD OF DESTINY.
ME TOO, ME TOO!
NO, NOT RED.
*FX: HA HA HA HA
*FX: HA HA HA HA
BY THE WAY, YOU BEEN CURED'A YOUR FEAR'A ELVES YET?
AH... NO...NOT YET...
THEN LATER ON I'LL STAKE MY LIFE ON TREATIN' YOU!
AH...NO... DON'T BOTHER...

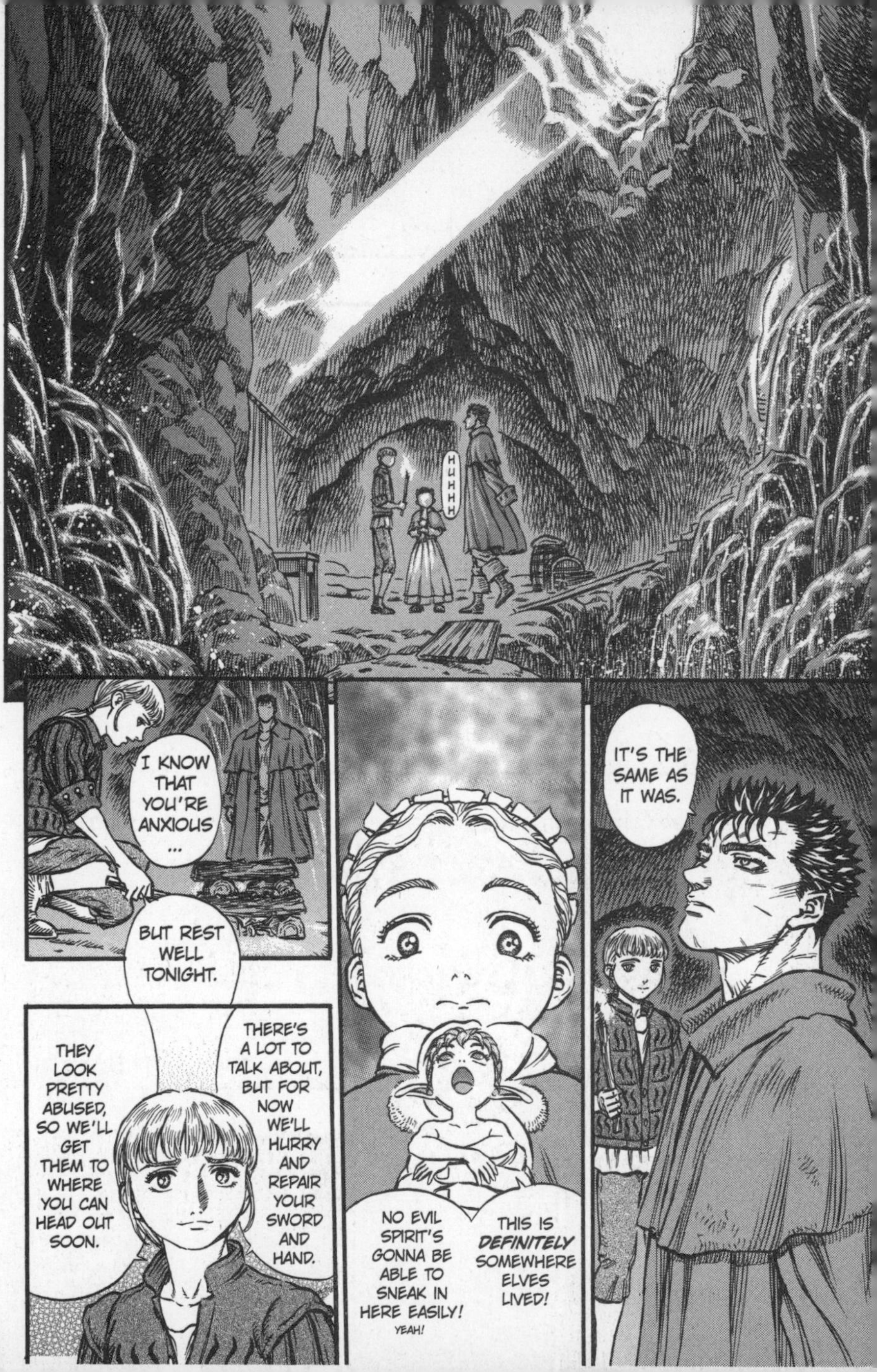
HUHHH
IT'S THE SAME AS IT WAS.
THIS IS *DEFINITELY* SOMEWHERE ELVES LIVED!
NO EVIL SPIRIT'S GONNA BE ABLE TO SNEAK IN HERE EASILY!
YEAH!
I KNOW THAT YOU'RE ANXIOUS ...
BUT REST WELL TONIGHT.
THERE'S A LOT TO TALK ABOUT, BUT FOR NOW WE'LL HURRY AND REPAIR YOUR SWORD AND HAND.
THEY LOOK PRETTY ABUSED, SO WE'LL GET THEM TO WHERE YOU CAN HEAD OUT SOON.

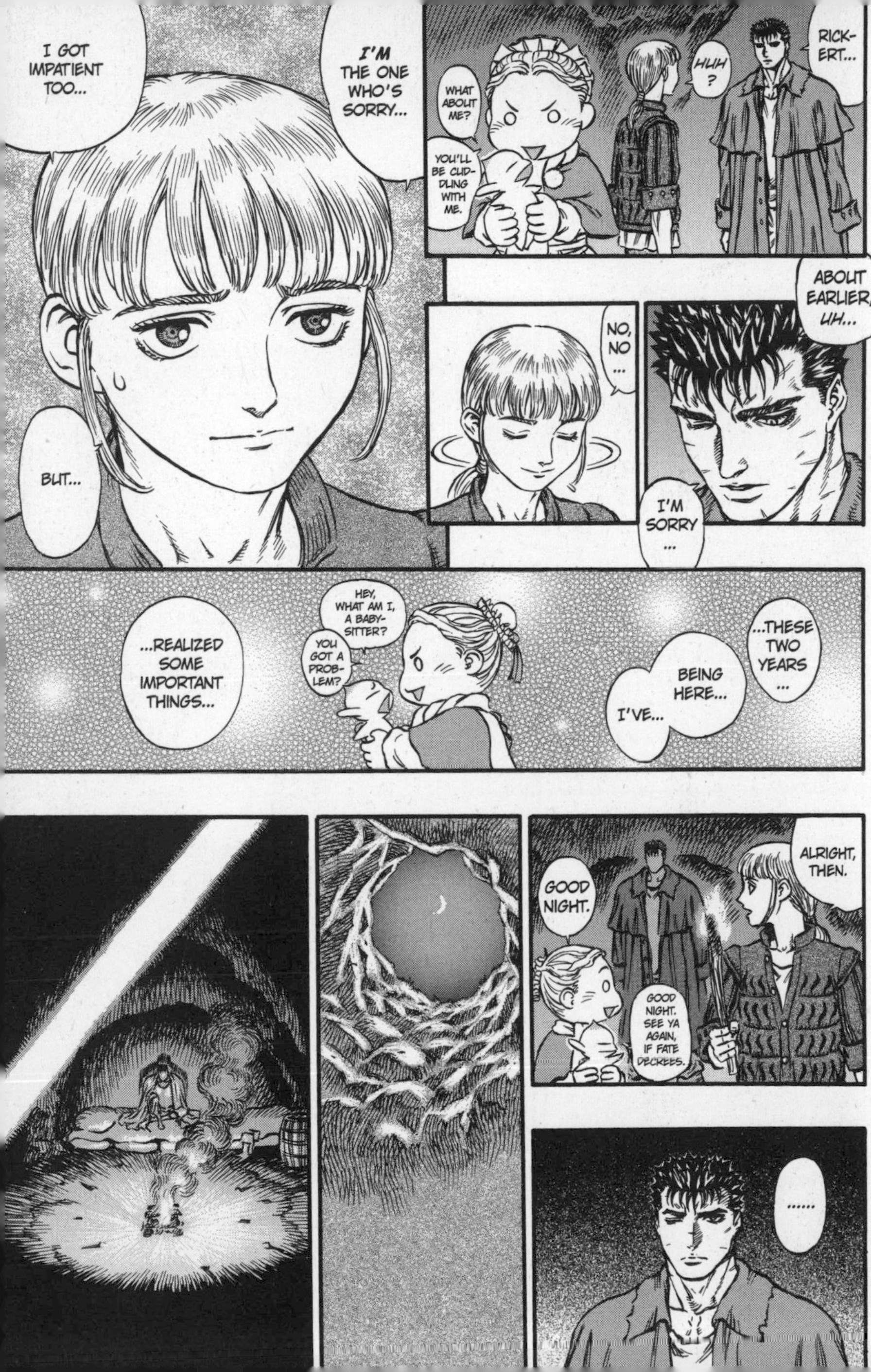
RICK-ERT...
HUH?
WHAT ABOUT ME?
YOU'LL BE CUDDLING WITH ME.
ABOUT EARLIER, UH...
I'M SORRY...
NO, NO...
I'M THE ONE WHO'S SORRY...
I GOT IMPATIENT TOO...
BUT...
...THESE TWO YEARS...
BEING HERE...
I'VE...
...REALIZED SOME IMPORTANT THINGS...
HEY, WHAT AM I, A BABY-SITTER?
YOU GOT A PROBLEM?
ALRIGHT, THEN.
GOOD NIGHT.
GOOD NIGHT. SEE YA AGAIN, IF FATE DECREES.
......

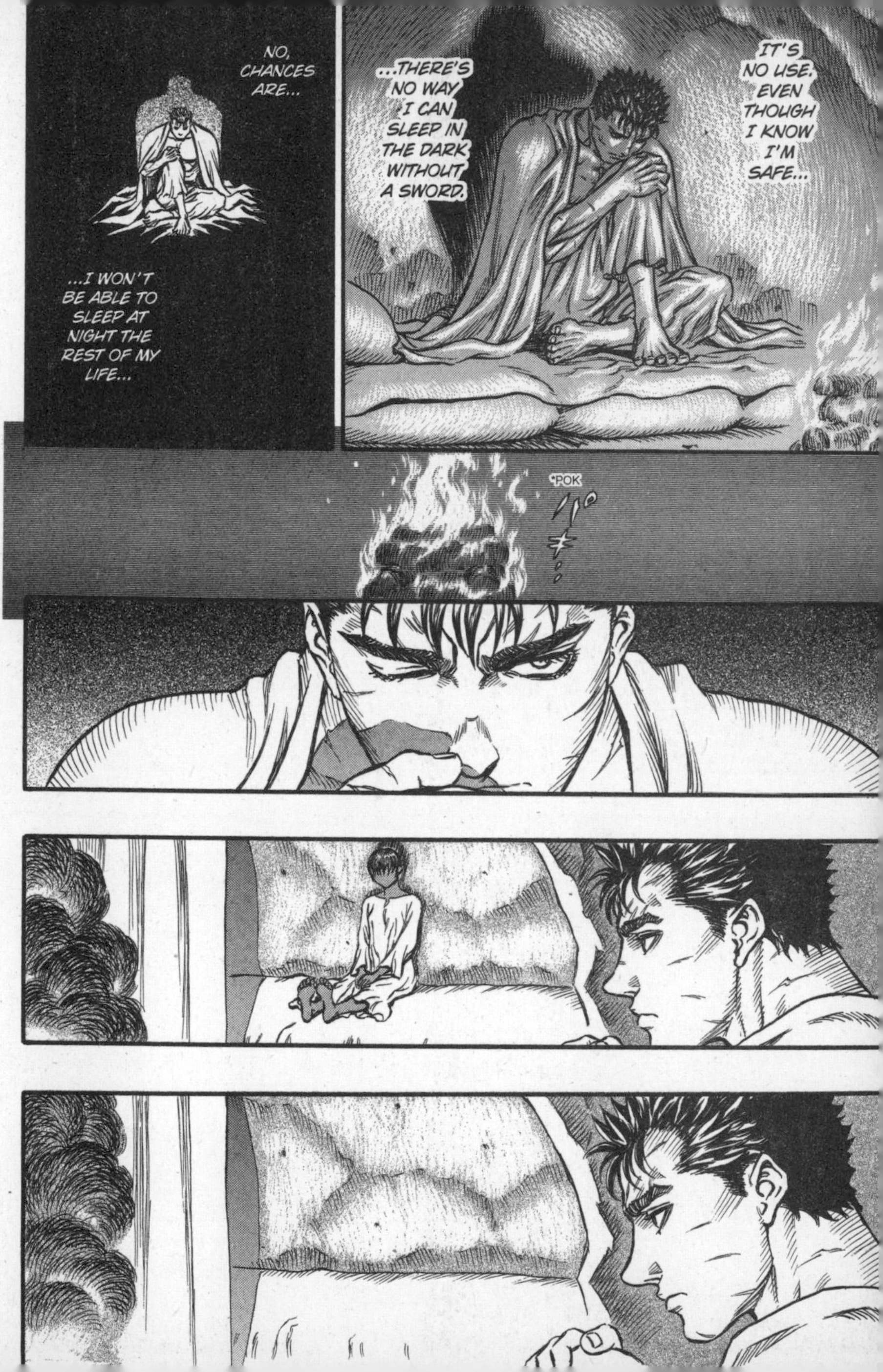
IT'S NO USE, EVEN THOUGH I KNOW I'M SAFE...
...THERE'S NO WAY I CAN SLEEP IN THE DARK WITHOUT A SWORD.
NO, CHANCES ARE...
...I WON'T BE ABLE TO SLEEP AT NIGHT THE REST OF MY LIFE...
*POK

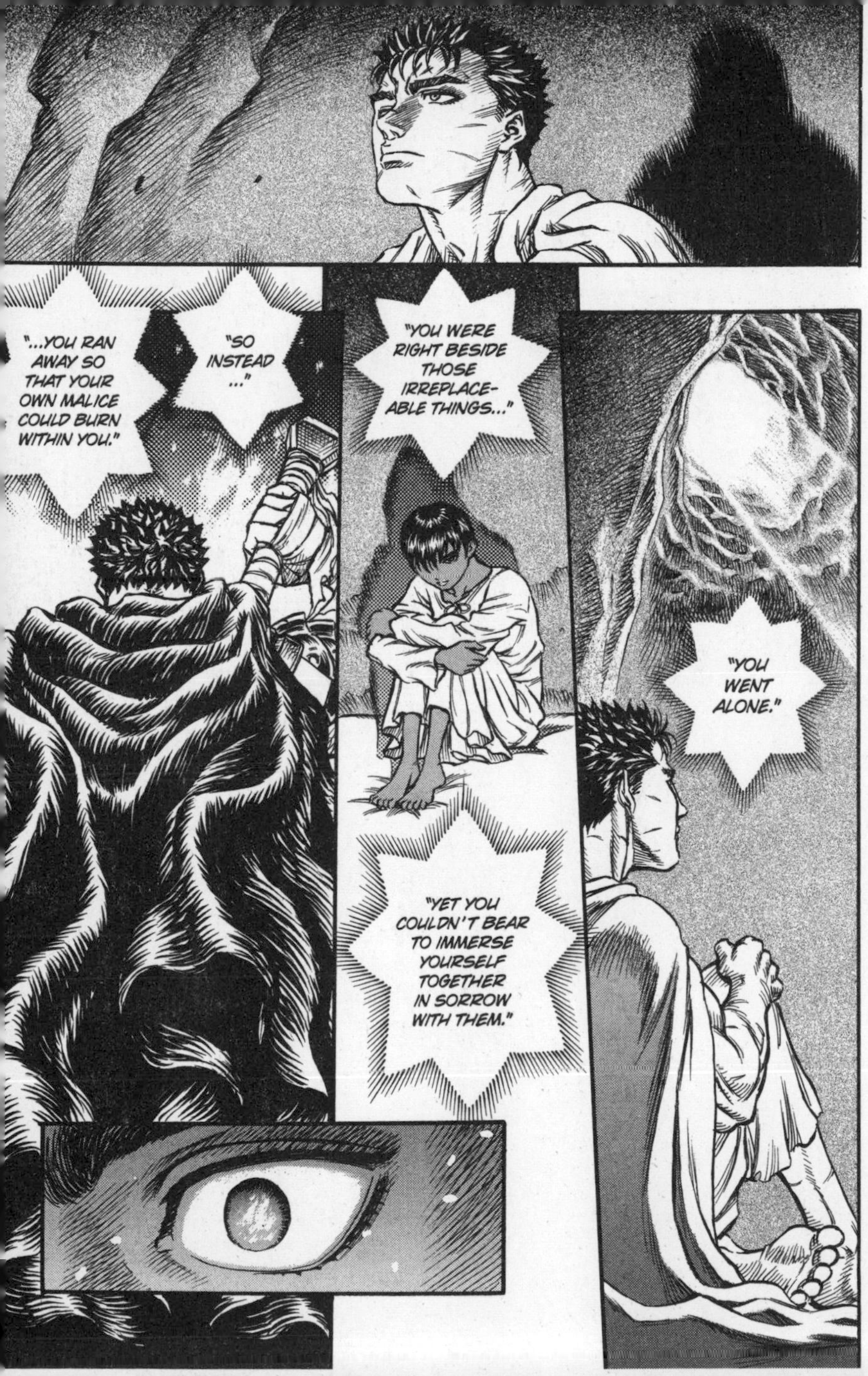
"YOU WENT ALONE."
"YOU WERE RIGHT BESIDE THOSE IRREPLACE-ABLE THINGS..."
"YET YOU COULDN'T BEAR TO IMMERSE YOURSELF TOGETHER IN SORROW WITH THEM."
"SO INSTEAD ..."
"...YOU RAN AWAY SO THAT YOUR OWN MALICE COULD BURN WITHIN YOU."

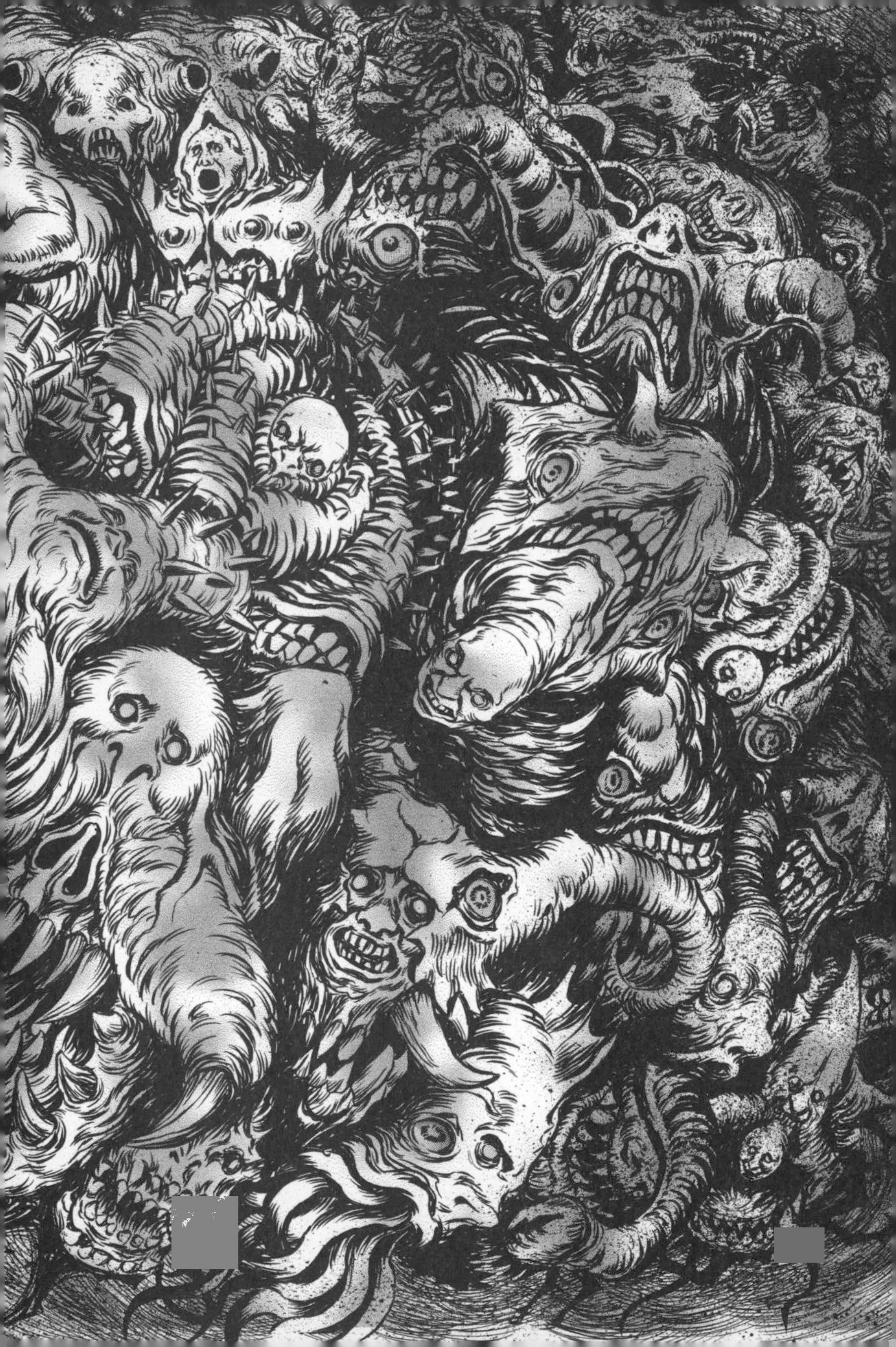

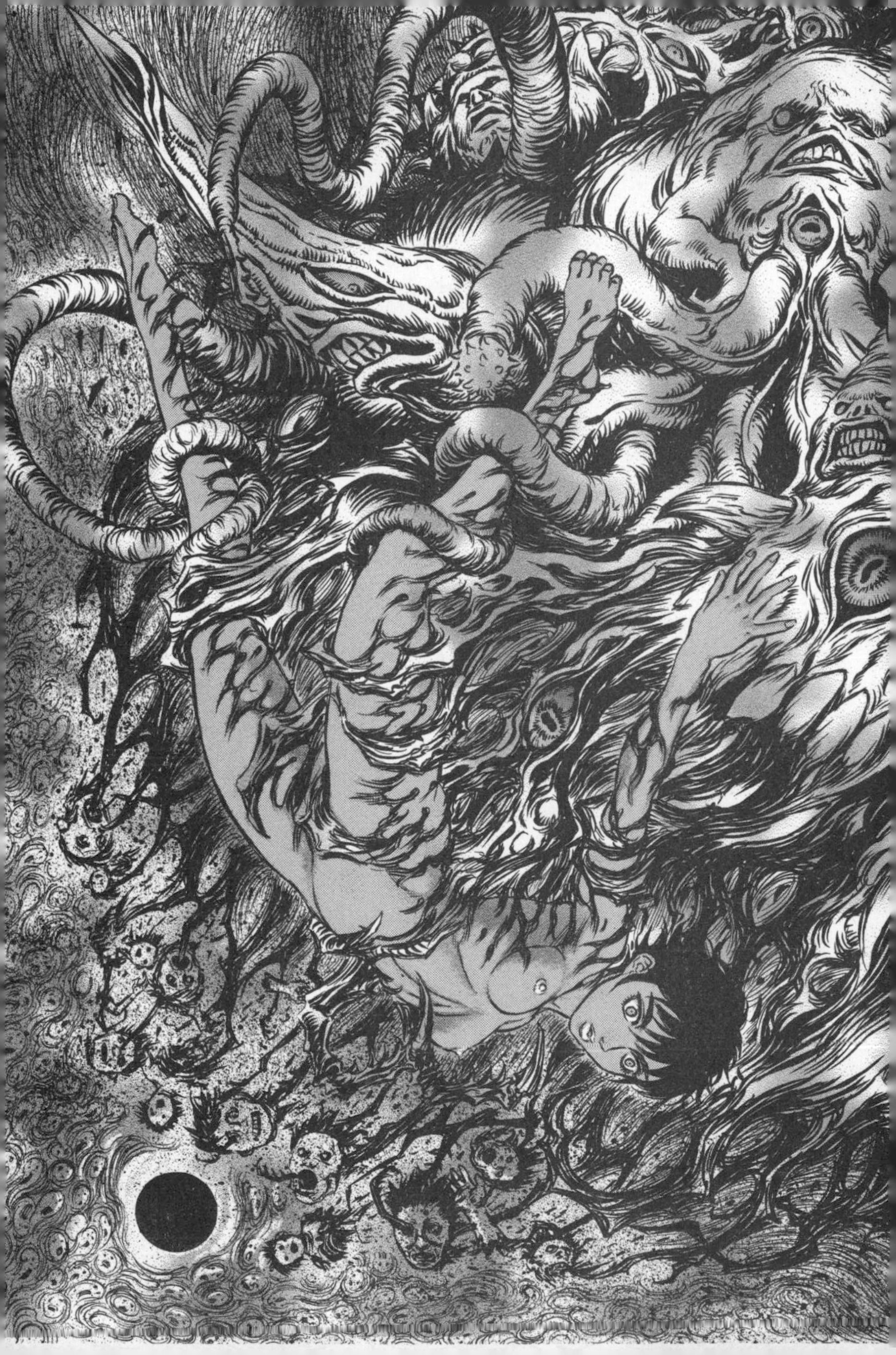

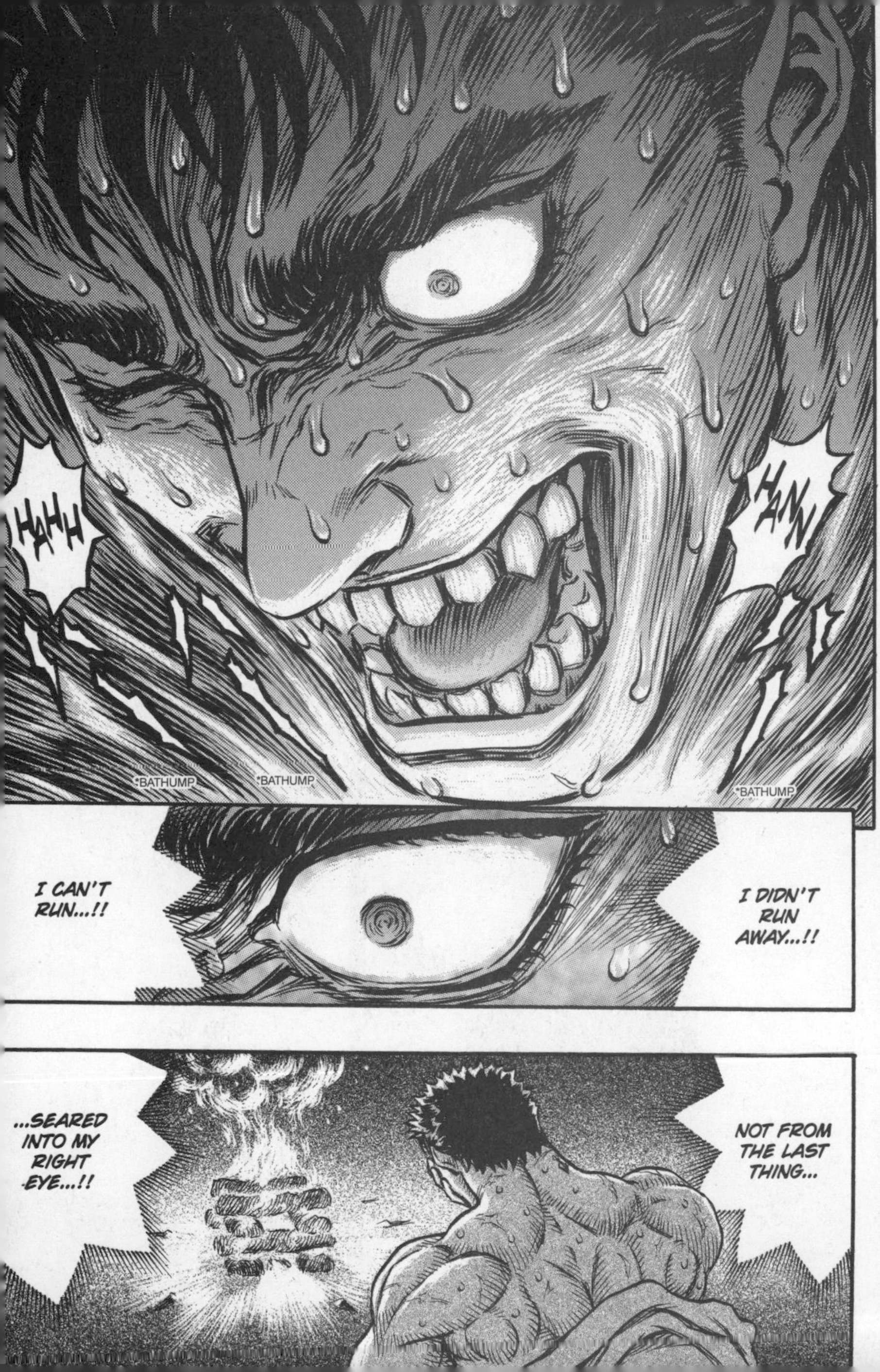
HANN
HAHH
*BATHUMP
*BATHUMP
*BATHUMP
I DIDN'T RUN AWAY...!!
I CAN'T RUN...!!
NOT FROM THE LAST THING...
...SEARED INTO MY RIGHT EYE...!!

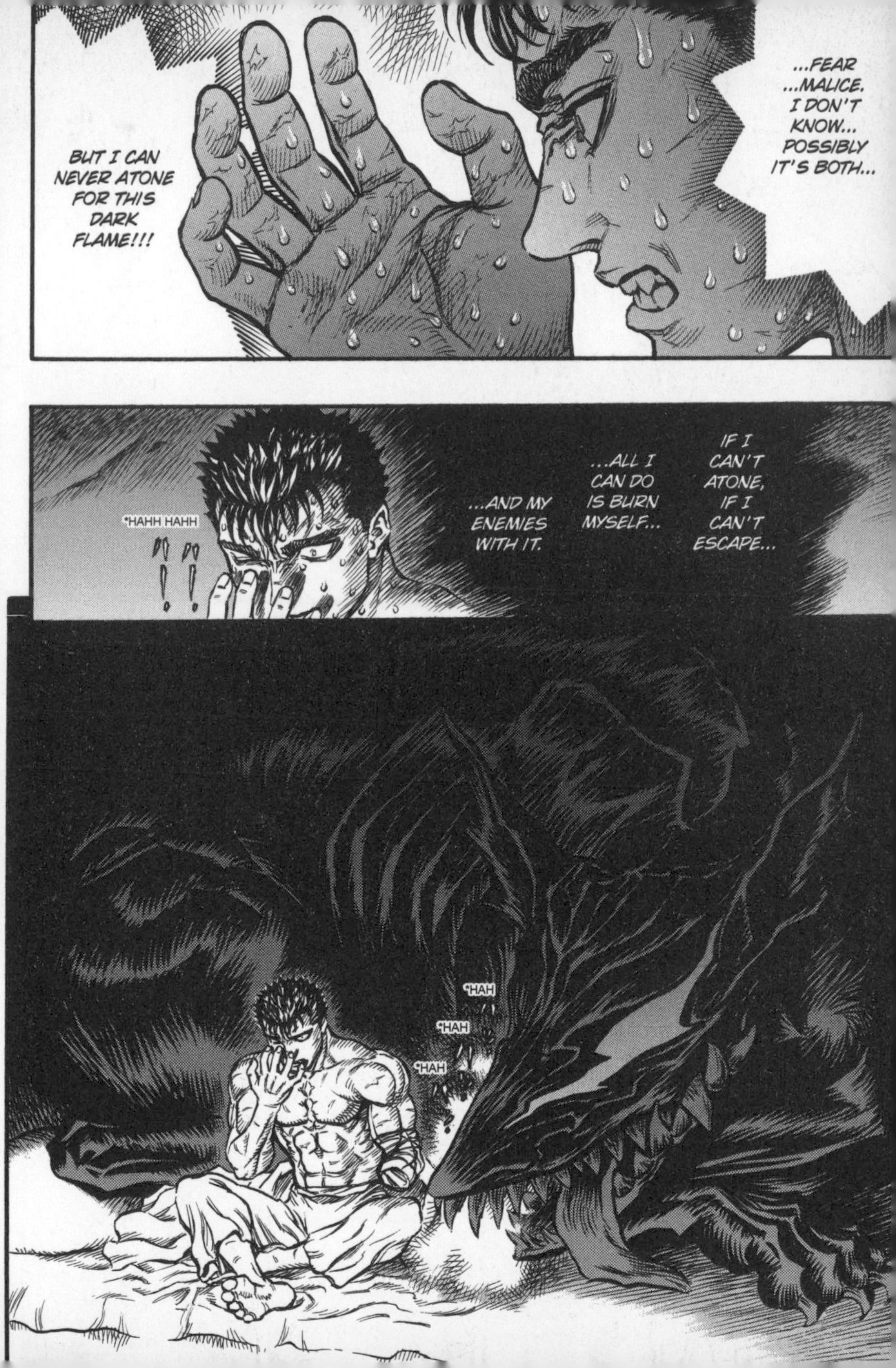
...FEAR ...MALICE. I DON'T KNOW... POSSIBLY IT'S BOTH...
BUT I CAN NEVER ATONE FOR THIS DARK FLAME!!!
IF I CAN'T ATONE, IF I CAN'T ESCAPE...
...ALL I CAN DO IS BURN MYSELF...
...AND MY ENEMIES WITH IT.
*HAHH HAHH
*HAH
*HAH
*HAH

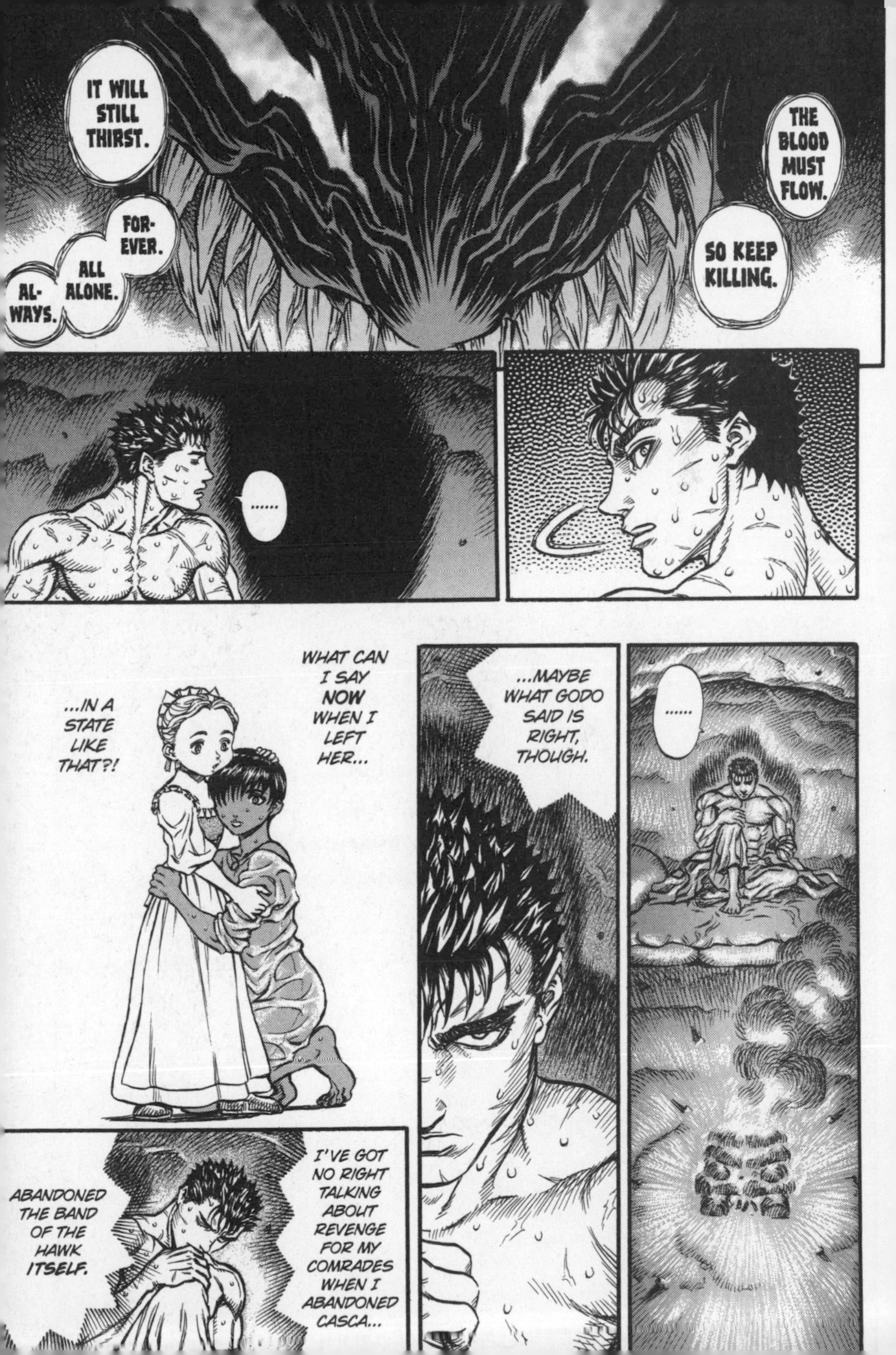
THE BLOOD MUST FLOW.
SO KEEP KILLING.
IT WILL STILL THIRST.
FOR-EVER.
ALL ALONE.
AL-WAYS.
......
......
...MAYBE WHAT GODO SAID IS RIGHT, THOUGH.
WHAT CAN I SAY NOW WHEN I LEFT HER...
...IN A STATE LIKE THAT?!
I'VE GOT NO RIGHT TALKING ABOUT REVENGE FOR MY COMRADES WHEN I ABANDONED CASCA...
ABANDONED THE BAND OF THE HAWK ITSELF.

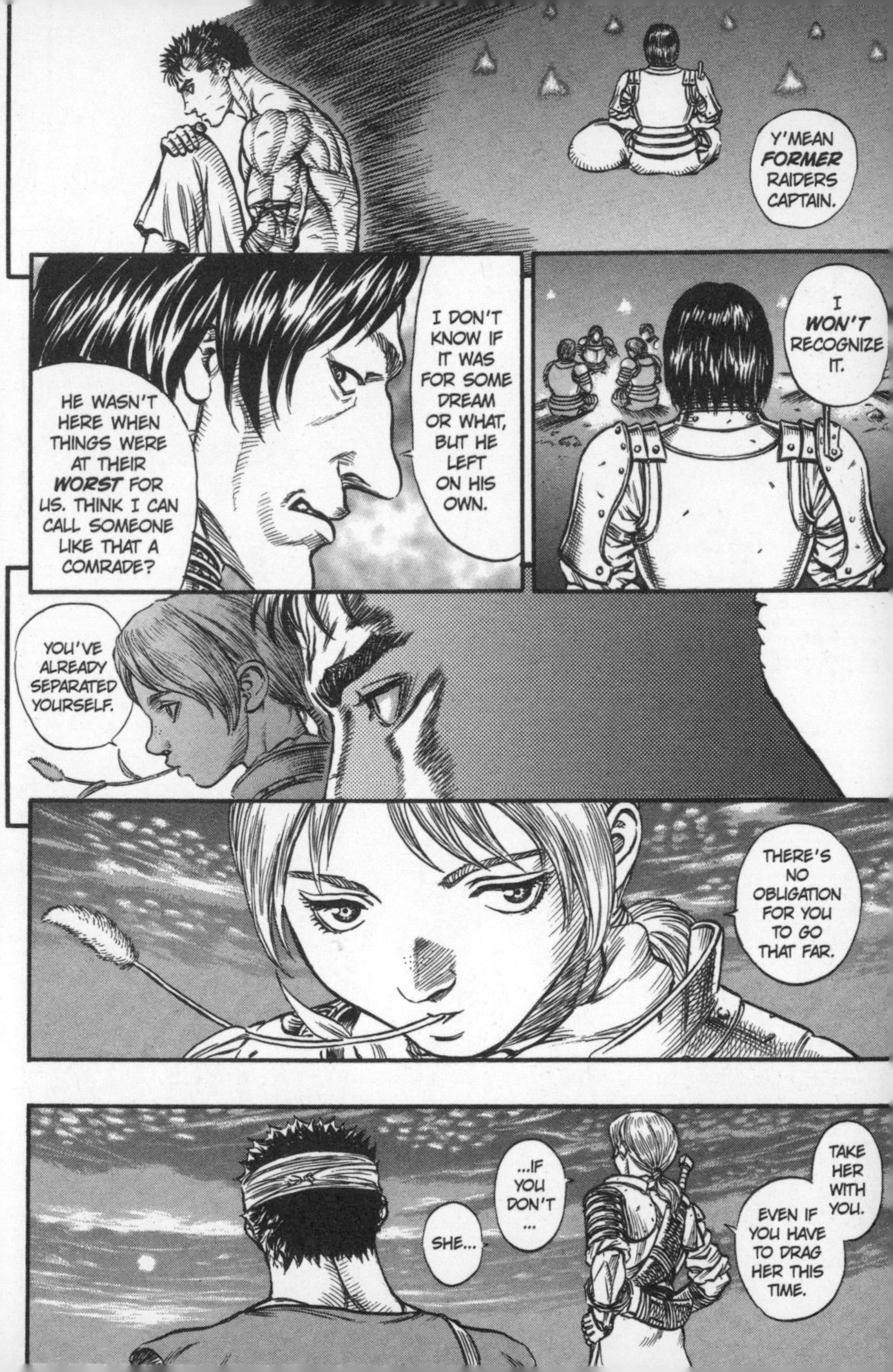
Y'MEAN FORMER RAIDERS CAPTAIN.
I WON'T RECOGNIZE IT.
I DON'T KNOW IF IT WAS FOR SOME DREAM OR WHAT, BUT HE LEFT ON HIS OWN.
HE WASN'T HERE WHEN THINGS WERE AT THEIR WORST FOR US. THINK I CAN CALL SOMEONE LIKE THAT A COMRADE?
YOU'VE ALREADY SEPARATED YOURSELF.
THERE'S NO OBLIGATION FOR YOU TO GO THAT FAR.
TAKE HER WITH YOU.
EVEN IF YOU HAVE TO DRAG HER THIS TIME.
...IF YOU DON'T ...
SHE...

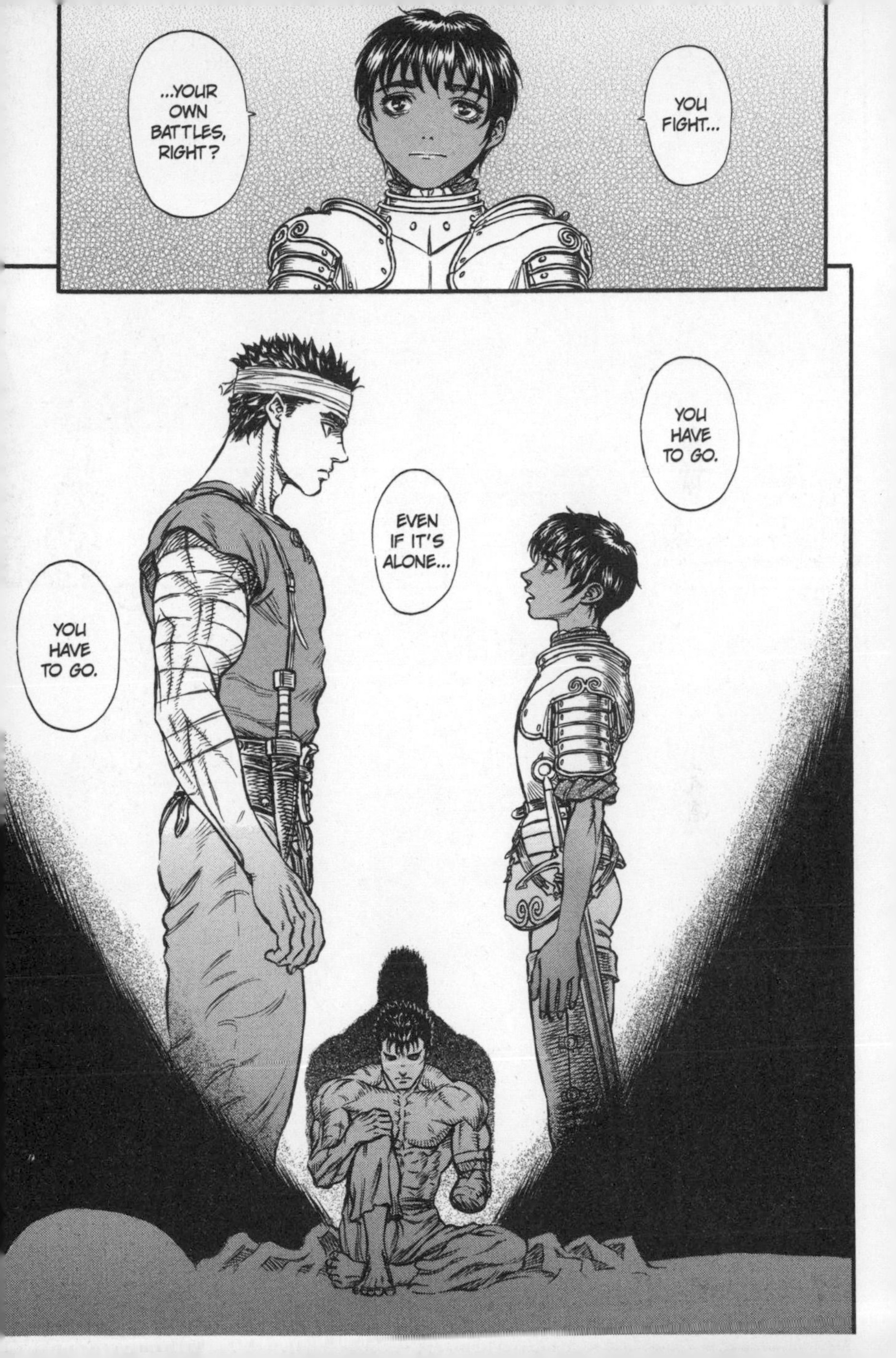
YOU FIGHT...
...YOUR OWN BATTLES, RIGHT?
YOU HAVE TO GO.
EVEN IF IT'S ALONE...
YOU HAVE TO GO.

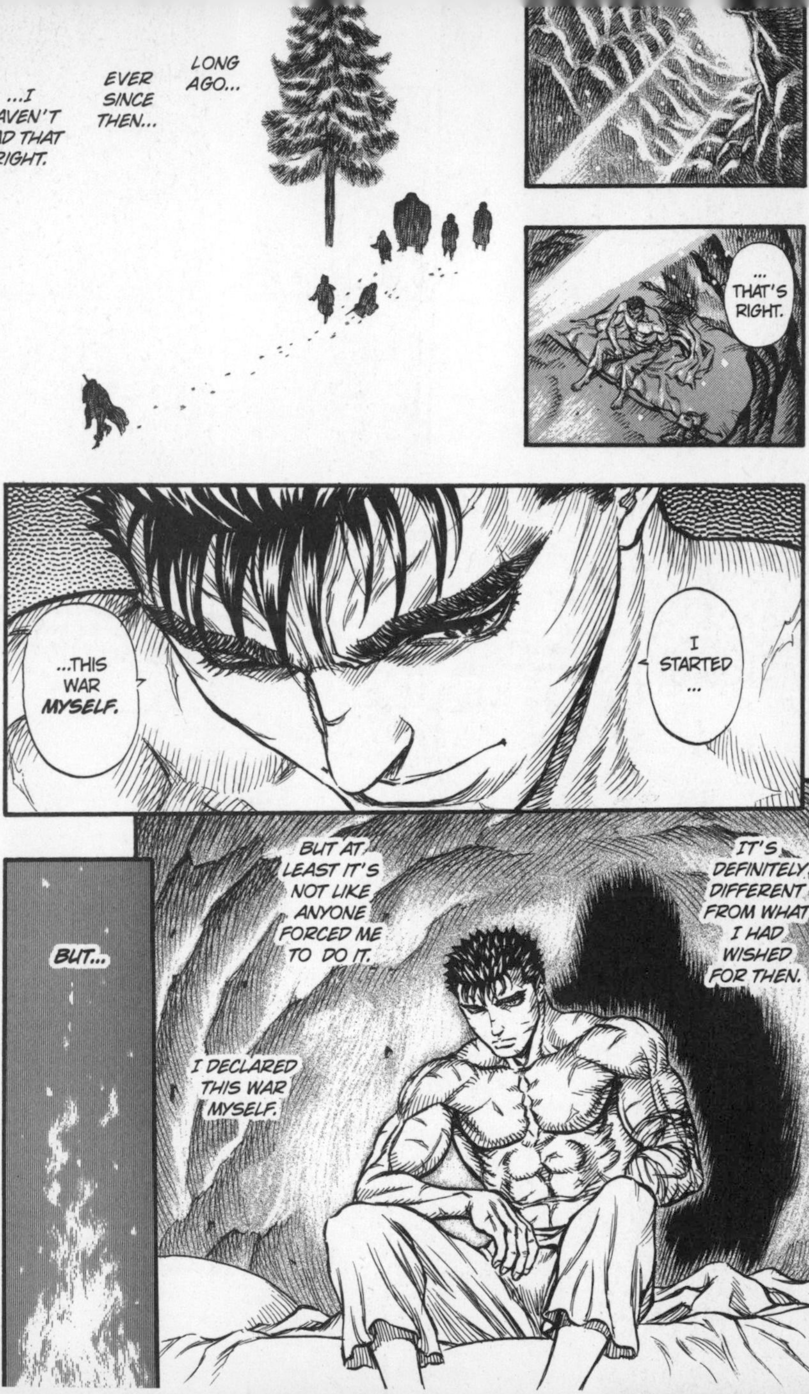
...THAT'S RIGHT.
LONG AGO...
EVER SINCE THEN...
...I HAVEN'T HAD THAT RIGHT.
I STARTED...
...THIS WAR MYSELF.
IT'S DEFINITELY DIFFERENT FROM WHAT I HAD WISHED FOR THEN.
BUT AT LEAST IT'S NOT LIKE ANYONE FORCED ME TO DO IT.
I DECLARED THIS WAR MYSELF.
BUT...

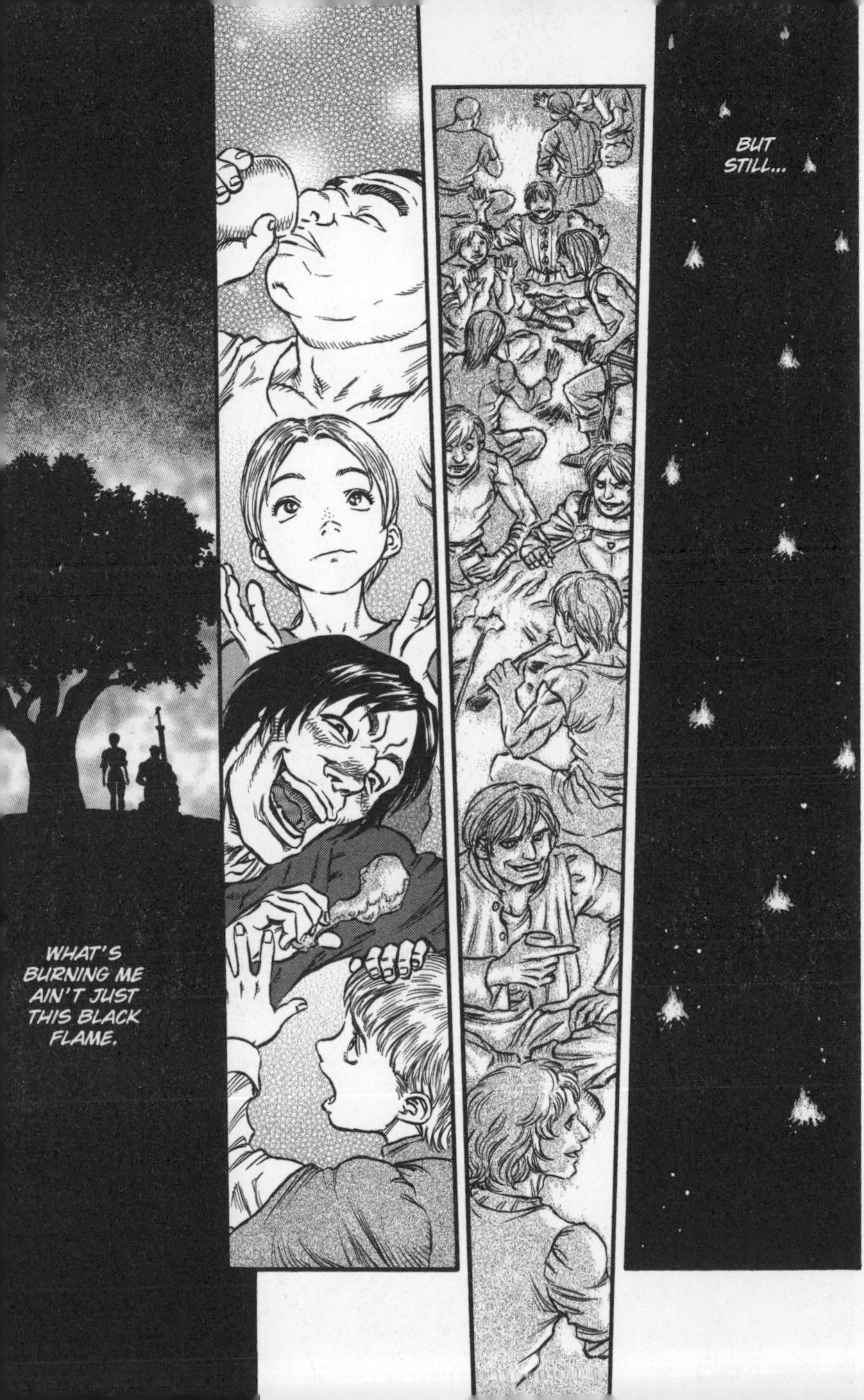
BUT STILL...
WHAT'S BURNING ME AIN'T JUST THIS BLACK FLAME.

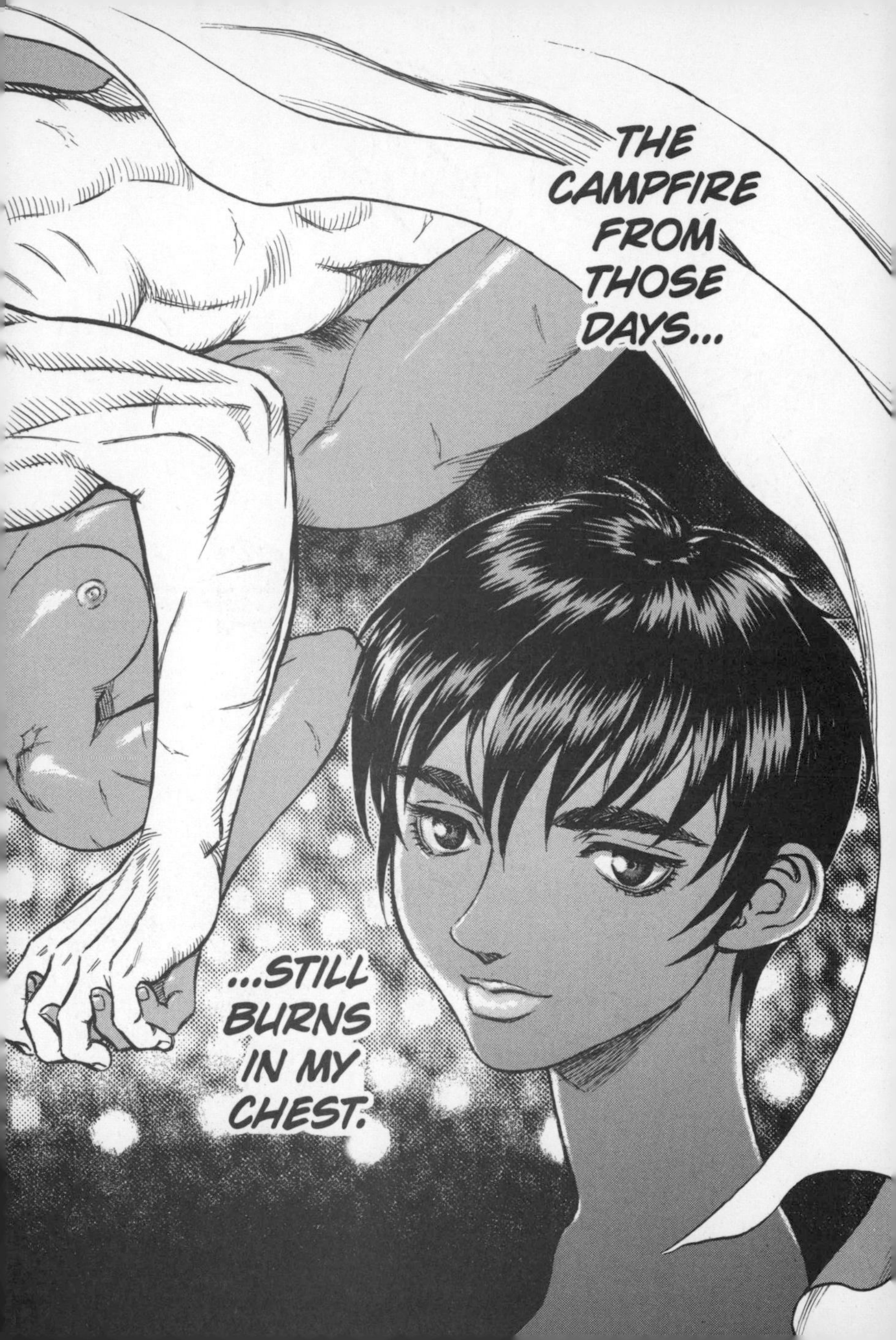
THE CAMPFIRE FROM THOSE DAYS...
...STILL BURNS IN MY CHEST.

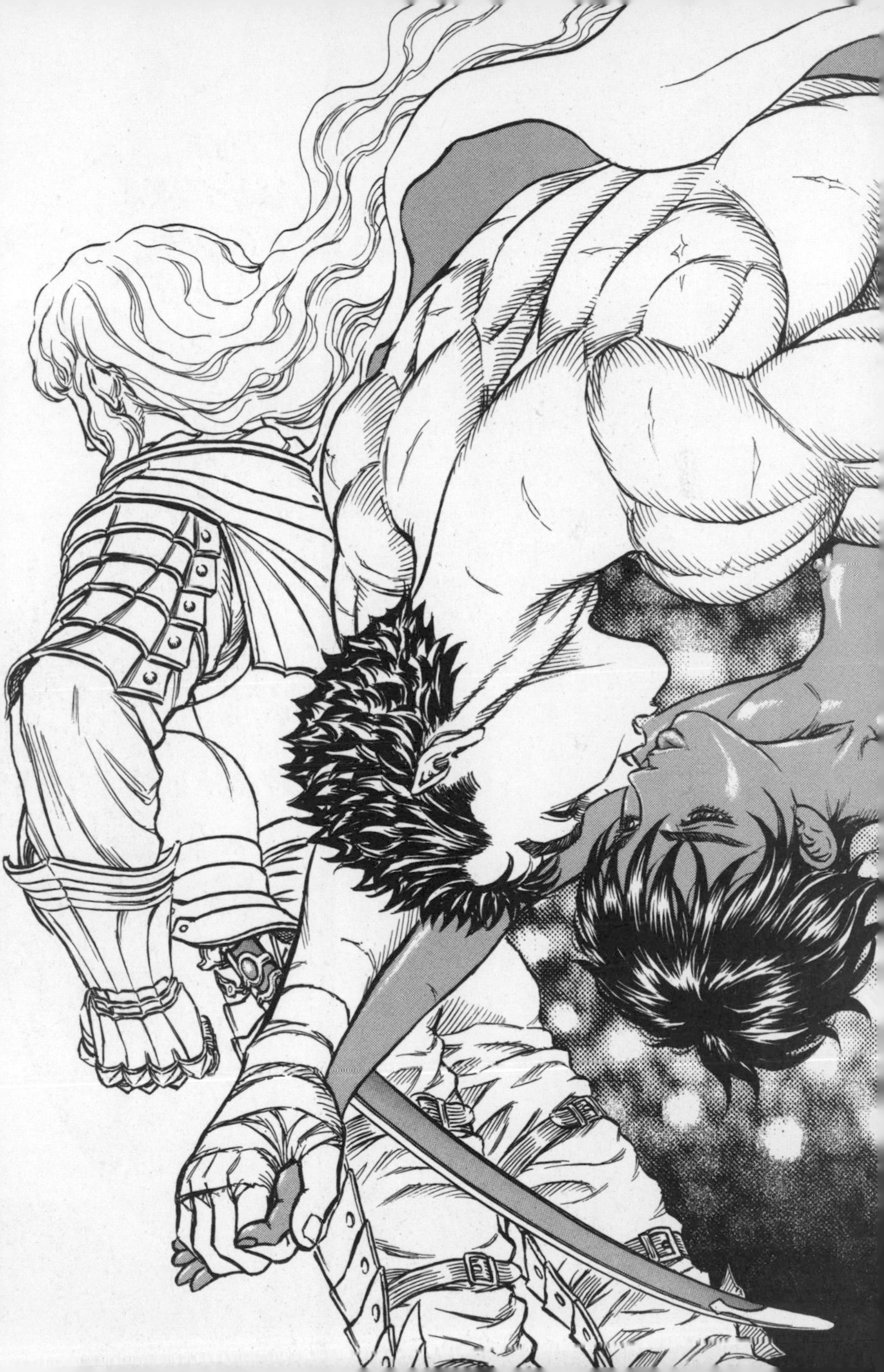

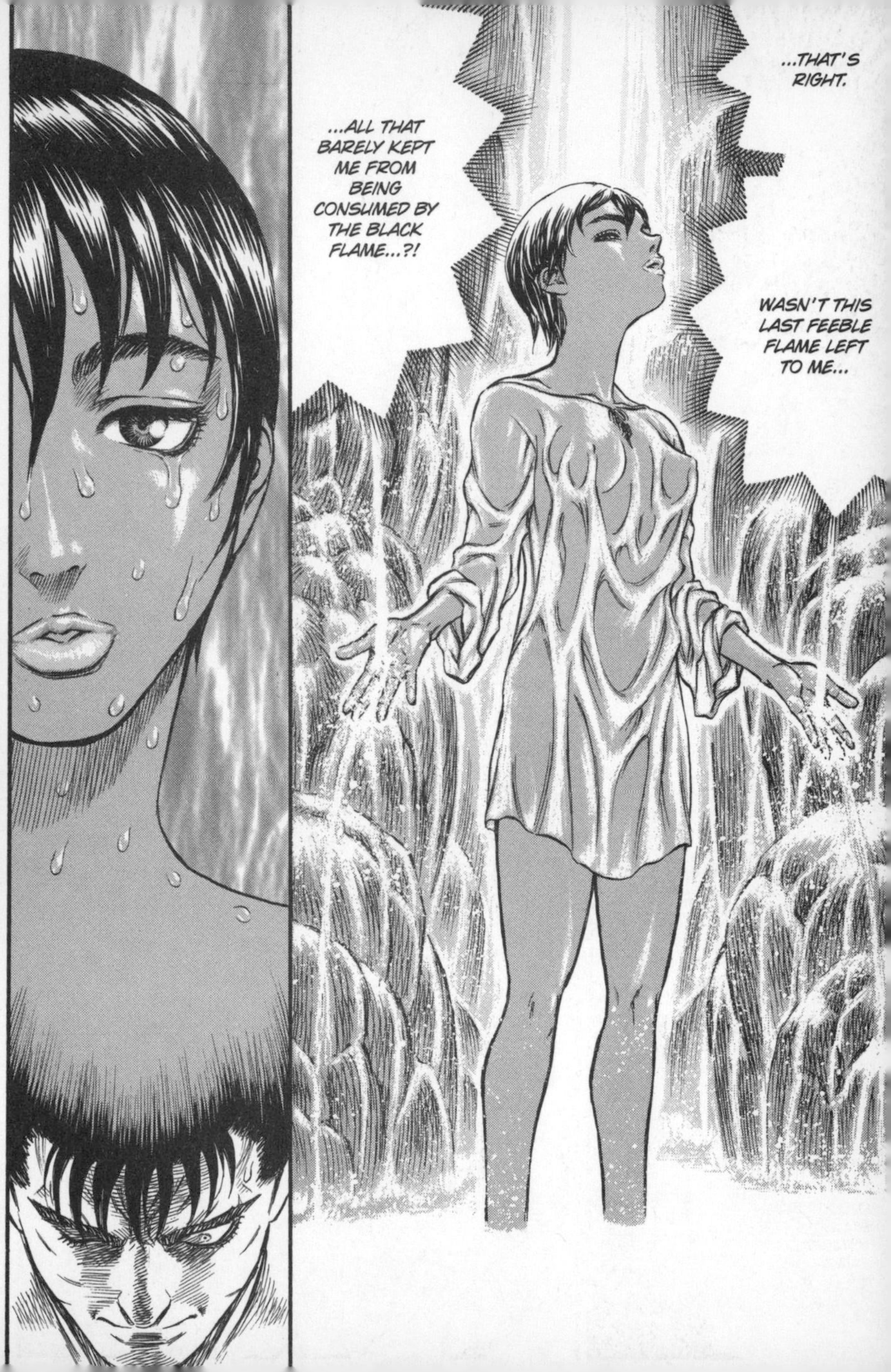
...THAT'S RIGHT.
WASN'T THIS LAST FEEBLE FLAME LEFT TO ME...
...ALL THAT BARELY KEPT ME FROM BEING CONSUMED BY THE BLACK FLAME...?!

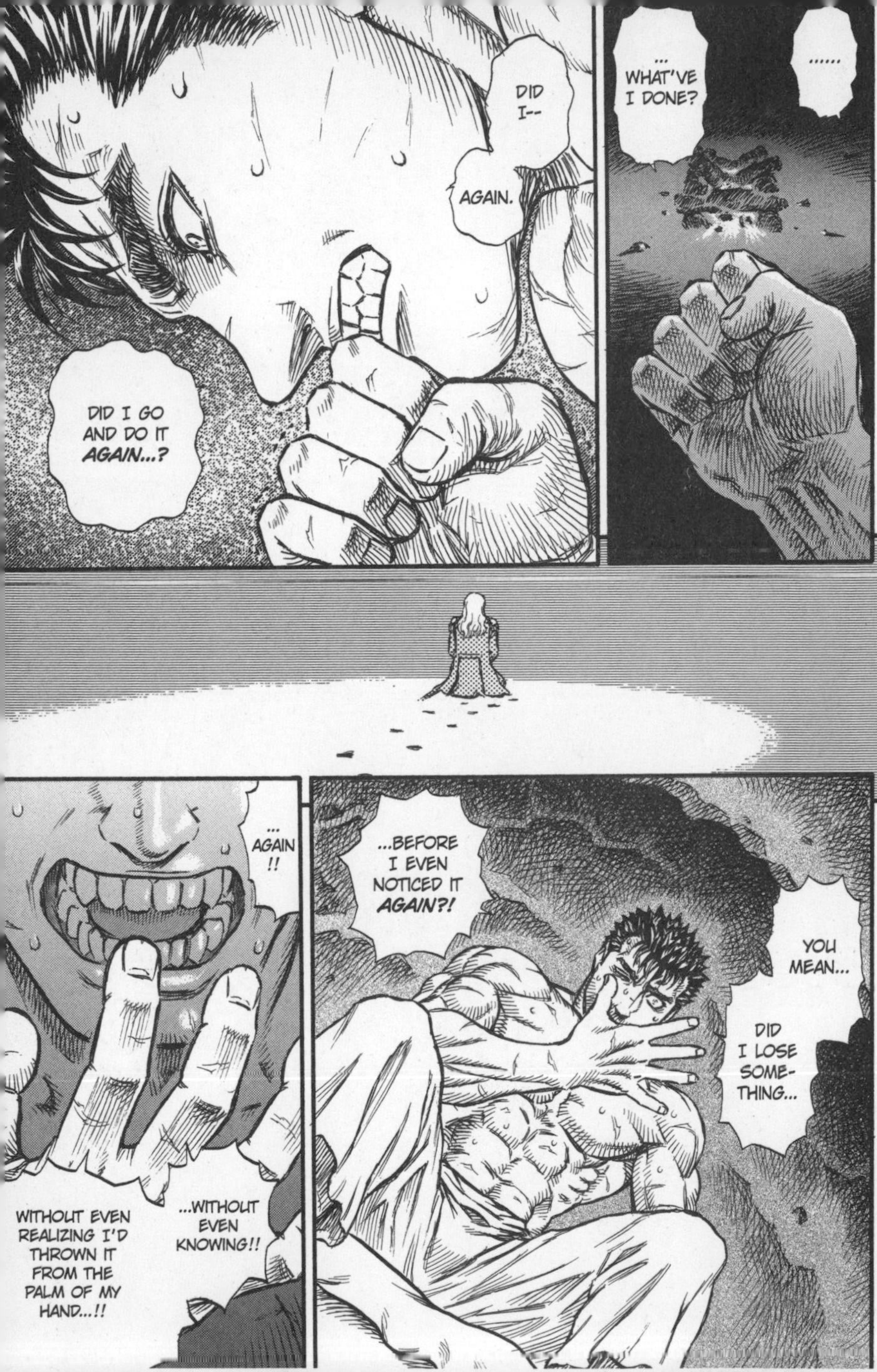
......
... WHAT'VE I DONE?
DID I--
AGAIN.
DID I GO AND DO IT *AGAIN...?*
YOU MEAN...
DID I LOSE SOME-THING...
...BEFORE I EVEN NOTICED IT *AGAIN?!*
... AGAIN !!
...WITHOUT EVEN KNOWING!!
WITHOUT EVEN REALIZING I'D THROWN IT FROM THE PALM OF MY HAND...!!

... GATHER AND ...

... BLIND SHEEP ...

WHEN THE SKY FALLS ...

... AT THE HOLY GROUND ...

... A PILLAR OF FIRE ...

... ERECT ...

NOT YET...

NO...

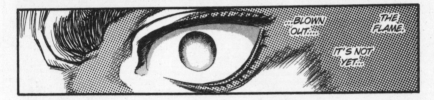

... BLOWN OUT...

THE FLAME.

IT'S NOT YET...

NOT YET!!

IT'S NOT TOO LATE!!

THIS TIME I SWEAR ...!!!

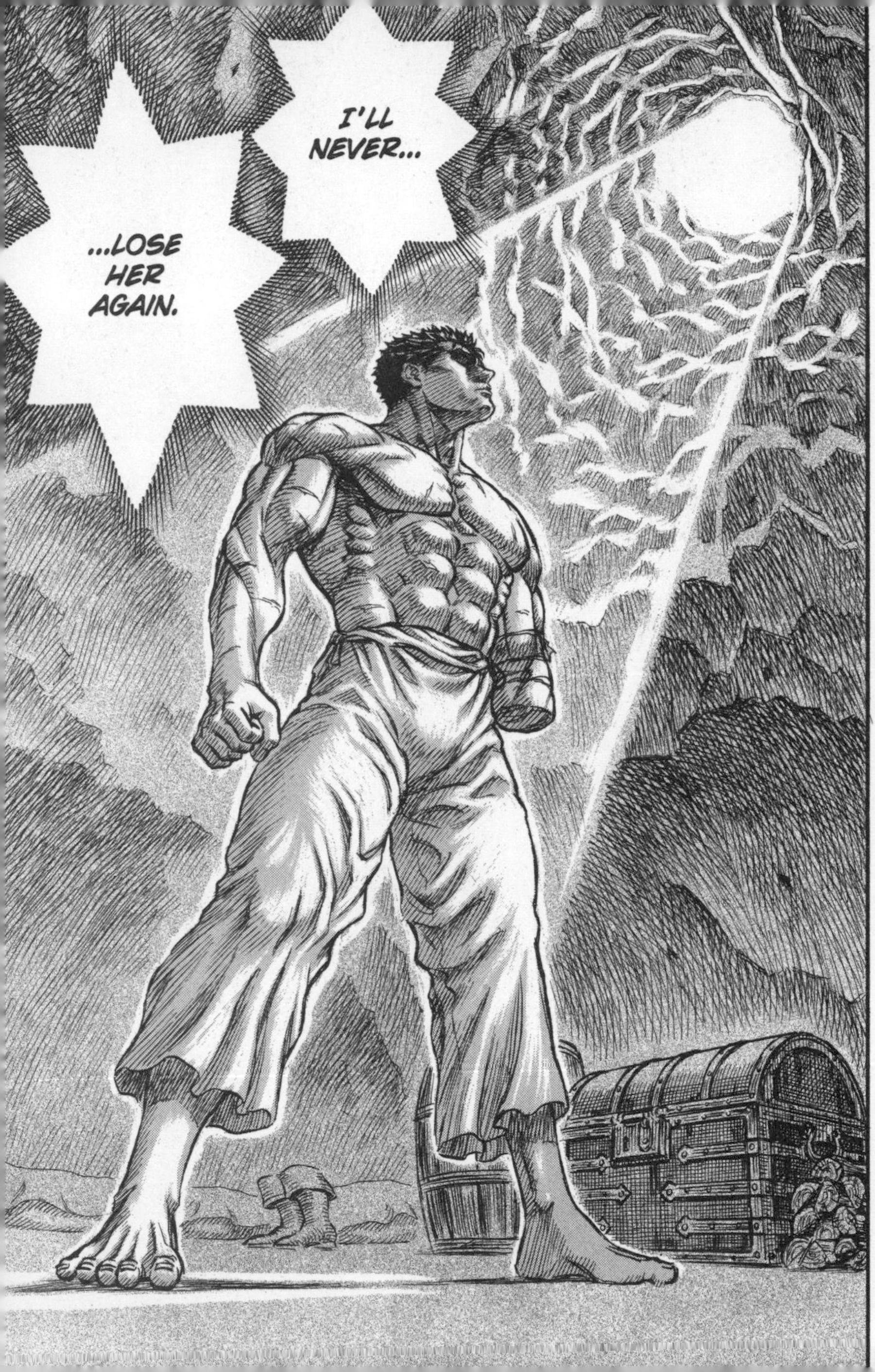
I'LL NEVER...
...LOSE HER AGAIN.

BERSERK

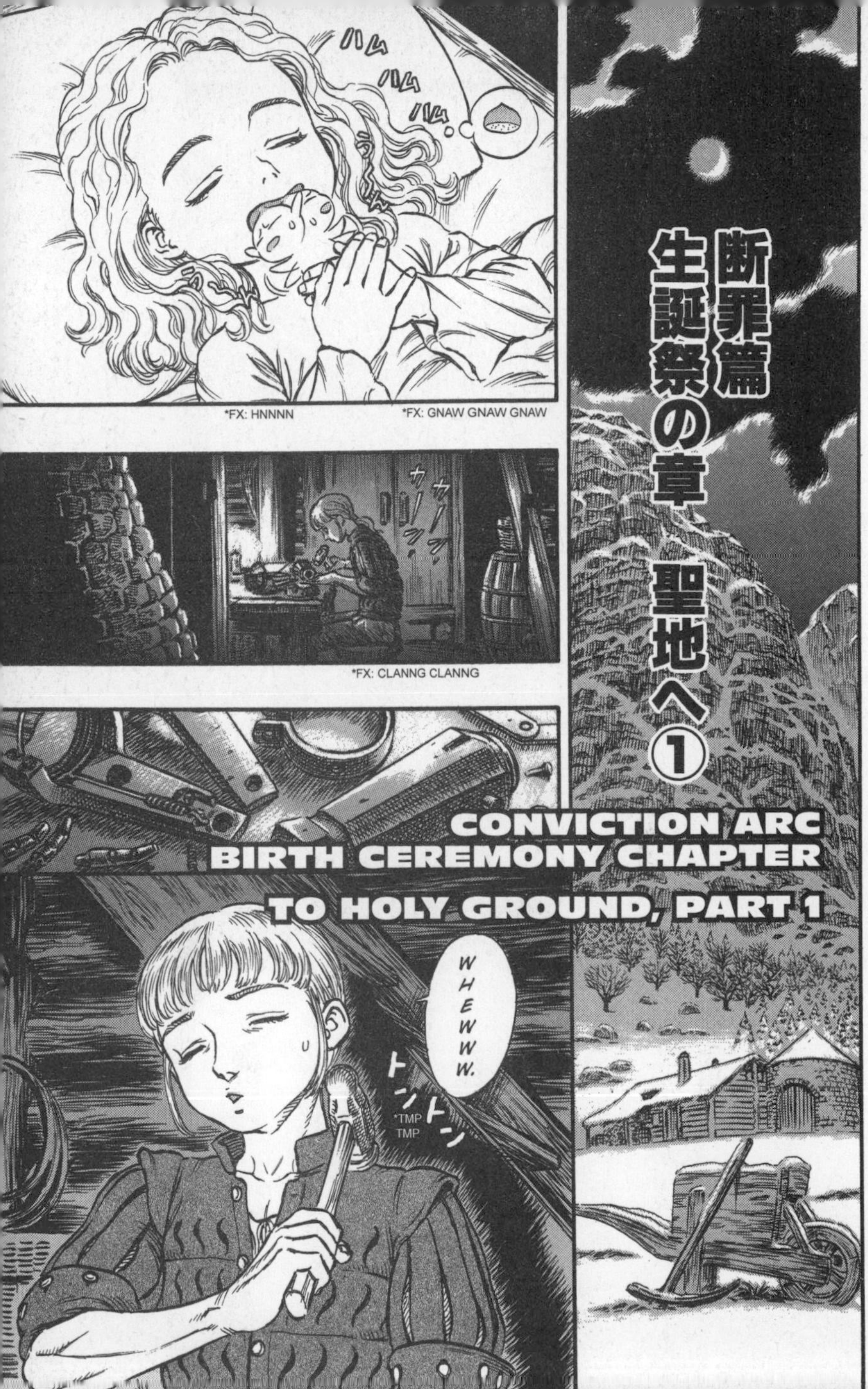
断罪篇
生誕祭の章 聖地へ①
CONVICTION ARC
BIRTH CEREMONY CHAPTER
TO HOLY GROUND, PART 1
*FX: GNAW GNAW GNAW
*FX: HNNNN
*FX: CLANNG CLANNG
WHEWWW.
*TMP TMP

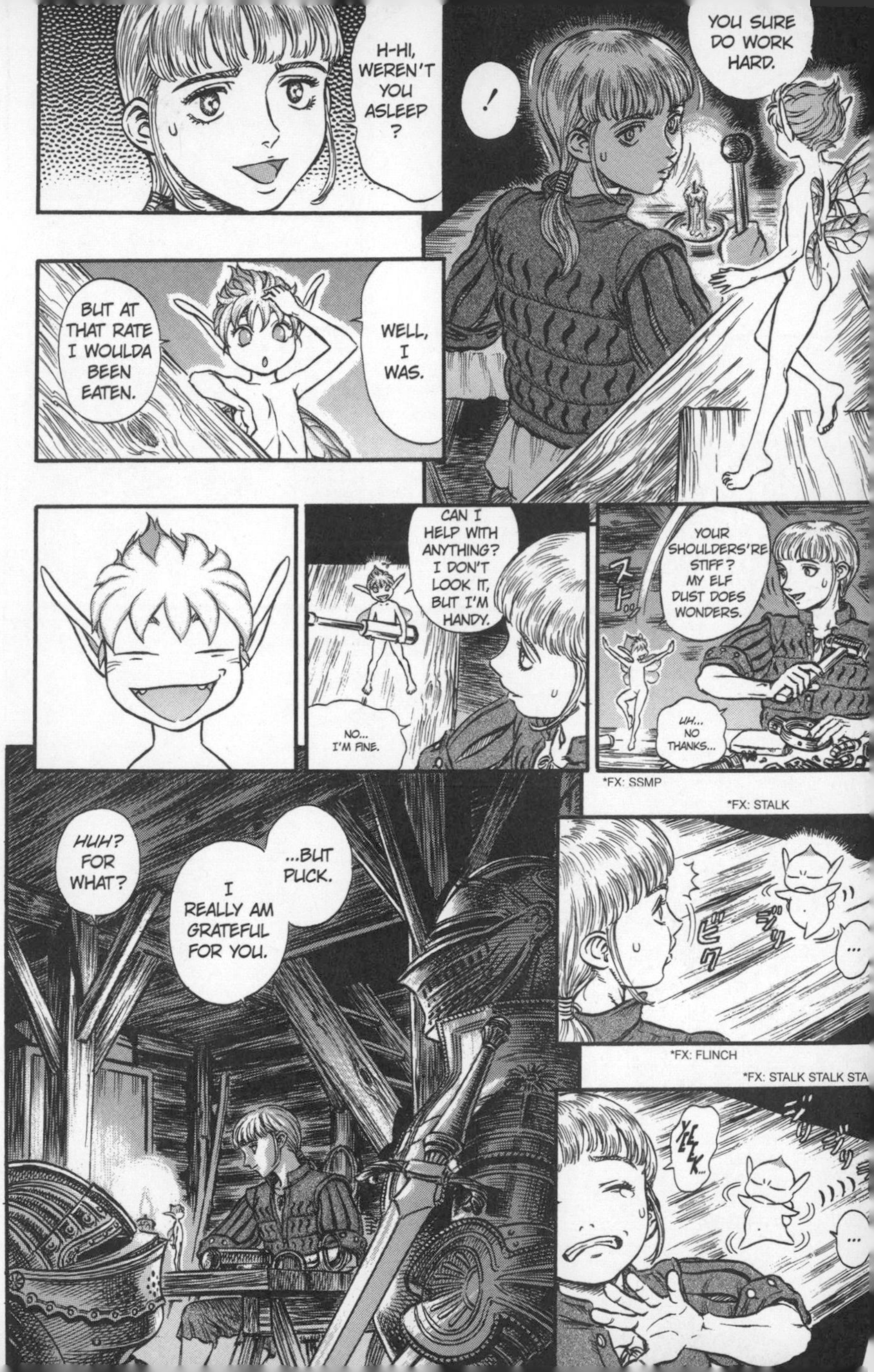

YOU SURE DO WORK HARD.
!
H-HI, WEREN'T YOU ASLEEP?
WELL, I WAS.
BUT AT THAT RATE I WOULDA BEEN EATEN.
YOUR SHOULDERS'RE STIFF? MY ELF DUST DOES WONDERS.
UH... NO THANKS...
CAN I HELP WITH ANYTHING? I DON'T LOOK IT, BUT I'M HANDY.
NO... I'M FINE.
*FX: SSMP
*FX: STALK
...
*FX: FLINCH
*FX: STALK STALK STA
YEESH...
...
...BUT PUCK.
I REALLY AM GRATEFUL FOR YOU.
HUH? FOR WHAT?

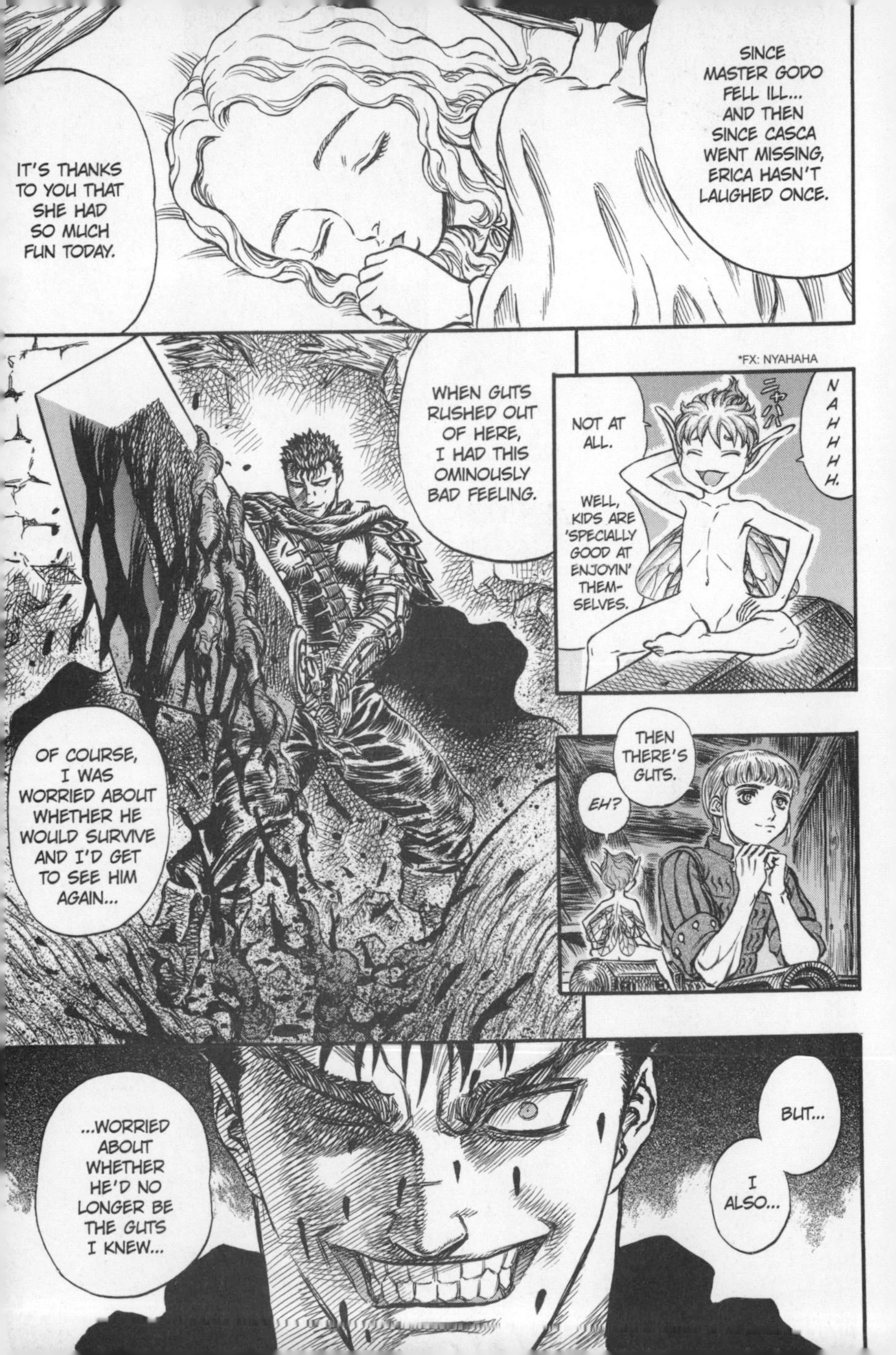
SINCE MASTER GODO FELL ILL... AND THEN SINCE CASCA WENT MISSING, ERICA HASN'T LAUGHED ONCE.
IT'S THANKS TO YOU THAT SHE HAD SO MUCH FUN TODAY.
*FX: NYAHAHA
NAHHHH.
NOT AT ALL.
WELL, KIDS ARE 'SPECIALLY GOOD AT ENJOYIN' THEM-SELVES.
THEN THERE'S GUTS.
EH?
WHEN GUTS RUSHED OUT OF HERE, I HAD THIS OMINOUSLY BAD FEELING.
OF COURSE, I WAS WORRIED ABOUT WHETHER HE WOULD SURVIVE AND I'D GET TO SEE HIM AGAIN...
BUT...
I ALSO...
...WORRIED ABOUT WHETHER HE'D NO LONGER BE THE GUTS I KNEW...

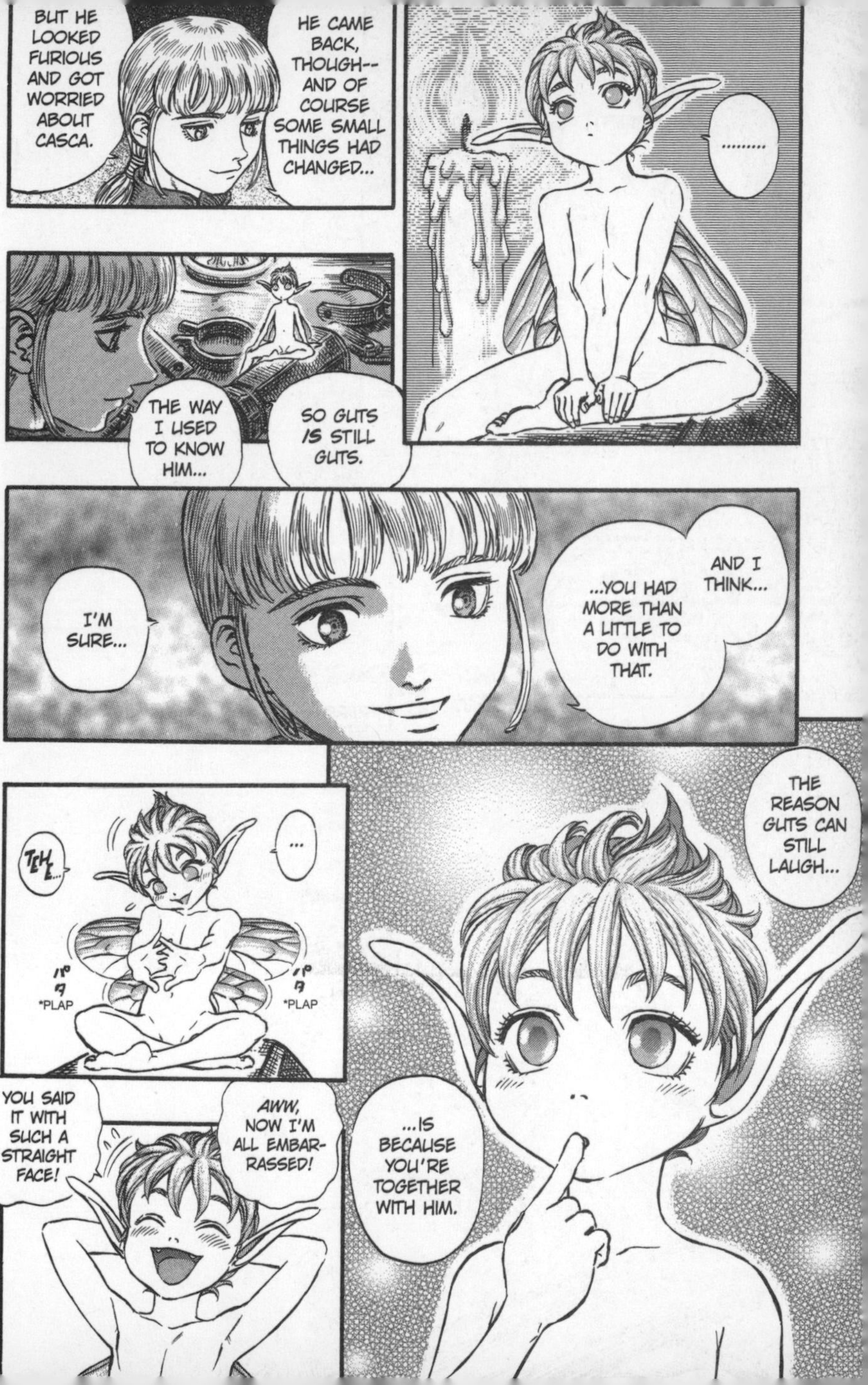

....
HE CAME BACK, THOUGH-- AND OF COURSE SOME SMALL THINGS HAD CHANGED...
BUT HE LOOKED FURIOUS AND GOT WORRIED ABOUT CASCA.
SO GUTS *IS* STILL GUTS.
THE WAY I USED TO KNOW HIM...
AND I THINK...
...YOU HAD MORE THAN A LITTLE TO DO WITH THAT.
I'M SURE...
THE REASON GUTS CAN STILL LAUGH...
...IS BECAUSE YOU'RE TOGETHER WITH HIM.
...
TEHE...
パタ *PLAP
パタ *PLAP
AWW, NOW I'M ALL EMBARRASSED!
YOU SAID IT WITH SUCH A STRAIGHT FACE!

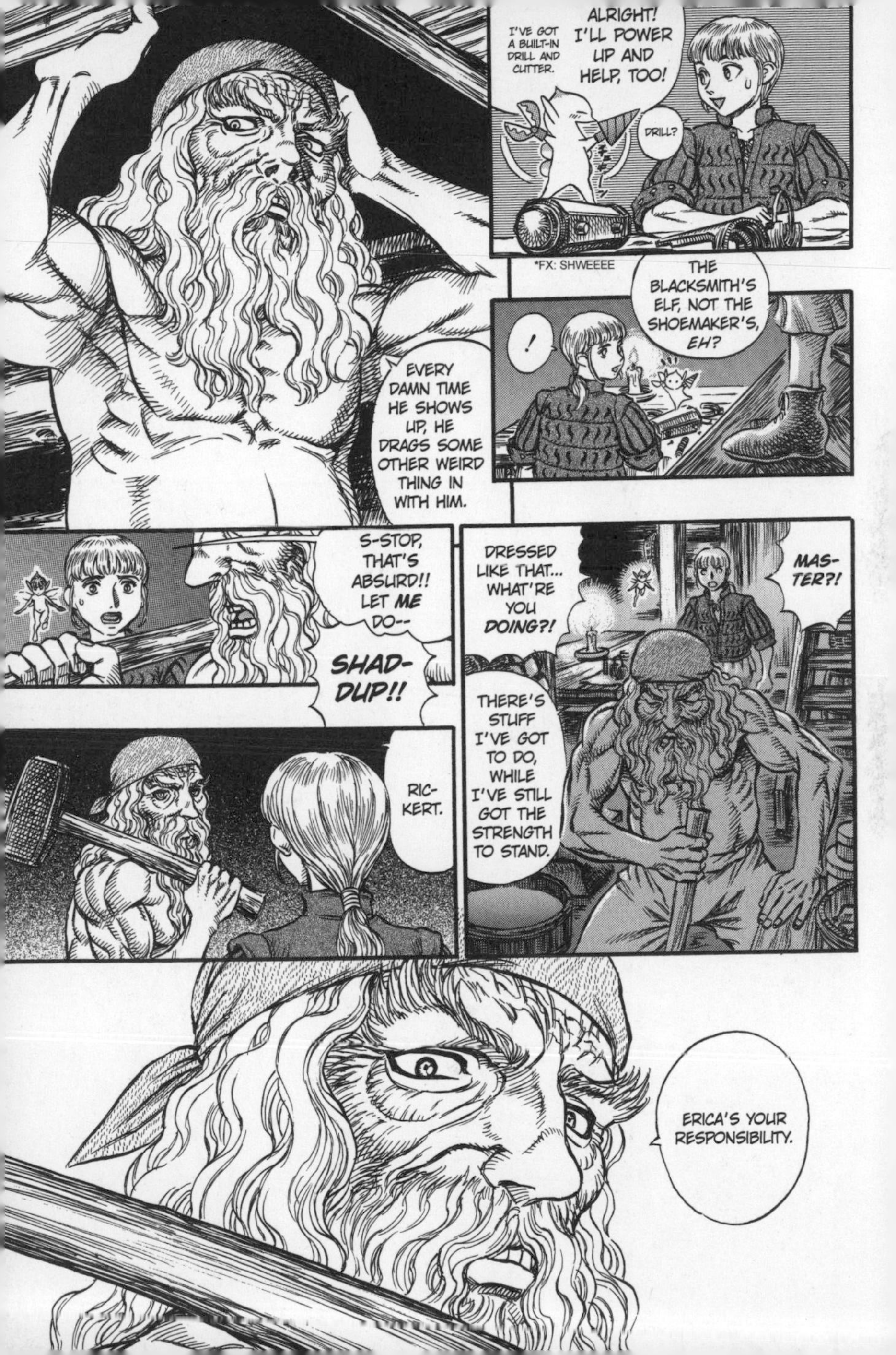

ALRIGHT! I'LL POWER UP AND HELP, TOO!
I'VE GOT A BUILT-IN DRILL AND CUTTER.
DRILL?
*FX: SHWEEEE
THE BLACKSMITH'S ELF, NOT THE SHOEMAKER'S, EH?
!
EVERY DAMN TIME HE SHOWS UP, HE DRAGS SOME OTHER WEIRD THING IN WITH HIM.
MAS-TER?!
DRESSED LIKE THAT... WHAT'RE YOU DOING?!
THERE'S STUFF I'VE GOT TO DO, WHILE I'VE STILL GOT THE STRENGTH TO STAND.
S-STOP, THAT'S ABSURD!! LET ME DO--
SHAD-DUP!!
RIC-KERT.
ERICA'S YOUR RESPONSIBILITY.

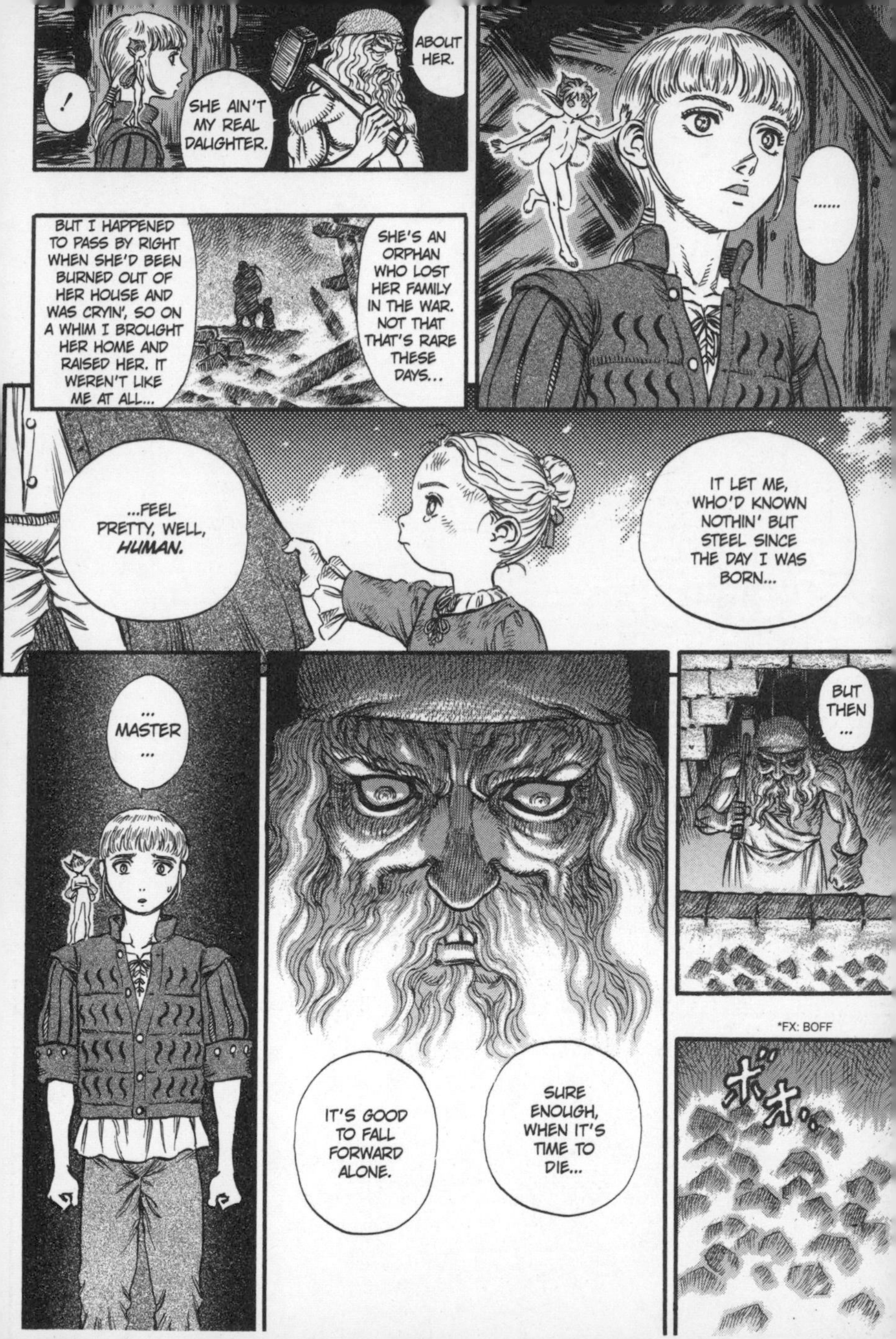

......
ABOUT HER.
SHE AIN'T MY REAL DAUGHTER.
!
SHE'S AN ORPHAN WHO LOST HER FAMILY IN THE WAR. NOT THAT THAT'S RARE THESE DAYS...
BUT I HAPPENED TO PASS BY RIGHT WHEN SHE'D BEEN BURNED OUT OF HER HOUSE AND WAS CRYIN', SO ON A WHIM I BROUGHT HER HOME AND RAISED HER. IT WEREN'T LIKE ME AT ALL...
IT LET ME, WHO'D KNOWN NOTHIN' BUT STEEL SINCE THE DAY I WAS BORN...
...FEEL PRETTY, WELL, *HUMAN.*
BUT THEN ...
*FX: BOFF
SURE ENOUGH, WHEN IT'S TIME TO DIE...
IT'S GOOD TO FALL FORWARD ALONE.
... MASTER ...

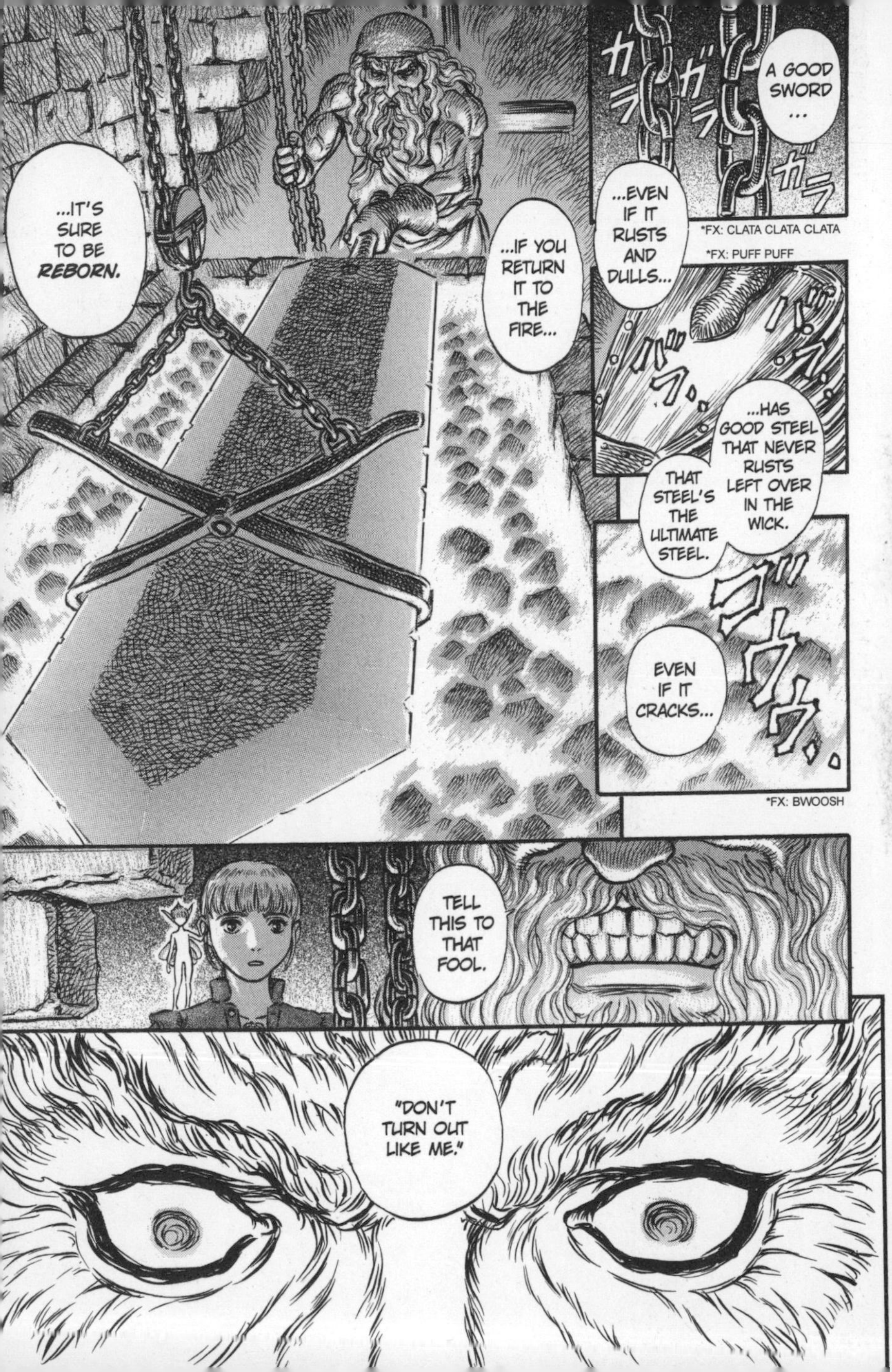
A GOOD SWORD ...
...EVEN IF IT RUSTS AND DULLS...
*FX: CLATA CLATA CLATA
*FX: PUFF PUFF
...HAS GOOD STEEL THAT NEVER RUSTS LEFT OVER IN THE WICK.
THAT STEEL'S THE ULTIMATE STEEL.
EVEN IF IT CRACKS...
*FX: BWOOSH
...IF YOU RETURN IT TO THE FIRE...
...IT'S SURE TO BE REBORN.
TELL THIS TO THAT FOOL.
"DON'T TURN OUT LIKE ME."

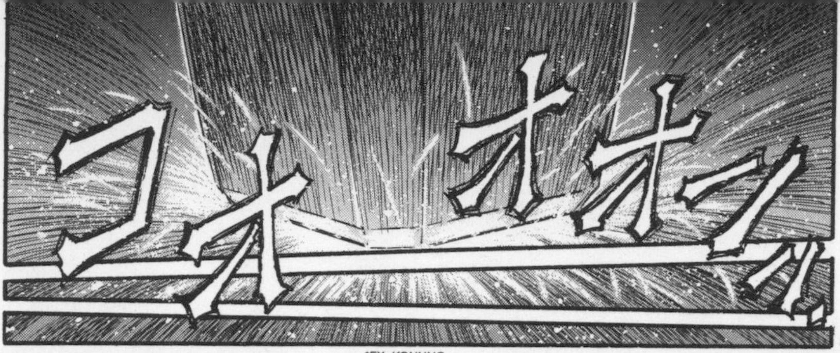
コオオオン

*FX: KONNNG

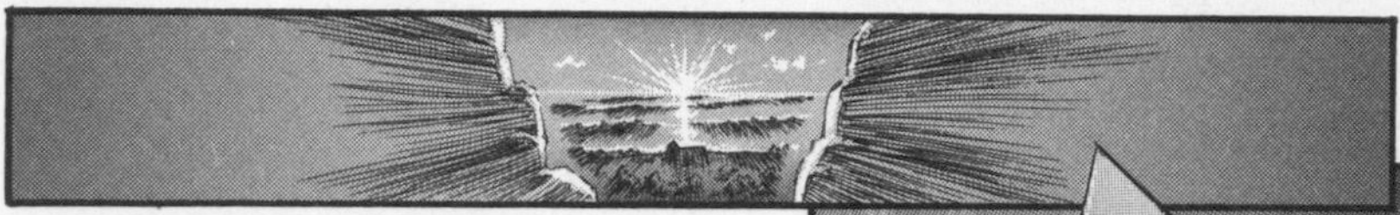

*FX: FLAP

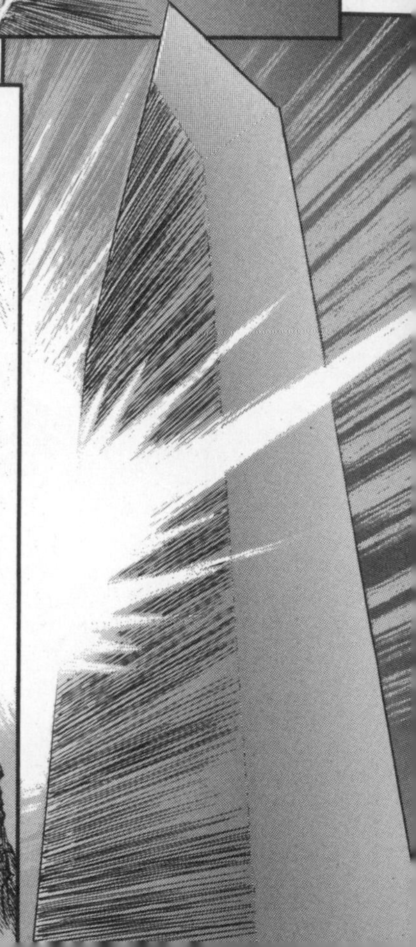

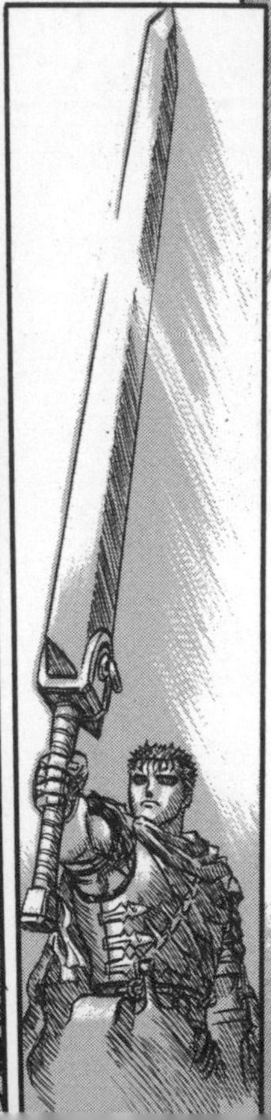

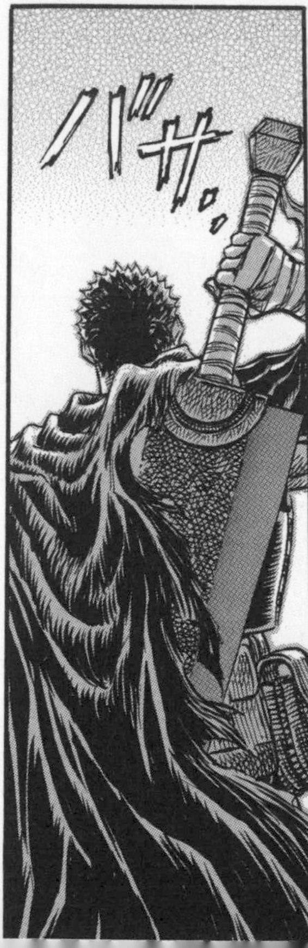
バサッ

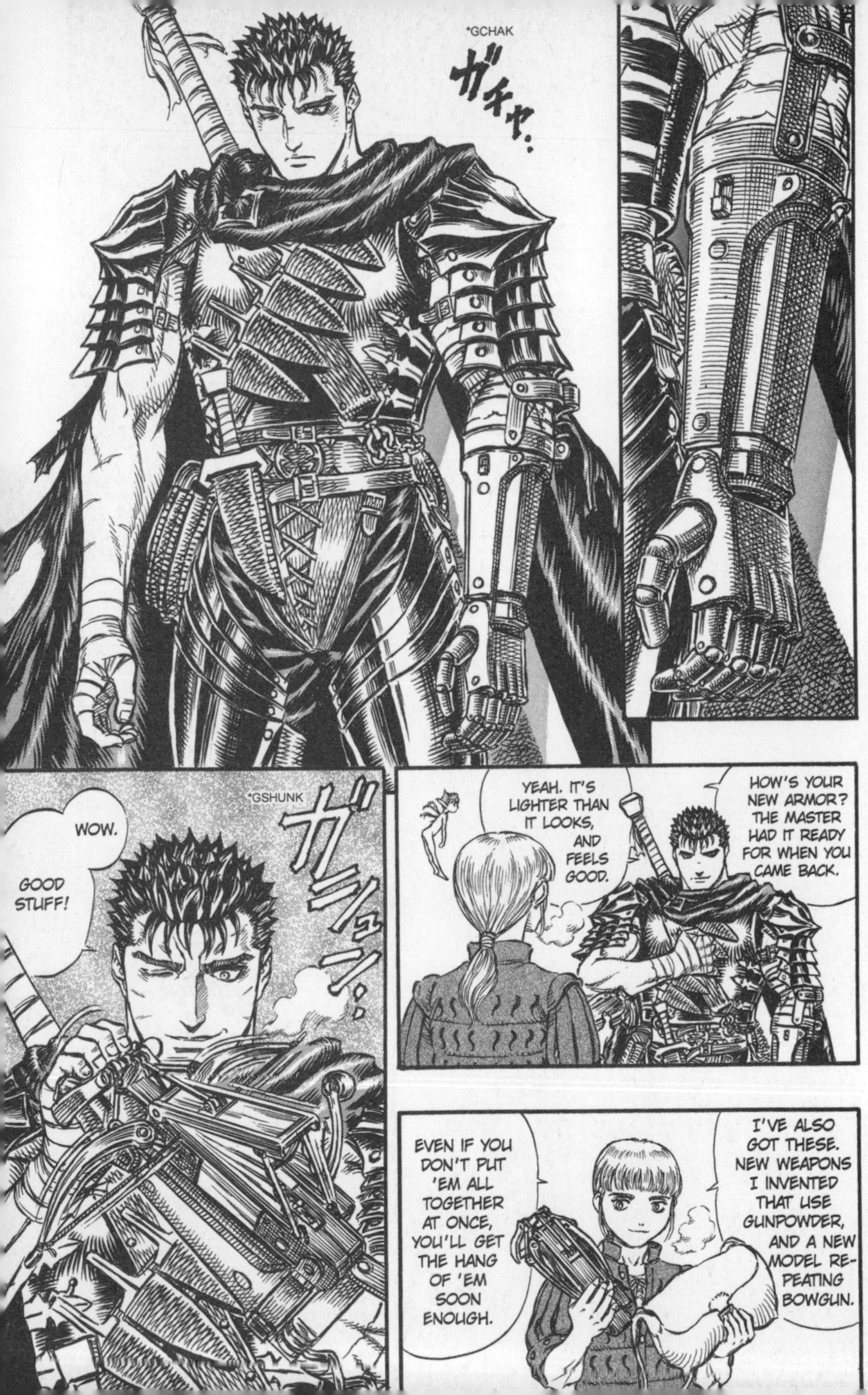
*GCHAK
HOW'S YOUR NEW ARMOR? THE MASTER HAD IT READY FOR WHEN YOU CAME BACK.
YEAH. IT'S LIGHTER THAN IT LOOKS, AND FEELS GOOD.
I'VE ALSO GOT THESE. NEW WEAPONS I INVENTED THAT USE GUNPOWDER, AND A NEW MODEL RE-PEATING BOWGUN.
EVEN IF YOU DON'T PUT 'EM ALL TOGETHER AT ONCE, YOU'LL GET THE HANG OF 'EM SOON ENOUGH.
*GSHUNK
WOW.
GOOD STUFF!

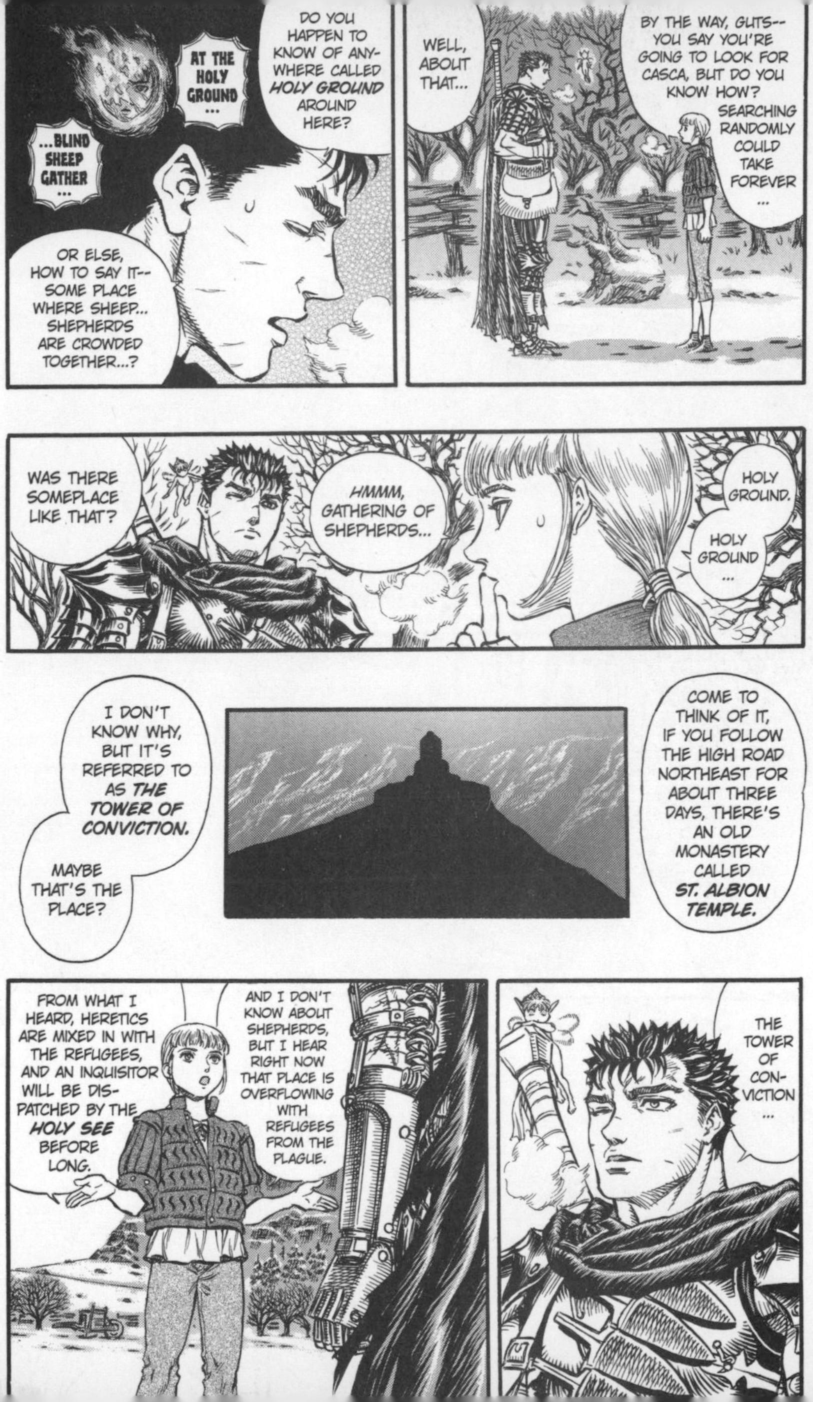
BY THE WAY, GUTS-- YOU SAY YOU'RE GOING TO LOOK FOR CASCA, BUT DO YOU KNOW HOW?
SEARCHING RANDOMLY COULD TAKE FOREVER ...
WELL, ABOUT THAT...
DO YOU HAPPEN TO KNOW OF ANY-WHERE CALLED HOLY GROUND AROUND HERE?
AT THE HOLY GROUND ...
...BLIND SHEEP GATHER ...
OR ELSE, HOW TO SAY IT-- SOME PLACE WHERE SHEEP... SHEPHERDS ARE CROWDED TOGETHER...?
HOLY GROUND.
HOLY GROUND ...
HMMM, GATHERING OF SHEPHERDS...
WAS THERE SOMEPLACE LIKE THAT?
COME TO THINK OF IT, IF YOU FOLLOW THE HIGH ROAD NORTHEAST FOR ABOUT THREE DAYS, THERE'S AN OLD MONASTERY CALLED ST. ALBION TEMPLE.
I DON'T KNOW WHY, BUT IT'S REFERRED TO AS THE TOWER OF CONVICTION.
MAYBE THAT'S THE PLACE?
THE TOWER OF CON-VICTION ...
AND I DON'T KNOW ABOUT SHEPHERDS, BUT I HEAR RIGHT NOW THAT PLACE IS OVERFLOWING WITH REFUGEES FROM THE PLAGUE.
FROM WHAT I HEARD, HERETICS ARE MIXED IN WITH THE REFUGEES, AND AN INQUISITOR WILL BE DIS-PATCHED BY THE HOLY SEE BEFORE LONG.

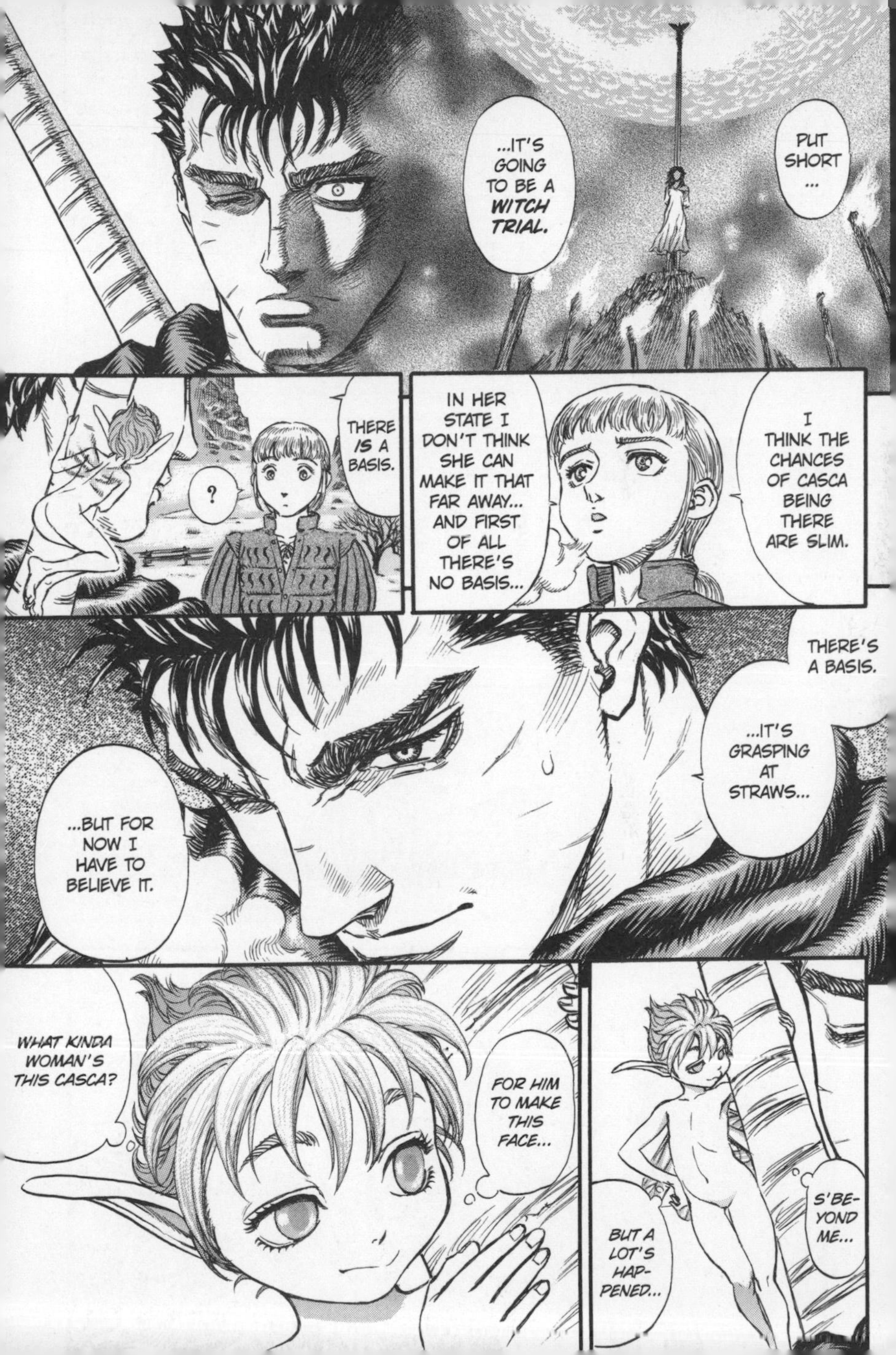
PUT SHORT ...
...IT'S GOING TO BE A *WITCH TRIAL.*
I THINK THE CHANCES OF CASCA BEING THERE ARE SLIM.
IN HER STATE I DON'T THINK SHE CAN MAKE IT THAT FAR AWAY... AND FIRST OF ALL THERE'S NO BASIS...
THERE *IS* A BASIS.
?
THERE'S A BASIS.
...IT'S GRASPING AT STRAWS...
...BUT FOR NOW I HAVE TO BELIEVE IT.
S'BE-YOND ME...
BUT A LOT'S HAP-PENED...
FOR HIM TO MAKE THIS FACE...
WHAT KINDA WOMAN'S THIS CASCA?

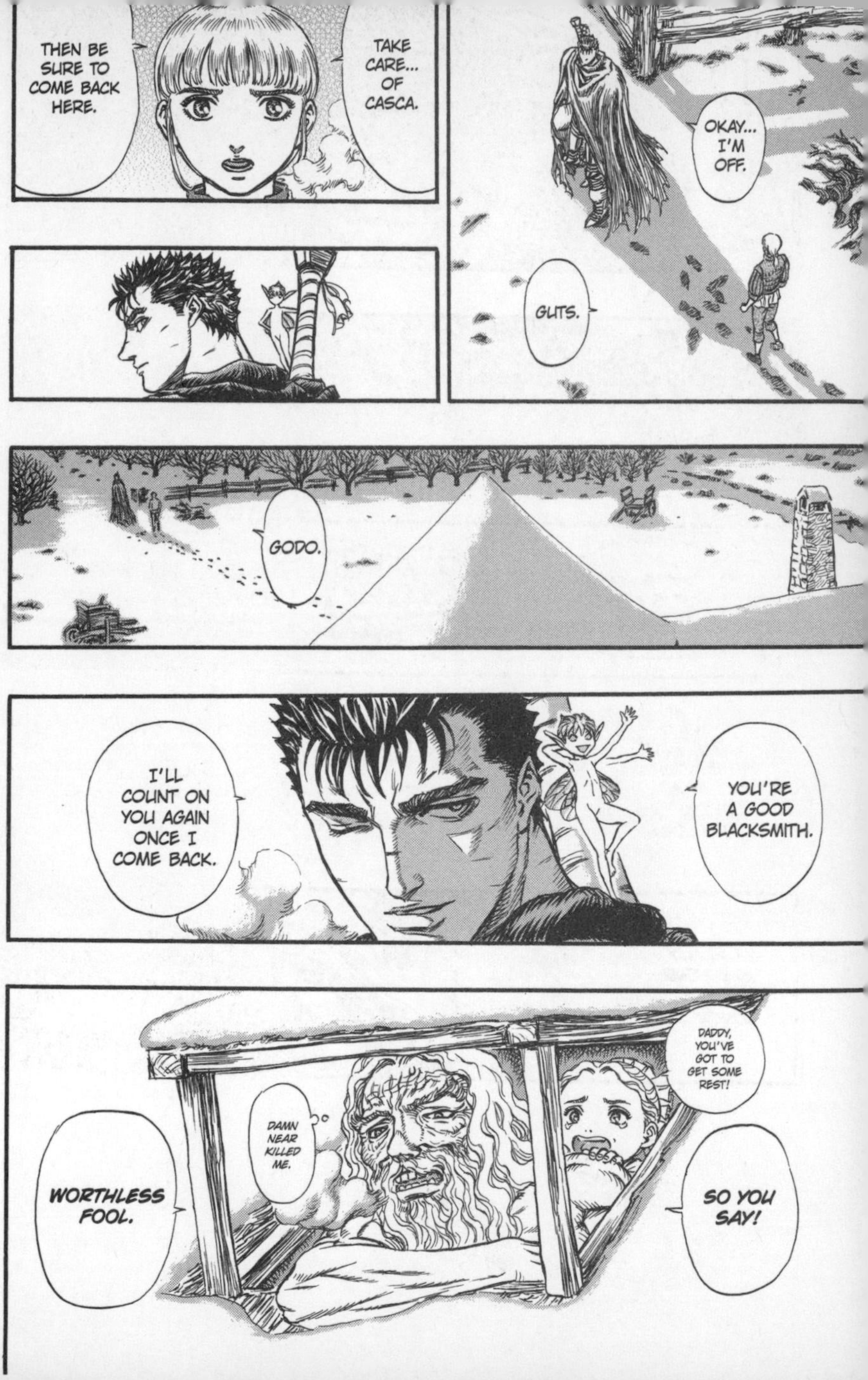
OKAY... I'M OFF.
GUTS.
TAKE CARE... OF CASCA.
THEN BE SURE TO COME BACK HERE.
GODO.
YOU'RE A GOOD BLACKSMITH.
I'LL COUNT ON YOU AGAIN ONCE I COME BACK.
DADDY, YOU'VE GOT TO GET SOME REST!
SO YOU SAY!
DAMN NEAR KILLED ME.
WORTHLESS FOOL.

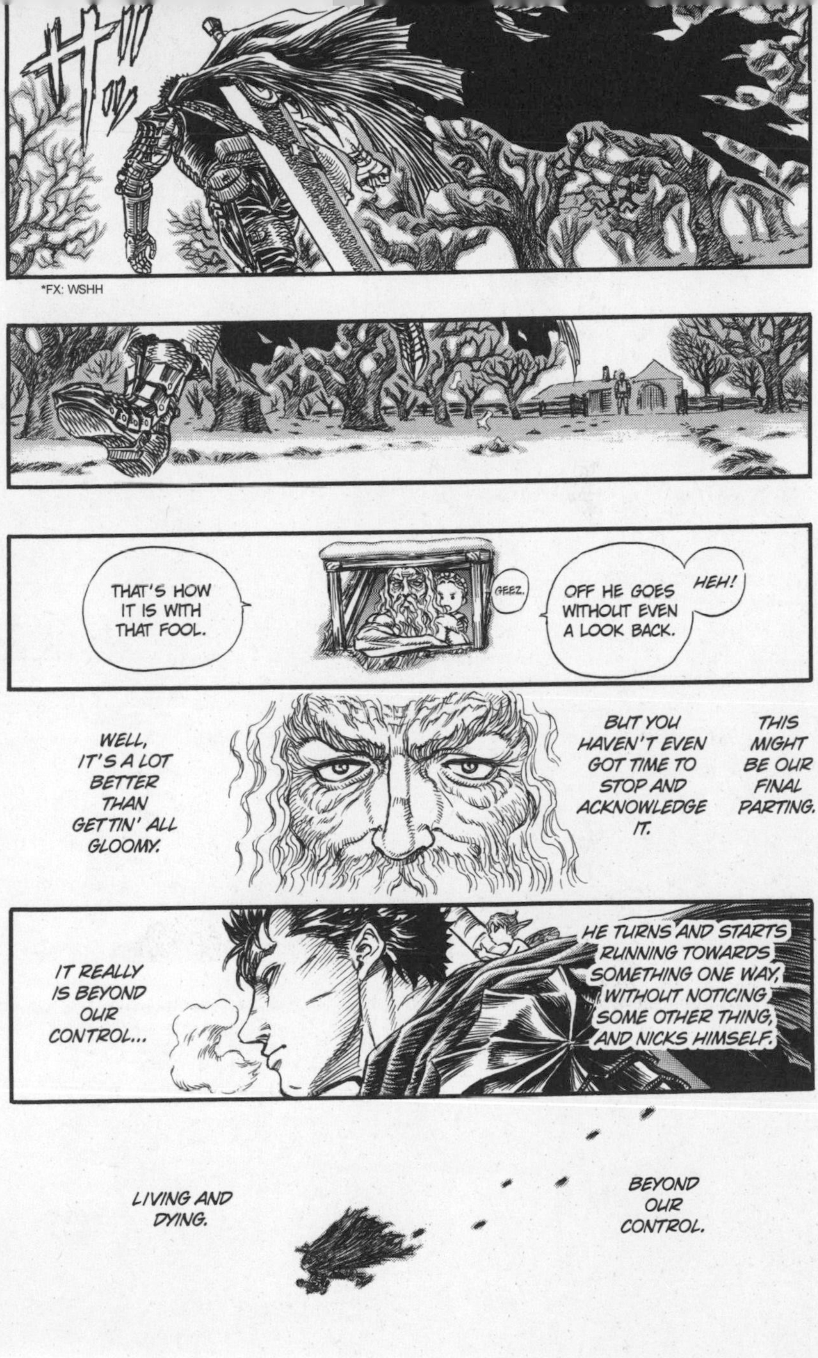
*FX: WSHH
HEH!
OFF HE GOES WITHOUT EVEN A LOOK BACK.
GEEZ.
THAT'S HOW IT IS WITH THAT FOOL.
THIS MIGHT BE OUR FINAL PARTING.
BUT YOU HAVEN'T EVEN GOT TIME TO STOP AND ACKNOWLEDGE IT.
WELL, IT'S A LOT BETTER THAN GETTIN' ALL GLOOMY.
HE TURNS AND STARTS RUNNING TOWARDS SOMETHING ONE WAY, WITHOUT NOTICING SOME OTHER THING, AND NICKS HIMSELF.
IT REALLY IS BEYOND OUR CONTROL...
BEYOND OUR CONTROL.
LIVING AND DYING.

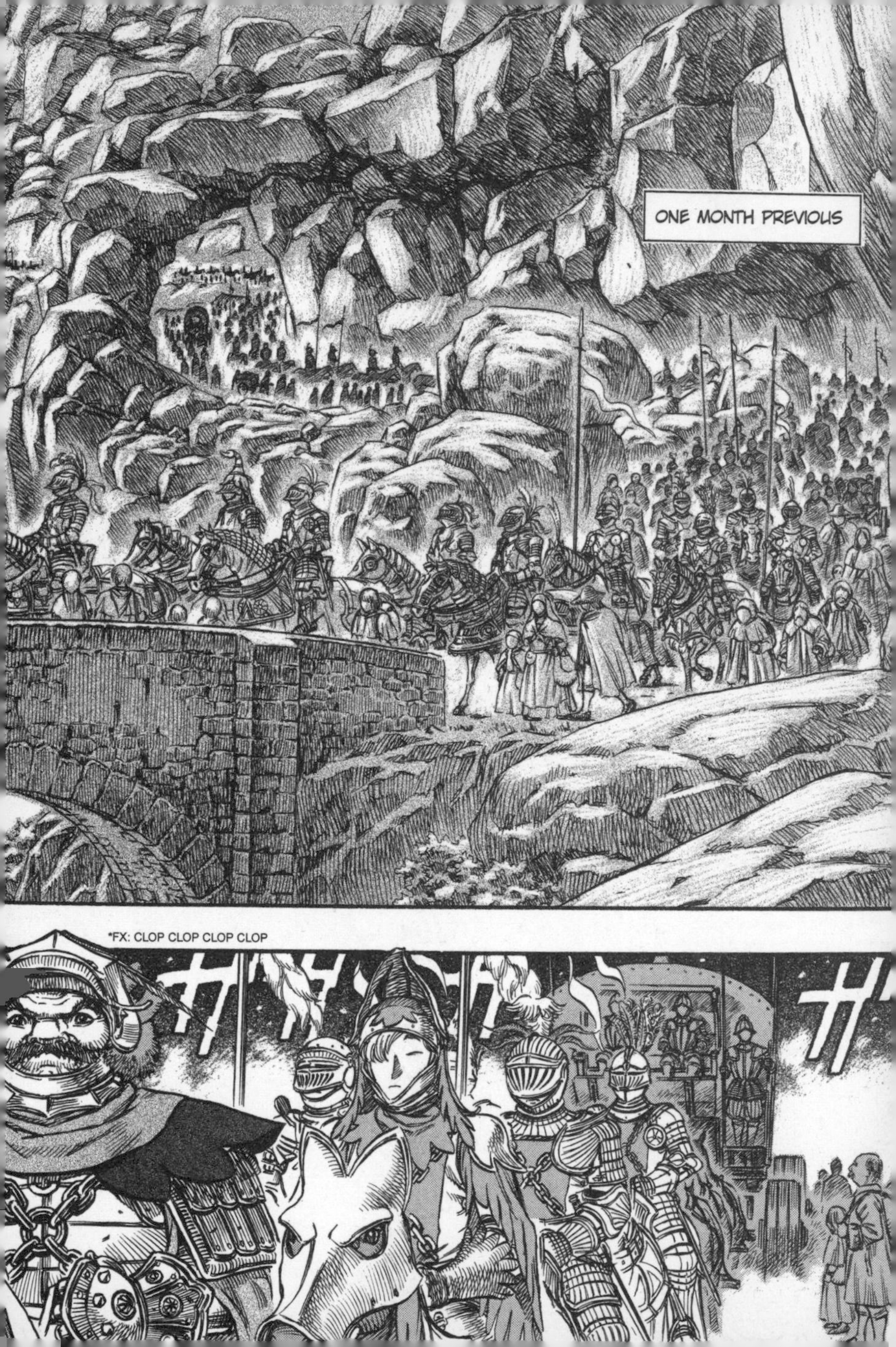
ONE MONTH PREVIOUS
*FX: CLOP CLOP CLOP CLOP

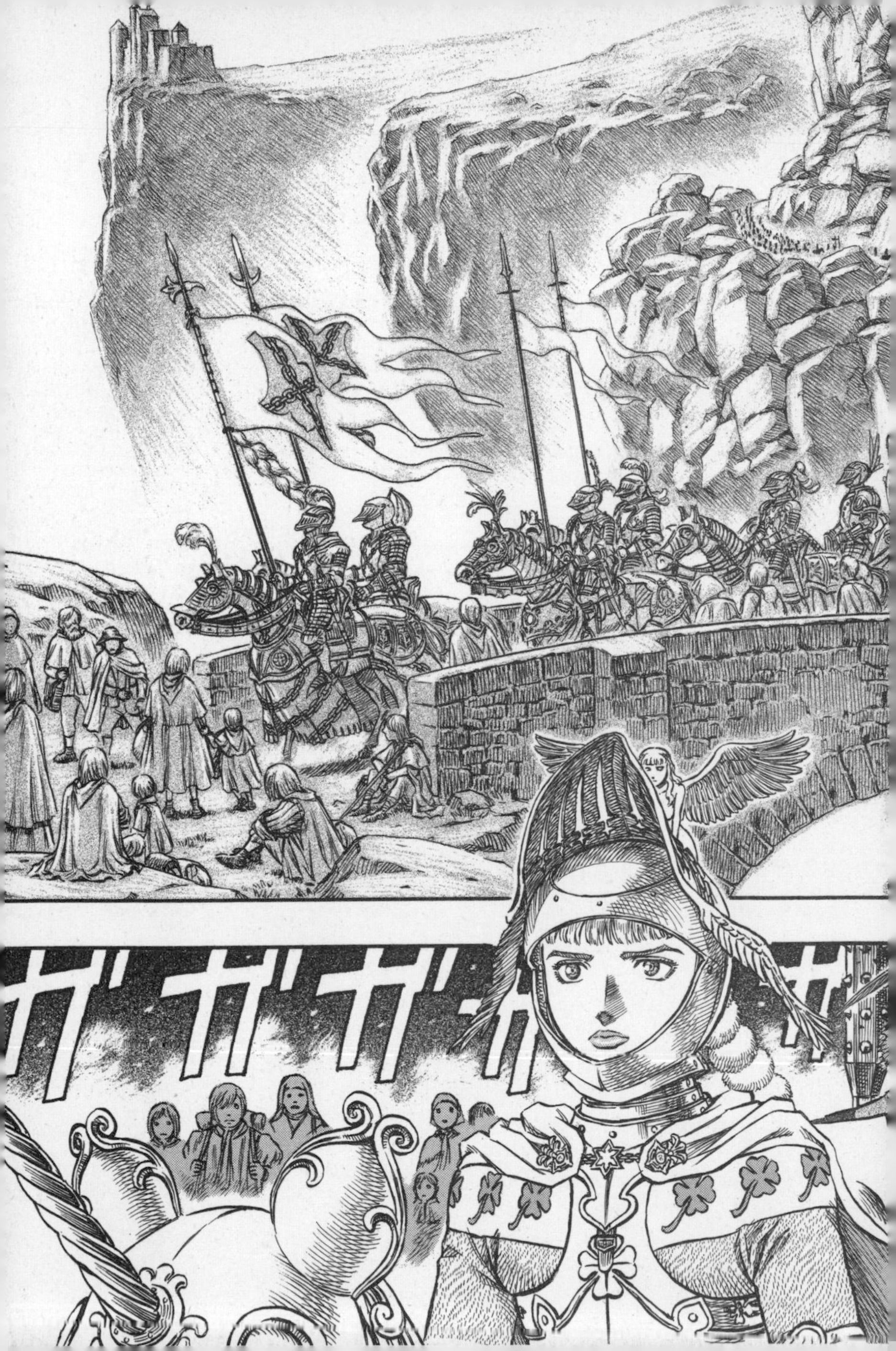
ガガガーガ ガ

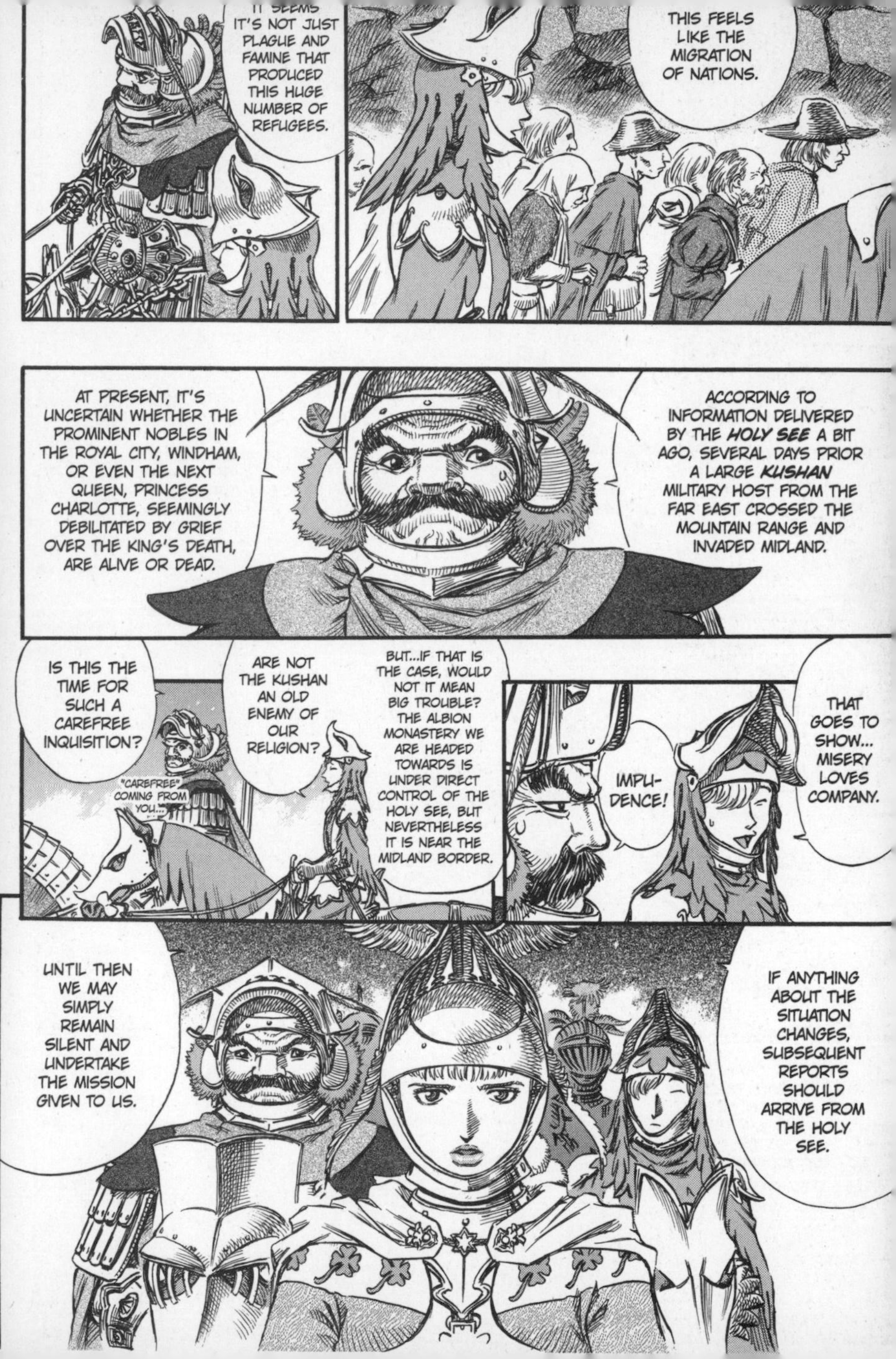
THIS FEELS LIKE THE MIGRATION OF NATIONS.
IT SEEMS IT'S NOT JUST PLAGUE AND FAMINE THAT PRODUCED THIS HUGE NUMBER OF REFUGEES.
ACCORDING TO INFORMATION DELIVERED BY THE HOLY SEE A BIT AGO, SEVERAL DAYS PRIOR A LARGE KUSHAN MILITARY HOST FROM THE FAR EAST CROSSED THE MOUNTAIN RANGE AND INVADED MIDLAND.
AT PRESENT, IT'S UNCERTAIN WHETHER THE PROMINENT NOBLES IN THE ROYAL CITY, WINDHAM, OR EVEN THE NEXT QUEEN, PRINCESS CHARLOTTE, SEEMINGLY DEBILITATED BY GRIEF OVER THE KING'S DEATH, ARE ALIVE OR DEAD.
THAT GOES TO SHOW... MISERY LOVES COMPANY.
IMPU-DENCE!
BUT...IF THAT IS THE CASE, WOULD NOT IT MEAN BIG TROUBLE? THE ALBION MONASTERY WE ARE HEADED TOWARDS IS UNDER DIRECT CONTROL OF THE HOLY SEE, BUT NEVERTHELESS IT IS NEAR THE MIDLAND BORDER.
ARE NOT THE KUSHAN AN OLD ENEMY OF OUR RELIGION?
IS THIS THE TIME FOR SUCH A CAREFREE INQUISITION?
"CAREFREE" COMING FROM YOU...
IF ANYTHING ABOUT THE SITUATION CHANGES, SUBSEQUENT REPORTS SHOULD ARRIVE FROM THE HOLY SEE.
UNTIL THEN WE MAY SIMPLY REMAIN SILENT AND UNDERTAKE THE MISSION GIVEN TO US.

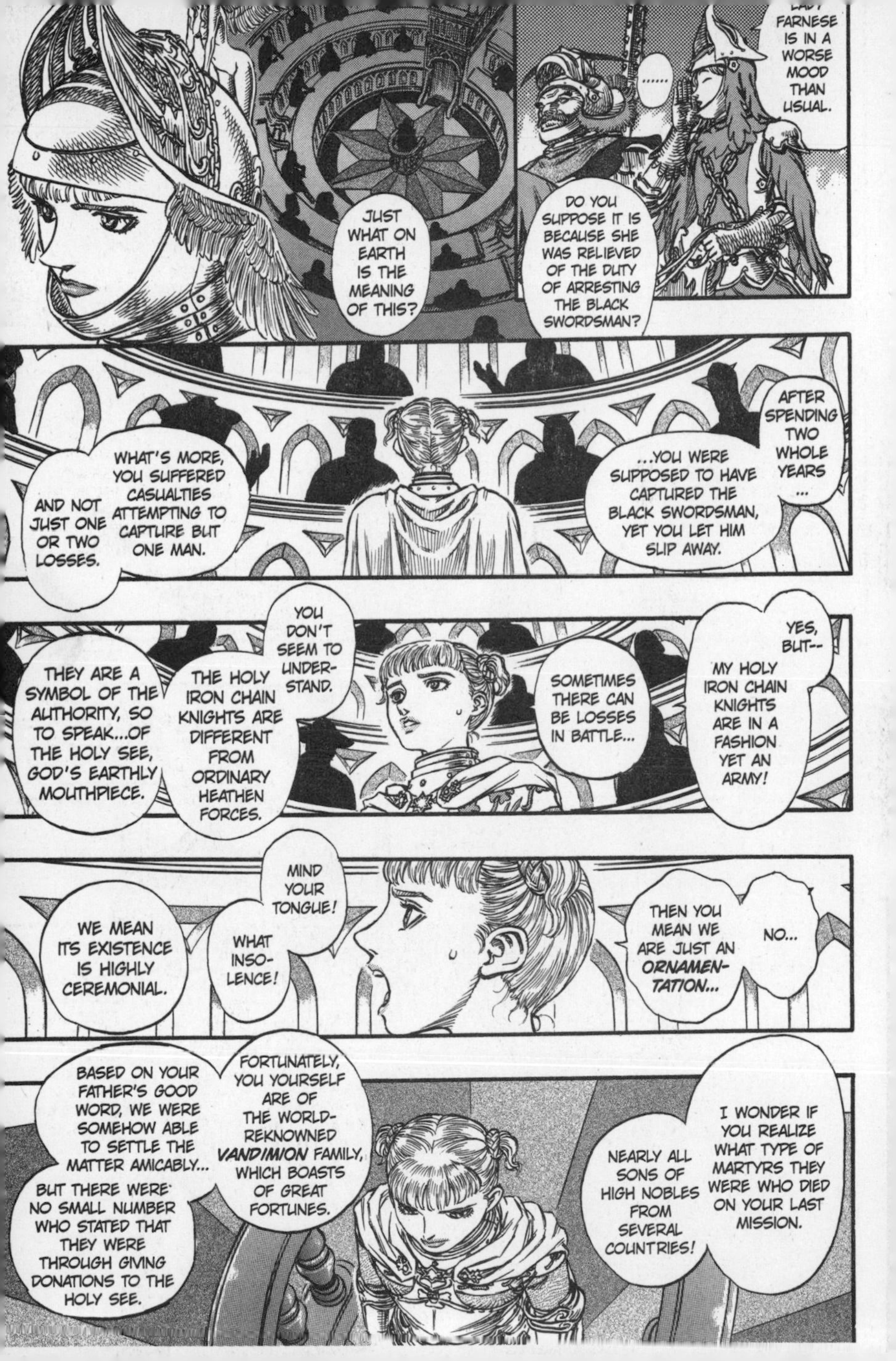
LADY FARNESE IS IN A WORSE MOOD THAN USUAL.
......
DO YOU SUPPOSE IT IS BECAUSE SHE WAS RELIEVED OF THE DUTY OF ARRESTING THE BLACK SWORDSMAN?
JUST WHAT ON EARTH IS THE MEANING OF THIS?
AFTER SPENDING TWO WHOLE YEARS ...
...YOU WERE SUPPOSED TO HAVE CAPTURED THE BLACK SWORDSMAN, YET YOU LET HIM SLIP AWAY.
WHAT'S MORE, YOU SUFFERED CASUALTIES ATTEMPTING TO CAPTURE BUT ONE MAN.
AND NOT JUST ONE OR TWO LOSSES.
YES, BUT--
MY HOLY IRON CHAIN KNIGHTS ARE IN A FASHION YET AN ARMY!
SOMETIMES THERE CAN BE LOSSES IN BATTLE...
YOU DON'T SEEM TO UNDER-STAND.
THE HOLY IRON CHAIN KNIGHTS ARE DIFFERENT FROM ORDINARY HEATHEN FORCES.
THEY ARE A SYMBOL OF THE AUTHORITY, SO TO SPEAK...OF THE HOLY SEE, GOD'S EARTHLY MOUTHPIECE.
NO...
THEN YOU MEAN WE ARE JUST AN *ORNAMENTATION...*
MIND YOUR TONGUE!
WHAT INSO-LENCE!
WE MEAN ITS EXISTENCE IS HIGHLY CEREMONIAL.
I WONDER IF YOU REALIZE WHAT TYPE OF MARTYRS THEY WERE WHO DIED ON YOUR LAST MISSION.
NEARLY ALL SONS OF HIGH NOBLES FROM SEVERAL COUNTRIES!
FORTUNATELY, YOU YOURSELF ARE OF THE WORLD-REKNOWNED *VANDIMION* FAMILY, WHICH BOASTS OF GREAT FORTUNES.
BASED ON YOUR FATHER'S GOOD WORD, WE WERE SOMEHOW ABLE TO SETTLE THE MATTER AMICABLY...
BUT THERE WERE NO SMALL NUMBER WHO STATED THAT THEY WERE THROUGH GIVING DONATIONS TO THE HOLY SEE.

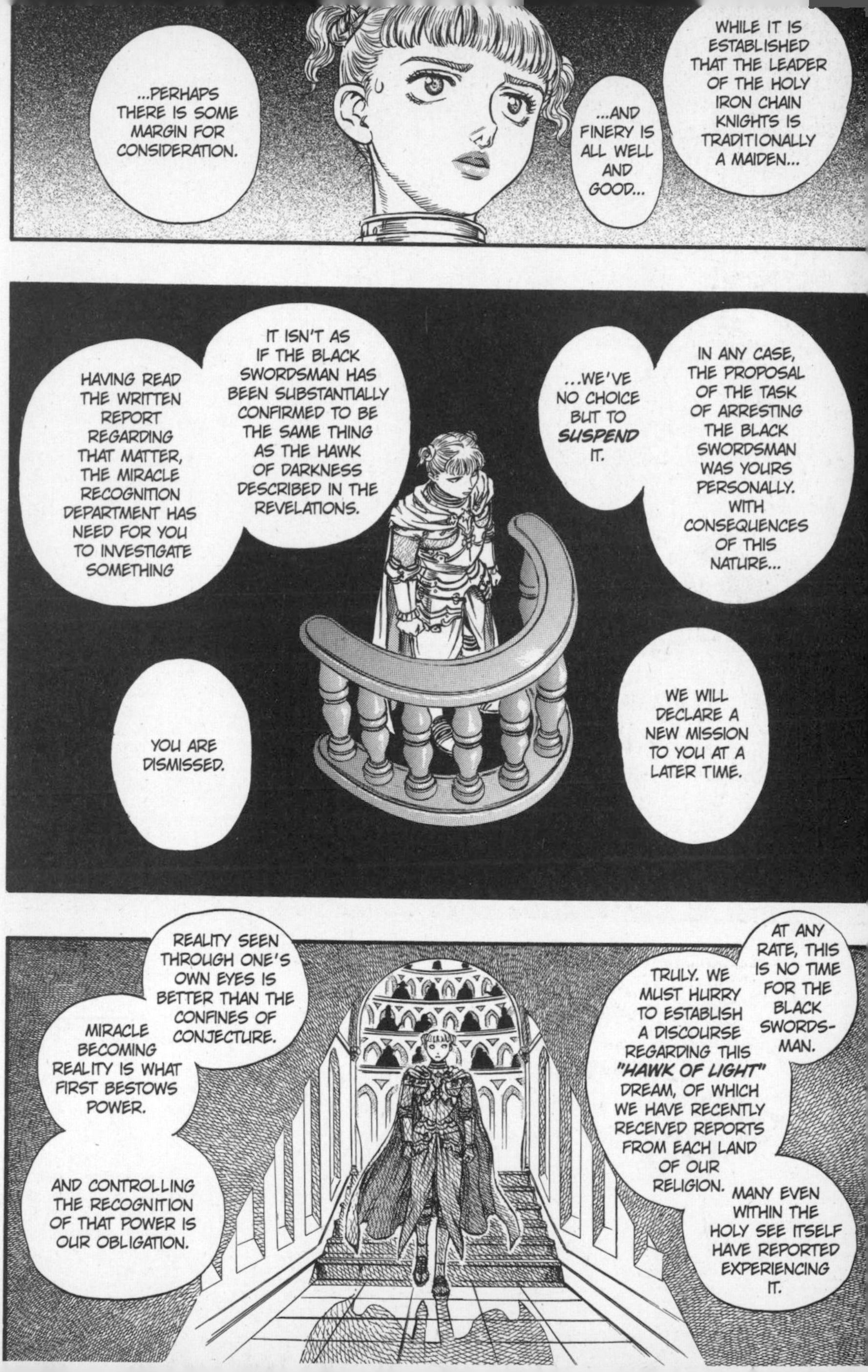
WHILE IT IS ESTABLISHED THAT THE LEADER OF THE HOLY IRON CHAIN KNIGHTS IS TRADITIONALLY A MAIDEN...
...AND FINERY IS ALL WELL AND GOOD...
...PERHAPS THERE IS SOME MARGIN FOR CONSIDERATION.
IN ANY CASE, THE PROPOSAL OF THE TASK OF ARRESTING THE BLACK SWORDSMAN WAS YOURS PERSONALLY. WITH CONSEQUENCES OF THIS NATURE...
...WE'VE NO CHOICE BUT TO *SUSPEND* IT.
IT ISN'T AS IF THE BLACK SWORDSMAN HAS BEEN SUBSTANTIALLY CONFIRMED TO BE THE SAME THING AS THE HAWK OF DARKNESS DESCRIBED IN THE REVELATIONS.
HAVING READ THE WRITTEN REPORT REGARDING THAT MATTER, THE MIRACLE RECOGNITION DEPARTMENT HAS NEED FOR YOU TO INVESTIGATE SOMETHING
WE WILL DECLARE A NEW MISSION TO YOU AT A LATER TIME.
YOU ARE DISMISSED.
AT ANY RATE, THIS IS NO TIME FOR THE BLACK SWORDS-MAN.
TRULY. WE MUST HURRY TO ESTABLISH A DISCOURSE REGARDING THIS ***"HAWK OF LIGHT"*** DREAM, OF WHICH WE HAVE RECENTLY RECEIVED REPORTS FROM EACH LAND OF OUR RELIGION.
MANY EVEN WITHIN THE HOLY SEE ITSELF HAVE REPORTED EXPERIENCING IT.
REALITY SEEN THROUGH ONE'S OWN EYES IS BETTER THAN THE CONFINES OF CONJECTURE.
MIRACLE BECOMING REALITY IS WHAT FIRST BESTOWS POWER.
AND CONTROLLING THE RECOGNITION OF THAT POWER IS OUR OBLIGATION.

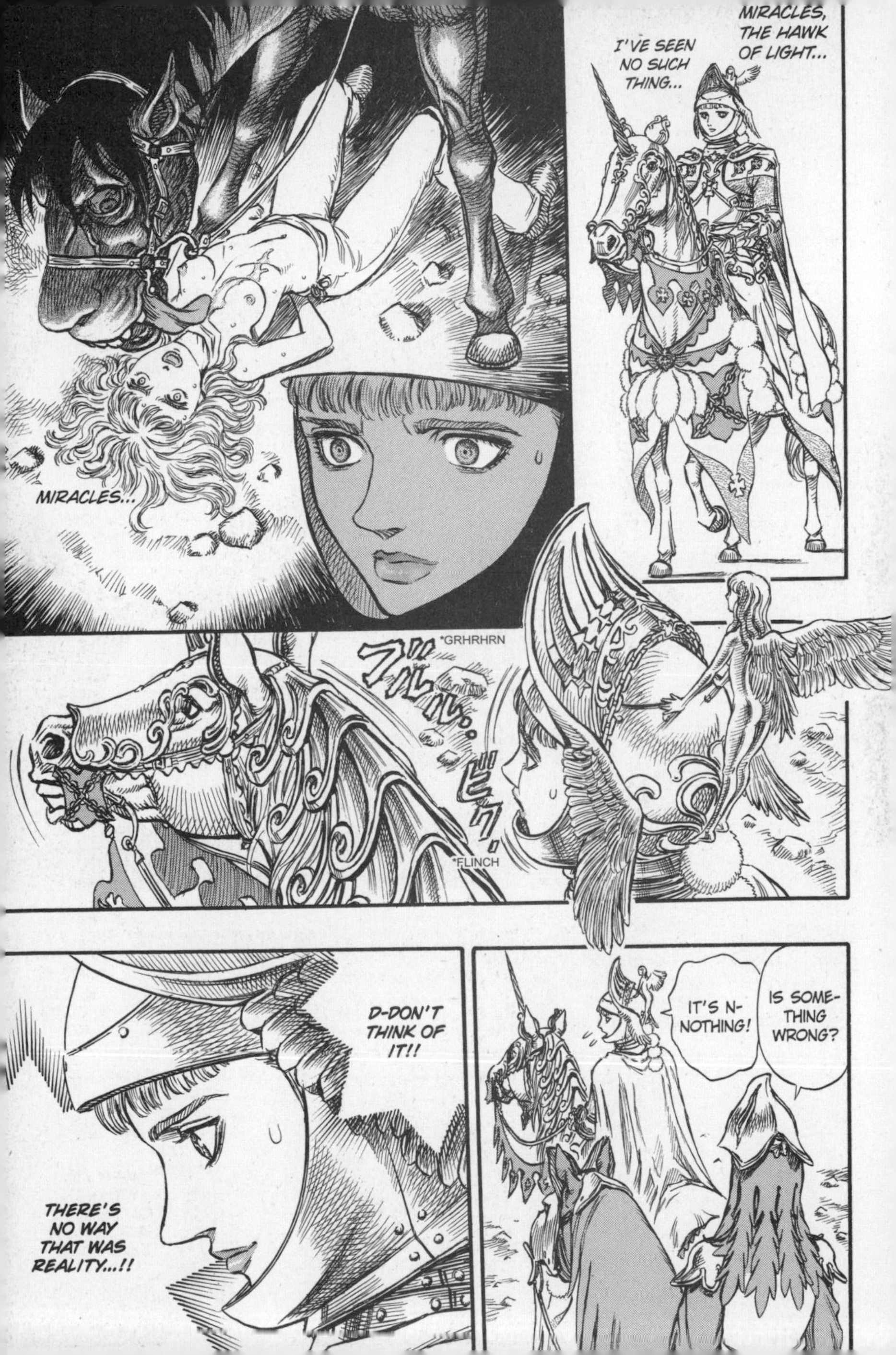
MIRACLES, THE HAWK OF LIGHT...
I'VE SEEN NO SUCH THING...
MIRACLES...
*GRHRHRN
*FLINCH
IS SOME-THING WRONG?
IT'S N-NOTHING!
D-DON'T THINK OF IT!!
THERE'S NO WAY THAT WAS REALITY...!!

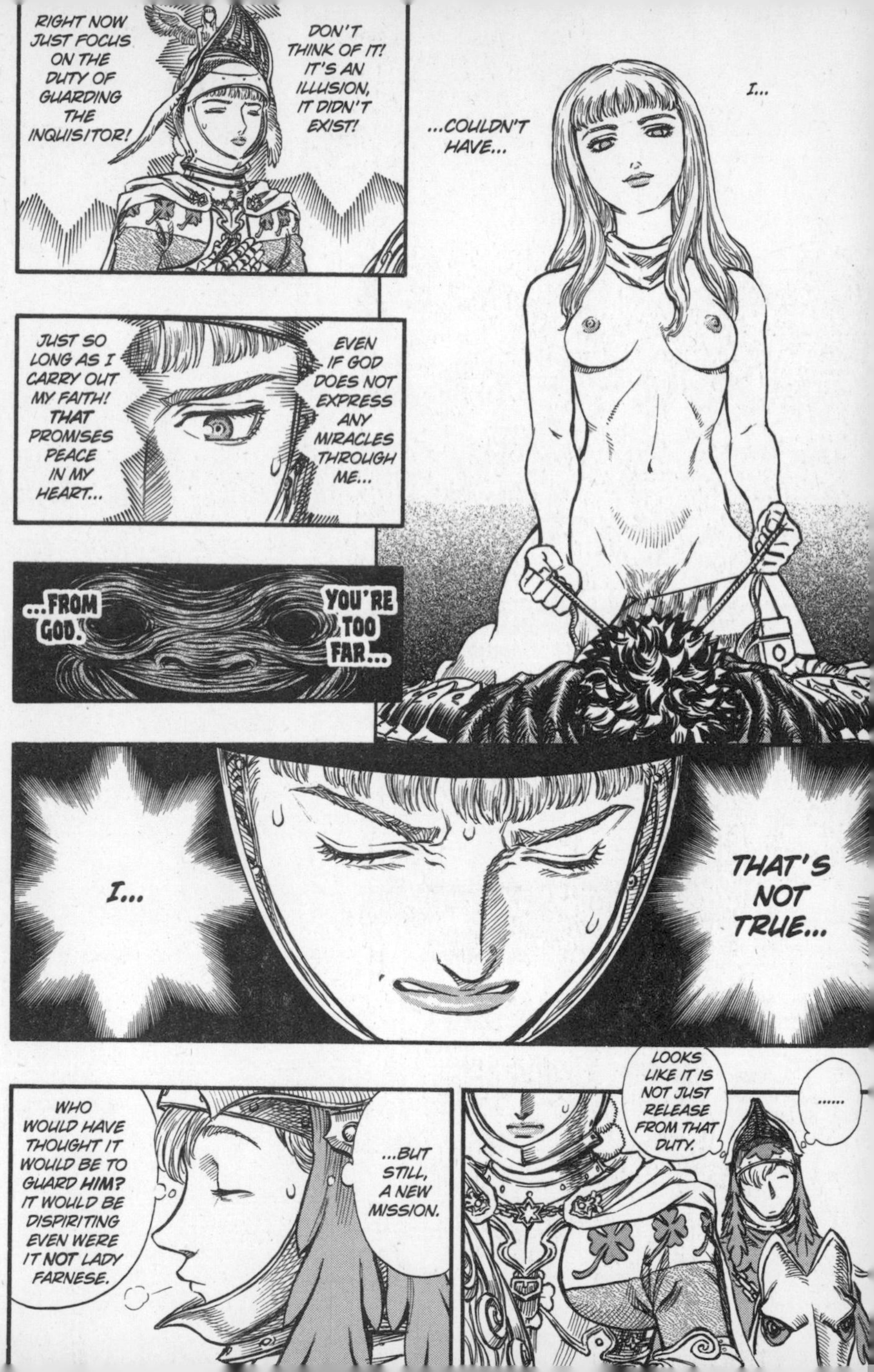
I...
...COULDN'T HAVE...
DON'T THINK OF IT! IT'S AN ILLUSION, IT DIDN'T EXIST!
RIGHT NOW JUST FOCUS ON THE DUTY OF GUARDING THE INQUISITOR!
EVEN IF GOD DOES NOT EXPRESS ANY MIRACLES THROUGH ME...
JUST SO LONG AS I CARRY OUT MY FAITH! THAT PROMISES PEACE IN MY HEART...
YOU'RE TOO FAR...
...FROM GOD.
THAT'S NOT TRUE...
I...
......
LOOKS LIKE IT IS NOT JUST RELEASE FROM THAT DUTY.
...BUT STILL, A NEW MISSION.
WHO WOULD HAVE THOUGHT IT WOULD BE TO GUARD HIM? IT WOULD BE DISPIRITING EVEN WERE IT NOT LADY FARNESE.

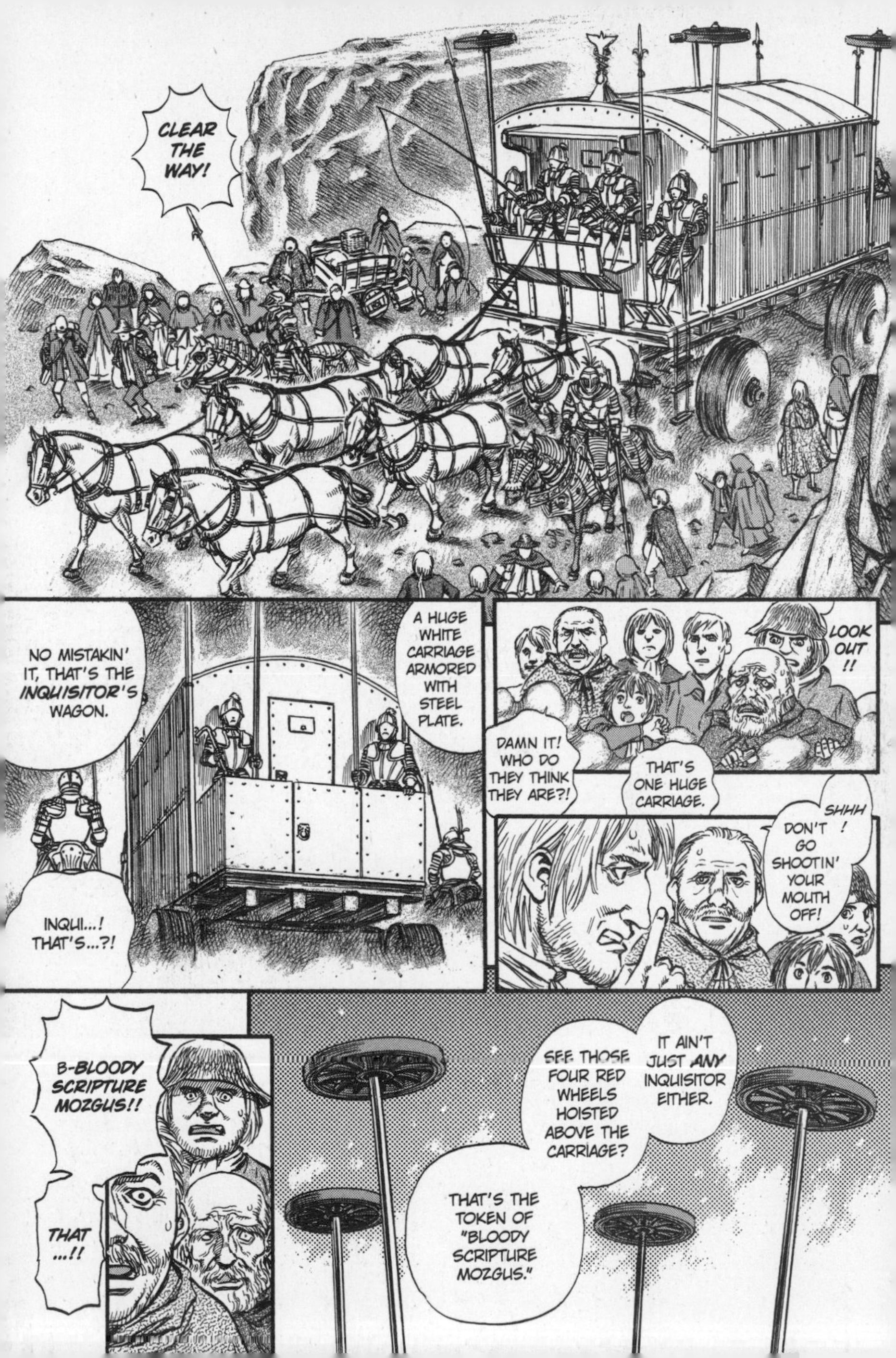
CLEAR THE WAY!
LOOK OUT!!
DAMN IT! WHO DO THEY THINK THEY ARE?!
THAT'S ONE HUGE CARRIAGE.
SHHH! DON'T GO SHOOTIN' YOUR MOUTH OFF!
A HUGE WHITE CARRIAGE ARMORED WITH STEEL PLATE.
NO MISTAKIN' IT, THAT'S THE *INQUISITOR*'S WAGON.
INQUI...! THAT'S...?!
IT AIN'T JUST *ANY* INQUISITOR EITHER.
SEE THOSE FOUR RED WHEELS HOISTED ABOVE THE CARRIAGE?
THAT'S THE TOKEN OF "BLOODY SCRIPTURE MOZGUS."
B-*BLOODY SCRIPTURE MOZGUS!!*
THAT ...!!

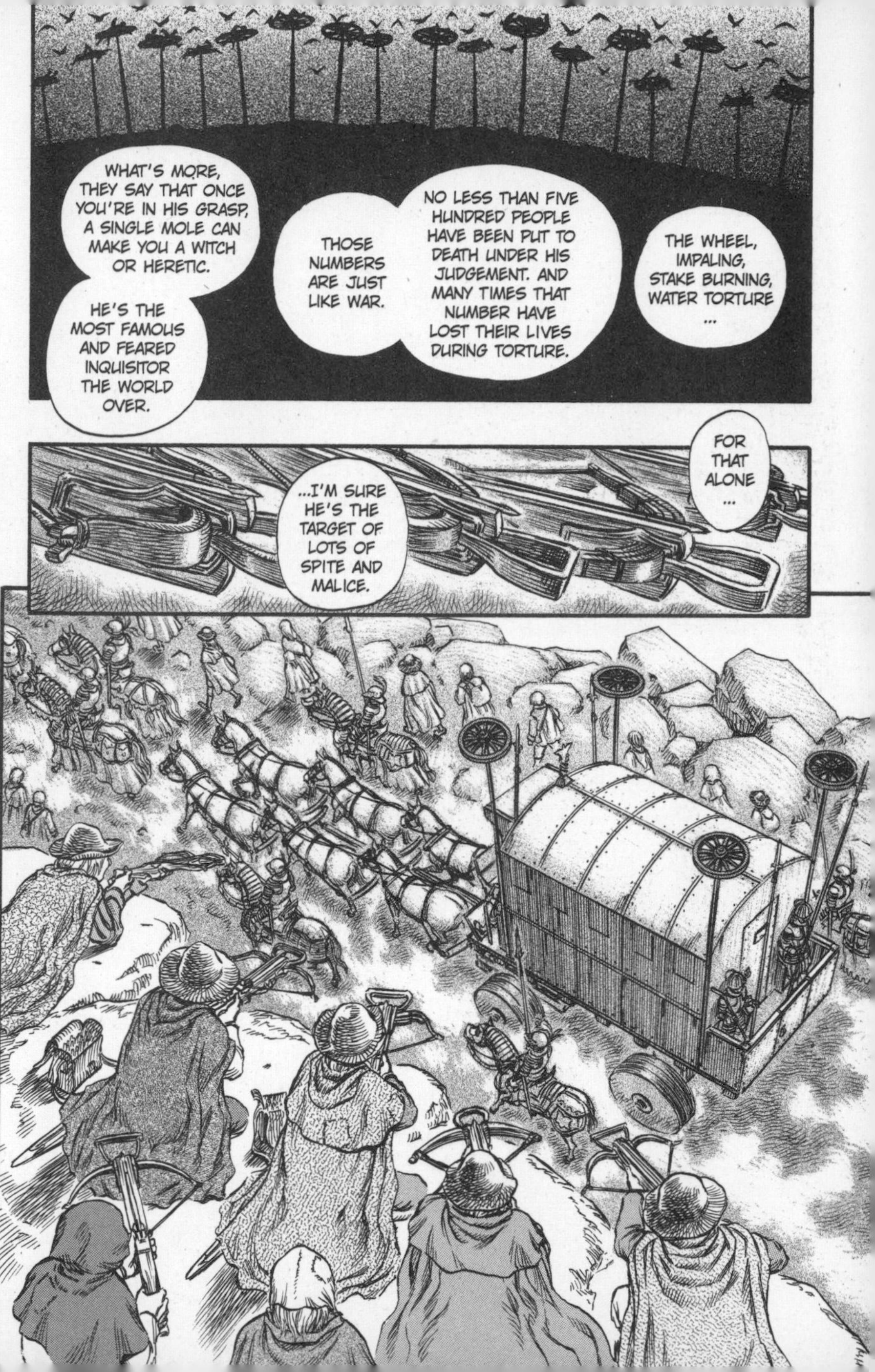
THE WHEEL, IMPALING, STAKE BURNING, WATER TORTURE ...
NO LESS THAN FIVE HUNDRED PEOPLE HAVE BEEN PUT TO DEATH UNDER HIS JUDGEMENT. AND MANY TIMES THAT NUMBER HAVE LOST THEIR LIVES DURING TORTURE.
THOSE NUMBERS ARE JUST LIKE WAR.
WHAT'S MORE, THEY SAY THAT ONCE YOU'RE IN HIS GRASP, A SINGLE MOLE CAN MAKE YOU A WITCH OR HERETIC.
HE'S THE MOST FAMOUS AND FEARED INQUISITOR THE WORLD OVER.
FOR THAT ALONE ...
...I'M SURE HE'S THE TARGET OF LOTS OF SPITE AND MALICE.

断罪篇 生誕祭の章 聖地へ②

CONVICTION ARC
BIRTH CEREMONY CHAPTER
TO HOLY GROUND, PART 2

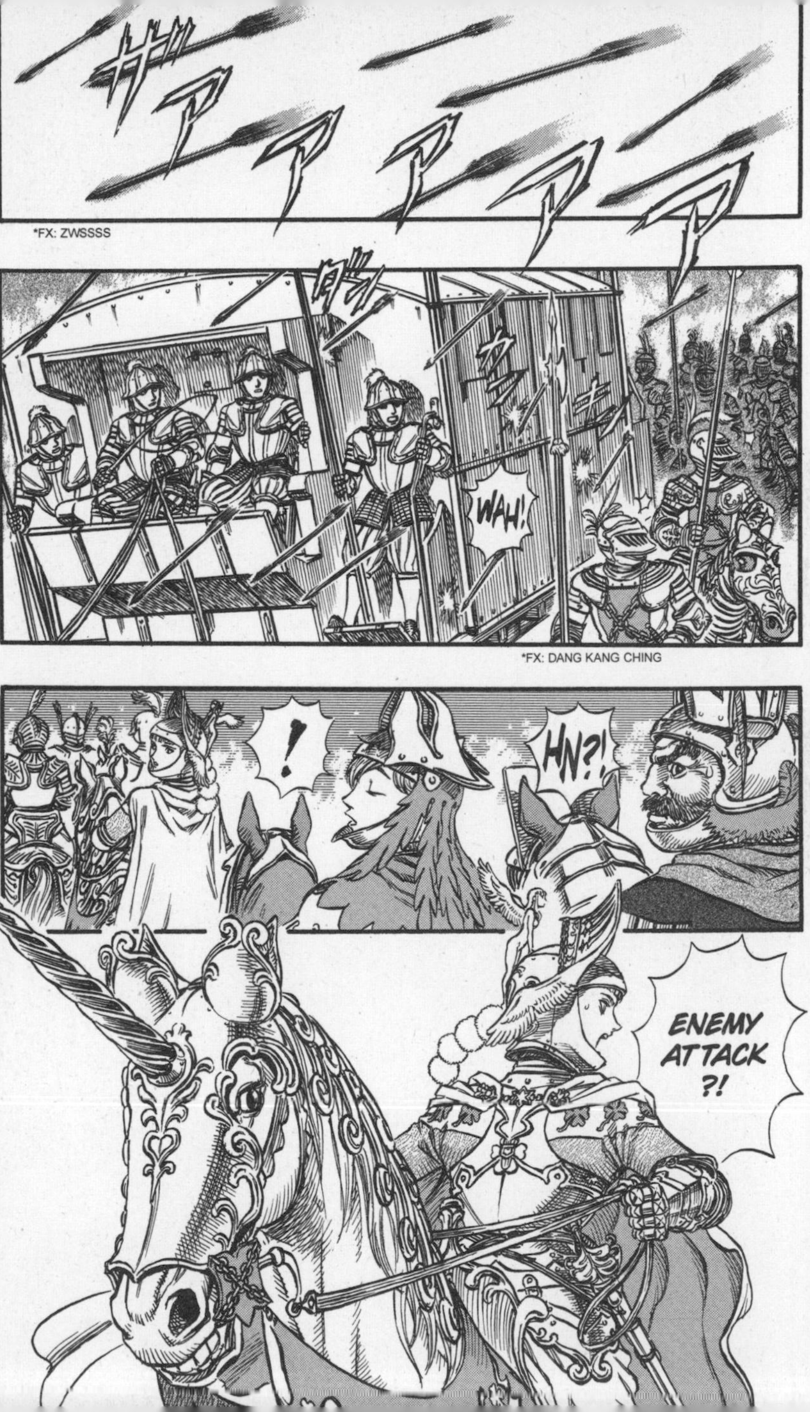
*FX: ZWSSSS
WAH!
*FX: DANG KANG CHING
HN?!
!
ENEMY ATTACK ?!

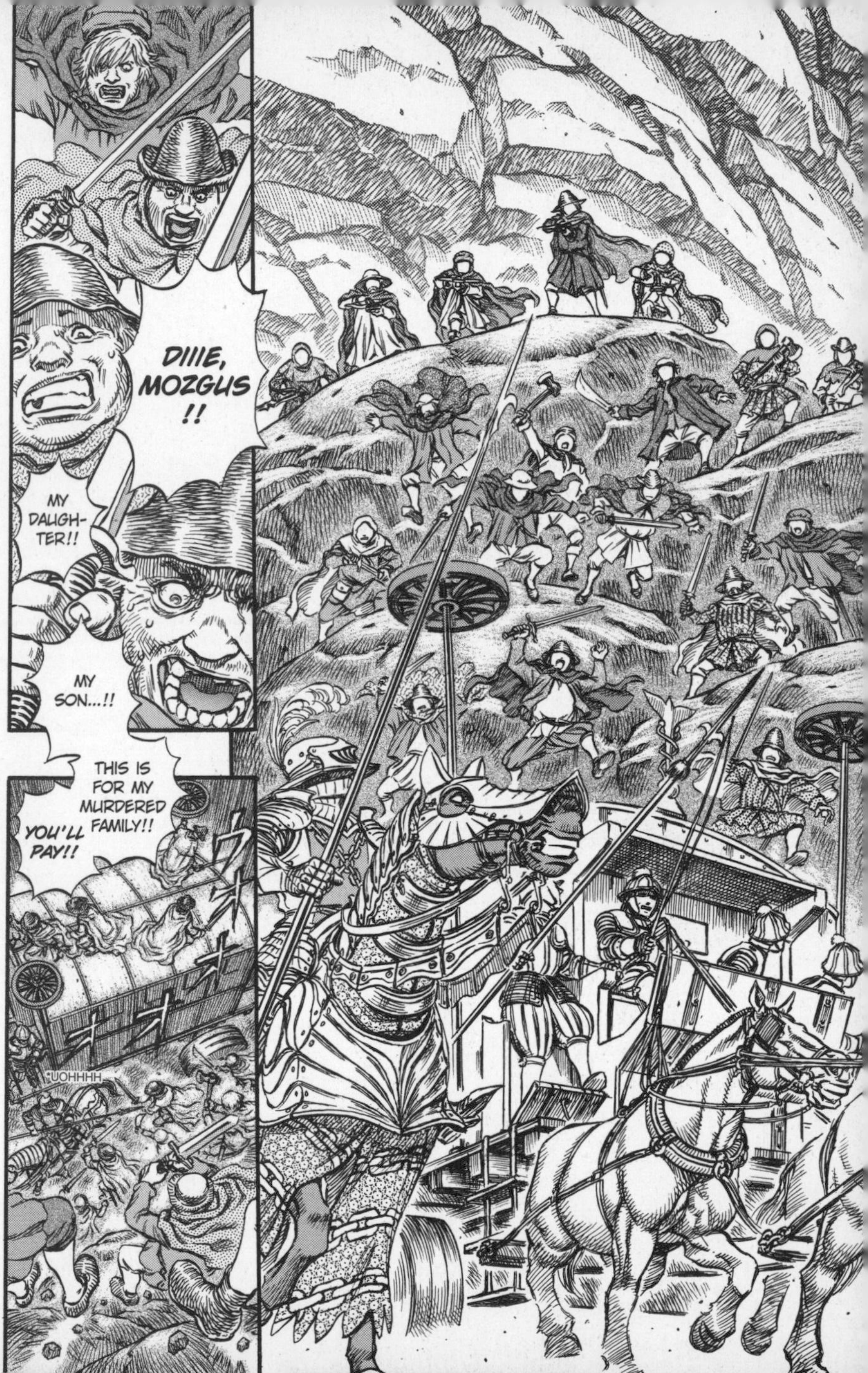
DIIIE, MOZGUS!!
MY DAUGHTER!!
MY SON...!!
THIS IS FOR MY MURDERED FAMILY!!
YOU'LL PAY!!
UOHHHH

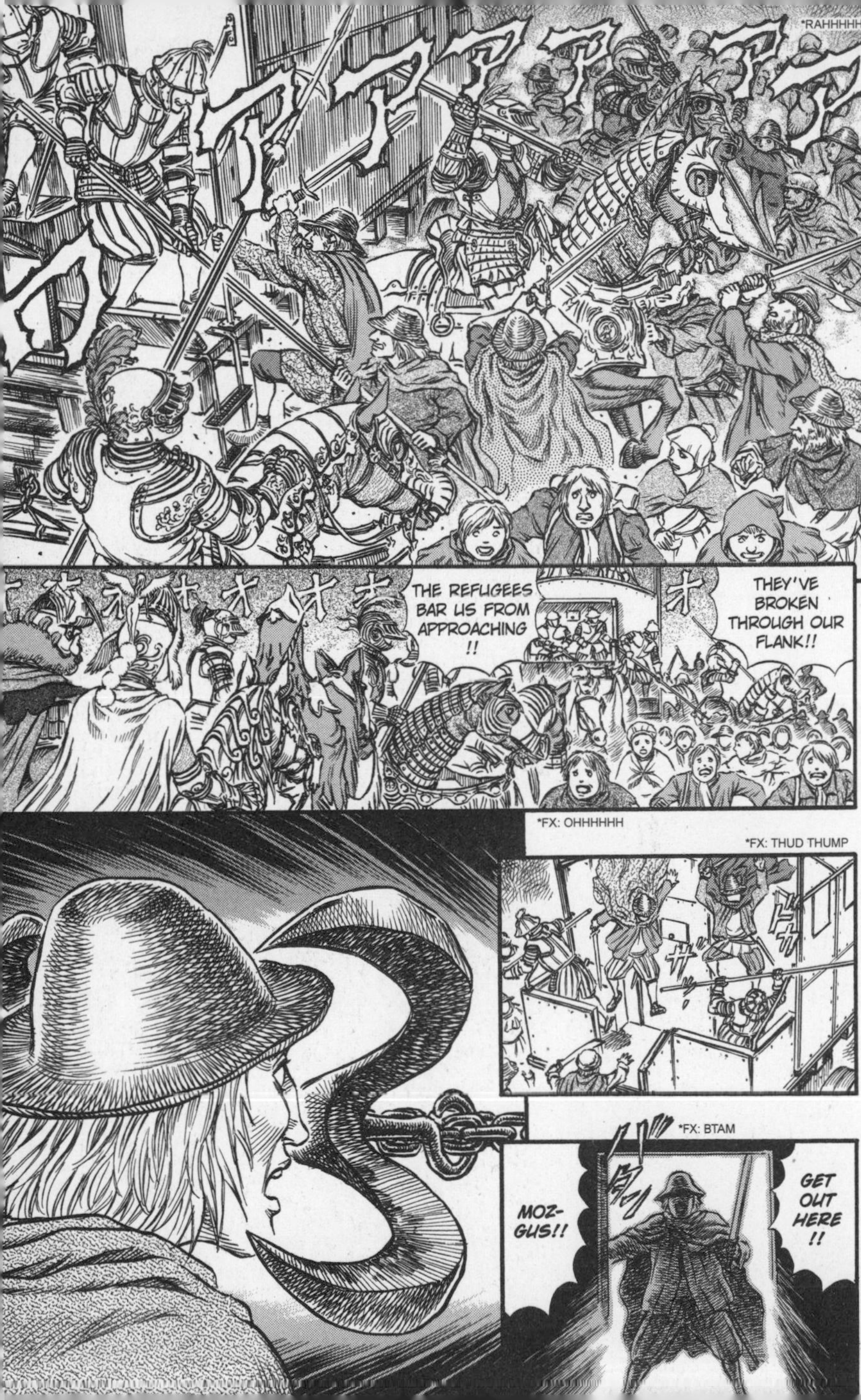
*RAHHHHHH
THEY'VE BROKEN THROUGH OUR FLANK!!
THE REFUGEES BAR US FROM APPROACHING!!
*FX: OHHHHHH
*FX: THUD THUMP
*FX: BTAM
GET OUT HERE!!
MOZ-GUS!!

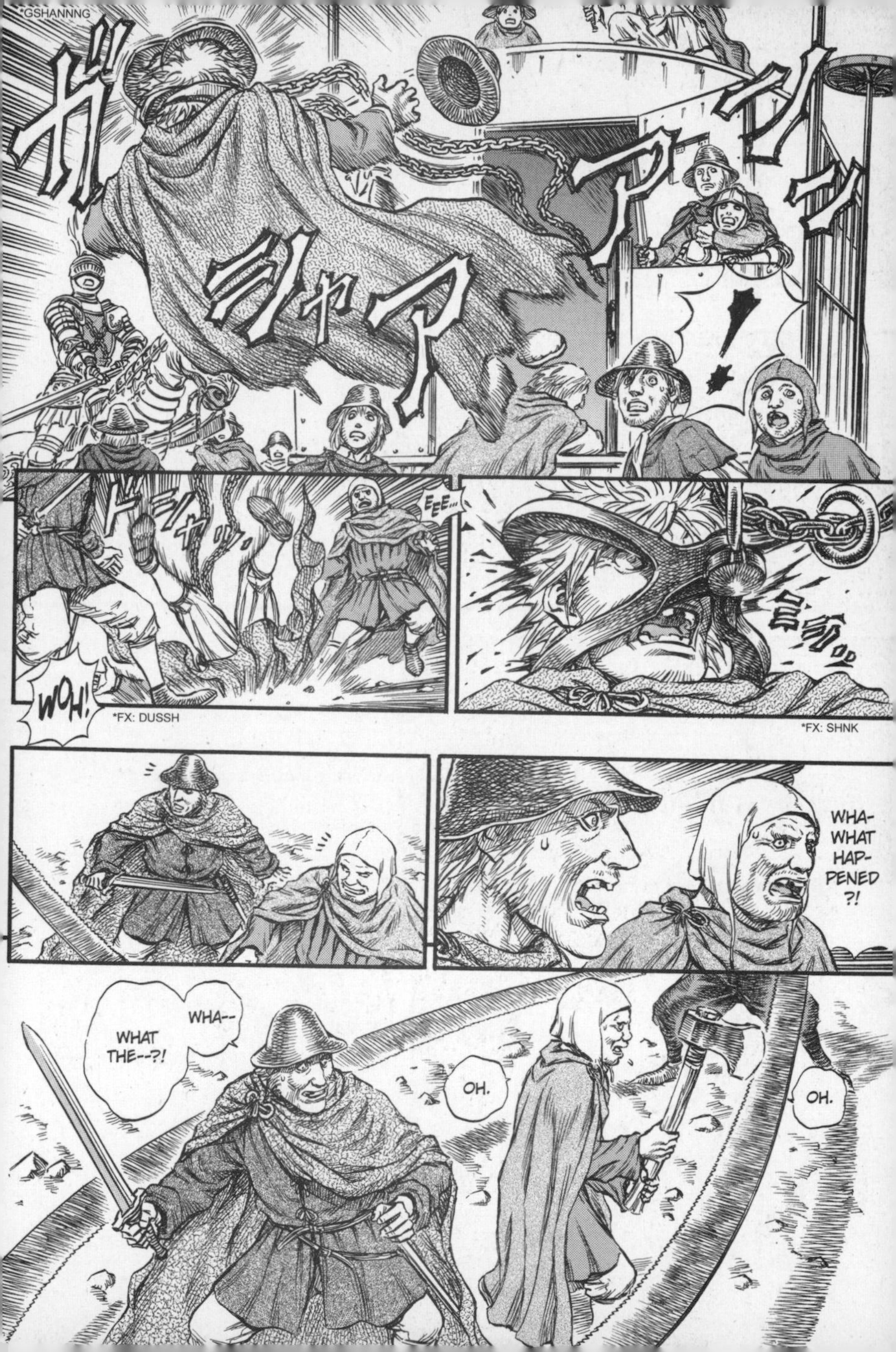
*GSHANNNG
*FX: SHNK
EEE...
WOH!
*FX: DUSSH
WHA-WHAT HAPPENED?!
OH.
OH.
WHA--
WHAT THE--?!

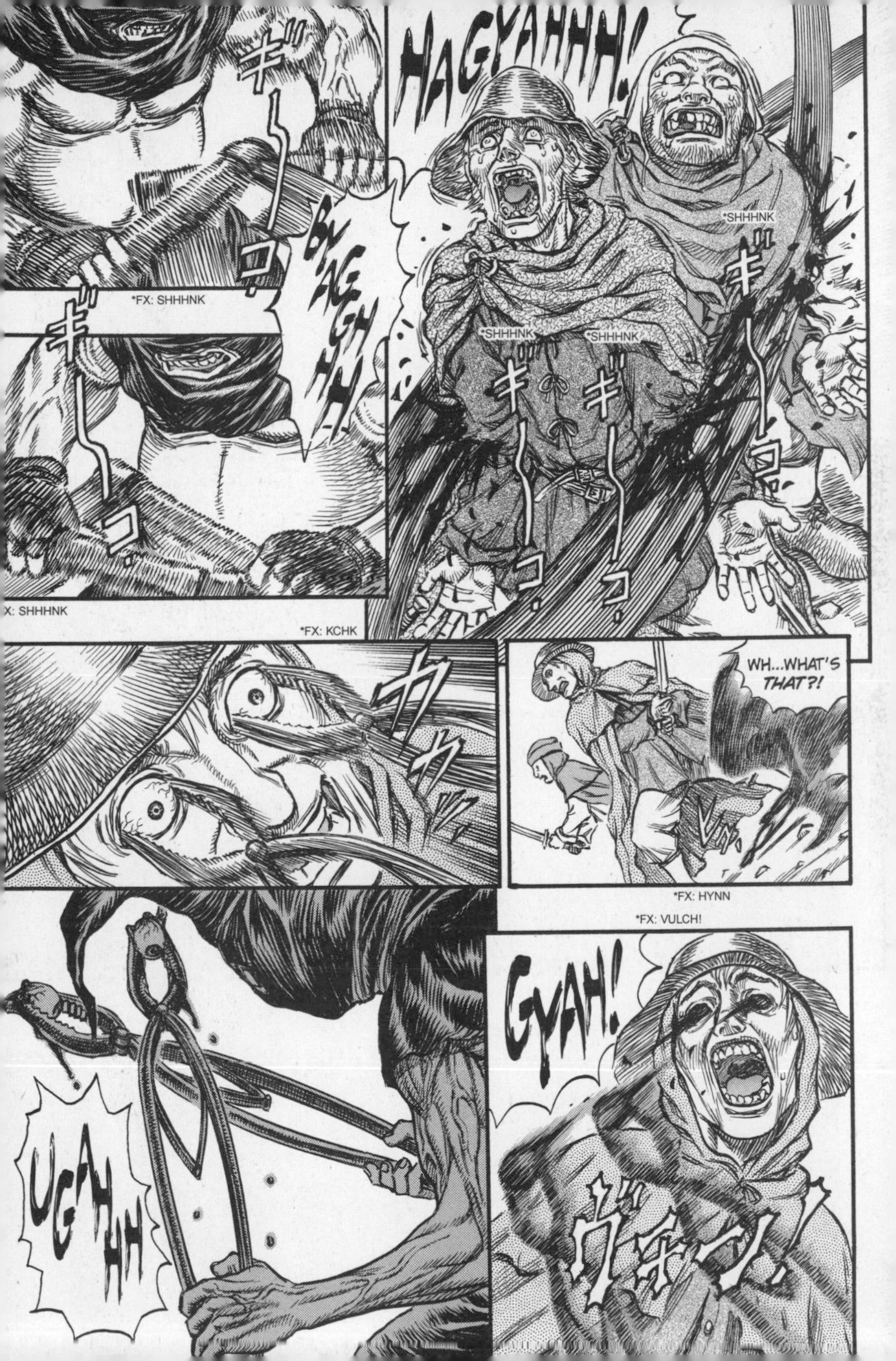
HAGYAHHH!
*SHHHNK
*SHHHNK
*SHHHNK
*FX: KCHK
BWAGHHH!
*FX: SHHHNK
X: SHHHNK
WH...WHAT'S THAT?!
*FX: HYNN
GYAH!
*FX: VULCH!
UGAHHH

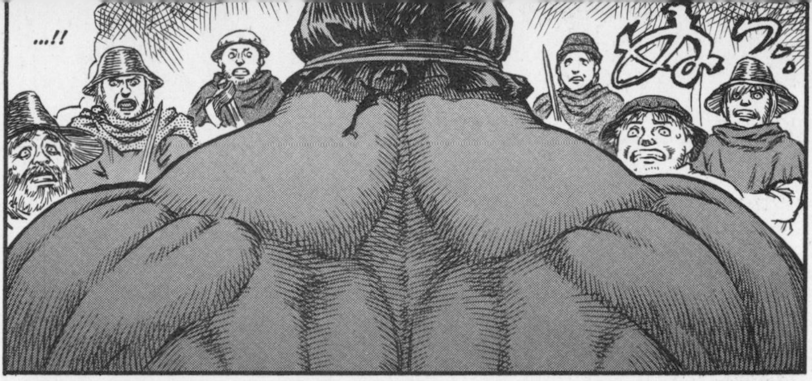
ぬっ
...!!

*FX: LOOM

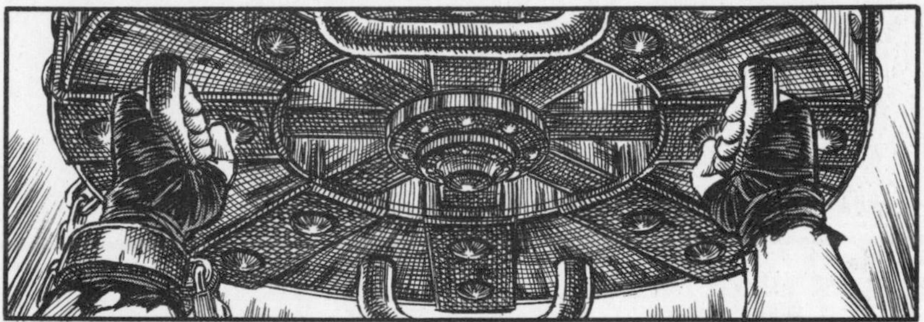

*FX: WHOMP

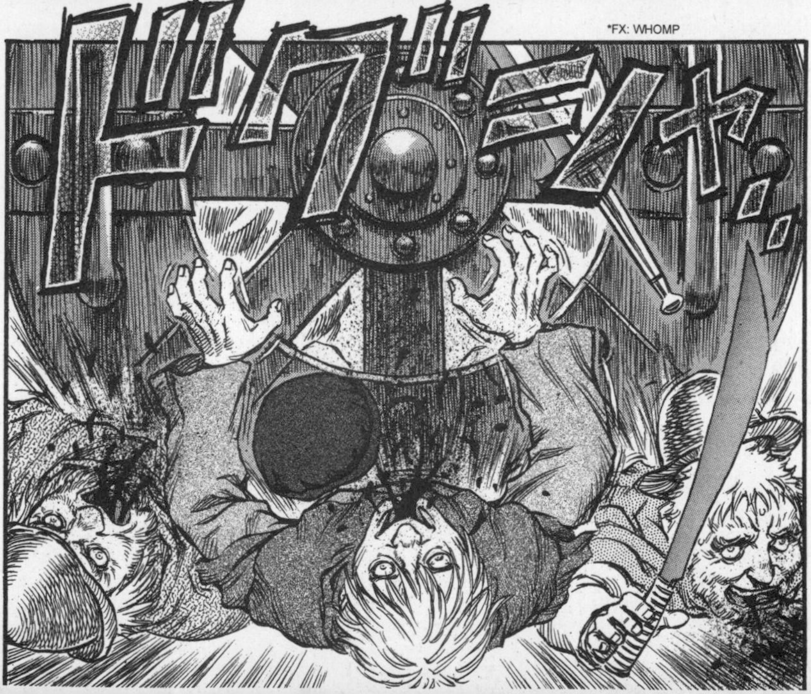
ドッグシャ

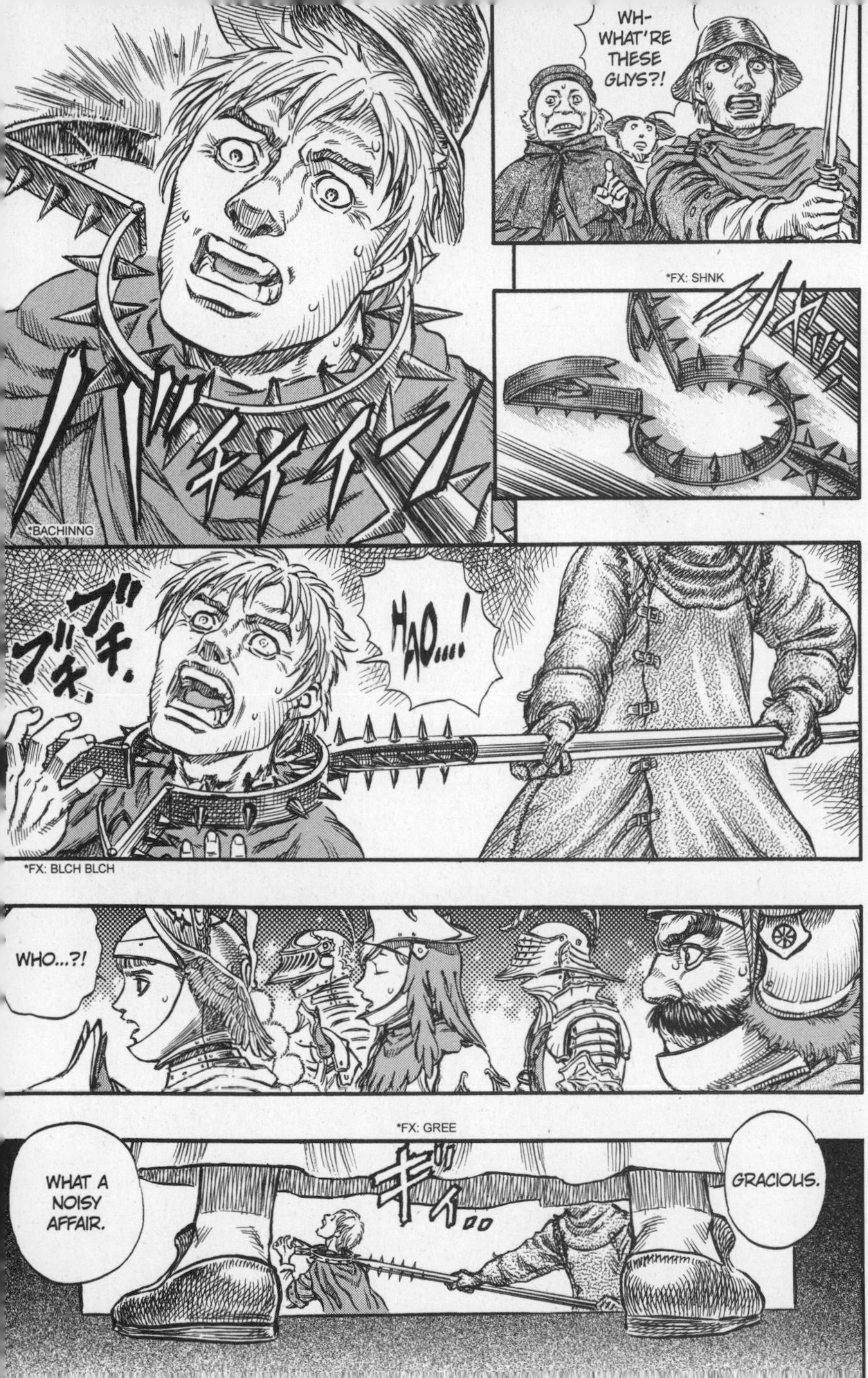
WH-WHAT'RE THESE GUYS?!
*FX: SHNK
*BACHINNG
HAO...!
*FX: BLCH BLCH
WHO...?!
GRACIOUS.
*FX: GREE
WHAT A NOISY AFFAIR.

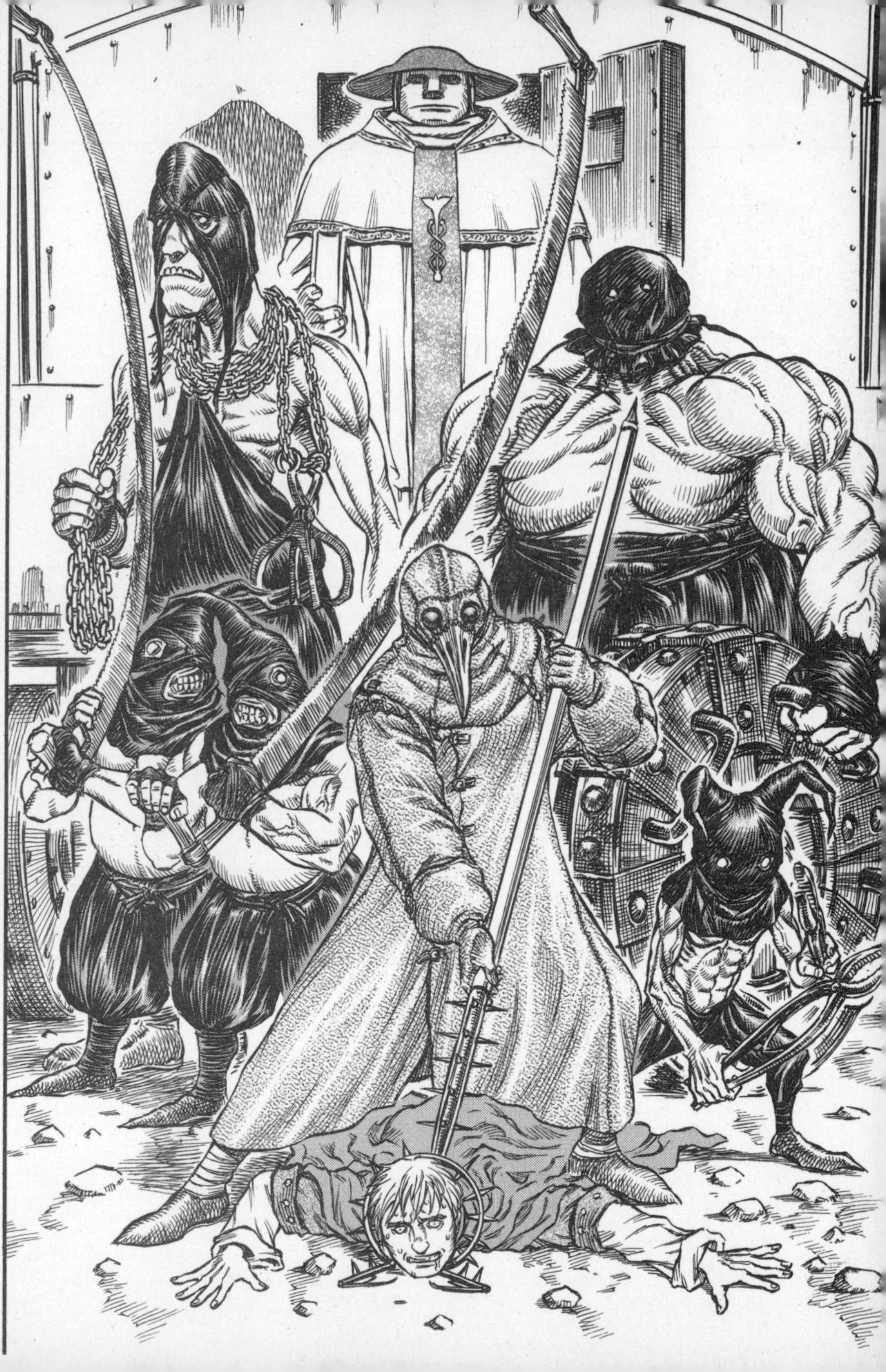

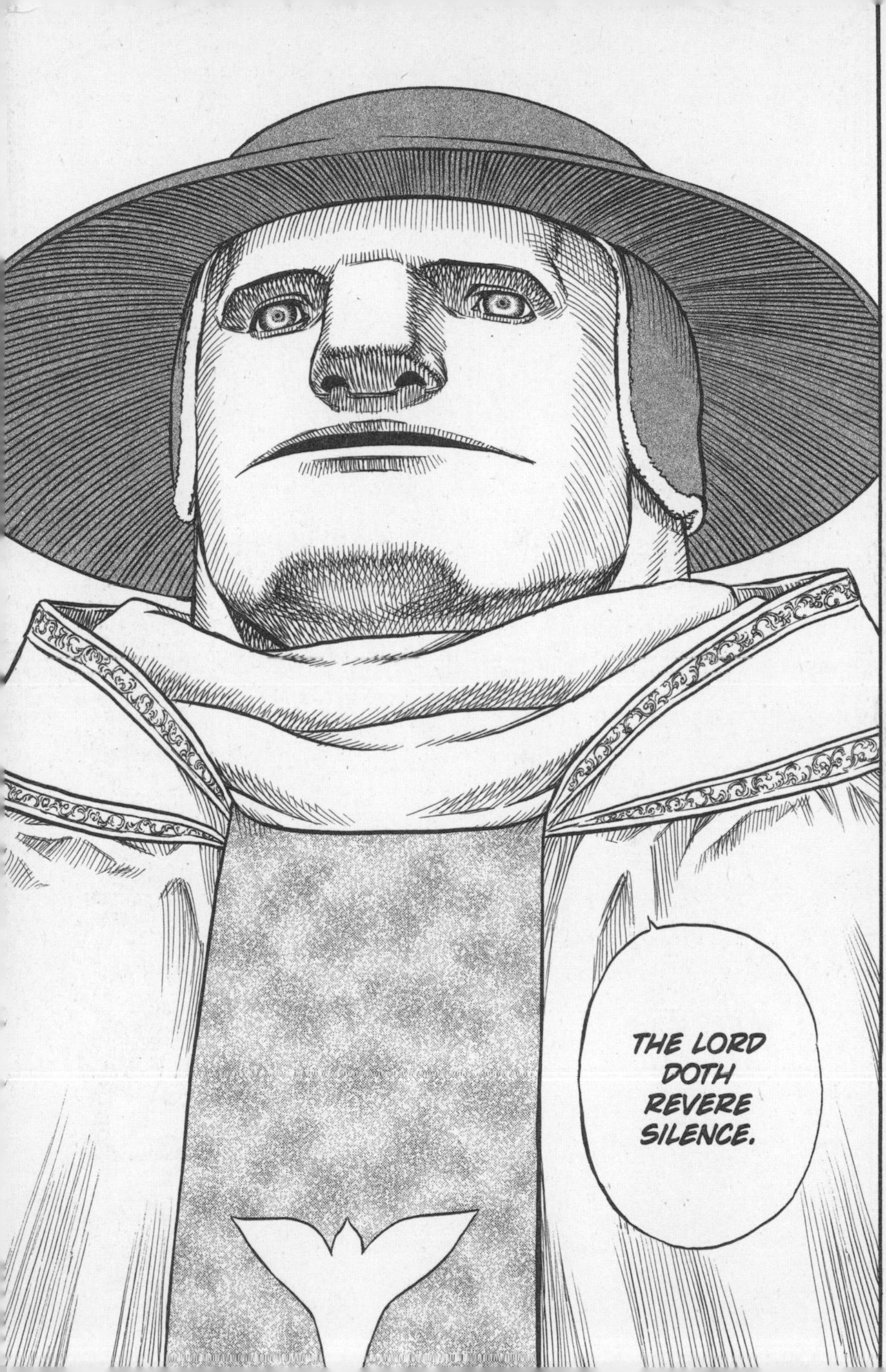
THE LORD DOTH REVERE SILENCE.

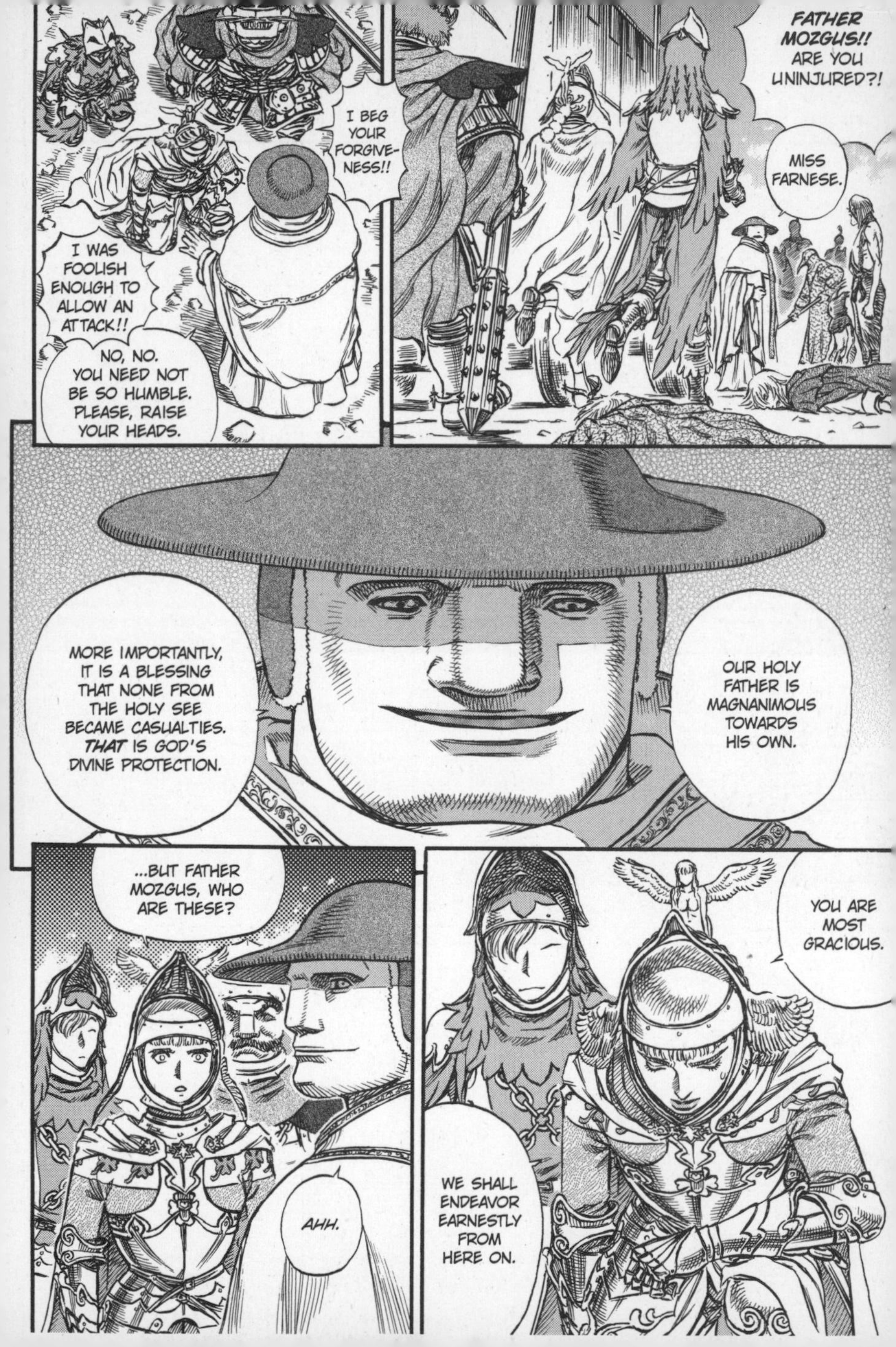
FATHER MOZGUS!! ARE YOU UNINJURED?!
MISS FARNESE.
I BEG YOUR FORGIVE-NESS!!
I WAS FOOLISH ENOUGH TO ALLOW AN ATTACK!!
NO, NO. YOU NEED NOT BE SO HUMBLE. PLEASE, RAISE YOUR HEADS.
OUR HOLY FATHER IS MAGNANIMOUS TOWARDS HIS OWN.
MORE IMPORTANTLY, IT IS A BLESSING THAT NONE FROM THE HOLY SEE BECAME CASUALTIES. THAT IS GOD'S DIVINE PROTECTION.
YOU ARE MOST GRACIOUS.
WE SHALL ENDEAVOR EARNESTLY FROM HERE ON.
...BUT FATHER MOZGUS, WHO ARE THESE?
AHH.

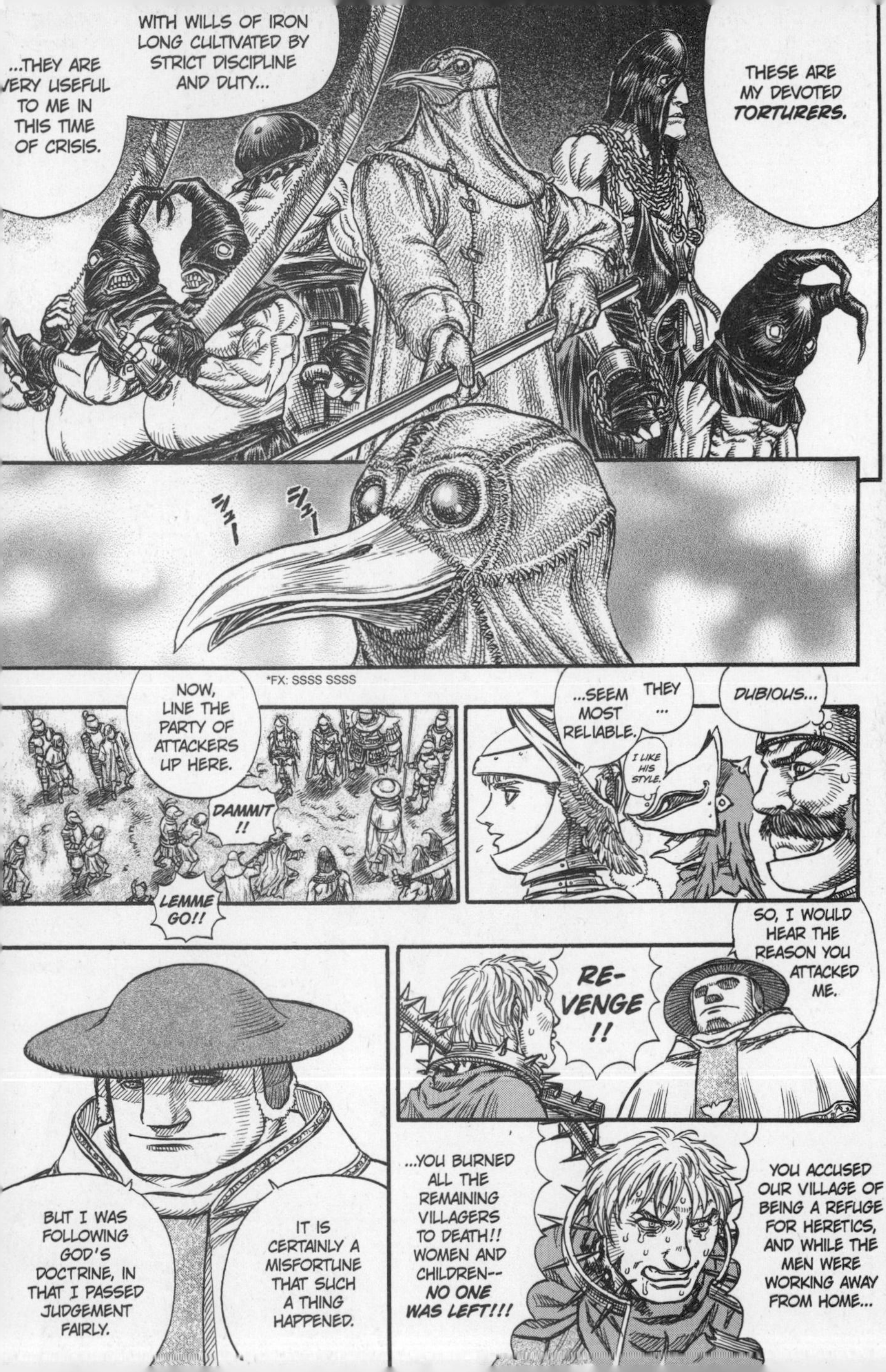
THESE ARE MY DEVOTED TORTURERS.
WITH WILLS OF IRON LONG CULTIVATED BY STRICT DISCIPLINE AND DUTY...
...THEY ARE VERY USEFUL TO ME IN THIS TIME OF CRISIS.
*FX: SSSS SSSS
DUBIOUS...
THEY ...
...SEEM MOST RELIABLE.
I LIKE HIS STYLE.
NOW, LINE THE PARTY OF ATTACKERS UP HERE.
DAMMIT!!
LEMME GO!!
SO, I WOULD HEAR THE REASON YOU ATTACKED ME.
RE-VENGE!!
YOU ACCUSED OUR VILLAGE OF BEING A REFUGE FOR HERETICS, AND WHILE THE MEN WERE WORKING AWAY FROM HOME...
...YOU BURNED ALL THE REMAINING VILLAGERS TO DEATH!! WOMEN AND CHILDREN-- NO ONE WAS LEFT!!!
IT IS CERTAINLY A MISFORTUNE THAT SUCH A THING HAPPENED.
BUT I WAS FOLLOWING GOD'S DOCTRINE, IN THAT I PASSED JUDGEMENT FAIRLY.

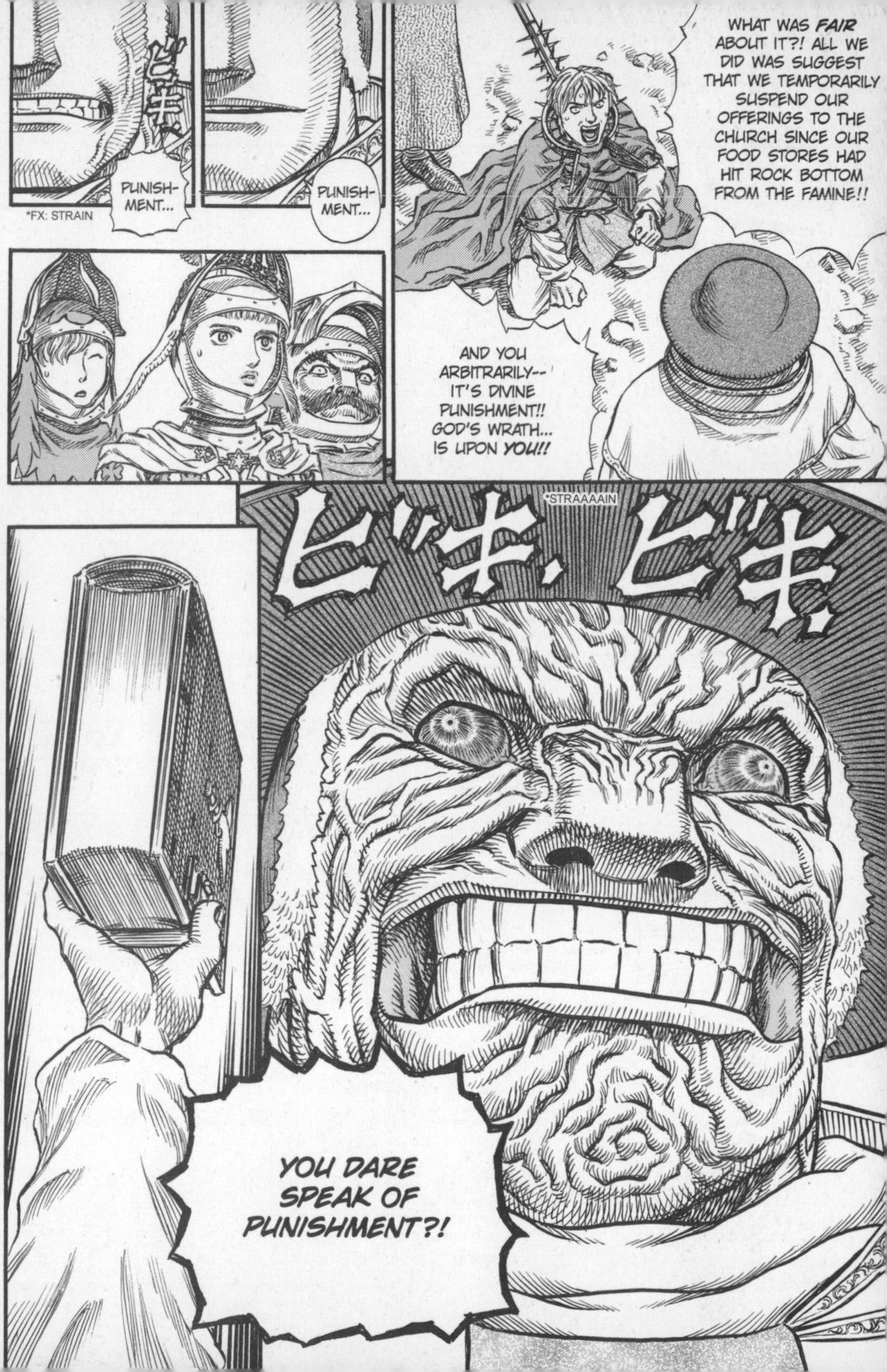
WHAT WAS FAIR ABOUT IT?! ALL WE DID WAS SUGGEST THAT WE TEMPORARILY SUSPEND OUR OFFERINGS TO THE CHURCH SINCE OUR FOOD STORES HAD HIT ROCK BOTTOM FROM THE FAMINE!!
AND YOU ARBITRARILY-- IT'S DIVINE PUNISHMENT!! GOD'S WRATH... IS UPON YOU!!
PUNISHMENT...
PUNISHMENT...
*FX: STRAIN
ビキ. ビキ.
*STRAAAAIN
YOU DARE SPEAK OF PUNISHMENT?!

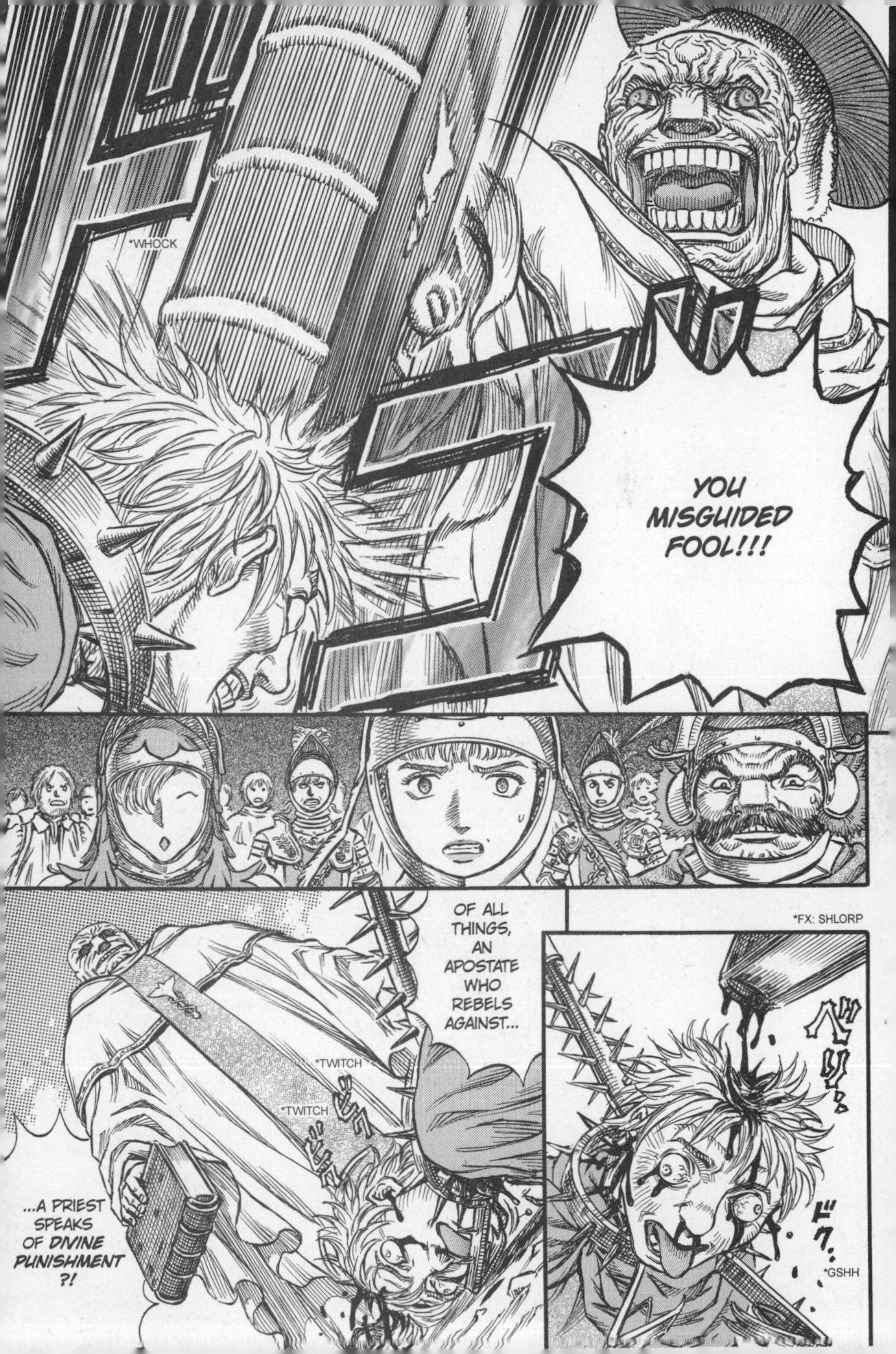
*WHOCK
YOU MISGUIDED FOOL!!!
*FX: SHLORP
*GSHH
OF ALL THINGS, AN APOSTATE WHO REBELS AGAINST...
*TWITCH
*TWITCH
...A PRIEST SPEAKS OF DIVINE PUNISHMENT?!

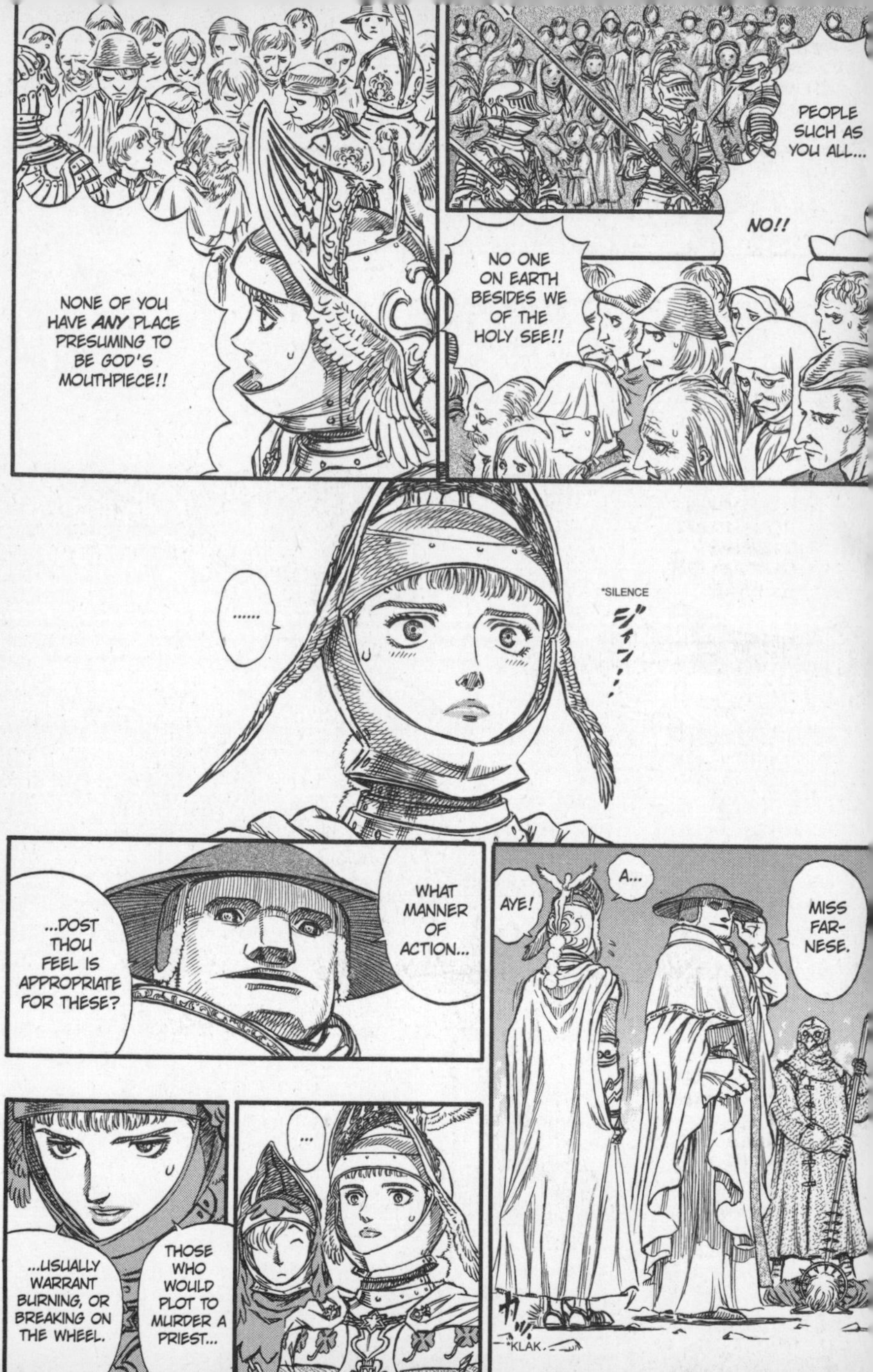
PEOPLE SUCH AS YOU ALL...
NO!!
NO ONE ON EARTH BESIDES WE OF THE HOLY SEE!!
NONE OF YOU HAVE ANY PLACE PRESUMING TO BE GOD'S MOUTHPIECE!!
......
*SILENCE
MISS FAR-NESE.
A...
AYE!
*KLAK.
WHAT MANNER OF ACTION...
...DOST THOU FEEL IS APPROPRIATE FOR THESE?
...
THOSE WHO WOULD PLOT TO MURDER A PRIEST...
...USUALLY WARRANT BURNING, OR BREAKING ON THE WHEEL.

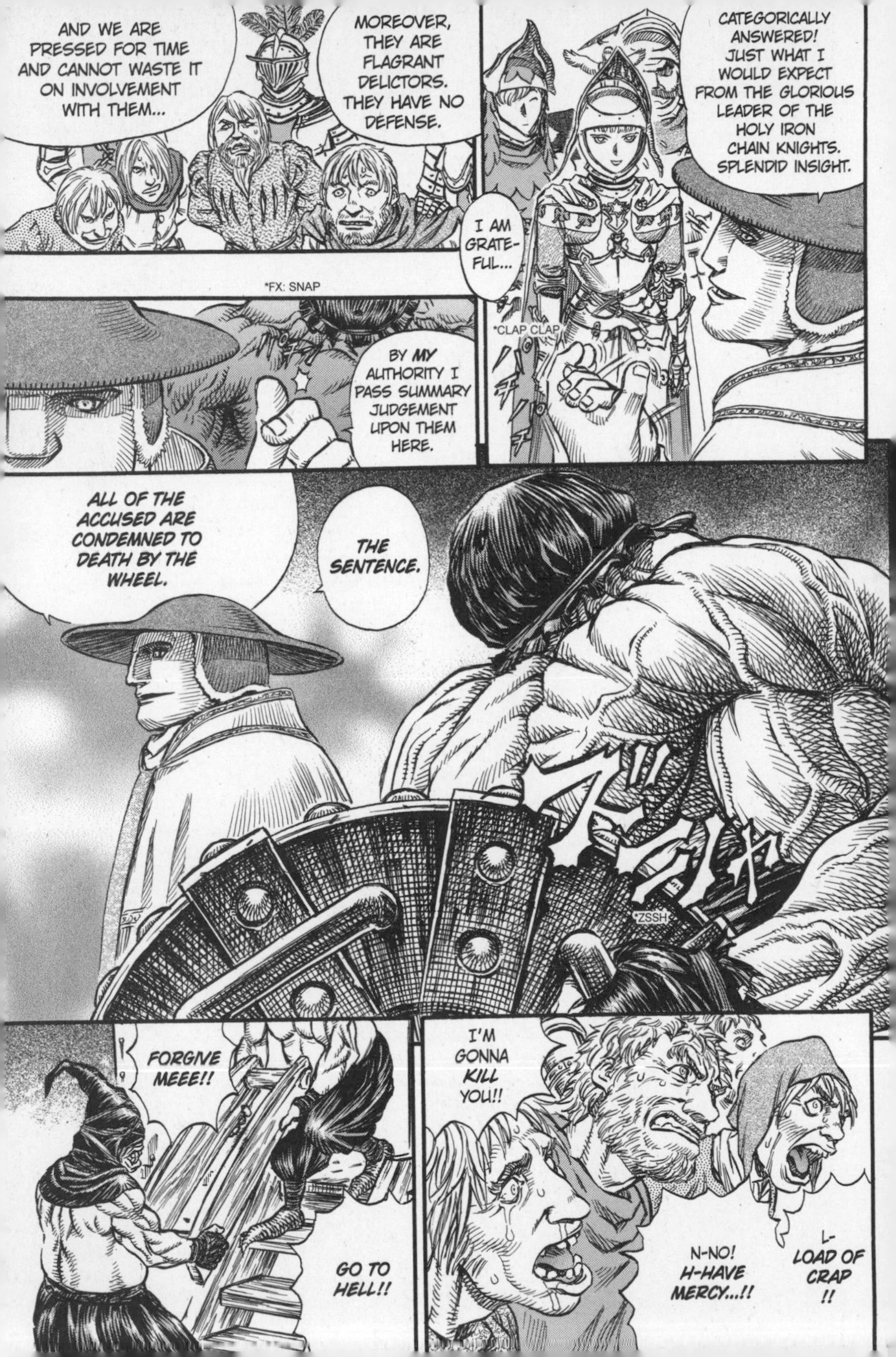
CATEGORICALLY ANSWERED! JUST WHAT I WOULD EXPECT FROM THE GLORIOUS LEADER OF THE HOLY IRON CHAIN KNIGHTS. SPLENDID INSIGHT.
I AM GRATE-FUL...
*CLAP CLAP
MOREOVER, THEY ARE FLAGRANT DELICTORS. THEY HAVE NO DEFENSE.
AND WE ARE PRESSED FOR TIME AND CANNOT WASTE IT ON INVOLVEMENT WITH THEM...
*FX: SNAP
BY MY AUTHORITY I PASS SUMMARY JUDGEMENT UPON THEM HERE.
THE SENTENCE.
ALL OF THE ACCUSED ARE CONDEMNED TO DEATH BY THE WHEEL.
*ZSSH
I'M GONNA KILL YOU!!
L- LOAD OF CRAP !!
N-NO! H-HAVE MERCY...!!
FORGIVE MEEE!!
GO TO HELL!!

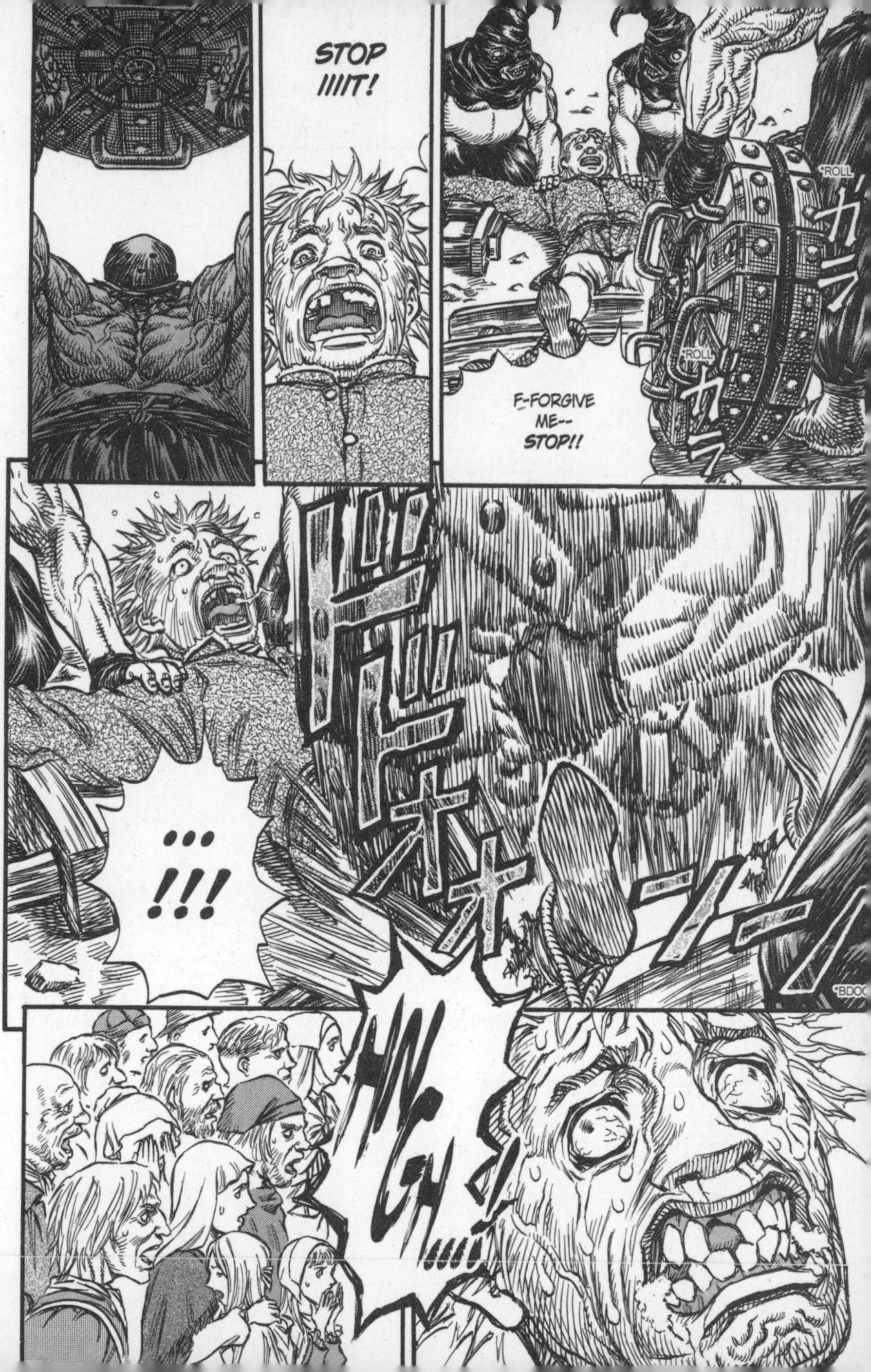
*ROLL
*ROLL
F-FORGIVE ME-- STOP!!
STOP IIIIT!
*BDOO
...!!!
HNGH...

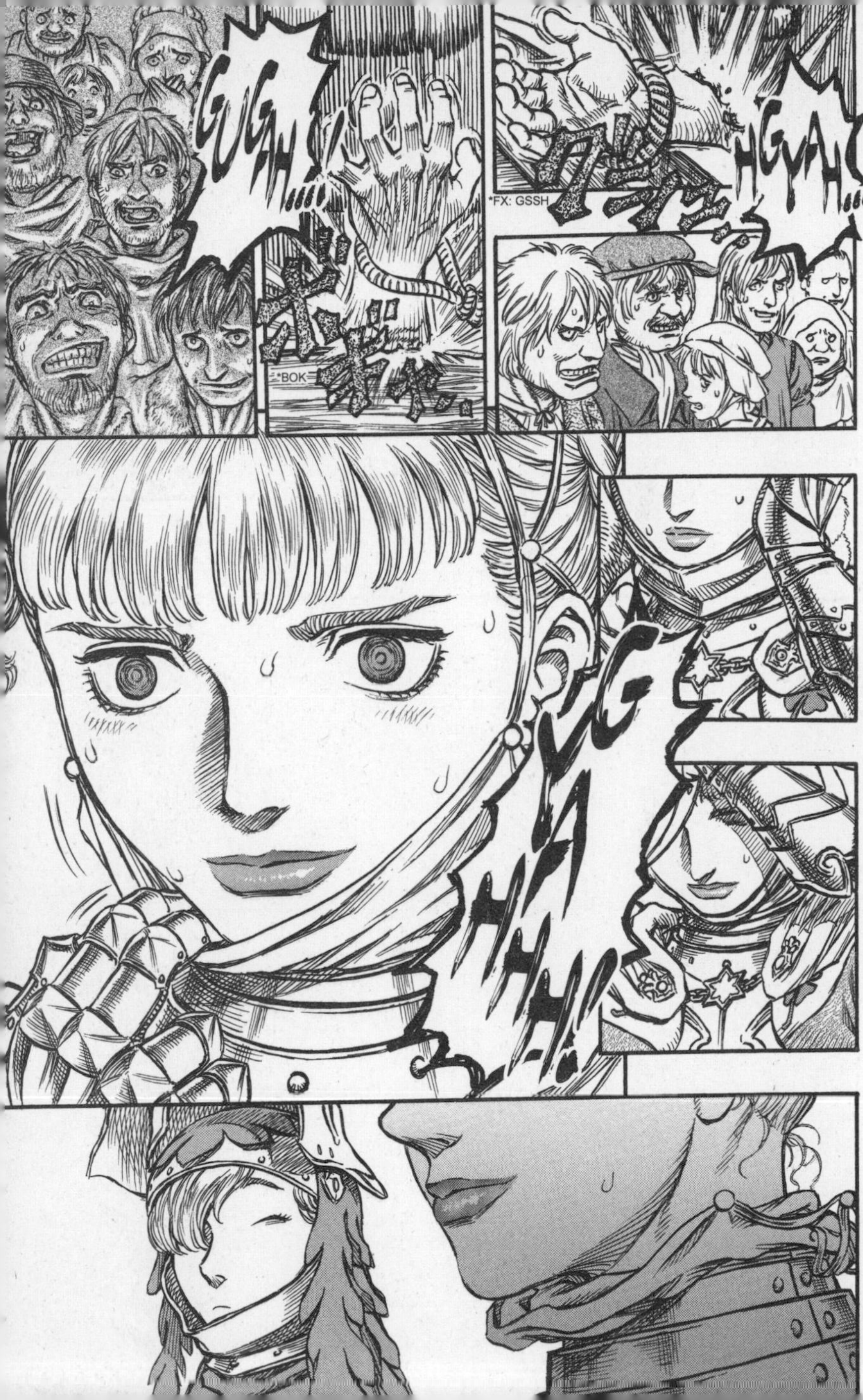
HGYAH...!
*FX: GSSH
*BOK
GUGAH...!
UGYAHHH...!

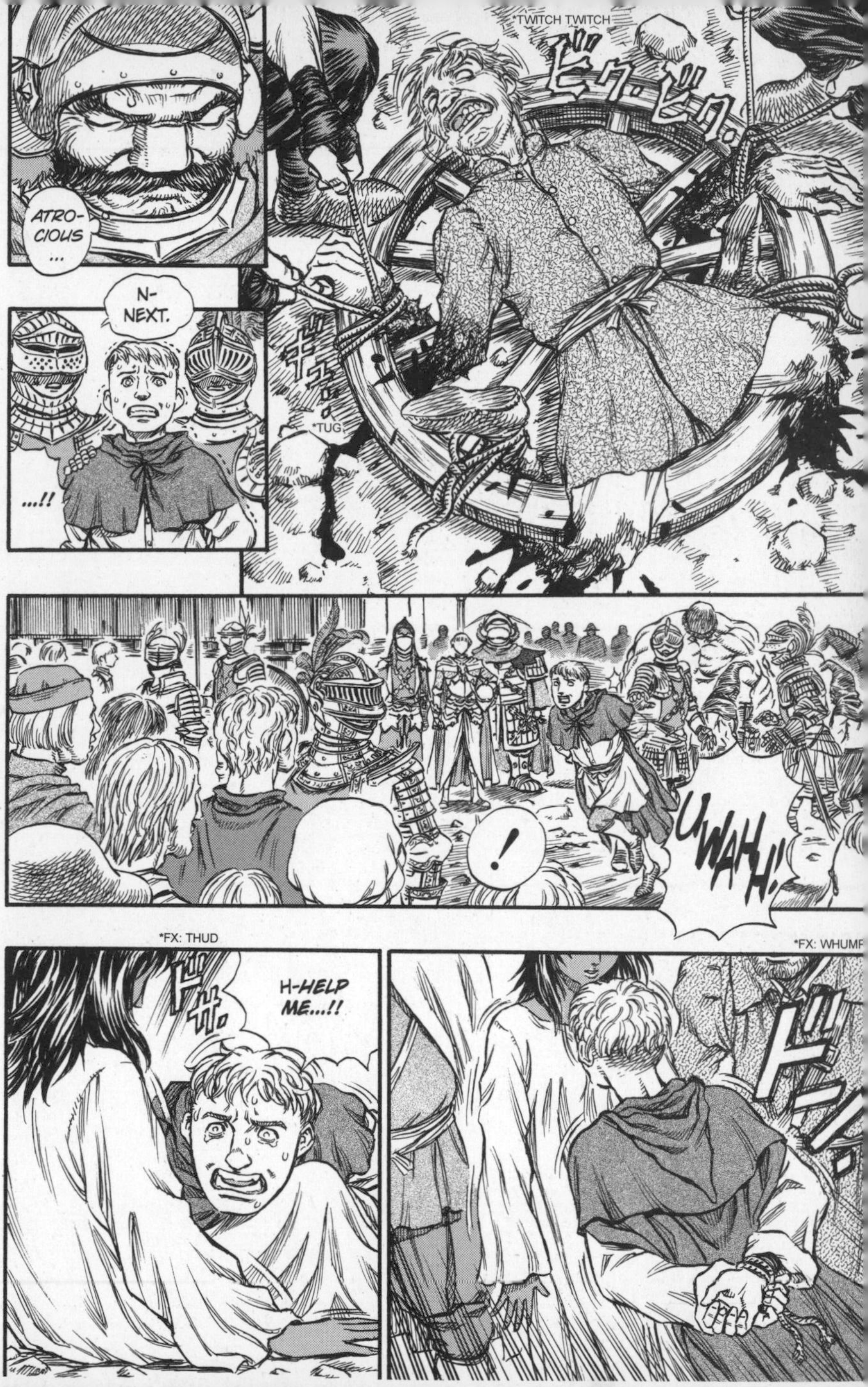
*TWITCH TWITCH
ビク。ビク。
*TUG
ATRO-CIOUS ...
N- NEXT.
...!!
UWAHH!
!
*FX: WHUMP
*FX: THUD
H-HELP ME...!!

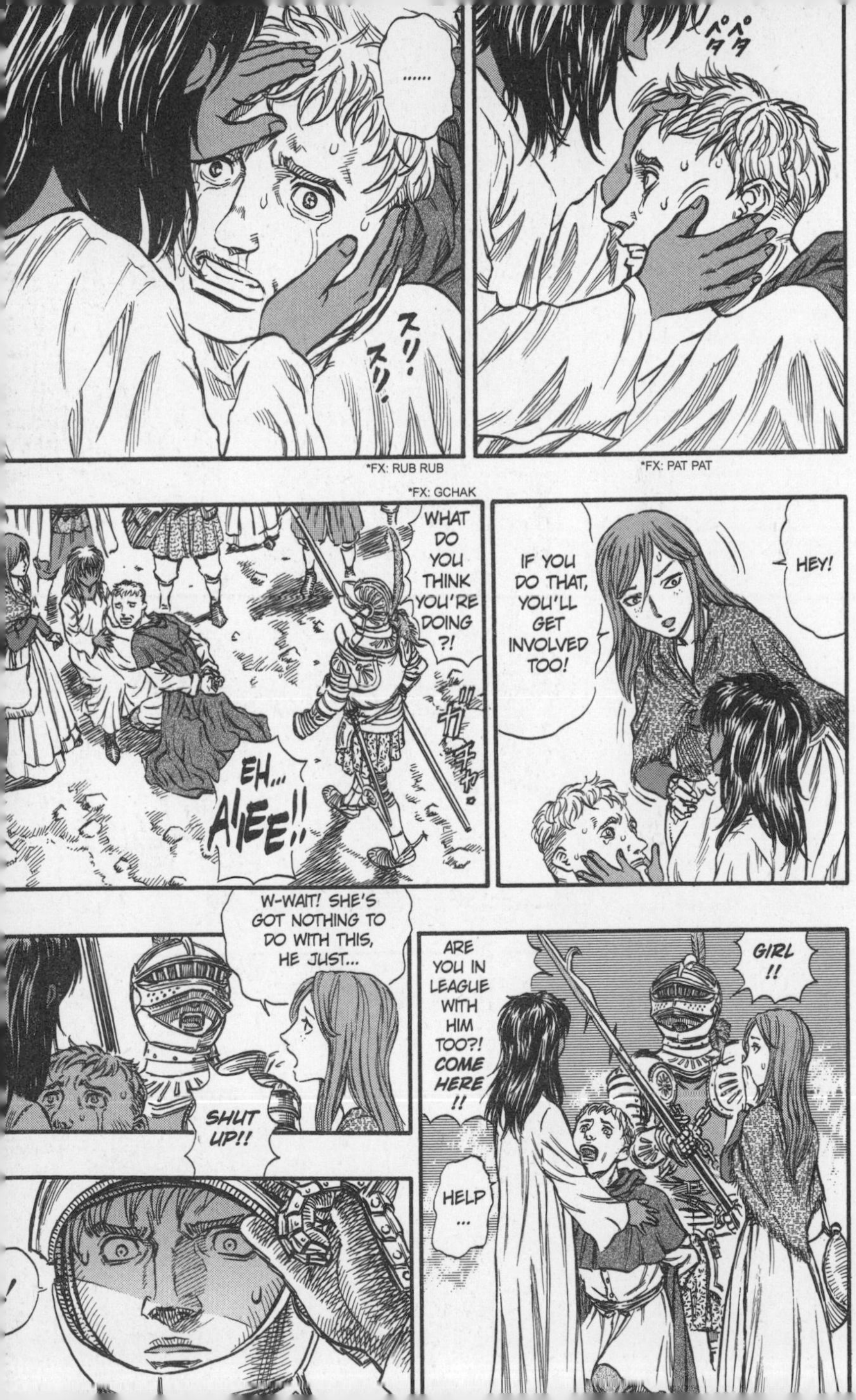
*FX: PAT PAT
......
*FX: RUB RUB
HEY!
IF YOU DO THAT, YOU'LL GET INVOLVED TOO!
*FX: GCHAK
WHAT DO YOU THINK YOU'RE DOING ?!
EH... AIIEE!!
GIRL !!
ARE YOU IN LEAGUE WITH HIM TOO?! COME HERE !!
HELP ...
W-WAIT! SHE'S GOT NOTHING TO DO WITH THIS, HE JUST...
SHUT UP!!

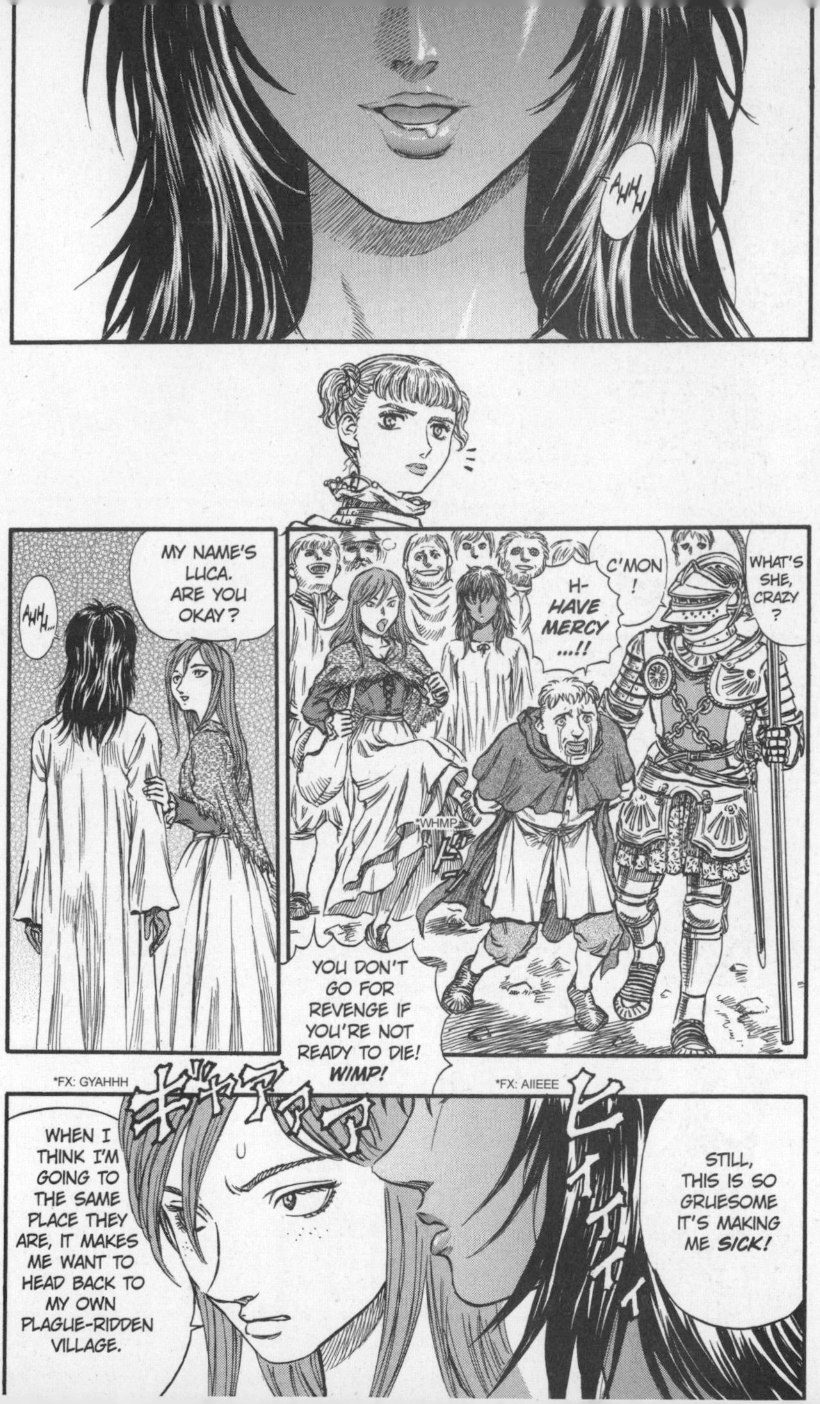
AHHH
WHAT'S SHE, CRAZY?
C'MON!
H- HAVE MERCY ...!!
*WHMP
YOU DON'T GO FOR REVENGE IF YOU'RE NOT READY TO DIE! WIMP!
MY NAME'S LUCA. ARE YOU OKAY?
AHHH...
*FX: AIIEEE
STILL, THIS IS SO GRUESOME IT'S MAKING ME SICK!
*FX: GYAHHH
WHEN I THINK I'M GOING TO THE SAME PLACE THEY ARE, IT MAKES ME WANT TO HEAD BACK TO MY OWN PLAGUE-RIDDEN VILLAGE.

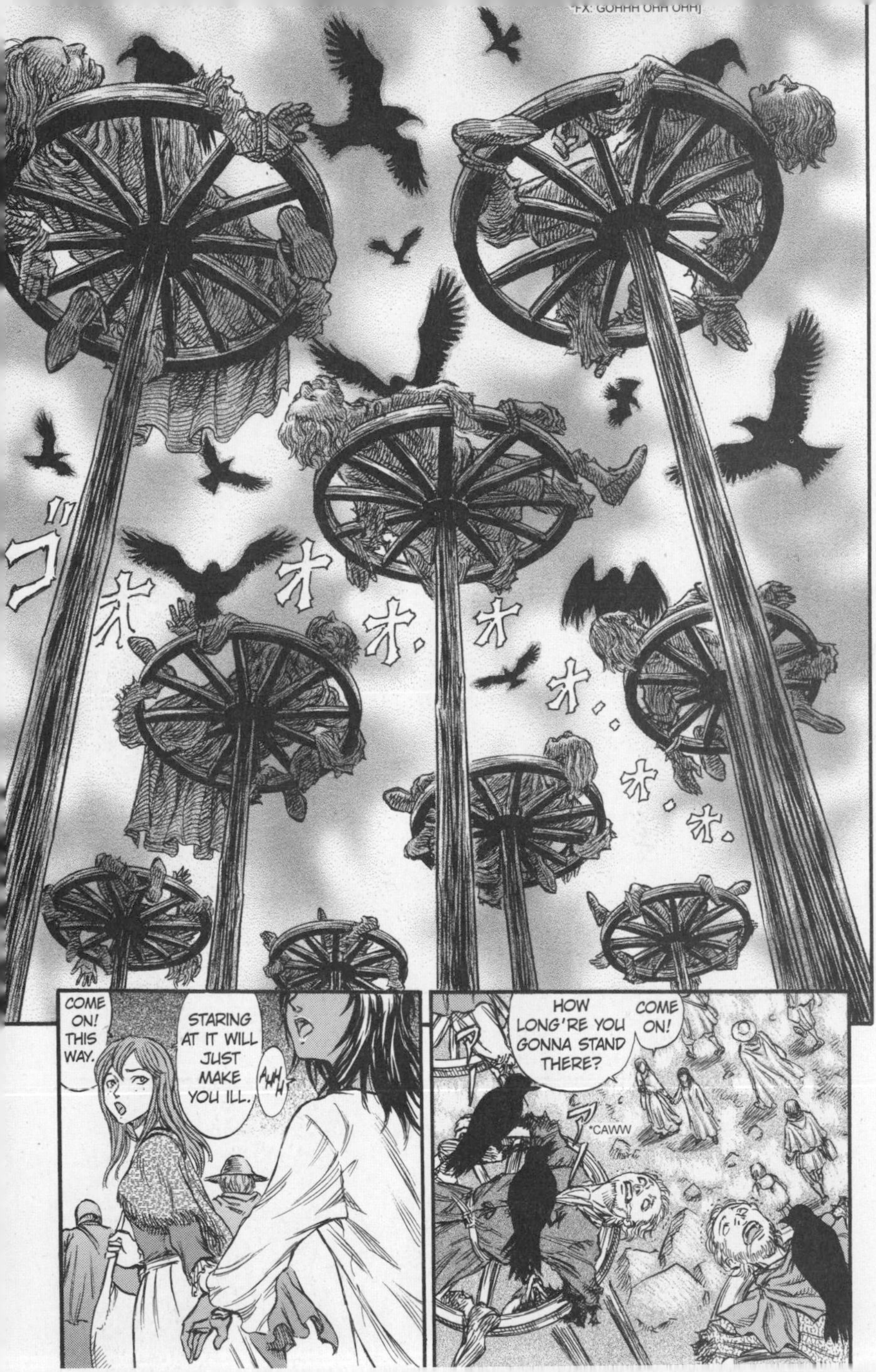
*FX: GOHHH OHH OHH]
ゴオオオオオオオ
HOW LONG'RE YOU GONNA STAND THERE?
COME ON!
*CAWW
COME ON! THIS WAY.
STARING AT IT WILL JUST MAKE YOU ILL.
AHH

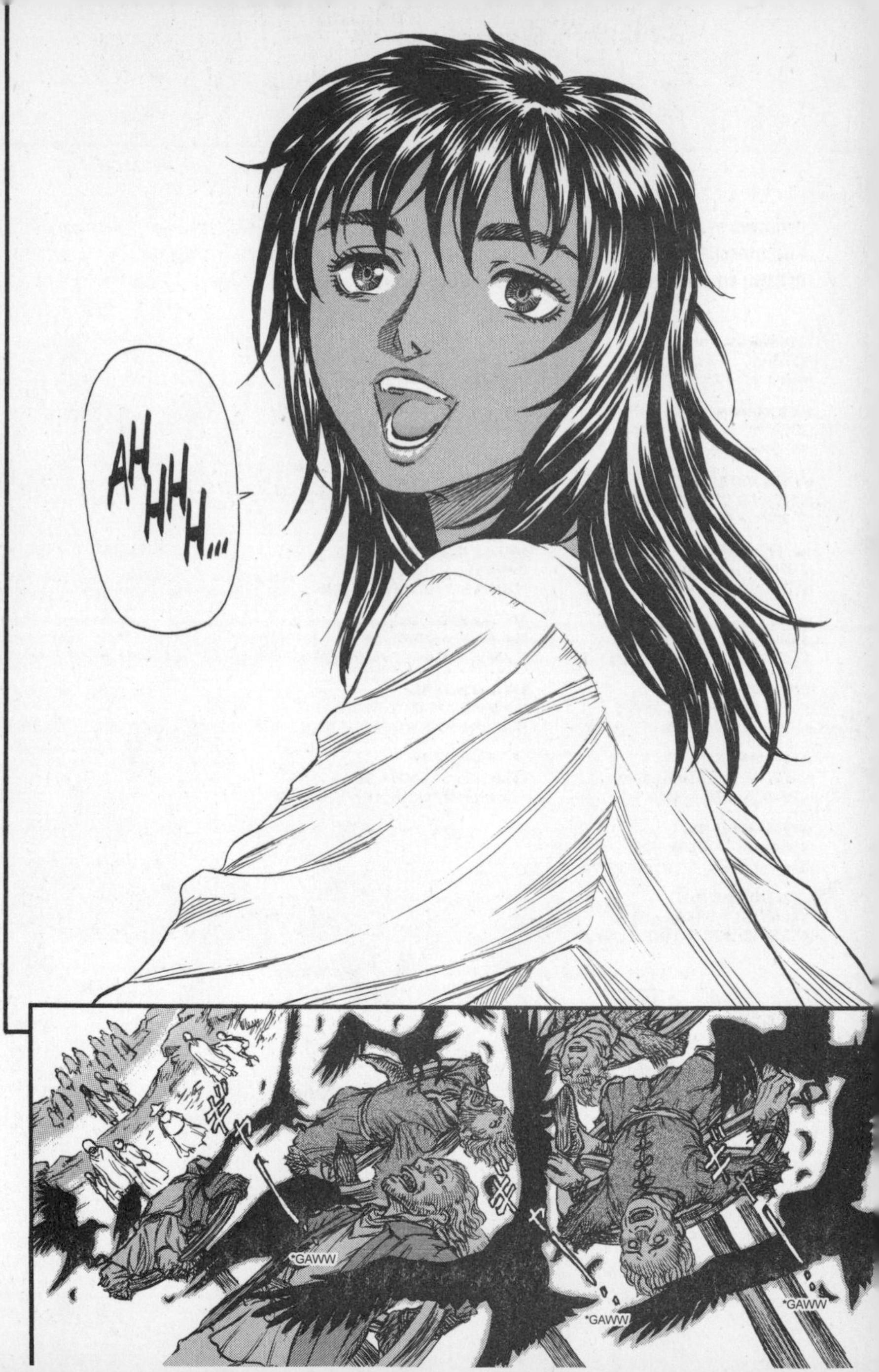
AHHHH...
*GAWW
*GAWW
*GAWW

BERSERK

Created by Kentaro Miura, *Berserk* is manga mayhem to the extreme—violent, horrifying, and mercilessly funny—and the wellspring for the internationally popular anime series. Not for the squeamish or the easily offended, *Berserk* asks for no quarter—and offers none!

VOLUME 1:
ISBN-10: 1-59307-020-9
ISBN-13: 978-1-59307-020-5

VOLUME 2:
ISBN-10: 1-59307-021-7
ISBN-13: 978-1-59307-021-2

VOLUME 3:
ISBN-10: 1-59307-022-5
ISBN-13: 978-1-59307-022-9

VOLUME 4:
ISBN-10: 1-59307-203-1
ISBN-13: 978-1-59307-203-2

VOLUME 5:
ISBN-10: 1-59307-251-1
ISBN-13: 978-1-59307-251-3

VOLUME 6:
ISBN-10: 1-59307-252-X
ISBN-13: 978-1-59307-252-0

VOLUME 7:
ISBN-10: 1-59307-328-3
ISBN-13: 978-1-59307-328-2

VOLUME 8:
ISBN-10: 1-59307-329-1
ISBN-13: 978-1-59307-329-9

VOLUME 9:
ISBN-10: 1-59307-330-5
ISBN-13: 978-1-59307-330-5

VOLUME 10:
ISBN-10: 1-59307-331-3
ISBN-13: 978-1-59307-331-2

VOLUME 11:
ISBN-10: 1-59307-470-0
ISBN-13: 978-1-59307-470-8

VOLUME 12:
ISBN-10: 1-59307-484-0
ISBN-13: 978-1-59307-484-5

VOLUME 13:
ISBN-10: 1-59307-500-6
ISBN-13: 978-1-59307-500-2

VOLUME 14:
ISBN-10: 1-59307-501-4
ISBN-13: 978-1-59307-501-9

VOLUME 15:
ISBN-10: 1-59307-577-4
ISBN-13: 978-1-59307-577-4

VOLUME 16:
ISBN-10: 1-59307-706-8
ISBN-13: 978-1-59307-706-8

Presented uncensored in the original Japanese format!
$13.95 Each!

dmpbooks.com darkhorse.com

AVAILABLE AT YOUR LOCAL COMICS SHOP OR BOOKSTORE
To find a comics shop near your area, call 1-888-266-4226. For more information or to order direct: •On the web: darkhorse.com •E-mail: mailorder@darkhorse.com •Phone: 1-800-862-0052 Mon.-Fri. 9 A.M. to 5 P.M. Pacific Time.

STOP

This is the back of the book!

This manga collection is translated into English but oriented in right-to-left reading format at the creator's request, maintaining the artwork's visual orientation as originally published in Japan. If you've never read manga in this way before, take a look at the diagram below to give yourself an idea of how to go about it. Basically, you'll be starting in the upper right corner and will read each balloon and panel moving right to left. It may take some getting used to, but you should get the hang of it very quickly. Have fun!

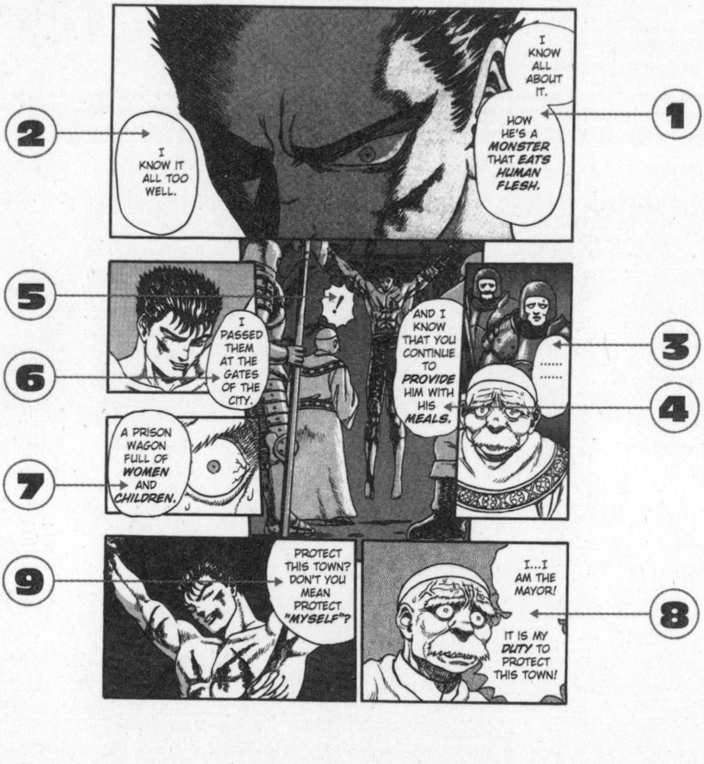
1
I KNOW ALL ABOUT IT.
HOW HE'S A MONSTER THAT EATS HUMAN FLESH.
2
I KNOW IT ALL TOO WELL.
3
....
4
AND I KNOW THAT YOU CONTINUE TO PROVIDE HIM WITH HIS MEALS.
5
!
6
I PASSED THEM AT THE GATES OF THE CITY.
7
A PRISON WAGON FULL OF WOMEN AND CHILDREN.
8
I...I AM THE MAYOR!
IT IS MY DUTY TO PROTECT THIS TOWN!
9
PROTECT THIS TOWN? DON'T YOU MEAN PROTECT "MYSELF"?